THE DESIGN PHILOSOPHY READER

THE DESIGN PHILOSOPHY READER

THE DESIGN PHILOSOPHY READER

Edited by

Anne-Marie Willis

BLOOMSBURY VISUAL ARTS
LONDON · NEW YORK · OXFORD · NEW DELHI · SYDNEY

BLOOMSBURY VISUAL ARTS
Bloomsbury Publishing Plc
50 Bedford Square, London, WC1B 3DP, UK
1385 Broadway, New York, NY 10018, USA

BLOOMSBURY, BLOOMSBURY VISUAL ARTS and the Diana logo are trademarks of Bloomsbury Publishing Plc

First published in Great Britain 2019

A catalogue record for this book is available from the British Library.

A catalog record for this book is available from the Library of Congress.

ISBN: HB: 978-0-8578-5349-3
PB: 978-0-8578-5350-9

Typeset by Deanta Global Publishing Services, Chennai, India
Printed and bound in Great Britain

To find out more about our authors and books visit www.bloomsbury.com and sign up for our newsletters.

CONTENTS

Contents

PREFACE AND ACKNOWLEDGMENTS

The idea for this book grew from the journal *Design Philosophy Papers*, an independent refereed journal founded in 2003 by Tony Fry, Clive Dilnot and I. It aimed to extend critical thinking on design especially by engaging disciplines beyond design. The concern was not so much with appropriating methods from social sciences and humanities to advance the activity of design research, there was also the ambition of a reverse appropriation: that the humanities and sciences needed to be engaging the increasingly designed character of modern world, directly, not just incidentally.

Design Philosophy Papers was neither the organ of a scholarly society nor affiliated with a particular institution. We announced calls for papers via networks such as PhD Design and Design Studies Lists. After the refereeing process, the chosen papers were published online in themed issues, and smaller selections were later published in print editions. The journal was published and distributed independently for the first ten years, and then Bloomsbury became the distributor, followed by Routledge.

When we discussed the idea of a Reader in design philosophy with Tristan Palmer, a former commissioning editor at Berg (now Bloomsbury), the assumption was that most of the material would be from the journal *Design Philosophy Papers*. However, on reviewing the output of more than a decade, though there were many strong papers, and revisiting the original ambition of the journal, it was recognized that deep philosophical engagement with design was still extremely under-developed. If the concept of the Reader had been "the best of *Design Philosophy Papers*" we could have included many excellent papers on, for example, participatory design, social design, user-centered design, and design history. Instead, it was decided to cast the net more widely, and to include texts from philosophy and other non-design disciplines.

Readers will note that some of the selected texts do not address design directly, rather they require to be brought to design, to designed things, and especially to unexamined assumptions that underlie a good deal of instrumental design theory and research. It needs to be emphasized that the choice of texts has been informed by what we perceive as the decline of informed critical thinking within the corporatized model of the university that is now the norm. Academic research has become a quantified output to feed the profiles of institutional education providers in the global marketplace, this accompanied by a huge increase in the number of academic journals with a vast output of mediocre papers written to formula. *The Design Philosophy Reader* is intended as an intervention into this dire situation, and to reiterate, if some of the included texts appear to have little to do with design, this is because we are less interested in design as it is now than in design as it needs to become. Sometimes this means reaching back to the past to retrieve resources for the making of better futures.

Therefore, my thanks go first to contributors to the larger project of design philosophy: the Editorial Board and all contributors to *Design Philosophy Papers*, as this Reader would not have been conceived of if not for the existence of the journal. To mention in particular the crucial input at various times of Clive Dilnot, Cameron Tonkinwise, Arturo Escobar, Erik Stolterman, Eli Blevis, Shana Agid, Mahmoud Keshavarz, Abby Lopes, Matt Kiem, Samer Akkach, Maria Cecilia, Glen Hill, Augustin Berque, Philippe d'Anjou, Carleton Christensen, Wolfgang Jonas, William McNeill, Albert Borgmann, Ezio Manzini, Carl Mitcham, and Karsten Harries.

For *The Design Philosophy Reader* itself, my thanks go to the authors and copyright holders of the included texts; to Tristan Palmer of Berg for support in the early stages; and in the later stages to Claire Constable and Rebecca Barden of Bloomsbury for their goodwill and infinite patience; to colleagues who reviewed the project at various stages, especially Duncan Fairfax; and last but not least, to my lifelong collaborator, Tony Fry, for his constructive criticism and continuous inspiration.

Anne-Marie Willis

INTRODUCTION
Anne-Marie Willis

What is Design Philosophy and why is it needed? This introduction will begin by outlining three inter-related contexts to which Design Philosophy is responding: first, the worldly pervasiveness of design; second, the state of thinking on design "from the inside"; and third, "the conditions of now" that are unable to be addressed by current thinking and practices of designing. Following this, the meta-project of philosophy will be briefly characterized, then the purpose of Design Philosophy will be introduced, showing it to have the potential to resonate with philosophy's purposes and its varying relations to other forms and fields of knowledge. Finally, a rationale will be presented for the texts that have been selected, and their manner of organization.

The pervasiveness of design

It has become almost mandatory to introduce a book on design by evoking the pervasiveness of design, usually along the following lines:

> *Design is everywhere. Just take a look around the room you're in now and see what's designed. Chair, table, book, computer, lamp, pens, power cords, light switches, door, window, the clothes you're wearing, your glasses, shoes, mobile phone, your bag and all the stuff in it, plus all the things you don't see right now, like the designed food packaging in the rubbish bin, or the data flying through time and space, satellites and servers, relay towers and however many billion computers and mobile devices, the data flow that now operationalizes economic, social and cultural existence, that can be turned on and off like water from a tap yet somehow is always on, and which has become as essential to the functioning of societal life as is water to biological life.*
>
> *OK, we got a bit carried away, so let's get back to your room. I want you to identify all the designed things in it; or, even better, find something that is NOT designed. The plant in the corner? Wrong. Hybridised, raised from tissue culture and cultivated for indoor environments, it would never survive if returned to the place where its ancestors flourished—so-called nature that is natural no more if it ever was.*

Designed things fill our worlds, they *are* our worlds; so thoroughly are we modernized, affluent people nested within the designed, within the naturalized artificial, neither would we survive if returned to the places of dwelling of our early human ancestors.

If philosophy is taken as enquiry into existence, and if the conditions of existence are increasingly designed, then "design" should be a major topic of philosophical investigation. In fact, *design*, named as such, is rarely engaged by philosophers. Yet designed things and designing practices have been addressed in philosophy, past and present, indirectly or without naming them as such. An example is where a philosopher might speculate on the nature of a physical object such as a chair but because their concern is with, say the question of perception or consciousness or materiality, the fact that the chair has come into being by design, is overlooked. This is a loss for philosophy, a loss that becomes increasingly significant; because any enquiry into "the conditions of now" will be deficient if it does not take cognizance of the extent of design as well as what Albert Borgmann, a philosopher who *has* engaged design front-on, calls "the depth of design." Another type of indirect engagement of design by philosophy comes into view if we move from the designed thing to the activity of designing. Design, as a separate practice from making, has only become widespread in the West since the Industrial Revolution. Before that, it was indivisibly part of skilled making, as the prefiguration of the made—as a drawing or plan, written or spoken instruction, or conversation and collaboration. Therefore philosophical writings that seek to define the arts, skill, or making are very relevant to the thinking of design.

Thinking design from the inside

Viewing the situation from the other side, that is, design's engagement with philosophy, is a different story, in which ideas from philosophy, as well as from Cultural Theory, Anthropology, Psychology, Mathematics, Biology, and many other science and humanities disciplines are serendipitously taken up by designers, and selectively appropriated by design scholars. This adoption intensified over the last three decades as design education shifted from technical colleges to universities and design research became an area of academic specialization encompassing design history (methods mainly drawn from art history), design studies (less defined and eclectic), and design methods. The latter has been dominant, its main object being "the design process," which at first was conceptualized by drawing on cybernetics and information theory, with the aim of establishing a systematic process able to be applied to any problem. This scientist approach was later modified and attention moved to studying the working processes of designers, which in turn were changing, as teamwork, user-centered, and participatory methods were being developed in response to market-driven needs to "humanize" the functioning of the information technologies that were being introduced into work places. Therefore, within the milieu of design research, when a question of a philosophical character is posed, such as "what is design?" the answer is mostly already over-determined by the model of professional design as the model of all designing. Furthermore, professional design itself is over-determined by its service role. As Clive Dilnot has written, "As a professional activity design does not occur, does not happen, only or even largely through its own volition. Rather, Design—modern design, professional design—is called into being by Industrialization."[1] This is precisely why it is not possible to give epistemological weight to designers' understanding of design. Professional designers' self-understanding of the nature of what they do may be of practical or sociological interest, but it is not the same thing as a philosophical understanding of design.

The difficulty of asking philosophical questions about design from the horizon of professional design is exemplified by a recent attempt to think "design beyond design" by the editors of a special issue of *Design Issues* on science, technology, and design. The editors introduce the essays by making a distinction between "proximate design," meaning the actions of professional designers and something larger that they call "design by society."[2] The latter sounds intriguing; but it immediately shrinks as soon as it becomes clear that "design by society" refers to no more than the institutions that shape the work of professional designers, such as codes and regulations, and no less than the influence of social norms on designers. This incoherent jamming together of the particular and general renders "society" an amorphous lump standing in the way, doing nothing more or less than blocking thinking.[3] "Proximate design" and "design by society" are incommensurable, forming a static binary that does not enable the putting into question of the bounded field "design"; it doesn't bring into visibility the contingent nature of professional design as socially and historically constituted and therefore not immutable; it doesn't allow for the possibility that design and designing could be otherwise.

The condition of "now"

At this point you could ask, "but what is wrong in defining design as what professional designers do? Why should it be otherwise?" I could reply by saying that humanity is in a crisis because its designs and inventions have been so successful in appropriating, transforming, using-up, and trashing the stuff of the given world (what was once called nature) that we have ruined the very things we need to sustain us and other forms of life, and that professional designers, as compliant service providers, bear some responsibility for this.

You may protest and say, "but that's not true, designers know about climate change and global warming and species extinction and pollution and toxic waste and war and disease and drugs and crime and violence and racism and persecution and the injustice of the over-consumption of the wealthy and the suffering of the poor . . . everyone knows these problems because they're on TV and all over the internet all the time." And you would be right, and therein lays the problem of the problems. A continuously streaming spectacle of videogenic symptoms of the condition of unsustainability as it structures the structures' contemporary existence now. And design is right there in the middle of it all, in the middle of this systemic unsustainability, a system of such vastness and complexity that it exceeds all attempts at representation. But design is not just there in the mix, it is active in its creation. Design channels, directs, focuses, crystallizes inchoate yearnings, anxieties, fears, insecurities. Desire for difference, for transformation, for a better life, to be respected, to live meaningfully, to be beautiful, to be admired, to be loved, to be entertained, amused, aroused, excited, to escape, to live, to fly, to be free of pain, to feel safe, to feel at home, to belong, to nest, to rest, to feel peace, to be still . . . design focuses, crystallizes, channels and directs yearnings, aspirations, feelings—noble and venal, reasonable and trivial—toward purchasable things, commodities, products, services, experiences. Branding, point-of-sale, packaging, promotion, advertising, free giveaways, product stories, emotional design, personas, look-and-feel, eye-appeal, target groups, viral marketing—this is the world of design, the milieu, the *habitas* of designers—and while these buzzwords and techniques are just as much part of marketing, and therefore, pedagogically, as much the province of schools of business and commerce as design, this is of little importance, for all of it is designing at a meta level—the gathering and marshalling, channeling and directing of creative ability, cognitive capital, market data, business knowledge, the assembly of project teams with targets, timelines, budgets all pointing toward the realization of more products and services.

Design as a service profession services capitalism: capitalism is a system that is inherently exploitive—of people, other living things, and the geophysical conditions upon which they all depend. This may sound like a moral judgment; it is not, it is a description. While there are ethical and unethical business owners, exploitive and less exploitive corporations, employers who treat workers well and badly, they (we) all operate within a system of production and exchange the very logic of which is to maximize profit no matter how damaging the consequences. Restraints on extreme harm do exist—labor laws, environmental regulations—but they are external to the system, and their imposition does not occur without a fight.

So, to continue to insist that this is what design actually is, that this is its legitimate locale, and to shape design research and education accordingly is to refuse what design could be, what it needs to be, and to become. Research, thinking, and theorization of design that cannot or is not willing to de-valorize "design as a service profession within the current economic status quo" simply contributes to the continuation of unsustainability: educating in error for designing in error. If "everything is designed," and "the designed goes on designing" and this, predominantly continues to drive unsustainability forward into defuturing, then design must become a far better informed, thoughtful type of practice. This is why there is a need for uncompromised thinking on design—a need for Design Philosophy.

Philosophy

At this point an obvious question arises, which is "what is philosophy?". One of the most common assumptions is that philosophy is an achievement of Western civilization, initiated by the early Greeks. This is erroneous on several counts. The modern academic discipline of philosophy established during the Enlightenment is not the same thing as early Greek philosophy, nor were the Greeks the sole founders of philosophy. We cannot know with certainty the origin of philosophy. Many histories of philosophy have been written; however they are not just retellings of something already formed, like all histories, they construct their object of engagement. Philosophy as developed by the early Greeks was not separate from other knowledge; it emerged out of a variety of sources including practical knowledge of, for example: medicine (diseases, cures, healing the body); and agriculture (cultivating edible plants, raising animals, knowing the seasons). Systemization of such knowledge was the beginning of what we now call science, and it was not separate from enquiry into underlying principles that we now call philosophy. But we need to be careful in back-loading our ways of understanding things onto the distant past: there is never a perfect fit, sometimes none at all. G. E. R. Lloyd, the noted historian of philosophy and science, tells us that what we call "astronomy" in both ancient Greece and China: "comprised not just calendar studies, and the descriptions of the constellations and investigation of the movements of the sun, moon and planets, but also—the study of celestial omens or other attempts to predict events on earth, in other words what we call astrology."[4]

The early Greeks built on knowledge from other civilizations of Persia, India, China, and Africa, but the exact circumstances of the transmission of knowledge are not always known and are debated by historians.[5] It is known that a number of Greek philosophers spent time in Egypt. Thales of Miletus, generally acknowledged as the first Greek philosopher is thought to have studied at the temple of Waset in Thebes (present day Luxor) in Egypt. Thales is credited with formalizing the practical geometry of the Egyptians into principles of geometry as well as explaining and predicting solar eclipses. He is viewed as a transitional figure between myth and philosophy/science, this particularly in relation to his claim that water is the fundamental substance out of which all things come and to which they all return. While this idea links with Egyptian and Babylonian myths of origin, it was a shift in thinking with important repercussions. Other Greek philosophers disagreed and put forward other candidates for the fundamental substance but Thales had established the proposition and initiated a line of enquiry that was pursued over many centuries, and according to Panchenko he adopted the procedure "which forms the basis of all theoretical knowledge: he inaugurated the tradition of arguable statements about the unobservable."[6]

Philosophy and banality

Bringing philosophy to design presents some challenges, not least the unfamiliarity of much philosophical writing. Let's take, for example, Emmanuel Levinas *Basic Philosophical Writings*. Picking this book off the shelf and flicking through it, the first impression for non-philosophers, is of extreme difficulty: the terminology, the complex sentences seem opaque. Yet at the same time, and this needs always to be kept in mind, philosophy is not about topics only comprehensible and relevant to academics, rather, the philosopher enquires into the obvious, that which is so obvious, that it never gets thought. One of the chapters in the book just mentioned is a lecture delivered by Levinas to the French society of philosophy, including a transcript of the discussion that followed it. Levinas argues that the presence of the Other for the "I" is the foundation of ethics. One of the discussants, Mikowski, presents this back to him as "the primitive human solidarity upon which our existence rests," others talk of degrees of proximity, of similarity and difference ("neighbour," "fellow human being"), in other words, they interpret what Levinas is saying sociologically. Levinas replies saying,

> You evoke differences of formation, culture, and character which distinguish men and their ways of understanding. All things considered, these are the different qualities, like colours, for example, which

distinguish men in the same way as one table is distinguished from another. What is unique in each man—and this is ultimately a banality—is that he is an I.[7]

There are many other banalities discussed in the texts of this Reader, such as world, care, animal, human, acting, and making. When encountering commonplace terms in philosophical texts, it is safe to assume that they either mean much more or much less or something other (like "Other") than their everyday meaning. Care, for example, as we will see in Part III, has nothing to do with emotions as felt ("I care about you") or commanded to be felt ("you should care about . . .") rather, it is something more basic—the intuitive, or barely susceptible forethought, in lifting a cooking pot from the fire or crossing a road, and as we shall see, care does not even require human presence. Banal terms are used by designers frequently in conceptualizing product ideas, in investigating or second-guessing the needs or motivations of potential users and in justifying or explaining their design concepts. Much of the language and therefore the thinking of designers (they are not alone in this) is overloaded with unexamined humanism and scientism, which is now irrelevant or erroneous. Designers need to engage philosophy not so much to gain more complicated "tools for thinking" but as a clearing.

From philosophy to theory

European philosophy itself has undergone a number of clearings (this gives the impression that things are erased, but they are not) over the last two and a half thousand years. It was subjected to a major clearing in the second half of the twentieth century from structuralism, post-structuralism, and deconstruction and postmodernism. Political movements of the 1960s and 1970s challenged the asserted neutrality of Western rationalism, and brought the questions of race, class, and gender to established bodies of knowledge, exposing that there were no value-free positions from which to make moral and aesthetic judgments or to determine what does or does not count as valid knowledge. Bodies of academic knowledge, their modes of valorization, their deployment beyond the academy—all of this was asserted as political, implicitly, or explicitly, in that it either supported or challenged existing social and institutional arrangements that were stacked in favor of one race, class, and gender against all others. In this, deconstruction initiated by Jacques Derrida was taken up as a powerful form of critique which exposed the foundation of the thinking upon which a text was based (whether a novel, a movie, an advertisement, a newspaper article, or an academic paper). Deconstruction exposes the work(ing) of language; it shows that rather than a writer or speaker "having a command of language" language speaks (through) us. Deconstruction affected most Humanities disciplines including philosophy, as did the thinking of Michel Foucault on power in the modern era as not just centralized and repressive but dispersed, operating at micro-level of surveillance, regulation, and organization of bodies, productive of forms of behavior and productive of knowledge that produces more power.

Design philosophy

Design Philosophy inherits this recent tradition. It is hybrid, trans, or even post-disciplinary and dominantly oriented toward a politicized reading of design. But Design Philosophy is still an infant, not yet formed.

Design Philosophy is a thinking of being with design in worldly ways. It is a disposition toward thinking that acknowledges the designed as the naturalized but problematic condition of existence now. Design Philosophy begins from the premise that everything is designed, and that the designed goes on designing.

Design Philosophy is not the same as design thinking, which is a form of instrumental thinking in which an array of methods and techniques are brought to problem situations.[8] Clearly it is not the same as the philosophy of individual designers. Design Philosophy shares some of the interests of the philosophy of technology, but the aim is not to establish it as a discipline or sub-discipline. Design Philosophy is the chosen designation rather than the philosophy of design because that naming is more prone to lead back toward an inward-looking focus on professional design. While Design Philosophy can and does take current design practice as an object of analysis, this is never its limit.

Design Philosophy opens design to be interrogated and theorized beyond the parameters of professional design, which, as argued above, is the horizon of limitation of most academic design research and thinking. Within this horizon, the ideas that "everything is designed" and "design is fundamental to being human" are either of little interest or felt to be threatening. When everything is design, does design disappear? When everyone is a designer do designers become redundant? From the perspective of Design Philosophy such questions are essential, pressing.

Design Philosophy is a meeting of design and philosophy; it could be written as Design/Philosophy to indicate a non-hierarchical relation, a condition of give and take, wherein one moment of a dialogue philosophy is dominant, at another design is dominant.

Rationale and organization of *The Design Philosophy Reader*

Backward and forward movements between design and philosophy characterizes the relation of texts published here: sometimes within a single text the connections between philosophy and design are obvious, sometimes this is not apparent until further texts are read. Design Philosophy, as should be clear from the foregoing discussion, is not a pluralist project. No attempt has been made to assemble a representative range of philosophers and philosophies. Nor has there been an attempt to represent the oft-cited design theorists such as Herbert Simon, Christopher Alexander, or Donald Schön, this because their work is available in several other edited collections of writing on design. Many of the contributors to this volume take these design theorists as a starting point to go beyond, and are less concerned with defining design process than with what designed things *do*. This also explains why anthropological and sociological studies of, for example, material culture and consumption are relevant to Design Philosophy. As said, Design Philosophy is still in formation, yet it doesn't claim to be "new," and regards many old texts as either still, or newly relevant. As well as a rough balance between old and new writing, texts have been selected across a range of difficulty, as it is presumed that most readers will not have a background in academic philosophy.

The selected texts are organized into eight Parts. These Parts have been formulated in terms of "what needs to be thought" in attempting to take the thinking of design beyond its discipline and professional boundaries. Yet the categories of what needs to be thought are difficult to contain, they intersect, are porous, overflow, and merge with one another, so there is an inevitable arbitrariness in the set-up of the parts and allocation of texts to parts. Yet this is not an argument for abandoning categories altogether. As Levi-Strauss said about "primitive" modes of thinking, "any classification is superior to chaos"[9] and we would do well to remember all our thinking whether "civilized" or "savage" is primitive in relation to the complexity of the totality of "what is." Many of the texts selected, as well as the texts they discuss, are neither from Design Theory nor Philosophy, but from anthropology, sociology, architectural theory, decolonial studies, science and technology studies, and other fields.

Each Part comprises between five and eight texts and an introduction to the issue or theme that the assembled texts address directly or indirectly. Additionally, each text has a very brief introduction. The texts are from journal articles and books; many have had some editing, such as removing sections not crucial to the main argument, this being indicated as ellipses (. . .). This has been done so as to present a good number of texts of varying levels of difficulty. At the end of each part are suggestions for further reading which are not intended to be comprehensive, but simply openings to explore the issues further or to relate them to other bodies of knowledge.

Part I, *The Essence of Design* asks "what is design fundamentally?" with different stories told of design's origins by Bernard Stiegler, Tony Fry, and Bruno Latour, all of which are argued to bear upon what design subsequently became and what it could yet be. "What designed things do" is central to Albert Borgman's essay and the second extract by Fry, setting this up for elaboration in Parts III, IV, V, and VI.

Part II, *The Practice of Design* shifts to the activity of designing, asking: what does it mean to design? Is it a special kind of making distinct from craft or art? Is design a set of skills to be applied or a mode of producing new knowledge? Engaging these questions takes us to consider some of the fundamental categories of thought created by Greek philosophers to define different human capacities of thought and action and determine relative significance. Their ideas of, for instance, *episteme, techne, praxis* and *phronesis* are revisited to better understand binaries (like theory/practice) that continue to stand in the way of developing new *practices* of design.

Part III, *The Ethos of Design* juxtaposes conventional understandings of professional ethics and design ethics with the deeper agenda of philosophical ethics, addressed in texts by Emmanuel Levinas and Judith Butler. Other selected texts, by Elaine Scarry and Cameron Tonkinwise open consideration of "an ethics of things," showing how a good deal of designed materiality already acts in ethical or unethical ways, providing care or harm, and inclining human beings toward certain actions and habits. Several of the contributors argue that the dominant condition of unsustainability requires design ethics to be remade.

Part IV, *Design and the Other* builds on the question of Otherness in the philosophy of Emmanuel Levinas, bringing it to the specificity of cultural, political, and economic power. The historically longstanding, violent relation between Same and Other that was produced by colonialism and its after-effects is briefly outlined in the Introduction to the selected texts which range across the coloniality of knowledge, Eurocentrism, modernity, and globalization, and three texts on modes of thinking, designing, and dwelling from China, Japan, and Egypt that have been misread or unable to be comprehended through Western eyes.

Part V, *Being Designed and Things* considers the relational structure of people and things. Most of the texts are informed by phenomenology or post-phenomenology, so some brief orientations are presented on two key ideas of phenomenological philosophy: object and world. The selected texts are a mix of Philosophy and design theory, chosen to bring out the many levels on which "we are designed by being with designed things," including being inducted into unsustainable modes of being in the world.

Part VI, *The Designing of Technology* extends the concerns of Part V, with texts selected to reveal the depth and complexity of the human-technology relation. In the selected texts, artisanal and industrial technologies are discussed, as well as technologies of writing and memory, but all go beyond functional considerations by posing ontological questions (Heidegger and Stiegler on "what is the being of technology?") or considering systemic effects (Simondon and Heim).

Part VII, *The Designing of Visuality* goes to the dominance of the visual in Western culture and its global diffusion; the visual as a mode of producing knowledge as in "making things visible"; and the image as seduction, as in "the spectacle of consumption" and the addictive visuality of screen-based entertainment. The texts, which include extracts from Plato, Heidegger, Baudrillard, and Bourdieu, consider visuality in relation to truth, power, social meaning, and the sign-driven economy.

Part VIII, *Designing After the End* assembles texts by contemporary philosophers including Rosa Braidotti, Isabelle Stengers, Claire Colebrook, and Benjamin H. Bratton, thinking the implications of the "condition of now" including new technological developments, as they are already shaping futures. One of the conditions of now is the ongoing legacy of industrial production as it impacts on climate futures and species extinction. New developments, such as artificial intelligence and genetic programming, are not so much new, but moving fast from speculation to actualization, hastening the arrival of the posthuman—an event feared and mourned by some, cautiously welcomed by others. What is clear is that the depth and scale of what is already underway cannot be responded to, shaped, or redirected by current forms of design thinking and practice. While there are a small number of designers and thinkers engaging with contemporary philosophy to better understand what needs thought, acted upon, made, remade, and eliminated, this needs to increase significantly. Conversely, contemporary philosophy needs to better understand the depth of the designed and the reconfigurative potential of designing, instead of stumbling over a few designed objects every now and again, or viewing the naturalized artificial as if it had dropped down from the sky.

Notes

1. Clive Dilnot, "The Matter of Design," *Design Philosophy Papers* Volume 13, Issue 2, 2015, 115–23.

2. Edward Woodhouse and Jason W. Patton "Design by Society: Science and Technology Studies and the Social Shaping of Design," introduction to *Design Issues* Volume 20, Issue 3, Summer 2004, 1–12.

3. This blocking of thinking is named by Isabelle Stengers as stupidity. "Stupidity is active, it feeds on its effects, on the manner in which it dismembers a concrete situation, in which it destroys the capacity for thinking and imagining of those who envisaged ways of doing things differently." Isabelle Stengers, *In Catastrophic Times: Resisting the Coming Barbarism* trans. Andrew Goffey, London: Open Humanities Press, 2015, p. 119.

4. G. E. R. Lloyd, *Adversaries and Authorities: Investigations into Ancient Greek and Chinese Science* Cambridge: Cambridge University Press, 1996, p. 2.

5. The establishment of philosophy as a distinct domain of knowledge involved the construction of its history. In surveying histories of philosophy written in different eras, Peter Park argues that there was a shift away from the paradigm of philosophy as a way of life to that of academic philosophy as a systematic explanation of everything. He shows how Enlightenment philosophers and historians excluded or downplayed the philosophies and religions of Persia, India, China, and Africa as sources of Greek philosophy, while the contributions of Islamic and Jewish philosophy to the development of European philosophy after the Middle Ages were marginalized. These erasures were used to justify the claim that philosophy was a uniquely European achievement. Peter K. J. Park, *Africa, Asia, and the History of Philosophy: Racism in the Formation of the Philosophical Canon, 1780–1830* Albany: State University of New York Press, 2011. Also see review of Park's book by Mohammad Azadpur in *SCTIW Review: Journal of the Society for Contemporary Thought and the Islamicate World*, March 5, 2015.

6. Dmitri Panchenko "Thales and the Origin of Theoretical Reasoning" 2005, unpublished translation of book published in Greek, artesliberales.spbu.ru/contacts-ru/publications/d_panchenko/d_panchenko_1 ; also see paper by D. Panchenko, "Thales and the Origin of Theoretical Reasoning," *Configurations* Volume 1, Issue 3, Fall 1993, 387–414.

7. Emmanuel Levinas, *Basic Philosophical Writings* eds. Adriaan T. Peperzak, Simon Critchley, and Robert Bernasconi, Bloomington: University of Indiana Press, 1996, pp. 26–29.

8. See Lucy Kimbell, "Rethinking Design Thinking Part 1," *Design and Culture* Volume 3, Issue 3, 2011 and "Rethinking Design Thinking Part 2," *Design and Culture* Volume 4, Issue 2, July 2012.

9. Levi-Strauss, "The Science of the Concrete" in *The Savage Mind* trans. George Weidenfeld and Nicolson, London: Weidenfeld and Nicolson, 1976, p. 15.

PART I
THE ESSENCE OF DESIGN

INTRODUCTION

What is design fundamentally, what is its essence?

There is an extensive literature stretching back over fifty years and constituting the field of design research that has sought to answer this question. As indicated in the Introduction, this was very much focused on the design profession and establishing design as a discipline within universities. So, the motivation of the inquiry into the nature of design from within institutionalized design is fundamentally different from philosophical enquiry.

Take the example of the often heard statement, "Designing is a fundamental human capacity." For someone whose interest is to define the nature of design as practiced by professional designers ("expert design," as Ezio Manzini calls it) this is a supplementary statement that is not much interested in defining human capacities as such or in locating designing among other human capacities, nor in the question that underlies this, which is what constitutes human beings *as* human. For example, Ezio Manzini states that on the one hand there is diffuse design: a generalized human ability; and on the other, there is expert design, that is, designers as those "endowed with specific design skills and culture."[1] The emphasis is on the expert designer, passing over diffuse designing as an under-developed version of expert designing, only of interest as the basis out of which "expert design" is built. Fry, in the extract published here from *Becoming Human by Design*, intentionally inverts this via a paleontological imagining of the origin of design.

One common definition of design is to prefigure something that doesn't yet exist. This could be a totally new invention, the modification of an existing thing to a new use, or even a different way of organizing resources or people or workflow. The common feature across this variety of situations is that of seeking to bring about change, major or minor, and devising a means to do this. One of the most frequently quoted definitions is Herbert Simon's "Everyone designs who devises courses of action aimed at changing existing situations into preferred ones."[2] This moves from a desire or perceived need for change, to a decision to bring it about, to a prefiguration of the changed situation as a concept, plan, visualization, model, drawing, specifications, as the "preferred situation" moves from the level of overview down to the detail. The assumption is that this process of prefiguration is coupled to a means of realization. The point here is design's difference from free-floating visions, dreams, utopias, or even day-dream doodles. Design can be visionary or mundane, but either way, it is directed toward realization in a form other than the design itself. Here is the crucial distinction between art and design. The artist's work is finished with the last brushstroke on the canvas, while the designer's completed design is just the start of a process—a set of plans for a building, CAD rendering, and data for the mass production of a product, a lay-out for a magazine to be printed. However, the demarcation between design and production, concept and realization is fast becoming erased by computation on many levels: with software, apps, and other digital commodities, the design, end product, and distribution all occur on the same plane, moreover the designing does not have to end because the digital medium allows for, in fact induces, continuous design of versions, updates, variations.[3]

To return to Herbert Simon's definition of design: "devising courses of action aimed at changing existing situations into preferred ones" makes clear that design is for a purpose, it is instrumental. The instrumental character of design predated the arrival of professional design to serve industrial production, nevertheless this event along with the spread of rationalist thinking, turned design toward instrumentalism, whereby everything must serve a purpose. Simon's definition is based on the idea that design is fundamentally about problem-solving. His statement can be, and frequently is, turned into a diagram showing "the design process" with separate stages for problem definition and exploration; solution generation, testing, feedback, re-iteration, and so forth. The flaw with the instrumental problem-and-solution model is first that most of what professional designers work on are not actually problems, except in a derivative sense; "we (the corporation) need a new look for our sportswear/frozen desserts/outdoor furniture/packaged holidays/whatever"; and the designer's "problem" is to generate ideas, concepts, visualizations for products/services directed toward a target market, within a given price range, plus various other constraints. Second, it is now acknowledged within design and management theory and beyond that problems are frequently ill-defined and complex. Horst Ritell's idea of "tame and wicked problems" is one registration of this,[4] another is that problem defining requires more attention, because so often, the first-named problem is a symptom of another, usually larger, problem. And this is connected to the crucial question of "for whom is this a problem?"

A different approach to the question of "what is design, essentially?" is to shift focus from the designer to the designed. This is what a number of philosophers of technology and design theorists do, and in this they take their cue from philosopher Martin Heidegger's interrogation of the nature of being. The being of some entity, for Heidegger, is not to be found in stasis, in the fixed properties of a thing, in its materials or chemical composition or molecular structure—that is, as science would describe it. Instead, the being of something is how it is acts in the world including how it interacts with a human being. The essence of a thing that exists to be used—which is the nature of all designed things—comes to be known in using it, rather than standing back and observing or making a theoretical or scientific study of it. As human beings our primordial understanding of things comes from pre-reflective engagement with them. And in engaging something, the thing itself makes demands on us—if it is a car we must use feet and hands to operate switches, pedals, and steering wheel; if it is made of glass we must handle it carefully. This is ontological designing and "the designing of the designed" as explained by Fry. Rather than designing as an intentional process that ends in a finished product, the process never stops—the designed thing doesn't just sit there in the world as a completed, finished thing—it prompts process—as people engage with it. And as Albert Borgman argues, the quality of that engagement is enhanced or diminished according to what the designed thing allows or doesn't allow those engaging with it to do.

Notes

1. Ezio Manzini, "Design in the Transition Phase: A New Design Culture for the Emerging Design," *Design Philosophy Papers* Volume 13, Issue 1, 2015.

2. Herbert A. Simon, *The Sciences of the Artificial*, 3rd ed., Cambridge, MA: MIT Press, 1996, p. 111. He goes onto say, "The intellectual activity that produces material artifacts is no different fundamentally from the one that prescribes remedies for a sick patient or the one that devises a new sales plan for a company or a social welfare policy for a state."

3. See Part V: Cameron Tonkinwise, "Is Design Finished?".

4. See Richard Buchanan, "Wicked Problems in Design Thinking," *Design Issues* Volume 8, Issue 2, Spring 1992, 5–21.

CHAPTER 1
THE FAULT OF EPIMETHEUS
Bernard Stiegler

Note from editor: In retelling a story of the origin of human beings as told by Plato, Bernard Stiegler is less interested in the drama of the fire-stealing Prometheus (this he shares with Bruno Latour) than in his not-so-clever brother, Epimetheus. The story starts with a mistake by the gods, as a result of which humans have no choice other than to make, with practical skills, the conditions of their existence from the raw materials of nature.

In the Greek mythology of technics, two ideas, *prometheia* and *epimetheia* which stem from the name of gods are handed down to everyday language.

(.....)

The tragic Greek understanding of technics ..... does not oppose two worlds. It composes *topoi* that are constitutive of mortality, being at mortality's limits: on the one hand, immortal [like the Gods], on the other hand, living without knowledge of death (animality); in the gap between these two there is technical life – that is, dying. Tragic *anthropogony* is thus a *thanatology* that is configured in two moves (*coups*), the doubling-up of Prometheus by Epimetheus.

(.....)

In the Platonic dialogue of his name, Protagoras narrates the myth of Prometheus and Epimetheus in the following terms:

> Once upon a time, there existed gods but no mortal creatures. When the appointed time came for these also to be born, the gods formed them within the earth out of a mixture of earth and fire and the substances which are compounded from earth and fire. And when they were ready to bring them to the light, they charged Prometheus and Epimetheus with the task of equipping them and allotting suitable powers (*dunameis*) to each kind. Now Epimetheus begged Prometheus to allow him to do the distribution himself—"and when I have done it," he said, "you can review it." So he persuaded him and set to work. In his allotment he gave to some creatures strength without speed, and equipped the weaker kinds with speed. Some he armed with weapons, while to the unarmed he gave some other faculty and so contrived means for their preservation. To those that he endowed with smallness, he granted winged flight or a dwelling underground; to those which he increased in stature, their size itself was a protection. *Thus he made his whole distribution on a principle of compensation, being careful by these devices that no species should be destroyed. . . .* Now Epimetheus was not a particularly clever person, and before he realized it he had used up all the available powers on the brute beasts, and being left with the human race (*non-aloga*) on his hands unprovided for, did not know what to do with them. While he was puzzling about this, Prometheus came to inspect the work, and found the other animals well off for everything, but man naked, unshod, unbedded, and unarmed, and already the appointed day had come, when man too was to emerge from within the earth into the daylight. Prometheus therefore, being at a loss to provide any means of salvation for man, stole from Hephaestus and Athena the gift of skill in the arts (*ten enteknen sophian*) together with fire—for without fire there was no means (*amekhanon*)

for anyone to possess or use this skill—and bestowed it on man. In this way man acquired sufficient resources to keep himself alive, but he had no political wisdom (*sophia*). This art was in the keeping of Zeus. . . . Through this gift man had the means of life, but Prometheus, so the story says, thanks to Epimetheus, had later on to stand his trial for theft.

Since, then, man had a share in the portion of the gods, in the first place because of his divine kinship he alone among living creatures believed in gods, and set to work to erect altars, and images of them. Secondly, by the art which they possessed, men soon discovered articulate speech (*phonen*) and names (*onomata*) and invented houses and clothes and shoes and bedding and got food from the earth. (Plato 1961, *Protagoras*, 320d—322a, my emphasis)[1]

It is immediately by deviating from the equilibrium of animals, from tranquility—a departure engendered by the fault of Epimetheus that mortals occur. Before the deviation, there is nothing. Then the accidental event happens, the fault of Epimetheus: to have forgotten humans. Humans are the forgotten ones. Humans only occur through their being forgotten; they only appear in disappearing.

Fruit of a double fault—an act of forgetting, then of theft—they are naked like small, premature animals, without fur and means of defense, in advance of themselves, as advance, and also as delay (no qualities are left, everything has already been distributed). They do not yet possess the art of the political, which will be made necessary by their prematureness directly ensuing from the technical. But this "not yet" does not imply that there will be two steps to their emergence, a time of a full origin, followed by a fall: there will have been nothing at the origin but the fault, a fault that is nothing but the de-fault of origin or the origin as de-fault (*le defaut d'origine ou l'origine comme defaut*). There will have been no appearance except through disappearance. Everything will have taken place at the same time, in the same step.

Source: Bernard Stiegler *Technics and Time 1: The Fault of Epimetheus* trans. Richard Beardsworth and George Collins, Stanford: Stanford University Press, 1998, pp. 185–88.

Note

1. Plato *The Collected Dialogues* ed. Edith Hamilton and Huntington Cairns, Bollingen Series LXX, Princeton N.J.: Princeton University Press, 1961.

CHAPTER 2
IN THE BEGINNING
Tony Fry

Note from editor: If what distinguishes human beings from other species is their ability to make, to shape found material into things for their own use, as suggested in The Fault of Epimetheus by Bernard Stiegler, just how far back does this go? Was the making of tools also the making of human beings? At what point does design arrive? Was it a flash of recognition – an augenblick – wherein a potential for making otherwise was seen? And what of the animal that remained, that has never departed?

There was no 'first man'. We did not arrive by virtue of originary *ur-time*; out of 'Adam and Eve', or from a noble or divine birth. Rather we arrived out of a now lost species over a vast expanse of time. The idea of a 'missing link' to apes and chimpanzees has now been abandoned by informed sources – it no longer serves any useful purpose.[1] What is known is that there were partially bipedal hominids walking the planet 6 million years ago and around two and a half million years ago there were hominids walking fully upright.[2] The earliest hominids, classified mainly as *Australopithecus*, were African, displaying what have been named as the three criteria of humanity: erect posture while walking; a free hand during this locomotion; and a 'short' face (identified by the size and position of teeth). The development of the brain came along with these characteristics and had a direct relation to them.[3] Development was dependent on processes of material evolution whereby the body and mind increasingly, if slowly, embraced higher levels of complexity. Paleo-archaeological information indicates that the more the hand was employed, the greater the demand was made on the brain. As a result of this demand, the more the cerebral structure improved (improvement being indicated by the increased size of the brain evidenced by an increase in size of the skull's brain cavity[4]) and the more the brain developed a capacity to advance social interactions, which in turn stimulated the brain.

The interactivity between the hand and the material world, together with the strengthening of social contact and structure established the key relations between the construction of a social world and those actions that started to form a world of proto-human existence within the world at large. But the slowness of the rate of change is hard for us to comprehend – incredibly small changes took hundreds of thousands of years.

World formation (of a world-within-the-world) was an ontological condition. There was no vision, just a deposit of change via process. The formation of an un-named world that evolves alongside its maker was central to the coming into being of the human, and was indivisible from the partial rupture of the human from its retained, but repressed, animality. Obviously, the more this activity became intrinsic, the more 'the world' that was being formed was prefigured by intent (by design at its most basic level) the more the gap and difference between other animals and hominids became.

(.....)

Contemporary debates on the human/animal relation have paid considerable attention to Heidegger's ideas, particularly from Part 2 of his *The Fundamental Concepts of Metaphysics* (a book based on lectures of 1929/30, first published in German among his collected works in 1983, and in English in 1995[5]). The main focus of attention has been on his explicated comment on the stone being worldless, the animal being poor of world and the human having a world.[6]

In essence, as the stone was viewed by Heidegger as independent and inanimate – as such it lacks sentient quality and in its unfeeling has no sense of its existence – hence it is deemed to be without a world. The issue of the animal 'being poor of world' is clearly more complex. It does have a limited world, but for Heidegger, the animal is constricted in a world as a condition of environmental confinement that for it is 'a fixed sphere that is incapable of further expansion or contraction'.[7] All animals are claimed to be captive to their conditions of existence, and while 'open' to other things they are (by degree) in a state of captivation within the 'nature' of their ecology – it is their *habitus*. Here again difference begs acknowledgement – a bird in a forest or ape in a jungle 'experience' the open in some form or another, while a steer in a feedlot or a chicken in a battery cage live in an environment of absolute ecological deprivation. At the same time, all animals are captive to what it is they are – they all have the individual or collective character of '*being absorbed*' within what it is they are (which means they cannot simply be individuated into that which has no existential selfhood).[8]

(.....)

A need to know is purely a human need. One could argue that what an animal lacks of world, we lack of environment. Both they and we are in our own ways held captive. Our openness, our freedom, is inappropriately generalised – our reality is relative. In many ways 'we' remain captive to our animality and as such share some of the environmental circumscription of animals. More than this: is not our condition of becoming open to becoming closed (job security, the domestic, urban life, etc.,) not the very essence of our being captured in a transmuting environment (once 'the world itself' now dominantly a condition mostly within the insecure settlement of the world-within-the-world)? So while in the context of the everyday, our animality remains mostly concealed. Yet it can instantly arrive in the open as lust, fear or violence. Moreover, 'the irresolvable struggle between unconcealedness and concealedness, which defines the human world, is an internal/eternal struggle between 'man' and/as animality'.[9]

(.....)

Emergence: Out of the phylum

We *Homo sapiens* emerged out of a phylum – the collectivity of all those hominoid beings before us as *they* accrued and developed intelligence, all gathered in a bequest of knowledge, materials, techniques and tools. All that 'we' achieved came from appropriation that was oblivious to any correlation between development and destruction (readable as a 'will to power'). 'We' have, in our coming into being (as it ruptured our relation to our zoological heritage) always, inherently and mostly unknowingly, been disposed toward the unsustainable. Of course, this condition did not become critical until we: (i) became of sufficient numbers and with a volume of 'productive output' to dramatically amplify our negative planetary impacts: and, (ii) created a way of life removed from directly observing the impacts of our actions upon the natural environment and thereby adjusting our actions accordingly (which is what hunter/gathers did). These impacts, while having planetary consequences, most fundamentally diminish our finitude.

As we shall consider in some detail, the crucial factor in our species emergence as creators and destroyers was the use of tools. Initially, something like 2.5 million years ago, a stone was picked up by a proto-hominoid animal and used to smash an object containing food (for instance, a coconut, other nuts or a marrow bone). The stone was simply a bodily extension 'much like an animal uses it claws'. But it was this use of the stone that emplaced the means to prefigure the arrival of stones as tools. We have now arrived at a point where the nature of the stone, the animal, the human and world evoked by Heidegger can be revisited.

The animal picks up the stone and slowly discovers, in its use, new capability. Slowly, oh so slowly (the paleontological consensus is that it was well over one and a half million years) two flint stones are picked up and smashed together to reveal something new. No doubt a huge number of stones would have been smashed together before this moment, but this time and in a flash – an *augenblick,* an instant moment of reflective thought arrives – a potentiality is seen. The stone is perceived as something else (retrospectively named as what we would now call a tool, a chopper) and the experiment of use begins – who knows for how long. But nonetheless this is the birth of a new skill. Now technics and ontological designing move from the prefigured (the object and idea with potential) to continually enacted innovation. But again the process is slow – very slow. Yet what has begun now will never stop.

Without the stone, the animal to become hominid would not have started on the path toward humanity. The inanimate was animated in a process that was to eventuate in the formation of the animal/human nexus and the world-within-the-world of 'its' creation. The determinate factor to emphasise was the arrival of a relational potential of becoming in which chance cannot be discerned from destiny. So while the stone can never materially become more than stone, it can become appropriated in use to become a material thing able to be directed toward 'thinging' in particular ways – thereby becoming an employed agent of change with symbolic value. As such it could, and did, acquire functionality as a designing object of use, innovation and causal change of its user. It was, as said, a crucial agent in the animal becoming other, and more than, itself. Appropriating the stone was the appropriative event par excellence!

Complexity of thought started to increase as a result of the continuing and dynamic interaction between mind, hand, tool, environment and the made. Over millennia, this developmental dynamic (which cannot be reduced to mere technics) established, along with the rise of the power of language and the symbolic, a brain that increased in size by a third. Our cognitive capacity could be said to have arrived out of the pre-linguistic encounter of the animal with the stone. The ontological designing journey that began in this moment has not ended. But what is now evident is that the complexity of the agency of what designs (us) is beyond our comprehension. What remains open is the question of our fate – is it actually sealed by this agency? The proposition that underpins almost everything said here is that, in large part, it is. What this means is that our destiny and design conflate. As all that has gone before tells us, the human is a product of the world of its own creation, and while this world impinges on the animal that we are, it remains much of what it always has been in the given world of biophysical natural, and unnatural change.

Source: Tony Fry *Becoming Human by Design* Berg: London, 2012, pp. 65–72.

Notes

1. See E. Delson, I. Tattersall, J.A. Van Couvering & A.S. Brooks (eds) *Encyclopedia of human evolution and prehistory* New York: Garland Publishing, 2000; and Carl Zimmer *Where Did We Come From?* Sydney: ABC Books, 2005, p. 43.

2. Ibid.

3. Andre Leroi-Gourhan *Gesture and Speech* (trans. Anna Bostock Berger) Cambridge (Mass): MIT Press, 1998, pp. 18–19.

4. Ibid., p. 59.

5. Martin Heidegger *The Fundamental Concepts of Metaphysics* (trans. William McNeill and Martin Walker) Bloomington: Indiana University Press, 1995.

6. Three years later (1933) Heidegger added the qualification that the human was also distinguished from the animal (and obviously the stone) via 'care'. Martin Heidegger *Being and Truth* (trans. Gregory Fried and Richard Polt) Bloomington: Indiana University Press, 2010, p. 167.

7. Heidegger *The Fundamental Concepts of Metaphysics* §47, p. 198.

8. Ibid., § 59, pp. 240–41.

9. Georgio Agamben *The Open: Man and Animal* (trans. Kevin Attell) Stanford University Press, 2004, p. 69.

CHAPTER 3
A CAUTIOUS PROMETHEUS? A FEW STEPS TOWARD A PHILOSOPHY OF DESIGN
Bruno Latour

Note from editor: Bruno Latour, a philosopher and sociologist of science and technology, is one of the founders of Actor Network Theory which emphasises the agency of 'non-human actors' such as designed artefacts. Turning his attention to design in this piece (a keynote talk to a conference of Design Historians) in a seemingly contradictory way he presents designing as something modest – the arrangement of already existing things. At the same time, he evokes the omnipresence of design. Thus design is powerful, but the practice of design doesn't realise this. The posited 'humility' of design, which he controversially juxtaposes with the Promethean ambitions of modernisation, leaves room for Latour's 'politics of things'.

When I was young, the word design (imported to French from English) meant no more than what we now call "relooking" in French (a good English word that, unfortunately, does not exist in English). To "relook" means to give a new and better "look" or shape to something – a chair, a knife, a car, a package, a lamp, an interior – which would otherwise remain too clumsy, too severe or too bared if it were left only to its naked function. "Design" in this old and limited meaning was a way to redress the efficient but somewhat boring emphasis of engineers and commercial staff. Design occurred by adding a veneer of form to their creations, some superficial feature that could make a difference in taste and fashion. Even if design could be greatly admired, it was always taken as one branch of an alternative: look *not only* at the function, *but also* at the design. This dichotomy was true even though the best design was one that, in good modernist fashion (as it did in "functionalism"), approximated function as closely as possible. "Design" was always taken in this "not only… but also" balance. It was as if there were really two very different ways of grasping an object: one through its intrinsic materiality, the other through its more aesthetic or "symbolic" aspects.

I know this is a very poor rendering of what you now want to mean by "design". (I am well aware that the French use of the word is much more restricted than the Scandinavian or the English one). However, I want to utilize this definition from my youth as a base line from which to fathom the extraordinary career of this term. From a surface feature in the hands of a not-so-serious-profession that added features in the purview of much-more-serious-professionals (engineers, scientists, accountants), design has been spreading continuously so that it increasingly matters to the very substance of production. What is more, design has been extended from the details of daily objects to cities, landscapes, nations, cultures, bodies, genes, and, as I will argue, to nature itself – which is in great need of being re-designed. It is as though the meaning of the word has grown in what logicians refer to as 'comprehension' and 'extension'. First, it has grown in comprehension – it has eaten up more and more elements of what a thing is. Today everyone with an iPhone knows that it would be absurd to distinguish what has been designed from what has been planned, calculated, arrayed, arranged, packed, packaged, defined, projected, tinkered, written down in code, disposed of and so on. From now on, "to design" could mean equally any or all of those verbs. Secondly, it has grown in extension – design is applicable to ever larger assemblages of production. The range of things that can be designed is far wider now than a limited list of ordinary or even luxury goods.

(.....)

If it is true as I have claimed that we have never been modern, and if it is true, as a consequence, that "matters of fact" have now clearly become "matters of concern", then there is logic to the following observation: the typically modernist divide between materiality on the one hand and design on the other is slowly being dissolved away. The more objects are turned into things – that is, the more matters of facts are turned into matters of concern – the more they are rendered into objects of design through and through.

If it is true that the present historical situation is defined by a complete disconnect between two great alternative narratives – one of emancipation, detachment, modernization, progress and mastery, and the other, completely different, of attachment, precaution, entanglement, dependence and care – then the little word "design" could offer a very important touch stone for detecting where we are heading and how well modernism (and also postmodernism) has been faring. To put it more provocatively, I would argue that design is one of the terms that has replaced the word "revolution"! To say that everything has to be designed and redesigned (including nature), we imply something of the sort: "it is a little tracer whose expansion could prove the depth to which we have stopped believing that we have been modern. In other words, the more we think of ourselves as designers, the less we think of ourselves as modernizers. It is from this philosophical or anthropological position on design that I address this audience tonight.

Five advantages of the concept of "design"

As a concept, design implies a humility that seems absent from the word "construction" or "building". Because of its historical roots as a mere addition to the "real" practicality, sturdy materiality and functions of daily objects, there is always some *modesty* in claiming to design something anew. In design there is nothing foundational. It seems to me that to say you plan to design something, does not carry the same risk of hubris as saying one is going to build something. Introducing Prometheus to some other hero of the past as a "designer" would doubtlessly have angered him. Thus, the expansion of the word "design" is an indication (a weak one to be sure) of what could be called a post Promethean theory of action. This theory of action has arisen just at the moment (this is its really interesting feature) when every single thing, every detail of our daily existence, from the way we produce food, to the way we travel, build cars or houses, clone cows, etc is to be, well, redesigned. It is just at the moment where the dimensions of the tasks at hand have been fantastically amplified by the various ecological crises, that a non- or a post- Promethean's sense of what it means to act is taking over public consciousness.

A second and perhaps more important implication of design is an attentiveness to *details* that is completely lacking in the heroic, Promethean, hubristic dream of action. "Go forward, break radically with the past and the consequences will take care of themselves!" This was the old way - to build, to construct, to destroy, to radically overhaul: "*Après moi le déluge!*" But that has never been the way of approaching a design project. A mad attention to the details has always been attached to the very definition of design skills. And 'skill' is actually a term that is also attached to design, in the same way that design is associated with the words 'art' and 'craft'. In addition to modesty, there is a sense of skilfulness, craftsmanship and an obsessive attention to detail that make up a key connotation of design. The reason why this is a point worth remarking is because it was unthinkable to connect these features of design with the revolutionary and modernizing urges of the recent past. To the contrary, a careful attention to detail, craft and skill, was precisely what seemed reactionary as this would only have slowed the swift march to progress. The expanding concept of design scale of what has to be remade has become infinitely larger (no political revolutionary committed to challenging capitalist modes of production has ever considered redesigning the earth's climate), what it means to "make" something is also being deeply modified. The modification is so deep that things are no longer "made" or "fabricated", but rather carefully "designed", and if I may use the term, precautionarily designed. It is as though we had to combine the engineering tradition with the precautionary principle; it is as though we had to imagine Prometheus stealing fire from heaven in a cautious way! What is clear is that at this very historical juncture, two absolutely foreign sets of passions (foreign for the modernist ethos that is) are having to be recombined and reconciled.

The third connotation of the word design that seems to me so significant is that when analyzing the design of some artefact the task is unquestionably about *meaning* — be it symbolic, commercial, or otherwise. Design lends itself to interpretation; it is made to be interpreted in the language of signs. In design, there is always as the French say, *un dessein*, or in Italian, *designo*. To be sure, in its weakest form design added only superficial meaning to what was brute matter and efficiency. But as it infiltrated into to more and more levels of the objects, it carried with it a new attention to meaning. Wherever you think of something as being designed, you bring all of the tools, skills and crafts of interpretation to the analysis of that thing. It is thus of great import to witness the depths to which our daily surroundings, our most common artefacts are said to be designed. To think of artefacts in terms of design means conceiving of them less and less as modernist objects, and conceiving of them more and more as "things". To use my language artefacts are becoming conceivable as complex assemblies of contradictory issues (I remind you that this is the etymological meaning of the word "thing" in English –as well as in other European languages).[1] When things are taken as having been well or badly designed then they no longer appear as matters of fact. So as their appearance as matters of fact weakens, their place among the many matters of concern that are at issue is strengthened.

The transformation of objects into signs has been greatly accelerated by the spread of computers. It is obvious that digitalization has done a lot to expand semiotics to the core of objectivity: when almost every feature of digitalized artefacts is "written down" in codes and software, it is no wonder that hermeneutics have seeped deeper and deeper into the very definition of materiality. If Galileo's book of nature was written in mathematical terms, prodigiously expanding the empire of interpretation and exegesis, this expansion is even truer today when more and more elements of our surroundings are literally and not metaphorically written down in mathematical (or at least in computer) terms. Although the old dichotomy between function and form could be vaguely maintained for a hammer, a locomotive or a chair, it is ridiculous when applied to a mobile phone. Where would you draw the line between form and function? The artefact is composed of writings all the way down! But this is not only true of computerized artefacts and gadgets. It is also true of good old-fashioned materiality: what are nano- or bio-technologies if not the expansion of design to another level? Those who can make individual atoms write the letters "IBM", those who implant copyright tags into DNA, or who devise nano cars which "race" on four wheels, would certainly consider themselves to be designers. Here again, matter is absorbed into meaning (or rather as contested meaning) in a more and more intimate fashion.

The fourth advantage I see in the word "design" (in addition to its modesty, its attention to detail and the semiotic skills it always carries with it), is that it is never a process that begins from scratch: to design is always to *redesign*. There is always something that exists first as a given, as an issue, as a problem. Design is a task that follows to make that something more lively, more commercial, more usable, more user's friendly, more acceptable, more sustainable, and so on, depending on the various constraints to which the project has to answer. In other words, there is always something *remedial* in design. This is the advantage of the "not only… but also" feature although I criticized it above. This split is a weakness to be sure (there is always the temptation of seeing design as an afterthought, as a secondary task, as a less serious one than those of engineering, commerce and science) but it is also an immense advantage when compared to the idea of creation. To design is never to create *ex nihilo*. It is amusing that creationists in America use the word "intelligent design" as a rough substitute for "God the Creator". They don't seem to realize the tremendous abyss that exists between creating and designing. The most intelligent designers never start from a *tabula rasa*. God the designer is really a redesigner of something else that was already there —and this is even truer for His Son as well as for the Spirit, who both are sent to redeem what has been botched in the first place… If humanity "has been made (or should I have said designed?) as the image of God", then they too should learn that things are never created but rather carefully and modestly redesigned. It is in that sense that I take the spread of the word design as a clear substitute for revolution and modernization. I do so furthermore, because there is always something slightly superficial in design, something clearly and explicitly transitory, something linked to fashion and thus to shifts in fashions, something tied to tastes and therefore somewhat relative. Designing is the antidote to founding, colonizing, establishing, or breaking with the past. It is an antidote to hubris and to the search for absolute certainty, absolute beginnings, and radical departures.

The fifth and decisive advantage of the concept of design is that it necessarily involves an ethical dimension which is tied into the obvious question of *good versus bad design*. In the modernist style, this goodness and badness were qualities that matters of fact could not possibly possess. They were supposed to sit there, undisputable, and removed from any normative judgment. This was so much so that their entire purpose was to make the fact/value distinction possible. "We are there whether you like it or not". But it is easy to understand that when you say that something has been "designed", you are not only authorized but forced to ask whether it has been well or badly designed. The spread of design to the inner definitions of things carries with it, not only meaning and hermeneutics, but also morality. More exactly, it is as if materiality and morality were finally coalescing. This is of great importance because if you begin to redesign cities, landscapes, natural parks, societies, as well as genes, brains and chips, no designer will be allowed to hide behind the old protection of matters of fact. No designer will be able to claim: "I am just stating what exists", or "I am simply drawing the consequences of the laws of nature", or "I am simply reading the bottom line". By expanding design so that it is relevant everywhere, designers take up the mantle of morality as well. …This normative dimension that is intrinsic to design offers a good handle from which to extend the question of design to politics. A politics of matters of facts and of objects has always seemed far fetched; a politics of designed things and issues is somewhat more obvious. If things, or rather *Dinge*, are gatherings, as Heidegger used to define them, then it is a short step from there to considering all things as the result of an activity called "collaborative design" in Scandinavia. This activity is in fact the very definition of the politics of matters of concern since all designs are "collaborative" designs – even if in some cases the "collaborators" are not all visible, welcomed or willing.

(.....)

Source: Keynote lecture by Bruno Latour, Sciences-Po, for the *Networks of Design* meeting of the Design History Society, Falmouth, Cornwall, 3rd September 2008. Original source: Brown Walker Press http://brownwalker.com/book/1599429063

Note

1. B. Latour *From Realpolitik to Dingpolitik. How to Make Things Public. An Introduction.*, in *Making Things Public. Atmospheres of Democracy* B. Latour and P. Weibel (eds). 2005, MIT Press: Cambridge, Mass. pp. 1–31.

CHAPTER 4
THE DEPTH OF DESIGN
Albert Borgmann

Note from editor: As a philosopher of technology, Albert Borgmann reflects upon what designed things do to human beings at a profound level. His concern in this piece is with what Fry names as "the designing of the designed". Working out of the phenomenological tradition, Borgmann attends to things as they are ordinarily encountered, noting the ways in which everyday life is shaped by material culture. He is troubled by the tendency of modern, designed devices to disburden, because this also entails a diminishment of possibilities for engagement.

The material culture of modern life is unique in its scale and sophistication. The most awesome and far-flung monuments of premodern life are modest, and its most sophisticated machines are crude, in comparison. In assembling our material culture, we have been much concerned with safety, efficiency, and commodiousness, and we have undertaken gigantic if often insufficient efforts to improve our material surroundings in these respects. At the same time, we almost entirely disavow responsibility for the moral and cultural excellence of our material surroundings.[1]

There is one heading, however, under which we discuss and judge the quality of our material culture, viz., design. Accordingly I propose we think of design as the excellence of material objects. Design in this objective sense is everyone's concern. So are health, justice, and education. And yet society especially entrusts the latter three concerns to particularly qualified people, to doctors, lawyers, and teachers. A group that has been so entrusted with a precious social good we call a profession, and typically such a group discharges its responsibility in a collegial and principled way.[2] Similarly design can be thought of as a professional practice, and designers as professionals.

To stress the coordination between design in its objective sense as the excellence of the material culture and design in its practical sense as a profession is eminently urgent and desirable. Design, taken as an objective quality, needs design as a professional practice because the quality of the material culture urgently needs the care and advocacy of professionals. Design as a practice needs design as an object because designers as professionals appear to suffer from an uncertain sense of identity that would be firmed up through the focus on the excellence of the material environment.

To be sure, daunting obstacles stand in the way of this mutual alignment. Perhaps the fundamental problem is the seemingly inexorable tendency of the excellence of the material culture toward attenuation, superficiality, and even disappearance. Consider the development of sound reproduction. The original Victrolas had an intelligible and dramatic shape and required constant and careful attention from their users. More sophisticated information retrieval by way of diamond pickups and the development of electronic amplification reduced the need for interaction and the intelligibility of the apparatus. There was less occasion for tangible and expressive design. The day is not far off when the daily presence of a sound system will have shrunk to a hand-held device consisting of a small keyboard and screen that allows you to call up whatever and however much music you desire. The musical information, the retrieval and amplification mechanisms, and the loudspeakers will be concealed behind opaque surfaces. The designer's scope will be reduced to making these surfaces as pleasing and the programming device as portable and functional as possible.

In other instances, the drift of technological development tends past reduction to invisibility. ….. The underlying phenomenon in these developments is a shift from aesthetic design to engineering design and a concomitant shift from user engagement to user disburdenment. To begin with the latter shift, should we worry about the disappearance of engagement? What is engagement?

"Engagement" is a term to specify the symmetry that links humanity and reality. Human beings have certain capacities that prefigure the things of the world; and conversely what is out there in the world has called forth human sense and sensibility. More specifically the most commanding and subtle things engage our talents most fully; and, conversely again, to employ our capacities most deeply we turn to the most powerful and intricate things. Engagement is to designate the profound realization of the humanity-reality commensuration. For example, a musical instrument normally engages a person deeply; a television program typically fails to do so.

(…..)

As engagement has declined, so has aesthetic design. More precisely, design as a practice has divided into an engineering branch and an aesthetic branch. Engineering devises the ingenious underlying structures that disburden us from the demands of exertion and the exercise of skills and leave us with the opaque and glamorous commodities that we enjoy in consumption. Aesthetic design inevitably is confined to smoothing the interfaces and stylizing the surfaces of technological devices. Aesthetic design becomes shallow, not because it is aesthetic, but because it has become superficial. It has been divorced from the powerful shaping of the material culture. Engineering has taken over the latter task. But it in turn conceals the power of its shapes under discreet and pleasant surfaces.

If we are concerned to revive engagement, we must try to recover the depth of design, that is, the kind of design that once more fuses engineering and aesthetics and provides a material setting that provokes and rewards engagement. Where is such depth to be found or opened up? The first possibility one might consider are those areas where design has depth of penetration, that is, the license to reshape things vigorously and from the ground up. Nowhere has this been more spectacularly so than in the reshaping of the urban environment. The two programs that have been particularly consequential in these last hundred years are the Garden City, whose design is due to Ebenezer Howard, and la ville radieuse, drawn up by Le Corbusier.[3] Both of these pioneers began by proposing a spacious, luminous, and orderly alternative to the crowded, dense, and untidy conditions of the traditional and industrial cities. Through the catalytic force of the automobile, this kind of hygienic and rigorous modernism eventually invaded and reshaped the cities' texture under the heading of urban renewal.

As we have since learned, many of us under the tutelage of Jane Jacobs, the vigor of design as a process does not always lead to equal vigor in the life that is shaped by the design.[4] In the case of urban renewal there is usually an inverse proportion. The more forceful the reshaping of the urban fabric, the more lifeless and even pathological the daily activities and practices in the new surroundings.

What has been filled in or leveled down by urban renewal is the depth of history. Most traditional cities in their irregular layout and diversity of buildings constitute something like a hallway that allows you to look down generations of different aspirations, styles, and levels of prosperity. Modernism was at pains to destroy or occlude this depth. But beginning in the late sixties, a shift and then a reversal took place. There was a rising concern to preserve the architectural heritage and a determination to revive in new buildings the architectural vocabulary of the classical and vernacular styles.[5]

This movement, whose architectural aspect has come to be called postmodernism, has led to the preservation and restoration of historic urban areas, ……

Historical preservation in downtown areas has made an important difference to urban life. …… But this urban activity is in large part simply a transplant of what used to go on in a suburban mall into a historic and urban setting. What people do here or there is eat and shop. "The background is history," it has been said, "but the foreground is late twentieth-century retailing."[6] History has become an essentially indifferent container. It has no genuine depth, like a lock that will respond to any key. The sensitivity and care of design are reduced to surface aesthetics after all.[7]

I am overemphasizing the problem. Walking, seeing, and comprehending are important ways of inhabiting a place, and those ways are much richer in a diverse and historic setting than in one where opaque glamor repels all comprehension. More important, comprehension shades over into engagement, and it is depth of engagement that truly allows and calls for depth of design.

The world of engagement that is the province of design has two principal settings, a large one in the city and a small one in the home; and both of these settings have a daily and a festive side. Daily engagement in the home is still vigorous. But it is endangered by lack of appreciation and by male chauvinism. Daily engagement is housework. Its value becomes clear when we consider its elimination. It might be eliminated technologically or socially. Technological elimination would be by way of a combination of automation and service industry. It is an arrangement that some professional people are approaching already. What is wrong with it? People who do housework extend themselves tangibly and subtly into the texture of their own most environment. They do so in furnishing, cleaning, repairing, adorning, and ordering their home. They lead a more extended and competent life than persons who are merely inserted into a prefabricated container. A home that shows the owners' housework is likely to be a more accurate and personable testimony to its inhabitants. Housework is eliminated socially when it is done by servants or a housewife. It is eliminated, of course, only for the lordly family or husband. For the privileged parties, social elimination is so tempting because it disburdens without the cost of anonymity. The only cost is injustice, a prohibitive cost as it happens.

Daily engagement in the home yields to festive engagement in the culture of the table. To clean and prepare food, to cook it, to set the table, and to clean up afterward, all this is a chore; it has the homely character of housework. But at the center of it is the celebration of a meal that engages and delights body and soul. The culture of the table in its central aspect is surely the most venerable and democratic kind of festive engagement in the home. Another is the culture of the word, conversing, telling stories, reciting poetry, and reading silently. Yet another is the culture of musicianship. And if someone wants to argue that the joint and thoughtful watching of a film can be festive, I will not demur.

Now what is the task of the designer in all this? It is twofold; there is a task of trusteeship and a task of artisanship. Designers are professionals in that they have been entrusted by society with a valued good and are hence accountable not only to the immediate desires of society but also for the well-being of the good that is in their care. The good of design is the moral and cultural excellence of the humanly shaped and built environment. More particularly, I want to urge, designers are charged with making the material culture conducive to engagement.

More particularly still, designers must constitute the common memory of practices of engagement. They must remind their clients of what has served the human family well and what has not. But in addition to this conservative task, there is a difficult innovative one. It follows from the fact that a life of full domestic engagement is impossible and undesirable today. We have neither the time nor the tolerance for all the hauling, scrubbing, sweeping, washing, darning, mending, canning, and preserving that used to engage householders. Daily domestic engagement must be selective, and festive engagement must be focal. What to select and focus on and how to secure and position the selected chores and focal things in their technological setting is not an easy task and should not be left entirely to the trials and errors of lay people.

Artisanship is required for the shaping of the engaging environment. Settings of engagement have a certain depth and unfoldedness. Consider the kitchen of a gourmet cook. There is a stove with four burners, a grill, and a hood, a row of hooks with eight pots overhead, a chopping block over to the side with six knives and two cleavers, a faucet and two sinks by the window, a ceramic pot with a bouquet of wooden spoons on the counter. These are the things that people want to move among and get their hands on. Each has a well-rounded shape, a tangible texture, a certain weight and motility, and all of them compose the setting we call the kitchen. Artisanship is the skill of creating, varying, and refining the shape, color, and texture of these things. Such designing has depth because of the wealth and disclosing power of the qualities a designer imparts to a thing. The experiential qualities of paradigmatic technological devices such as a microwave oven, a stereo set, or a refrigerator are, apart from the commodities they are intended to provide, primarily visual. The tactile and motile properties are so subordinated to ease of operation that they are nearly effaced.

In the case of a cooking pot, however, not only the colors matter, but even more so the shape, weight, heat conductivity, surface texture, even the sound it makes when you stir in it or set it down. The handling and use of a pot disclose the wealth of its properties even when its ultimate constitution is veiled by technological sophistication, as it is in a pressure-cast, ceramic-plasma-coated aluminum pan with the heat-resistant, springlock mounted, Bakelite handles.[8]

Things that invite engagement are distinguished not only by the wealth of their experiential properties but also by the disclosing power of those properties. A car does not really allow for engagement although it has a fair number of different kinds of experiential qualities. But normally the tendency is to make a car as insensitive as possible to the wider world, to outside noise and temperature and to the surface, grade, and curves of the road.

The kitchen utensils of the gourmet cook, to the contrary, disclose the texture, color, and taste of the food. The depth of the utensils opens on the depth of the world at large. They do not represent the world, as technological devices do; they allow the world to be present in its own right. Things, however, can have and hold this deeply disclosive power only if they are so designed.

(......)

There are frequent complaints that the contemporary city lacks an engaging public life.[9] ...... Not that the engaging qualities of daily city life have been without their admirers. Jane Jacobs and William Whyte have sung the praises of the vitality and charms that are to be seen in the daily errands and practices of city folk, in the ways they appropriate and animate public spaces as they do in walking, sitting, reading, eating, conversing, shopping, and playing.'[10]

As in the home, such engaging activities require an unfolded and open texture. Its principal strands are the streets, interwoven in small city blocks. This fabric must contain distinct and articulate places, shops, stores, bars, cafés, restaurants, apartments, plazas, generous sidewalks, and street furniture. ...... But what is often lacking is the substantial dailiness of city life. Many people come to an urban mall as mere tourists or shoppers. They come for pleasure, and then they leave. They do not live there and so cannot give the place the fullness of daily life, the habits, practices, chores, and errands that enact the substantial and serious side of life.

Here again designers are the guardians of common practical wisdom and the experts who help urban traditions to adapt to the advances of technology and to prosper in their midst. And here too design is deep and consequential. It is not confined to the cosmetics of a skyscraper's skin. The dimensions of spaces, the form and arrangement of street furniture, the distribution of economic and cultural functions, all these are intricate and consequential matters. If ignorantly or thoughtlessly designed, they can impede or destroy daily city life. (.....)

Source: The Depth of Design, Albert Borgmann *Discovering Design (ed. R. Buchanan & V. Margolin)* University of Chicago Press, 1995, pp. 13–22.

Notes

1. See my 'The Invisibility of Contemporary Culture' *Revue internationale de philosophie* 41(1987): 234–47.

2. Paul Starr *The Social Transformation of Medicine* New York: Basic Books, 1982, pp. 15–16.

3. Vincent Scully *American Architecture and Urbanism* 2nd ed. New York: Holt, 1988, pp. 161–73.

4. Jane Jacobs *The Death and Life of Great American Cities* New York: Random House, 1961.

5. Scully *American Architecture* pp. 257–93.

6. Bernard J. Frieden and Lynne B. Sagalyn, *Downtown, Inc.* Cambridge, MA: MIT Press, 1989, p. 175.

7. Frieden and Sagalyn *Downtown* pp. 199–213.

8. I am talking about Scanpans.

9. See 'Public Space' *Dissent* (Fall 1986): 470–85, with contributions by Michael Walzer, Michael Rustin, Gus Tyler, and Marshall Berman; and 'Whatever Became of the Public Square?' *Harper's* 281 (July 1990): 49–60, with contributions by Jack Hitt, Ronald Lee Fleming, Elizabeth Plater-Zyberk, Richard Sennett, James Wines, and Elyn Zimmerman.

10. Jacobs, *Death and Life* pp. 27–140. William H. Whyte *City: Rediscovering the Center* New York: Doubleday, 1988, pp. 8–102.

CHAPTER 5
DESIGN AS AN ONTOLOGICAL QUESTION
Tony Fry

Note from editor: Written to introduce a book that presents a series of historical studies on the power of designed things, this extract lays out a definition of 'Meta-Design', seeking to capture three crucial aspects and their inter-relation: designed things as such; the means by which they come into existence (which doesn't reduce to just 'the designer'); and what designed things do (which doesn't reduce to just their intended function). This comprehensive understanding of design, while it enormously complicates design scholarship and design education, is absolutely necessary to embrace, argues Fry, so as to grasp how unsustainability has come to be the dominant condition.

The question of design is always an ontological question, which is a question of what it does in the ways that it acts. Equally, design is also a domain of metaphysical knowledge. Design always arrives as the way something acts as, in and on the world, and as a learnt thinking (theory) that informs practices which bring something into being. It is always more than its reified forms, immediate applications or applied functional acknowledge. What the relational ensemble that is design actually determines, what it actually sets in motion as an assemblage, goes unseen. Design is everywhere as the normality of the made world that is rendered background as soon as 'design' becomes an individuated object of focus. There is not a single thing around us that is not designed — door, walls, ceiling, window, curtains, desk, lamp, computer, books, bookshelves, chairs, pens, radio, clock, pictures, waste bin, carpet, heater and a myriad of other things. Thus the world of designed objects and processes that are present for us constitute the designing environment. This pre-designed environment over-determines the designing of design processes and the products of design, all of which are deeply embedded in a circular process. The operational world, design process, designed objects, the agency of the designed and world creation constantly flow into and transform each other. To reify design, which is to present it in an objectified form removed from its dynamic in process, is to misconstrue the very nature of what design is.

There are three points of focus for this presented understanding of the design complexity:

1. the designed object that results from the design act or process (be it a city, building, industrial product, dress, visual image or garden);
2. the design agency: that is the designer designing, or the designing tool created by a designer for the design act (software, a pattern, a drawing, instructions, specifications);
3. design in process, which is the on-going designing that is the agency of the designed object as it functions or dysfunctions.

Of the third point it can be elaborated that all designed objects have determinate consequences, which may be great or small, as they constitute active environments and impacts. This is to say, all design in process futures or defutures, and that the environment out of which designing and the designed object come is a designing that prefigures the design act and the design form. Put succinctly; designers design in a designed world, which arrives by design, that designs their actions and objects, or more simply: we design our world, while our world designs us.

From what has been said, it follows that the way in which a new philosophy of design is manifested is not via an articulated system or theoretical framework but by an ontological shift that transforms how design is viewed, heard, felt, thought, understood, explained and done. Philosophy comprehended in this way is an embodied change that can only think the old through the new.

This meta-view of design (hereafter capitalised as Design) then is that which gathers the expressed particular forms of design, as object, agency and process as they exist conjuncturally and relationally in a specific time and space. Overlaying and underpinning the disposition of all elements of Design is its non-neutrality. Whatever we say Design is, it is also direction, force, power, imposition. This is why, in its omnipresence, it begs to be taken so seriously and is so implicated in, and between, the plurality of sustain-ability, the pluralism of the unsustainable, and the concealment of the crisis of unsustainability as it is misrepresented as a desirable standard of living, quality of life, needed economic growth and the like.

Anthropologically, designing is able to be recognised as omnipresent and integral to every intentional act we take. It is therefore elemental to our being and, as such is one of the defining qualities of what we are. In this respect we are all designers. We live in and by Design — our choices, be they of homes, lifestyle, dress, actions, perceptions, employment practices or environments are directed by the employment and consequence of Design. Its non-discreteness makes it seem an impossible object of study, and so legitimises its oversight.

Design always strays across fields, it always bleeds into, and travels with, the banners of work/labour/production, and consumption/culture/pleasure/lifestyle. Here is the impossibility of a history of design, since its options cover everything, or scattered fragments existing outside any regime of meaning.

No matter what its character, the activity of Design (and its application to structures, objects, forms, functions or appearances, as well as Design as thinking) has predominantly concerned itself with 'being-in-space'. In contrast, defuturing as a mode of inquiry, takes temporality as its major preoccupation, not on the basis of a wish to create the 'timeless' but rather the 'timemaking' that is bonded to the project of sustain-ability.

Restating, a critical engagement with unsustainable Design, as it defutures, has the ability to expose the profound dysfunction of the seeming functionality of now. A frontal encounter shows how Design is inscriptively posited in forms of power, exercised operationally as technology and implicated in those social, political and economic forms of industrial, post-industrial and consumer culture, which have made unsustainability a structural feature of the environment of the making of our 'natural' world.

The kind of thinking about Design exposed above will be developed in various ways later. What, however, we especially want to emphasise is that gaining an understanding of Design is of enormous critical importance to understanding how unsustainability has been created, how it defutures and what one needs to think if one is to work to create an ability to sustain. Approaching Design in this way by implication undercuts, and thus deconstructs, the agency of its existing foundations of authority in designer education, practice and scholarship. What is learnt in this exposé demands that we gain a far better grasp of how to make sense of our world, its un-freedoms and the impacts of our actions, This in turn implies that designing across the board itself be re-designed.

(.....)

… what has to be learnt is how to conserve (including conserve time) rather than taking away. Design has to be turned (by becoming informed by defuturing) from being the unwitting tool of unsustainability to become the means of making the sustainments that make time, and so serve futuring.

In order to move from the way design is presently constituted as an object of inquiry and practice, an ontological theory of design (Design) is needed. Such a theory allows questions about the consequences of the design of things and worlds (past, present and future) to be asked, and for Design, as an agency and site of a practical philosophy, to be constituted …..

An ontological theory of Design is not confined to ontological questions of philosophy or to questioning existing professional design practices. On the contrary, it presumes that thinking about and engaging with Design has to spill over into every situation in which it is possible to embrace responsible action. In sum, ontological Design is a theory and a practice concerned with the being of things (designed objects, environments, processes, texts or appearances) and the way these things create and sustain the time of the future.

Ontological Design brings into question the very division between embodied and disembodied matter by an exploration of reciprocal relations. It renders problematic the separation between us and things, subjects and objects, designing and being, world, self and others. Quite clearly, Design can make no appeal to the essential being of a thing. It cannot appeal to a ground upon which the essence of a thing can be disclosed, for it is the world rather than the thing that conceals essences. The being of a thing has no beginning, original form or foundation outside the explanatory framework of the world that its maker makes present.

'The product' (the produced thing) acts as the causal and directional focus, and limit of view, of existing design thought and practice. In contrast, Design foregrounds the relationality of the designed material or immaterial thing in or as process. However, Design does not pose itself as an absolutely determinate model able to understand or mobilise design. At the same time the relational complexity it can muster is able to shatter the frame of containment of design action, its institutional underpinning, professional application and economic direction. Such a theory exposes the limited capabilities of reason to control designing, and as such it goes well beyond current ecological design thinking and practice. What it does is to broaden views of fields of actions, effects, structures, time and objects to allow a contemplation of circumstantial remakings of 'the thing' as it changes by being in use, exchange, process, system and environment. Design, when linked to sustain-ability, does not function with certainty but with learning to change. While all design (and designing) is directional, ontologically biased Design comprehends direction. It is always multiple, relational and within a field of force: it knows everything is force (from Hegel), and power is everywhere (from Foucault).

Source: Tony Fry *A New Design Philosophy: An Introduction to Defuturing* Sydney: UNSW Press, 1999, 5–7, 73–4.

GUIDE TO FURTHER READING

A good general reference for philosophy is the internet-based *Stanford Encyclopedia of Philosophy*. For topics covered in the Introduction and Part I see the entries in the *Bloomsbury Encyclopedia of Design* (2015) on design methods (Elaine Kalantidou), design futures (Cameron Tonkinwise), futuring/defuturing (Matt Kiem), and instrumentalism (Cameron Tonkinwise). Many of the classics of design theory and methods can be found in *Design Studies: A Reader* (2009), see essays by Herbert Simon, Donald A. Schön, Victor Papanek, Abraham Moles, Buckminster Fuller, Henry Petroski, John Chris Jones, Richard Buchanan, and Donald Norman. Other key works on design methods and design process include Donald A. Schön, *The Reflective Practitioner* (1983); Nigel Cross, *Designerly Ways of Knowing* (2006); Nelson and Stolterman, *The Design Way* (2012), and going beyond professional designing, Ezio Manzini's *Design When Everybody Designs* (2015). For a critical account of Herbert Simon's extreme rationalism see D. J. Huppatz, "Revisiting Herbert Simon's 'Science of Design'" in *Design Issues* (2015). The aforementioned works and authors are theorizing desigin*ing* while works that focus on the design*ed* include Tony Fry's *Design Futuring: Sustainability, Ethics & New Practice* (2009), *Design as Politics* (2011), and *Becoming Human by Design* (2012); Anne-Marie Willis, "Ontological Designing" (2006). *The Shape of Things: A Philosophy of Design* (1999) by media theorist Vilem Flusser insightfully evokes the prefigurative power of design, especially in the essay "The Designer's Ways of Seeing." Though Latour's theory of design in "A Cautious Prometheus" published here is very different from Fry's, there is more convergence in his extended discussion of specific designed things in "Where are the Missing Masses?" (1992) and "From Realpolitik to Dingpolitik: How to Make Things Public" (2005). Albert Borgmann's analysis of disburdenment and engagement is brought to information and communications technologies in his books *Technology and the Character of Contemporary Life* (1984) and *Holding On to Reality. The Nature of Information at Turn of the Millennium* (1999), see also the critique by Peter-Paul Verbeek, "Devices of Engagement: On Borgmann's Philosophy of Information and Technology" (2002). Bernard Stiegler is a more recent and divergent thinker on technology drawing on Deleuze, Freud, Marx, Heidegger, and Simondon, see his three-volume work *Technics and Time*, English translation published by Stanford University Press. Further references on technology are given in Parts VI and VIII.

PART II
THE PRACTICE OF DESIGN

INTRODUCTION

The key question for the readings gathered in this section is "what kind of *practice* is designing?".

A common-sense approach to this question would be to ask whether designing is a talent of only some people, or a set of techniques and skills that can be taught. To answer that question, we need to examine the underlying categories—what is meant by talent, skill, and technique? A more informed approach might ask the following: Is designing a human capacity, a skill, a practice, a mode of making, or a form of knowledge? These categories also need defining, for their meanings have changed over time: activities and knowledge that were once together and regarded as complementary became separated over many centuries. A significant example is the division between theory and practice, as inscribed in the curricula of art and design schools and taught separately, on the assumption that theory equates with abstract principles while practice involves application of such principles by "doing." This goes back to a division that developed in Greek philosophy between *epistêmê* (knowledge of principles) and *technê* (art/design, skill, know-how). In early Greek philosophy—Xenophon, Socrates—knowledge was described as knowing how to do something, with no distinction between *epistêmê* as theoretical knowledge and *technê* as craft or skill. Thus it was said that Socrates could speak of the *technê* of such diverse activities as playing the harp, generalship, piloting a ship, cooking, medicine, managing an estate, smithing, and carpentry."[1] Aristotle is often blamed for initiating the opposition between theory and practice, yet, as Richard Parry says, "Aristotle refers to *technê* or craft as itself also *epistêmê* or knowledge because it is a practice grounded in an 'account'—something involving theoretical understanding."[2]

Aristotle codified other forms of knowledge—or ways that "the soul can know truth." There is *praxis*—informed practical knowledge—involving deliberation to decide a course of action whose product is the action itself as opposed to the *technê* of the craft worker whose activity of making is directed toward an end product. Then there is *phronesis*, or practical wisdom, which is not the same as *epistêmê*, because *phronesis* is not the application of a body of knowledge but action that is situation specific—and deemed to be ethical action, thus it is a virtue. These modes of knowledge and their inter-relation are discussed in Will McNeill's text in this section.

While design was not named by the Greeks or by subsequent Western philosophers as a distinct or separate activity, we can find descriptions in their writings that resonate with contemporary understandings of design. Explanations of the nature of permanence and change, of the animate and inanimate, of the faculties of human beings, and of how they can come to know the truth about such things, and how they should best conduct themselves among themselves were some of the preoccupations of Greek philosophy. Here was the genesis of certain fundamental ideas that travelled across time and still form the basis of much of our thinking today. Spanning several centuries, there was contestation of ideas (Socrates' method of dialogical questioning is famous) so some lines of thought survived, others were abandoned, and many more were transformed.

Subsequent philosophers built on, re-interpreted, selectively rejected, or recovered the Greek thinkers. So, while Aristotle and later Medieval philosophers sought to define the various human faculties, and speculated upon what exactly the thinking substance of the mind was comprised of, for seventeenth-century philosopher Rene Descartes, the only certainty was the thinking self—"the mind that I am," distinct from the body, all other bodies, and in fact everything else. This radical move, and the radical doubt it implied, set the stage for the opposition between idealism and realism, and ushered in a series of binaries that are still commonplace in thinking today: the mind/body; subjectivity/objectivity. These developments influenced what design was thought to be, as it emerged as a separate practice toward the end of the Enlightenment. Both the science-inflected model of the designer as a technical problem solver and the romanticist version of the designer as a quasi artist are regarded as irrelevant by Coyne and Snodgrass, as well as by d'Anjou who, drawing on existentialist philosophy, argues for design practice driven by a (life) project of substance.

Cartesian thinking validated "objectivity and neutral" observation: truth was to arrive by standing back and observing. This was challenged in the twentieth century by philosophy of phenomenology and hermeneutics, on two important counts: that human understanding comes from everyday immersion in the world, it is situated, it is primarily interpretive, and that it never starts from a clean slate, zero point, every observer (scientists included) comes to a situation with pre-knowledge that will frame what they encounter; they (we) are prejudiced but as philosopher Georg Gadamer pointed out, this "pre-judgment" is not a bad thing but inescapable: "Prejudices are our biases of our openness to the world. . . . They are simply the conditions whereby we experience something-whereby what we encounter says something to us."[3] If situatedness and pre-understandings are inevitable this clearly affects all actions including deliberation, designing, making. Rather than trying to overcome this with the imposition of a solidified *epistêmê*, it has to be made apparent—especially as these pre-understandings are the totality of who each and every one of us are, and as such, are generally invisible, part of "how we get on in and make sense of the world." The implication is that in situations of deliberation for action (praxis) and for designing (*technê*)—as both have the character of bringing about change—the pre-understandings of the social actors need to be made visible to themselves and others.[4]

Within academia in recent decades, the quest to understand the nature of design, in the main, has focused in closely on the designed object, and the design act as methods of designing or the "design process" as researchers and educators call it, while not entirely agreeing on what it does and doesn't entail. Still staying with the designer designing, we could shift the angle of view to ask "what is designing as *a practice*?". Practice, as in having a professional practice, being a practitioner of martial arts, or being a medical practitioner implies having a set of specialized skills. Additionally, practice suggests habits of mind, extension over time, therefore repetition, refinement (or degeneration) of skill, and accumulation (or loss) of knowledge.

Practice also has other meanings—as in social practices or the practices of everyday life. Here we note the influence of phenomenology in the social sciences and the emergence of "practice theory," which moves away from seeking to understand human behavior in terms of generalized social structures and norms, and looks instead to the performance of sociality in time and space, to the "nexus of doings and sayings" involving bodily actions, routines, equipment, material environments, and practical knowledge.[5]

This moves us from the designer to the designed object as it acts in the world (i.e., point number three in Fry's characterization of design: designed object/design agency/design in process). This, because everyday practices occur via the mediation of designed things, spaces, and procedures. This is not to say that everyday practices are deterministically designed. Rather, practices have designing agency—practices design practitioners. And in turn, those who have been inducted into a specific practice act as "carriers" "of patterns of . . . certain routinized ways of knowing-how that are historically and culturally specific."[6] Moving around the circle to point once again at the designer turns the question around—not "how do designers design?" but "what designs designers?".

Notes

1. Richard Parry, "Episteme and Techne," *The Stanford Encyclopedia of Philosophy* (Fall 2014 Edition), ed. Edward N. Zalta http://plato.stanford.edu/archives/fall2014/entries/episteme-techne/

2. Parry "Episteme and Techne." For a different account of *technê, epistêmê* and other Ancient Greek designations of knowledge see "Technology" by Cameron Tonkinwise in *Bloomsbury Encyclopedia of Design*, ed. Clive Edwards, 2015.

3. Hans Georg Gadamer, *Truth and Method* London: Sheed and Ward, 1996, p. 9. For further discussion of Gadamer, see text in Part V by Winograd and Flores.

4. See, for example, Marcus Jahnke, "Revisiting Design as a Hermeneutic Practice: An Investigation of Paul Ricoeur's Critical Hermeneutics," *Design Issues* Volume 28, Issue 2, Spring 2012, 30–40.

5. Jacqueline Lorber Kasunic, "Practices, Practice Theory," *Bloomsbury Encyclopedia of Design*.

6. Lorber Kasunic "Practices."

CHAPTER 6
SCIENCE, ART AND PRACTICAL WISDOM
Aristotle

Note from editor: Aristotle defines five types of knowledge, "The Chief Intellectual Virtues", which vary according to their object, and the means by which the knowledge is acquired and exercised. He posits these as fundamental capacities of human beings ("the states by virtue of which the soul possesses truth") and all of them involve reason ("by way of affirmation or denial"). The following extract from The Nicomachean Ethics *elaborates three of them: Science (episteme), Art (technê) and Practical Wisdom (phronesis). It is important to note that "Art" for the Greeks included all the skills of making – thus craft was not separate from painting and sculpture – the arts of visual representation that in later times, from the Renaissance onwards gained elevated status over the practical arts. For the Greek philosophers, design had not yet arrived as a separate category. However, what is of interest is that Aristotle's definition of Art fits more closely with what we now call design: "contriving and considering how something may come into being which is capable of either being or not being."*

Science—demonstrative knowledge of the necessary and eternal

… Let it be assumed that the states by virtue of which the soul possesses truth by way of affirmation or denial are five in number, i.e. art, scientific knowledge, practical wisdom, philosophic wisdom, intuitive reason; we do not include judgment and opinion because in these we may be mistaken.

Now what scientific knowledge is, if we are to speak exactly and not follow mere similarities, is plain from what follows. We all suppose that what we know is not even capable of being otherwise; of things capable of being otherwise we do not know, when they have passed outside our observation; whether they exist or not. Therefore the object of scientific knowledge is of necessity. Therefore it is eternal; for things that are of necessity in the unqualified sense are all eternal; and things that are eternal are ungenerated and imperishable. Again, every science is thought to be capable of being taught, and its object of being learnt. And all teaching starts from what is already known, as we maintain in the Analytics also; for it proceeds sometimes through induction and sometimes by syllogism. Now induction is the starting-point which knowledge even of the universal presupposes, while syllogism proceeds from universals. There are therefore starting-points from which syllogism proceeds, which are not reached by syllogism; it is therefore by induction that they are acquired. Scientific knowledge is, then, a state of capacity to demonstrate, and has the other limiting characteristics which we specify in the Analytics; for it is when a man believes in a certain way and the starting-points are known to him that he has scientific knowledge, since if they are not better known to him than the conclusion, he will have his knowledge only incidentally.

Let this, then, be taken as our account of scientific knowledge.

Art—knowledge of how to make things

In the variable are included both things made and things done; making and acting are different (for their nature we treat even the discussions outside our school as reliable); So that the reasoned state of capacity to act is different from the reasoned state of capacity to make. Hence too they are not included one in the other; for neither is acting making nor is making acting. Now since architecture is an art and is essentially a reasoned state of capacity to make, and there is neither any art that is not such a state nor any such state that is not an art, art is identical with a state of capacity to make, involving a true course of reasoning. All art is concerned with coming into being, i.e. with contriving and considering how something may come into being which is capable of either being or not being, and whose origin is in the maker and not in the thing made; for art is concerned neither with things that are, or come into being, by necessity, nor with things that do so in accordance with nature (since these have, their origin in themselves). Making and acting being different, art must be a matter of making, not of acting. And in a sense chance and art are concerned with the same objects; as Agathon says, 'Art loves chance and chance loves art'. Art, then, as has been said, is a state concerned with making, involving a true course of reasoning, and lack of art on the contrary is a state concerned with making, involving a false course of reasoning; both are concerned with the variable.

Practical wisdom—knowledge of how to secure the ends of human life

Regarding practical wisdom we shall get at the truth by considering who are the persons we credit with it. Now it is thought to be a mark of a man of practical wisdom to be able to deliberate well about what is good and expedient for himself, not in some particular respect, e.g. about what sorts of thing conduce to health or to strength, but about what sorts of thing conduce to the good life in general. This is shown by the fact that we credit men with practical wisdom in some particular respect when they have calculated well with a view to some good end which is one of those that are not the object of any art. It follows that in the general sense also the man who is capable of deliberating has practical wisdom. Now no one deliberates about things that are invariable, or about things that it is impossible for him to do. Therefore, since scientific knowledge involves demonstration, but there is no demonstration of things whose first principles are variable (for all such things might actually be otherwise), and since it is impossible to deliberate about things that are of necessity, practical wisdom cannot be scientific knowledge or art; not science because that which can be done is capable of being otherwise, not art because action and making are different kinds of thing. The remaining alternative, then, is that it is a true and reasoned state of capacity to act with regard to the things that are good or bad for man. For while making has an end other than itself, action cannot; for good action itself is its end. It is for this reason that we think Pericles and men like him have practical wisdom, viz. because they can see what is good for themselves and what is good for men in general; we consider that those can do this who are good at managing households or states. ('This is why we call temperance (*sophrasune*) by this name; we imply that it preserves one's practical wisdom (*sözousa ten phronesin*). Now what it preserves is a judgment of the kind we have described. For it is not any and every judgment that pleasant and painful objects destroy and pervert, e.g. the judgment that the triangle has or has not its angles equal to two right angles, but only judgments about what is to be done. For the originating causes of the things that are done consist in the end at which they are aimed; but the man who has been ruined by pleasure or pain forthwith fails to see any such originating cause—to see that for the sake of this or because of this he ought to choose and do whatever he chooses and does; for vice is destructive of the originating cause of action.)

Practical wisdom, then, must be a reasoned and true state of capacity to act with regard to human goods. But further, while there is such a thing as excellence in art, there is no such thing as excellence in practical wisdom; and in art he who errs willingly is preferable, but in practical wisdom, as in the virtues, he is the reverse. Plainly, then, practical wisdom is a virtue and not an art. There being two parts of the soul that can follow a course of reasoning, it must be a virtue of one of the two, i.e. of that part which forms opinions; for opinion is about the variable and so is practical wisdom. But yet it is not only a reasoned state; this is shown by the fact that a state of that sort may be forgotten but practical wisdom cannot.

Source: Aristotle *The Nicomachean Ethics* (trans. David Ross), Rev. ed., Oxford: OUP, 1991, pp. 141–2.

CHAPTER 7
THE COMPLICATION OF PRAXIS
William McNeill

Note from editor: Philosopher and translator of Heidegger, William McNeill, in this extract from his book Glance of the Eye[1] *explains why theory and practice are not separate, and that paradoxically, theory may be the highest form of practice. His elaboration of techné, praxis and phronēsis via Heidegger's reading of Aristotle exposes 'making' as more complex than the application of learnt skills, involving 'eidos' (idea) and deliberation towards material realization – this has parallels with 'design as prefiguration'. Other concepts discussed here, such as* practical *aisthesis and prohairesis can also be brought to the task of understanding of design, both in its limitations and possibilities.*

…. Practical knowledge and its most excellent form, *phronēsis* or practical wisdom, seems to differ in principle from theoretical or speculative knowledge simply because practical knowledge is always already involved in a particular *praxis*. It does not have time to turn away or take a contemplative distance from the concrete situation of its immediate involvement. The horizon of *praxis* thus seems to lie outside that of *theōrein*. And we might therefore expect practical knowledge to be different in principle from that "desire to see" which marks the starting point or *arche* of Aristotle's investigation into speculative knowledge. But is this in fact the case?

For Aristotle *praxis* is the highest and most distinctive possibility of human existence. Unfolding in the midst of the temporal and the contingent, such existence can in no sense transcend the intrinsic finitude of its situation so as to attain directly an outside perspective on itself. Such a perspective would be possible only if one were to commit the hubris of identifying the human condition with that of the divine. Aristotle's account of the *praxis* of human life emphasizes the worldly character of human involvements and the inevitable unpredictabilities to which such an existence is exposed. Nevertheless, it remains striking that Aristotle will ascribe the fullest disclosure of human existence as such not to the kind of vision that remains attentive to and most fully apprehends such contingencies —the vision of *phronēsis* or practical wisdom—but to the "theoretical" vision belonging to the *sophia* of the philosopher. The philosophical vision sees most transparently what human existence is as such. And yet the relation between theoretical knowledge and *praxis* is not a simple opposition for Aristotle. As a kind of knowing, *theōria* may indeed be contrasted with *phronēsis* but, as we shall appreciate more fully later, this contrast is not an opposition. Aristotle not only identifies the activity of *theōria* as itself a *praxis*: he regards it as the highest *praxis*. Yet it is not as though *theōria* were merely one possibility or form of human *praxis* among others; rather, as we shall try to show, *theōria* is that kind of vision which first sees and thereby knows what *praxis* itself most truly is. *Theōria* as a *praxis* is so far from being severed from *praxis* and *phronēsis* that it proves, on Aristotle's account, to be the most originary self-disclosure of *praxis* as such.

(.….)

Aristotle describes five ways in which the soul attains truth (*alētheia*) in affirmation or denial, that is, by way of the logos. These are identified as *technē, epistēmē, phronēsis , sophia*, and *nous*. …

Truth is here considered insofar as it can be apprehended by the soul itself. The soul, according to Aristotle, has two parts, one having logos, the other without it. Furthermore, there are two ways of having logos:

a) *epistēmonikon*, the epistemic or "scientific" faculty, and b) *logistikon*, the deliberative faculty. The first is concerned with episteme, the second with deliberation … The distinction is made on the basis of the kind of knowledge that each provides, the epistemic faculty is concerned with the contemplation (*theōrein*) of those things whose *archai* are invariable, the deliberative faculty with things that are variable: not simply things that can "change" or move, as Heidegger explains, but things that in their very being can he otherwise than they are.

(…..)

…. the knowledge pertaining to *epistēmē* can be taught; and "all teaching proceeds from that which is already known." In other words, *epistēmē* presupposes our already being in explicit possession of certain *archai* as learnable and teachable. Episteme constitutes an independent kind of knowledge—its *logos* remains true whether or not its objects are present for it, and yet precisely because of this it does not in itself provide access to the ultimate disclosedness or true being of its objects. Such truth can be apprehended only by *nous*, for it concerns a truth of being and not merely a "logical" … truth.

The second form of knowledge Aristotle considers is *technē*, here understood in the restricted sense of know-how that pertains to making or producing. *Technē* has as its object something that undergoes change. Its object (the product) undergoes change in the specific sense that prior to the productive process it does not yet exist in its eventual form. In this sense, the object of *technē* is something that can be other than it is. *Technē*, like *epistēmē*, entails a kind of *theōrein*, but one specifically concerned with how to bring a thing into existence. Yet unlike episteme, this kind of seeing apparently contains the ultimate *archē* of its object within itself. Heidegger here refers to Aristotle's account from Book VII of the *Metaphysics*. Before producing something, a kind of deliberation is required which entails that the artisan must first contemplate how the product will look in its *eidos*. In the *Metaphysics*, Aristotle states that "that which properly produces that from which movement begins, is the *eidos* in the soul." More precisely, it is the "seeing" of this *eidos*, its presence in the soul, which is there referred to as *noesis*. This means, however, that the *archi* does not lie in the work or artifact itself, as does the *archë* of those things which exist "by nature". Furthermore, the end of the activity of making is other than the activity itself; the finished work lies outside the productive process. As finished and completed the artifact thus no longer falls within the purview of *technē*, but has been set forth and freed for other ends. In other words, the knowledge or *theōrein* specific to *technē*, as concerned with poiesis, with the process of making, cannot wholly preserve within it the full *archē* of its object. The object of *technē*, as something made, is other than *technē* and as such already falls prey to contingency and chance in the very process of making. The product may turn out to be a failure, even though the artisan had a clear vision of what he or she wanted to make. The disclosure in *technē* of the being of its object is intrinsically deficient.

(…..)

The third kind of knowledge considered by Aristotle (is) *phronēsis* (which) refers to knowledge belonging to human *praxis* insofar as such activity constitutes an end in itself. It is described as " a disclosive disposition that occurs by way of logos concerned with action in relation to what is good and bad for human beings ."

…. In *technē*, knowledge is directed toward the finished product as the end or telos of that knowledge. In *phronēsis*, on the other hand, knowledge is directed toward action itself as constitutive of the being of the person of practical wisdom. *Phronēsis* is a knowledge attuned to human beings in their singularity and communal being with one another, concerned with the human being as "an origin of actions." Accordingly the ontological disclosure of the object of *phronēsis*, the disclosure of the being of the self as an acting is preserved in this direct and immediate relatedness. *Phronēsis* discloses … the truth of my own being as acting here and now. Unlike the ontological disclosure of true being in episteme, this disclosure is bound to the finite temporality of the moment: it is nor a general truth already accessible in principle to an independent or supposedly neutral observer.

Aristotle notes that *phronēsis* too is commonly associated with a kind of theorem concerned with what is good for oneself and for human beings in general. Yet since the object of *phronēsis* is none other than oneself. Aristotle points out that this kind of knowing does not constitute an independent body of knowledge in which we might come to excel. *Phronēsis* is not like *technē* in this regard: it is not an independent knowledge that could he applied to different cases. We cannot therefore speak of excellence in *phronēsis* , as we can in the case of *technē* rather, *phronēsis* itself is an excellence or virtue. …. Furthermore, whereas technë is learned and perfected by a process of trial and error, this is not the case in *phronēsis*: in ethical action, one cannot, fundamentally, experiment with oneself in the manner in which a *technē* experiments with its object, namely, in such a way as to be capable of an indifference toward that object . For *phronēsis* is a seeing ("knowing") of oneself *as an acting self* as the self that is acting in any particular situation, and not a seeing of oneself as an object whose very being is other than that of oneself. …

Phronēsis is an intrinsic relation to one's own being. To formulate it in terms that parallel Heidegger's characterization of Dasein in *Being and Time* … *phronēsis* entails a seeing in which the being of the human being that I myself am is in question (and thus in some sense open, at stake, yet to he decided). It entails a kind of seeing whose own mode of being is not indifferent to it; its activity is structured as an ontico-ontological care for self …. *Phronēsis* thus seems to be a complete and self-contained form of knowing …. In our doing and acting, we "see" ourselves and are thus in a sense present to ourselves immediately without any contemplative distance or objectification.

Nevertheless, our originary, worldly relation to ourselves as acting beings not only presupposes concealment; this relation and its attendant concealment can themselves become concealed and covered over in and through our guiding interpretations of ourselves and of the world. *Phronēsis* is disclosive ….precisely because concealment is intrinsic to the being of the self as acting. … Furthermore, concealment of oneself is not only a possible result of a particular self-interpretation. As Aristotle indicates by reference to pleasure and pain, a mood or attunement can conceal the human being from himself, so that the *archë* "does not show itself" as such. And for this reason, *phronēsis* must repeatedly be retrieved by a certain composure.

…

But the fact that *phronēsis* remains a task, and not a perfected accomplishment, points to something else that is important, namely, the fact that this kind of knowing is not an independent mode of disclosure.

(….)

…. the disclosure that occurs deliberatively in *phronēsis*, by way of logos is itself dependent upon and directed toward, that is, subservient to, a more originary disclosure. *Phronēsis* , as we shall see, indeed guides an action, but in its deliberative capacity neither first discloses the practical situation of action, nor indeed does it disclose the primary end toward which an action is directed in advance …

The glance of the eye

Central to *phronēsis* is what Aristotle in the *Nicomachean Ethics* identifies as a practical *aisthesis*, a practical vision or "perception" that discloses the ultimate *archë* and *telos* of *praxis*, namely the concrete situation of action in all the particularity of its givenness. *Phronēsis* , as Aristotle puts it, "concerns what is ultimate (*eschaton*) …. Yet the kind of *aisthesis* in question not that of the mere sense-perception of sense-objects, but is something like the sort of *aisthesis* whereby "we perceive that the ultimate figure (*eschaton*) in mathematics is a triangle." Two things are distinctive of the kind of *aisthesis* belonging to mathematics: first, we perceive the object—the figure of the triangle—as a whole; and second, our perceiving reaches a kind of end or stop (*stësetai*) in this perception.

(....)

But what exactly is the role of the practical *aisthesis* in *phronēsis* ? *Phronēsis* ... occurs by way of deliberation, of talking something through in the logos. This deliberation follows the form of a practical "syllogism" or deduction. However, as Heidegger constantly emphasises in his interpretation of Book VI, it is crucial to keep in mind that this syllogism, as the way in which *phronēsis* unfolds, is not something undertaken independently of our actions. The practical syllogism is what happens in and as *praxis*. it is *praxis* in its very accomplishment. in the movement of tis unfolding and actualization. A practical syllogism consists of the following steps: (1) The particular action or immediate end desired. that is, held in advance in a *prohairesis* (for the sake of some further end or good ...) is such and such (major premise); (2) The concrete situation is this (minor premise); (3) Therefore. I shall act in the following way (conclusion). Yet it is not only the minor premise—that is whatever is disclosed in the moment of practical *aisthesis* —that first has to be given in order for deliberation to occur. The major premise—the end projected or intended—also has to be given: indeed it is prior to, and even appears to organize the practical *aisthesis* itself: I "see" the present situation in the light of a projected end. We thus find the following moments intrinsic to *praxis*: (1) the particular end or action projected or "chosen in advance" (*prohairesis*) as the specific goal of desire; (2) the disclosure of the factical situation, via a practical *aisthesis*, with respect to this end; (3) the projected end as modified via deliberation, this third moment marking the beginning of a particular action, the moment of correct deliberation and decision when desire is correctly directed toward the appropriate action in accordance with the logos of the one deliberating. The logos thus belongs to the action; the action itself, if appropriate. should unfold as a true disclosure (*alētheia*) that is homologous with desire. This moment at which deliberation has been correctly accomplished and is conclusively directed toward the end desired is the moment of judgment that enables a decision. Heidegger thus translates boule as "open resolve" or "resolute openness" comprising the "transparency" of an action. insofar as this resolute openness has indeed been appropriated and achieved. that is, insofar as I am openly resolved, the action is there in its most. extreme possibility." Openness here means a disclosedness, being resolved in a certain disclosedness. Yet this conclusion of the syllogism Heidegger indicates, is also a closure or coming to an end: "it is not some proposition or piece of knowledge, but the breaking-forth of whoever is acting as such."

Yet how, if at all, is *praxis* as an end in itself, as an unconditional end, present in *phronēsis* ? Is it something toward which we orient ourselves in advance of the logos of a more primary projection —the result, perhaps of a prior philosophical, theoretical, or calculative-technical reflection on the nature of the good? If such were the case, *praxis* could not be an end in itself, distinct from *poēsis*, as Aristotle argues but would become subservient to an extrinsic end, thereby inscribing itself within the means-end schema of calculative deliberation characteristic of *technē*. ....

What the practical *aisthesis* discloses is more precisely the various "given" (the various factors to be taken into account in deliberation) within the temporal particularity... The particular situation. moreover, is something ultimate, something so singular and unique that it cannot he apprehended by logos, hut only by the practical *aisthesis*. It constitutes the proper end or *eschaton* of the practical vision, and thereby of *praxis* itself. What Heidegger finds especially significant is that Aristotle describes this practical *aisthesis* as a form of *nous* - a term otherwise reserved for the pure apprehending, in *sophia*, of universals that remain constant.

(.....)

Nous is present in both *sophia* and *phronēsis* . And what is grasped by nous is in each case something ultimate: either the universal delimitations ... that remain the same and comprise the starting point of demonstration in scientific knowledge, or the 'ultimate fact or state of affairs that can be otherwise and at which all deliberation in the logos ends. Practical vision is intrinsically eschatological in that it discloses and thus itself comprises in its very operation, an *eschaton* that marks the limit of logos and that logos itself cannot reach. … *phronēsis* … remains dependent on something other than itself, namely, "the action itself." and is thus … not an independent form of disclosure …. Whether we are concerned with deliberation, calculation, or demonstration discursive thought can only set to work on what has already been disclosed via a finite and unique act of nous.

What this means on Heidegger's reading, is that the intrinsic structure of *phronēsis* is "the same" as that of *Sophia*….

> The practical vision that informs *phronēsis* occurs in a momentary glance; it is a moment of "most extreme concretion," a moment that, as Heidegger puts it, orients or directs itself toward what is most extreme", catches sight of the absolute *eschaton*:

> The nous of *phronēsis* aims at what is most extreme in the sense of the absolute *eschaton*. *Phronēsis* is a catching sight of the here-and-now of the concrete here-and-now character of the momentary situation as aesthesis, it is the glance of the eye, the momentary glance (der Blick den Auges. der Augen-blick] at what is concrete in each specific case and as such can always be otherwise. The *noein* in *Sophia*, by contrast, is a contemplating of that which is *aie*, that which is always present in its sameness.

Certainly, the moment of vision or glance of the eye intrinsic to *phronēsis* has, by virtue of a guiding *prohairesis*, always already let the situation he seen in a determinate respect. *Praxis* itself, human existence , as the hesitant yet ongoing transformation of *praxis* in each case, is hereby always already seen with respect to a guiding "not yet" a futural possibility and directionality for its transformation. Yet amid this "kairotic" vision in which, in the unfolding of *praxis*, what has been has always already turned into and toward the future, practical insight peaks in opening onto something that cannot be calculated or appropriated by deliberation. As deliberative, *phronēsis* is, as Heidegger (echoing Aristotle) puts it, "epitactic" it issues commands, it orders and directs what is seen in the *Augenblick*, giving it a determinacy, letting it he seen in a particular light. But this 'epitactic illumination" only brings our *praxis* into a "readiness for" something, a "breaking-forth toward" something for the *eschaton* of the practical vision. the point at which the latter stops and comes to an end or halt, is also the end of *logos*, a standstill and a stilling It is "that moment of being which is concerned with concrete beings and at which the intervention of the doctor engages and conversely, that moment at which deliberation and talking things through come to a standstill" This *eschaton* is "the most extreme limit" of deliberation, at which "an action engages."

In *phronēsis* the practical *aisthēsis* informs every moment in the ongoing transformation of *praxis* that human existence is. It discloses *praxis* itself in its momentary character, its exposure to a particular situation. Yet does the practical aesthesis thereby disclose *praxis* itself as such, *praxis* as *praxis*? The glance of the eye that informs *phronēsis* sees what it sees in terms of a "good" that has already been decided upon beforehand, but this may be just a particular end or good (e.g., promoting health in the case of a doctor), or it may be the good in itself, that is, the absolute good with respect to human existence as a whole, the practical good as an end in itself. Only if it deliberates with a view to the latter will deliberation be the kind of deliberation appropriate to *phronēsis*, namely, deliberating well. As deliberating well, *phronēsis* must already have the *agathon* "in view" at every moment it must act knowingly with a view to the good. Yet this means that *phronēsis* itself (as deliberating on what is disclosed in the practical *nous*) is powerless to decide the ultimate end or good toward which it is directed: *phronēsis* is possible only for someone who is already good. And this in turn implies that the practical *aisthēsis*, oriented in advance toward a particular end, yet given over to the particularity of a here-and-now situation, is in itself unable to disclose the practical good (*praxis* itself) as such. The disclosure of the latter. rather, is contributed by *sophia*.

In other words, the glance of the eye belonging to genuine *phronēsis* (as deliberating well) has already seen more than what is given in any practical situation. It sees the "givens" in the context of a whole (the temporal particularity of the situation) but thus "whole" has itself been seen in advance in a very specific respect: not just with a view to any particular good but with respect to the practical good as such, to *praxis* as an end in itself: presence or actuality itself as fleeting, unstable, open to the possibility of change at any moment. But this implies that intrinsic to *phronēsis* there is a vision that already "sees" not only the possibility of change but actuality itself as that which remains constant that which always returns as the same, that is, as presence, in and throughout all change. …..

Note

1. This is a shortened extract from chapter 2, pages 30–47, with in-text references and footnotes removed, this because many of them are lengthy and detailed. Reprinted by permission from *The Glance of the Eye: Heidegger, Aristotle and the Ends of Theory* by William McNeill, the State University of New York Press (c) 1999, State University of New York. All rights reserved.

CHAPTER 8
TECHNICITY AND PUBLICNESS: STEPS TOWARDS AN URBAN SPACE
Stephen Read

Note from editor: Phenomenology pays attention to human beings as they are already immersed in their worlds of activities, material and immaterial things. Our relation to the worlds we inhabit are always interested, directed towards, involved, yet as Read argues, drawing on Heidegger, this is not the same as subjectivism. The phenomenological approach is dynamic and relational: we create material things and meanings that constitute worlds that in turn create us. Read contrasts a phenomenological understanding of space as concrete and lived with space considered as abstract or empty, revealing a circular co-determining relation between space(s) as designed and practices, which can reconfigure how public and private might be understood. This extract can be read along with Lefebvre's 'Production of Space' in Part VII, Mitchell's 'Enframing' and Keshavarz's Violence of Humanitarian Design both in Part IV, all of which deal with spatial practices.

The Stanford Encyclopedia of Philosophy defines phenomenology as 'the study of structures of consciousness as experienced from the first-person point of view'.[1] This has led to phenomenology being characterised as 'subjectivist' and 'introspective' (as opposed to being objective and concerned with the 'external' communicable reality of things). The point that Don Ihde makes in proposing a post-phenomenology[2] – and one that will be reinforced here in looking at Heidegger's space – is that phenomenology, properly understood, is not about subjectivity in the conventional sense we think of it at all. It is relational and concerned first and foremost with the relations humans have with the world around them.

It is not so much about introspection either, but about reflexivity, in that what one experiences is derived from the real and embodied relations (characterised as 'intentionality' in phenomenology) of the subject with other people and things in the environment. These relations have nothing to do with any internal or private Mind, but are lived out beyond the skin of the subject – and already in public. Phenomenology is concerned before anything else with these relations, and investigates not so much real things 'in themselves' as the conditions under which subject-object relations (things to people) appear. Ihde goes on to emphasise the roles of objects, settings and technologies.[3] ....

(.....)

The idea of us and our world being co-constituted in a relational and dynamic unity may be held up by both phenomenology and cybernetics as an alternative metaphysics to the 'ontological dualism' of the Cartesian system, which understands matter and mind or substance and spirit as belonging to essentially separate realms – across the boundaries of which we have to travel in order to make this us-world connection. ...... In our more conventional view of the urban world we inhabit, we set ourselves against the world as an indifferent materiality to be overcome by way of intelligence or wayfinding. Also, in our conventional view of our relations with other people we understand ourselves as joining with them in direct social bonds of affinity or dependence. Both of these conventional views may have to be modified in the sort of urban space that emerges out of Heidegger's thinking. I will argue that we may begin to understand the city much more precisely as fields of places or technical settings which emplace us in very particular and public and political ways.

Relationality is on the agenda in urbanism today. At the same time it is fair to say that most 'network thinking' comes nowhere near addressing the full consequences of relationality, which includes I will argue the idea that the city is not just an artefact in the sense that it is planned and designed by us, but also that it itself constitutes an unplanned but perfectly coherent dynamic, relational 'body politic' with an order and a unity born out of the technologically mediated practice of everyday life within it. ....

The intersubjective realm in spaces of intentionality

Rather than trying to find experience in the gap between our situation in some external and absolute space on the one hand and our psychological state on the other, Heidegger proposes we think of experience as well as the genesis of our being public and with others in terms of the way the world discloses itself to us differently from different situations. Heidegger uses in fact no concept of consciousness at all in his system but replaces it with 'a concept of existence as the mode of being of an entity for which the things with which it deals are there ... in the mode of perceptual presence'.[4] This involves a direct relation between subject and the object of perception, action or attention in fields of presence where different things are revealed or disclosed from different positions. Certain things may become possible or coherent from particular positions while others remain foreclosed or incoherent. And there may be a certain objectivity or systematicity about these fields in which perceptions emerge as a public factor in a 'politics' of situated presence and appearance.

In phenomenology, 'structures of consciousness' are approached, if we are to take our lead from Heidegger, in the first instance by recognising the enormous, though not obvious to us most of the time, gulf between things and the 'being' of things – between things and the way things are disclosed to us. Heidegger calls this 'ontological difference' and his argument really sets the tone for the whole question of our experience of reality. Basically, Heidegger argues, things themselves and independently of us are quite beyond our imagination, because in bringing them to our imagination, or even to our knowledge of their being, we incorporate them in an indissoluble unity (that intentional relation) with ourselves.[5]

From this point on, we begin relating to things in a direct active and spatial relation that is integral, personal and significant. Things may exist in some abstract sense apart from our consciousness of them, but the reality we deal in simply cannot be the absolute reality, Descartes imagined. Things always exist for us – and things also exist for us in a way they simply cannot for things that cannot develop intentional relations with other things. For Heidegger, Being itself '"is" only in the understanding of those entities to whose Being something like an understanding of Being belongs'.[6] Existence is neither an absolute or a neutral issue; existence matters for us, and as embodied, active, inquisitive beings, things 'are' in some very important sense in the way we form a relation with them and take them into our lives. Things are disclosed to us in this relation, and in our encounter with the world; they come to Being in this encounter, and it is here that a practical non-abstract (and pre-reflective or pre-representational) realism begins. I will propose that we may build a space of this encounter, and characterise the city as a space of encounter that brackets and specifies our experience of things and people in the world.

This encounter works both individually, in a space of things 'ready' for immediate active incorporation in our lives – and then potentially collectively, in a space of things 'present' to us and for our more generalised, communicable and collective knowing of them. For Heidegger, our first relation with things in perception and action is an integral ecological relation with things 'ready-to-hand' or *zuhanden*. On the other hand we also construct spaces of relations with things in the world which makes them communicable and part of our knowledge. This is our relation with things 'present-at-hand' or *vorhanden*. *Zuhanden* space could be understood (in the sense that it works from a singular perspective) as being 'subjective', while *vorhanden* space could be seen as being 'collective' or 'public' (again in a way that needs to be qualified as spatial). Heidegger therefore reverses the Cartesian priority of 'objective' or absolute space coming before 'subjective' space, insisting that our encounter with the world by way of the ready-to-hand or *zuhanden* comes first, and the present-at-hand or *vorhanden* is a derivation or construction out of this immediate active involvement with things.[7]

In other words, we encounter the world first, for the most part quite unproblematically, immediately and practically – and we then begin, as and if the need arises, to order and make better sense of it. In fact, there is no place to begin outside of our actions and movements in real situations in the world, and these are in a continuous engagement not only in space but in a practical time which connects our past through the present to a future shaped by the intention of the movement itself. The key to understanding Heidegger's theory of space therefore is his attempt to describe spatial experience without presupposing objective space, or in his own terms, 'world-space'. He attempts instead to describe a lived space from within the finite perspective of an active being. This is the space of a being continuously engaged and to a large extent already familiar with the world through previous engagement with it. It is also a 'subjective' space in the sense that it represents a singular situated perspective on the world.

A question arises therefore about where the 'public' and the 'social' may be in all of this ready-to-handness and direct and individual relations with an environment. The question is significant because Heidegger does not address himself simply to the private experience of reality Husserl was concerned with (*Erlebnis*), but also to *Erfahrung*, a notion of experience that addresses itself to a more collective understanding of what experience might be. ……………

Heidegger's prioritisation of the intentional relation of situated people with their environment – the space of 'being-there' or Dasein – does not relate at all …. to 'subjectivism', and the direct intentional relation may be also already part of collective experience. Heidegger simply cannot be seen, according to Olafson, as an existentialist who places the perspective of the individual at the centre of the problem of being and of being social. Rather, our being in the world with others (Mitsein) is a much more fundamental part of our being than we normally see or acknowledge: 'Our being with other like entities is … a constitutive element in our own mode of being as it is in theirs; and it is one to which we cannot do justice as long as we approach it via traditional philosophical routes like the theory of empathy'.[8]

The mutual bonds of intersubjectivity involve in other words not so much specific agreements, empathies and dependencies, as a more general agreement about the nature of the world between us. Olafson proposes we find a common 'ground' in the realm of what lies between human beings rather than in sets of rules or values or 'strong ties'. He emphasises that this mode of being in the world as subject-entities with other entities, is one within which subjects and things develop a reciprocal presence to each other and where both self and others are disclosed. This reciprocity is so familiar to us, is so much what we are immersed in, that we lose sight of it and of the power it has to determine what the things around us are in their relations with other present things. This realm of commonality may even begin to be understood as having its own existence at a material and organisational level from which we cannot escape without losing vital components of what we are. We could begin to understand there to be something here that is concrete and historical, making of the collective and the public something that is developmental, fashioned in a relational space and in time between people – never in addition to 'subjective' life but always integral with it.[9]

……. This has to do with the peculiar nature of the relationality of Dasein, including the fact that individual intentionality relates to a public or collective realm of entities (including people) in a way that makes them mutually constitutive of each other. What is 'out there' – what we know and respond to – is a function, to a great degree, of us, while what is 'out there' also conditions us as we encounter it. ……. If we live in relations of reciprocal presence, then the recognition of other beings and things as complementing and completing one's own being is prior to substantive or absolute essences or rules of conduct or definitions of justice or whatever, and according to Olafson this strange mutually constituting individualisation of self and other needs far more attention than it has thus far received.

Heidegger's space

Heidegger himself offers an alternative to three older theories of absolute space, relational space, and Kantian space. He sets his own space against absolute space but incorporates aspects of both other spaces in his own. Absolute space is the familiar Cartesian space as 'container'. It serves as the framework for defining the positions and motions of objects within it. But absolute space itself exists independently of these objects and has a homogeneous structure and existence of its own. According to Leibniz on the other hand, space is relative, an order of coexistences. Relational space depends on its objects rather than coming before them, as it is nothing more than the relations between these objects. Space here is a property of the objects and there is no space above and beyond the configurations of the objects themselves. However both absolute and relational ideas of space understand space to be, if not strictly material in the case of relational space, certainly absolutely objective and real.

Kant however claimed that space was subjective rather than objective. He believed that space comes to existence in our knowing of things – actually in our intuitions based in our experience of the world. Space is an 'internal' representation of the things given in our senses and the way we make our experiences of things 'outside' ourselves coherent. According to Kant it is only from a human standpoint that we can speak of space: space depends on an intuition and an oriented sense of the world which can only come from us. Without this intuition of coherence, which must be subjective, and therefore for Kant 'interior', 'space stands for nothing whatsoever'. Two important points with regard to this 'coherence' is that in being subjective it is taken to be 'internal' and essentially a private experience, setting up the problem of the communication between an 'interior' consciousness and 'external' reality.

Heidegger rejects the metaphysical dichotomy of subject and object along with the presuppositions of interiority and exteriority that go with it. The question of the interiority of the subjective experience is one that had already been dealt with by Brentano and Husserl, who understood intentionality as a 'breaking out' rather than a 'dissolving' of the world in consciousness. According to them, we are in the world, between things, amongst others, and consciousness is no more than a relation with the world. 'Every mental phenomenon includes something as object within itself'[10] – it is that intentional relation. Heidegger acknowledges therefore the human character of space and its role as a condition of experience, but sees it emerging in our action and our practical involvement in the world rather than as an interior construction or representation of an exterior reality. Heidegger is therefore not much interested in the Kantian question of whether space is intrinsically subjective or objective (or private or public); he is looking for the conditions under which our ideas of objectivity and subjectivity (or public or private) appear. He begins by looking at spaces in which concrete, historical human existence expresses itself and the way it is produced in everyday actions. He looks especially for example at pre-reflective activities, such as walking and reaching for things, in order to begin to elucidate a theory of lived space. Objective and subjective views of space turn out in his view to be practical orientations to the world rather than abstractions from these more primordial spatialities of lived action.

Heidegger sees three different types of space being produced in our actions and perceptions. These are world-space, regions (Gegend), and the spatialities of situated action. These last are divided into that 'breaking out' (Ent-fernung; translated as 'de-severance') and directionality (Ausrichtung). '"De-severing" amounts to making the farness vanish – that is making the remoteness of something disappear, bringing it close'.[11] De-severance is what happens when I reach for something, but it is also what happens when I set out for the supermarket or when I speak to someone on my phone or send an email. De-severance is the impulse of an action directed to a specific goal. It is directional, aimed toward something specific and within a region which references and is prepared for that action and makes it coherent. All action happens from a centre, towards completion, and through a region.

World-space is our commonsense conception of space as a container: 'the bench is in the lecture-room, the lecture-room is in the university, the university is in the city, and so on, until we can say the bench is "in world space"'.[12] Heidegger also calls this space present-at-hand (*vorhanden*) and he understands it as being not so much always and already there, as Cartesian space is, but as something that emerges out of – or that we produce out of – the more primordial spatialities of action that we start with. Heidegger would understand Cartesian absolute space as being world-space, but the objects 'in' world-space come to be understood or intuited by us as being independent of the space that contains them. World-space is not the most original and primordial space therefore, but is rather the most synthetic, the most fabricated – and it remains founded on the spatiality of the actions of situated people. 'It is because we act, going to places and reaching for things to use, that we can understand farness and nearness, and on that basis develop a representation of world-space at all. ... our spatial notions such as "distance", "location", etc., [come] from a standpoint within the spatial relation of self (Dasein) to the things dealt with'.[13]

Regions are the spaces which distribute and locate the things we are involved with in our everyday activities. The places we inhabit are defined not as bounded areas but as regions which emplace 'equipment' that we deal with on an everyday basis. 'Equipment' is the stuff we have or bring ready-to-hand (*zuhanden*) in action, but that we also organise and take care of in a present-at-hand (*vorhanden*) space. Regions are both the spaces of action and the functional spaces of work and everyday living that are themselves part of the organisation of those activities. They are already formalised and organised for action, and one of the most basic functions of regions, I will argue, is to reference or index the things we need and use in relation to other complementary things. Things don't and cannot exist in isolation: they exist in relation to other things in our active engagement with them, and these relations contribute both to their constitution and their locations. Regions are backgrounds to the things we use in action but not neutral backgrounds; rather they are the backgrounds out of which things emerge as what and where they are. Regions are therefore fundamental to the being of things and places – they are in a sense the necessary other side of things; the 'ground' from which the 'figure' of the thing is disclosed.

What Heidegger is trying to capture here is a space which is a mode of our active existence, rather than a space independent of that existence. Any space of action and active knowing, he is saying, is already part of that action, and any space which doesn't begin with that action will leave us again having to cross a gulf between intention and action, between knower and known. These spaces of action are not any 'internal' subjective construction or representation, but are out there in the world along with the action – and already in the present-at-hand spaces of the world we encounter. Things and their places become therefore very quickly not just relational but referential or indexical with respect to regions in our activities – they become spatial organisations which emplace things in relation to other things such that they are not just ready-to-hand in actions but also present-at-hand for action – that we may act on them knowingly, knowing where things are, where we are with things and how or where to go further. The thingness of things and the placeness of their places begin to be significant simply and only in the context of our involvement with them – while this involvement is about things in the world and not things in our heads. But this involvement with things also draws in the other things and their places that contribute to making that thing what it is for us in that particular context. What Heidegger is not talking about here is a subjective attitude in which something seems to be 'close' when it is actually far. The 'closeness' he is talking about is that which is the achievement of a specific perception or action in the course of doing things and in a region which locates both actions and things. It is tied up not with thinking or feeling as much as with a practical doing. It is a partially reflective, or even unreflective, practical getting on with things in a real world context of real things important for – and prepared for – the completion of real tasks. The region orients and organises the intention, attention and concern developed in the action, but the region also has a reality, or a mappability let's say. Heidegger's space becomes both subjective and objective.

But these are also much more than spaces that simply are there. They are spaces we are involved with in our actions, and into which we put our attention and our intention. These spaces may be encountered in action, but they are already practical spaces for action before we encounter them. They are also spaces we care about and care for; we may and do construct, reconstruct, organise and reorganise them to make them ready and fit for the patterns of our activities. Heidegger used the example of the carpenter's workbench, but we could imagine the office of an importer-exporter, or a well-provisioned and ordered kitchen – even the mobile telephone of a well-connected teenager. These spaces are prepared and equipped for our action – they are about doing things efficaciously as well as about knowing where things are and where we are with things, and are thus 'cognitive' in the sense that the spatial organisation itself is also part of our knowledge. But they are also entirely 'exterior' and there is nothing here that corresponds to our conventional view of an 'interior' subjectivity.

(.....)

Both the relationality of Leibnitz's space and the subjectivity of Kant's space are to be found in this space, but in such a way that they become inseparable and begin to define the subject and the object in relational and situational terms. Subjectivity and awareness has become spatialised and distributed – taken out of some absolute realm defining self and identity – and has become a situated perspective on an intersubjective world from which the self presents itself and to which things and other subjects are disclosed. This situated perspective works across regions that are already prepared for particular kinds of action – and which are not containers for shared activities, but rather repositories of shared reference. Everything an active 'subjectivity' is capable of becomes bracketed by this perspective as place and access become politicised – setting the framework for Hannah Arendt's further work on appearance and the polis.

Finding common ground

But when we think of action we are still speaking of the integral couple (in intentionality) of subject and world, creating a centred space of our own activity, organised in a region but centred on a situation or centre of action which is our own. These are the spaces of our encounter with the world, and especially with the environments familiar to us – those of our own office or workbench, of our own kitchen, or of our own mobile phone – though someone else may with more or less difficulty use our kitchen or try to make a call on our mobile phone. Our own spaces are again not neutral or set against our action, they are equipped and readied for our action and the environments of our actions become conjoined with those actions. Heidegger's central insight was in seeing just how much of what supports our being and action slips out of sight in its readiness-to-hand. He saw how much of our world consists of 'equipment' for action and how the relation between the ready-to-hand and the present-at-hand was therefore crucial to understanding the spatial mode of our existence, while recognising that relationship would always be difficult for us to see. The being of things incorporated in our actions consists in their efficacy, not in any particular aspect of their make-up or even in the combination of those aspects understood outside of the subject-environment relation. ....

(.....)

The subjectivity in all this lies in an orientation to a region of elements constituting and referencing a certain action and the directionality and specificity of the action itself. The publicness is a dense web of ties to 'indeterminate others' that constitutes a common world of co-reference. Our actions and subjectivities exist in webs of intersubjectivity that have a grounding and a levelling effect, creating a commons and a public. In fact, in acting, in interacting, in using tools or equipment, Dasein (being there) becomes Mitsein (being with) others, even when other people are not immediately present and when actions do not immediately involve other people. The problem of a 'relation of minds' does not arise because a world common to us all, understood and even built as present-at-hand, intervenes. We can begin to understand ourselves becoming public between things and others in a realm de Certeau characterises as 'the oceanic rumble of the ordinary … the place from which discourse is produced'.[14]

Common spaces of action

One plugs in fact, not just into regions but also into the webs of indexicality, sociality and significance invested in them and their elements, as objects and people partake in communicative webs of co-reference with other objects and people. In our regions and places we are constantly involved with things and people which refer to other things and people, and as Heidegger points out, this involvement may be with indeterminate others. Even when there are no other people directly part of any particular action, the elements of regions are themselves already 'socialised' by being made part of a whole that communicates through cross-linking with other wholes that involve people.[15] Taking a simple example: a chair may be involved directly in a particular action, but it participates by analogy with other similar actions involving chairs through time – the chair comes to the action already marked by its significance as a chair. Actions and objects form relational totalities that are significant and which are 'disclosed … with a certain intelligibility'[16] and regions become the backgrounds against which people act and are 'that wherein the intelligibility of anything is sustained'.[17]

The world is already intelligible and significant to us, intelligibility coming with the process of disclosure in an integral whole. And action doesn't just happen in a space of communicative intersubjectivity, it finds itself involved with and supported by countless items of equipment involved (right alongside the actor) in the cybernetic totality of the action. This equipment includes multitudes of things that escape our attention precisely because they are ready-to-hand (until they break down and reveal their presence to us): floors, keys, doors, spectacles, walls, switches, ventilators, corridors, chairs, bicycle paths, bus timetables, fish tanks, restaurant menus, watches, knees, mobile telephones. We incorporate multitudes of things in use in our lives on an everyday basis, things that we both count on and take for granted. …..

A shared cultural or professional space, if we look at a region like the carpenter's bench, is something that is a factor of the region's facilitation of particular shared practices – and the workbench is a setting, regularised and standardised to the support of the practice of carpentry. The fact that the carpenter makes his own workbench to the support of practices learned from his master nicely explains how regions and actions become joined – the fact that he uses a measure clinches the type of space he is constructing. Here is where the normalisation of space to present-at-hand and eventually to world-space begins, and this space normalised for the practice of carpentry is the workbench. We live in a world prepared for our action and 'equipment is its context … every implement exerts a determinate and limited range of effects in each instant, and is equally determined by the equipment that surrounds it'.[18] Practices become themselves normalised in relation to already mapped out and constructed settings. More refined and abstracted practices, like the practice of measuring itself, will contribute to a further normalisation and 'worlding' of space. This is the *vorhanden* space that facilitates a particular Dasein for a particular skilled practitioner, who needs to rely on his equipment in action. This makes the space 'public' in the sense that it becomes common to a practice, and shared by a bounded group of people who have both access to and the skills to use that space.

There is something a little strange and circular about these equipped, user-included totalities we call regions however, because we find ourselves acting in a world to a very significant extent prepared and 'made to measure' for practices already practiced.[19] Here, if we take Heidegger's example of the carpenter's workbench, we can begin to see how a regularisation of the equipment and the work processes using that equipment could mean that indeed, a carpenter, with a few adjustments and adaptations, could begin work on another carpenter's bench. It would be the same for a professional cook in another cook's kitchen – but probably less so for the kitchen of the enthusiastic but undisciplined amateur! The spaces for action are already at least partly prepared against the breakdown of action – and the actions become transportable to other places where the skills and settings exist. Spaces are concrete settings constructed and formed to regularised 'cultural' and 'everyday' practices, and even more so perhaps when we consider specialised and professionalised practices. We could also imagine regularised and less specialised spaces for action, for more generic activities and practices like walking in the city. It is this 'preparation' that I am taking to be the most important character of the *vorhanden* spaces we use.

It is difficult to see therefore where in the region of space itself we could find a character or marker for publicness or privateness. Publicness and privateness will be a matter of access to different sets of mutually referring 'implements' held in different spatial 'commons' – access therefore for different 'publics' to the prepared *vorhanden* spaces facilitating specific or generic practices. The preparedness of regions means that qualities and degrees of publicness will be factored into that preparation. While both public and private spaces are necessarily 'shared' or 'common' by virtue of the communicative regions all actions are necessarily part of – they are more or less accessible to, or secured against, the access of those included or excluded from a particular 'commons'. It may be decided for example that slaves and women are simply not 'public'! Some regions will be prepared for a broad public, others will be secured (and all too many are today) and will be 'public' to a select few. We can begin to see how the domains of 'public' and 'private' become contingent on practices of publicness as well as the rights and provisions of access made for different people to different equipped and facilitating regions. The confusion about Heidegger's understanding of the public and the private may be cleared up when we resist finding any essential public and private: the public and the private remain a contingent matter of access and rights, and the politics of their construction, negotiation, contestation and placement in wider webs of intersubjectivity. ....

© Stephen Read / first published in *Footprint: Architecture and Phenomenology*, Autumn 2018, pp 7–22. / DOI: http://dx.doi.org/10.7480/footprint.2.2.683

Notes

1. Stanford Encyclopedia of Philosophy; entry on 'Phenomenology': http://plato.stanford.edu/entries/phenomenology/ (accessed 21 July 2008).

2. Don Ihde 'If phenomenology is an albatross, is postphenomenology possible?' in D. Ihde and E. Selinger (ed.) *Chasing Technoscience* Bloomington: Indiana University Press, 2003.

3. Many urbanists concerned with the city as a human environment will recognise close parallels at a conceptual level with James Gibson's relational environmental psychology and I will continue to footnote some of this in passing (see James Gibson *The Ecological Approach to Visual Perception* Hillsdale: LEA Publishers, 1986). One of the main points the cyberneticians were making at the Macy Conferences in the 1940s and 50s, was that in talking of human-technological systems, the observer or the user is always indissolubly part of the system. James Gibson's parallel interests in perception and the relations between humans and their environment mediated through

human-environment optics and technologies – and especially his work with pilots – was exemplary of this tradition. For Gibson, what came first was the direct 'psychophysical' relation with the object of perception. The pilot becomes locked in an indissoluble unity of relation with his aircraft and with the landing strip he is approaching. In the same way the blind man became blind-man-with-white-stick in the 'cybernetics of self' of Gregory Bateson (in Gregory Bateson *Steps to an Ecology of Mind* Chicago: University of Chicago Press, 2000), and in Ihde's discussion of Galileo's contribution to the progress towards modern science, Galileo becomes Galileo-with-telescope (Ihde (2003)).

4. Frederick Olafson 'Heidegger à la Wittgenstein or "Coping" with Professor Dreyfus' *Inquiry* vol 37, 1994, 52.

5. The 'ontological primacy' of the human-environment relation in 'intentionality' reminds us of the 'ontological primacy' of 'affordances' in James Gibson's environmental psychology (see John T. Sanders 'An ontology of affordances' *Ecological Psychology* vol 9, no 1, 1997, 97–112.

6. Martin Heidegger *Being and Time* (trans. J. Macquarrie & E. Robinson) Oxford: Blackwell, 1962, p. 228 [183].

7. Ibid. secs. 22–24. 16. See Frederick Olafson *Heidegger and the Ground of Ethics: A study of Mitsein* Cambridge: Cambridge University Press, 1998, ch. 1; see also Pierre Keller and David Weberman 'Heidegger and the source(s) of intelligibility' *Continental Philosophy Review* vol 31, 1998, 369–86.

8. Olafson (1998), pp. 3–4, 7.

9. I will be arguing later that a common world of places may be what the urban specifically and simply adds to this 'world between people'.

10. Franz Brentano *Descriptive Psychology* (trans. Benito Müller) London: Routledge, 1995, p. 88.

11. Heidegger (1962), p. 139 [105].

12. Ibid. p. 79 [54].

13. Arisaka (1995) p. 460.

14. Michel de Certeau *The Practice of Everyday Life* (trans. by S. Rendell) Berkley: University of California Press, 1984, p. 5.

15. See Dan Zahavi 'Beyond empathy: Phenomenological approaches to intersubjectivity' *Journal of Consciousness Studies* vol 8, no 5–7, 2001, 151–67.

16. Heidegger (1962), p. 119 [86].

17. Ibid. p. 193 [151].

18. Graham Harman *Tool-being: Heidegger and the Metaphysics of Objects* Chicago: Open Court Publishing, 2002, p. 23.

19. We find parallels again with Gibson who recognised that the perceiving organism and the environment are already related through the co-evolution and co-adaptation of each to the other. The environment therefore offers conditions commensurate with the organism's needs. As a result, perception for the organism is the pickup of information on the go that supports the organism's perception and action. Gibson called this action-supportive information 'affordance'. It is the affordance the environment offers that is the proper object of perception, and this affordance may be directly perceived, according to Gibson, without intervening mental representation.

CHAPTER 9
THE EXISTENTIAL SELF AS THE LOCUS
OF SUSTAINABILITY IN DESIGN
Philippe d'Anjou

Note from editor: The idea of design having a purpose beyond itself is one of the crucial aspects that distinguishes it from art. But the rhetoric of the noble purposes of design are usually gestural and vague, such as notions of design serving people's needs, as if these existed pure, simple and uncontested; or the injunction to designers to "be sustainable." This is where D'Anjou's text is of value in bringing the more limited concept of 'project' within design practice into collision with Jean Paul Sartre's notion of life project. What he writes raises the question: is it possible to be committed to the self-identity of designer while also being committed sustainability as a life project, or do the contradictions overwhelm?

Perhaps the only way to apprehend the problematic of sustainability and what is really at stake regarding it, is via a theory of the agency of design; and the student in the situation of design learning in the context of the design studio represents a crucial agency.[1] The studio is of primary importance because it represents a core pedagogical paradigm of design education.[2] It is indeed where professional designers are formed, where the individual *becomes* a designer.

The stance from which sustainability is comprehended stems from addressing the relationship between design and sustainability in a different way than is usually envisioned. Instead of apprehending sustainability as a sort of 'utensil' – to be used when needed and most of the time as a technological add-on, 'applied' to a design project, it is the other way round. The question becomes not what sustainability can do for design but rather what design can do for sustainability.[3]

Also, the designer is to be considered as a conscious self that defines the self and his/her being-in-the-world through the design project and the act of design, and not as a problem-solving agent aiming only at the making of artifacts. Herein lies the main point of interest concerning the relationship between sustainability, design and the designer. The means and the end are reversed. Instead of sustainability (the means) serving design (the end), it is design (the means) benefiting sustainability (the end). This stance changes everything when we address the issue of sustainability in design education as well as in design practice and design research. Indeed, from this standpoint, sustainability is not anymore something exterior to the design act and consciousness of the student-designer in the act and learning of design. It is instead an attitude that discloses the self, others, and the world through the design of artefactual oriented projects such as buildings, cities, systems, objects, etc.

In that sense, sustainability can become a conscious and freely chosen attitude that takes place within the dialectical process between the *existential project* and the *design project* of the student. That attitude consists of being a being that chooses being so there can be *sustainment* through design and the act of design, and as such, is the cornerstone of the problematic of sustainability in design education, and therefore in design practice and research. Thus it is in the dialectical situation that takes place between the project of defining the self (the existential project) and the design project, that sustainability might be approached.

The theoretical frame proposed here is based on a consideration of Sartre's distinct but interrelated theories of freedom, project and responsibility. According to Sartre, the self is never determined and it is not a static essence that fixes once and for all the identity of the person. The self is rather a continuous project grounded in our being-in-the-world as embodied freedom in situation, i.e., in the ways we concretely engage realities or the world – things, people, time – through choices and actions. The ways we engage realities constitute the existential projects. The individual transcends facticity due to consciousness that can change continuously the relation of the individual with the world. Thus, all human experience and action may be discussed in terms of existential projects of the individual, i.e., a being with consciousness that creates the self by pursuing the fulfilment of lacks that consciousness generates.

Sustainability as an issue of the self in the act of design within design education can benefit from considering the philosophy of Jean-Paul Sartre.[4] Therefore, a theoretical frame for comprehending the phenomenon and issue of sustainability in design in the context of design learning is proposed through the Sartrean ontology. A Sartrean perspective has the ability to inform our understanding of the existential relationship between sustainability, self, and design.

Approaching the study of design in design education in relation to the issue of sustainability through a Sartrean perspective is relevant and timely. On the one hand, many aspects of Sartre's philosophy provide a framework that is meaningful and useful for design concerns in general, and design in relation to sustainability in particular. On the other hand, the continuous debate regarding sustainability in design cannot find an in-depth and fresh epistemological renewal if it is not addressed from an existential ground where the self is at the center of the phenomenon in terms of its existential relation to the self itself and to the other, through the envisioning and making of the built world, i.e., the *design project*. Sartre's ontology offers such an opportunity.

To figure this out, it is important to look to the structure that constitutes the person or the self. Sartre offers a comprehensive theory of the person in which individual responsibility is a constant underlying reality. He writes that man:

> carries the weight of the whole world on his shoulders; he is responsible for the world and for himself as a way of being. We are taking the word responsibility in its ordinary sense as consciousness (of) being the incontestable author of an event or object. In this sense the responsibility of the for-itself is overwhelming since he is the one by whom it happens that *there is* a world.[5]

Sartre's theory of responsibility rests upon his existential ontology, in which reality is made of two types of being, *being-in-itself* and *being-for-itself*. Being-in-itself is the world without consciousness whereas Being-for-itself is human consciousness.[6] Because consciousness is always consciousness of something, the two types of being are, for Sartre, inextricably related. From this, Sartre provides his ontological proof: the fact that consciousness is always consciousness of something means that consciousness is supported by a trans-phenomenal being (being-for-itself), which is not itself.[7] Also, consciousness creates distinctions within the otherwise undifferentiated non-conscious world (being-in-itself). Consciousness organises the world in terms of instrumental complexes or means-end relationships that are an expression of its overall goal or *project*.[8]

Sartre claims that without human consciousness there would be no world but only an undifferentiated plentitude of being-in-itself; thus human consciousness is individually and collectively responsible for the state of the world.[9] What we know as the world is the conglomerate of human projects. Human consciousness causes the world to be as it is, and so it is entirely responsible for the world, in both its material and immaterial forms.

Thus, Sartre's conception of a person is primarily concerned with the moral problems involved in human action.[10] At the root of Sartre's analysis is the conviction that persons are morally responsible agents. Sartre rejects the view that persons are reducible to material objects obeying deterministic laws, as well as the view that a person is essentially an immaterial subject distinct from the body.

Sartre's concept of intentionality is central to his notion of a person since it explains why conscious phenomena are irreducible to physical phenomena and why consciousness is not an independent thing or substance. By intentionality, Sartre means that consciousness, unlike physical objects, is a relation or reference to objects beyond it, even when these objects do not exist. What is distinctive about the intentionality of consciousness is that only human consciousness can imagine possible alternative purposes and choose between them.[11] Intentionality of consciousness is the center from which persons intend the world. We have here the very situation of the student as consciousness and the design project as object of the student's consciousness. The student intents a non-existing artefactual reality and carries out its outcome through a series of design choices and actions. In doing so, the student intents the world.

It is relevant here to situate the issue of the existential project in the context of the question of sustainability in design education. Indeed, the 'design project' in the disciplines of design represents the pedagogical paradigm of design education.[12] The students in such education are put in a design learning sequence through the development of a series of projects that are related to artefactual environments such as buildings, cities, objects, etc. In general, the project-oriented design pedagogy takes place within a studio setting where the students are assigned a series of project problems that they have to conceptualise and materialise in an analogical representation of built forms that respond to some program problem that manifests the lack of something.

Although this is a very basic description of the learning situation in design education, it summarises the reality of design education and design learning in most of the design discipline programs worldwide. In order for students to materialise, through models and graphics, the idea of a built environment, i.e., an artefactual oriented project, they must go through steps of design learning, in dialogue with an instructor, that refer to choosing and acting towards an end, i.e., the artifact proposal.[13] Hence a dialectical process is initiated between the student and the design project through design action and reflection.

Thus the students engage the world through the envisioning and making of an artifact that arises from the envisioning of its lack, through which they (seek to) transform the world. We can consider at this point, from a Sartrean perspective, that the students are individuals that define themselves and the world by means of design choices and actions. And the design project is the anchor of these choices and actions. As such, the design project is *per se* an existential project where the student defines the self. The design project is a lack that the student engages with in a certain manner, therefore it becomes the object of his/her consciousness toward which choices and actions are undertaken and it establishes a situation. It is a situation that the student creates so he/she can define the self and there can be being-in-the-world.

Indeed, for Sartre, humans create themselves through actions that are freely chosen and that are embodied in a set of existential projects. For Sartre, "man is nothing else but what he purposes, he exists only in so far as he realises himself, he is therefore nothing else but the sum of his actions, nothing else but what his life is."[14] This is why it can be said that in design education the student creates him/herself through the design projects that he/she carries out, as these are the result of intentional design choices and actions. At the moment of engaging with it, the design project, for the student, is an existential project.

But Sartre adds that all projects (existential projects) of an individual are circumscribed within what he calls a *fundamental project* or an original choice of being. For instance, in the case of the student in design education, the project of engaging with a design project in a studio can be seen as the most immediate project to carry out an activity. This project is inspired by a larger project such as graduating with a degree in a specific design discipline. This project in turn is motivated by a more basic project such as becoming a design professional, which is motivated by the project of being socially part of a certain category of people. The series of projects, each time more encompassing, ends with a project that is not contained by a more basic project. This ultimate project discloses the person's fundamental project and it has no justification *per se*, it faces the contingency of human existence. The fundamental project is defined as the general predisposition that has been chosen towards one's way of being in the world and of making the world be.

The fundamental project consists in a *desire for being*; it is the project of providing the individual with being.[15] Hence "all the trivial expectations of the real, all these commonplace, everyday values, derive their meaning from an original projection of myself which stands as my choice of myself in the world ... the unique and original project which constitutes my being."[16]

The fundamental project is distinguished from the particular projects of different individuals – because these particular projects derive from the fundamental project. That way of being in the world, through choices and actions, is a habitual or, as Sartre would put it, a 'pre-reflective' attitude underlying all subsequent projects and actions. This means that the fundamental project structures, in an invisible manner, the everyday life of the individual in terms of choices, thoughts and actions. It directs as a blueprint the individual in the reality of the world consisting of both objects (the artefactual) and other humans (the free subjects or projects). It is the fundamental project of the student that determines his/her design choices and actions in a design project. Thus, for instance, the resolution of a design project will be clearly different whether the student operates within a fundamental project based on hedonism or on philanthropy. The fundamental project that drives the way the individual engages the world through actions and choices represents the key dimension of being. It is where it is possible to intervene in order to reinvent the being of the self and therefore the way we act and choose. Sartre asserts that humans are free to change or modify their fundamental project as long as they move from a pre-reflective to a reflective mode of consciousness and way of being in the world. Indeed, the pre-reflective mode keeps us from being aware of how we carry on our fundamental project and all projects related to it. In that sense, it becomes almost impossible for the individual to transform his/her fundamental project. It requires a 'radical conversion' as Sartre puts it.

Here rests the importance of studio project exercises and design pedagogy in regard to the dialectic that takes place between the design instructor and the students. For the design instructor is key in providing the student in the design learning process, through reflective design choices and actions, with the insights and opportunity of radical conversion where sustainability can be considered as a freely chosen option of a fundamental project. In that sense, the student would continuously freely choose sustainability so as to be authentic in the choice of the self. This is a very important issue in regard to the ethical stance in Sartrean terms.

By addressing the concept of project through a Sartrean lens we can comprehend the student as a self in relation to the experience of design action in design education. Considering the Sartrean notion of project that refers to the grounding from which the individual chooses and acts and therefore creates him/herself, the self can be seized as the organic totality of the projects that the individual is.[17] Also, the fundamental project of the individual, which is his/her way that he/she has chosen to exist in the world, represents an anchor from which the individual organises the world, defines the meaning of the self within its relationship to the world and to other human beings. The student in design is therefore a self that defines itself, in the exercise and choice of a design project, through its design choices and actions that are projects manifesting the fundamental project. The design project is, in that very sense, the engagement of the student, as a self in the making, with the world and others. The experience that the design project is for the student may be considered as the dialectic that Sartre identifies between self and world, between the student's fundamental project as signifier and the world as signified.[18] There lies the threshold of significance in regard to the problematic of sustainability in design education. For any change to the student's fundamental project, such as the choice of sustainment, would lead to the redefinition of the self and the world in a reciprocal manner.

Whereas any change that is deliberately brought to the fundamental project of the student has to come from an inner conversion, the change that can be brought on by the issue of sustainability would involve a radical modification from an external source. This source is the design instructor. Let's see what is involved in that change of the student's fundamental project if it is to happen. In this regard it has to do with the issue of what is at stake and its value. The key question is: "I could have done otherwise, but at what price?"[19] Indeed, the person's project determines the existential value of the action. Also, the more encompassing an existential project is in relation to other projects, the higher the cost for changing or altering that level of project. Such a change would ask for changes to all levels of the encompassed or inner projects. In the situation that is considered here, i.e., design learning in design education, it would be costlier for a student to give up a studio course than to change the way he/she engages a design problem.

The highest existential cost is one that relates to any modification or transformation imposed on the fundamental project of the student. This refers to what Sartre calls a 'global change' since such a change involves changing the student's whole being-in-the-world.

In the case of sustainability, the existential cost of radically altering the student's fundamental project can be very important because it involves the global change in question and, more importantly, it is a 'price' that the student may not want to pay. In considering sustainability as fundamental project, the student's fundamental project would be disrupted in some respects, such as his/her professional project, i.e., his/her chosen professional being-in-the-world would definitely be modified; hence all of the other levels of projects like the student's relation to others, the student's capacity to get future commissions, etc., would be equally affected. Ultimately, what is truly transformed is the student's relation to himself as a for-itself – the person in the becoming of being. This in turn affects the student's being-for-others and the others' being-for-him/her.

In summary, sustainability involves a radical alteration of a student's fundamental project from outside, a change that disrupts directly the student's professional being-in-the-world. Sartre's idea of consciousness, in which self and world form a unity that is defined by a chosen fundamental project, allows us to understand sustainability as the breaking of this unity, rooted in the design project exercise, and therefore the redefining of the student's fundamental project. The role of the design instructor consequently would be to bring up sustainability within the dialectic between the existential project and the design project of the student – where the student is constantly defining the self, the world, and the relationship between the two – in order to bring out sustainability as a freely and continuously chosen fundamental project. In this way, being freely and reflectively chosen, we ensure that the choice of sustainability be authentic and therefore ethical in Sartrean terms.

As Sartre points out, by choosing, the person commits not only him/herself, but the whole of humanity.[20] Although there are no a priori values for Sartre, the agent's choice creates values in the same way as the artist does in the aesthetic realm. The values thus created by a proper exercise of the designer's freedom have a universal dimension, in that any other human being could make sense of them were he/she to be placed in his/her situation. There is therefore a universality that is expressed in particular forms in each of the existential projects, which definitely include the design projects of the designer's fundamental project.

Source: *Design Philosophy Papers Collection Four,* ed. A.M. Willis, 2008, pp. 13–20.

Notes

1. Although, in this paper, only the individual as designer is considered as agency, it should be understood that the agency in design is both the person acting as designer and the designed; both are involved ontologically in the designing of the world. For a more detailed study of that issue see the insightful paper by Anne-Marie Willis in which she presents and develops the concept of *Ontological Designing*. See A-M Willis 'Ontological Designing' *Design Philosophy Papers* no. 2, 2006 and 'Ontological Designing: Laying the Ground' in *Design Philosophy Papers Collection Three* Ravensbourne (Aust): Team D/E/S Publications, 2007.

2. The context of the design studio in education is probably the most relevant locus for an enquiry regarding the dialectical reality between the existential project and the artefactual project, and the problem of the articulation

of sustainability from the standpoint of the student as self-reflectively and consciously involved through the act of design in that dialectic. Indeed, the studio pedagogy is grounded in what Donald Schön calls *reflection in action* and it offers, upstream in the education of the professional, an ideal moment to have the student reach beyond the immediate apprehension of what it means to be a designer that engages a project that will transform the self and the others. For a more detailed account of the notion of *reflection in action* see Donald Schön *The Reflective Practitioner: How Professionals Think in Action*, Burlington: Ashgate Publishing, 1995.

3. See A-M Willis 'The Limits of Sustainable Architecture', paper delivered at *Shaping the Sustainable Millennium*, Queensland University of Technology, July 2000. The works by Anne-Marie Willis and Tony Fry argue for a radical conceptualisation of design in regard to sustainability. Design is conceptualised from being an activity of designing structures and buildings to one of designing what they call *sustainments*, i.e., environments with the ability to sustain that which needs to be sustained. This is the notion of sustainability adopted in the paper I present here. See this notion of sustainability, *sustainment*, developed and exposed in the works of Willis and Fry published in several issues of *Design Philosophy Papers* particularly Tony Fry 'The Voice of Sustainment: Design Ethics' *Design Philosophy Papers*, no. 2, 2004. See also Tony Fry *A New Design Philosophy: An Introduction to Defuturing*, Sydney: UNSW Press, 1999 and Tony Fry 'A Total Rewriting of the Past, Present and Future of Design' Public Lecture Program, School of the Art Institute of Chicago, 2001.

4. The seminal work of Jean-Paul Sartre regarding ontology is *Being and Nothingness: An Essay on Phenomenological Ontology*. Another of his works *Existentialism is a Humanism,* addresses some ethical implications of his ontology.

5. J-P Sartre *Being and Nothingness: An Essay on Phenomenological Ontology* trans. Hazel E. Barnes, New York: Philosophical Library, 1956, p. 553.

6. *Ibid* pp. 73–105.

7. *Ibid* p. lxi.

8. *Ibid* pp. 171–180, 433–553.

9. *Ibid* pp. 433–600.

10. Many scholars argue that the whole philosophy of Sartre is concerned with the ethical dimension of the human being. Sartre himself tends to assert that ethics is a major concern in his work. This is the perspective adopted in this paper. Two interesting studies on that issue are: T.C. Anderson *Sartre's Two Ethics* Chicago: Open Court, 1993; and J. Marchand *Introduction à la lecture de Jean-Paul Sartre*, Montréal: Liber, 2005.

11. P. Morris *Sartre's Concept of a Person: An Analytic Approach*, Amherst: University of Massachusetts Press, 1975, p. 27.

12. The concept of project has been recognised as an epistemological paradigm in architecture and in design disciplines in general. See J-P Boutinet *Psychologie des conduites à projet*. Paris: PUF, Que sais-je, 1993; J-L LeMoigne 'Recherche scientifique en architecture?' *La recherche architecturale: un bilan international*, (ouvrage coll.) Marseilles: Parenthèses, 1986, 97–102; and R. Prost *Concevoir, Inventer, créer: réflexions sur les pratiques*, Paris: L'Harmattan, 1995.

13. See Donald Schön *The Reflective Practitioner: How Professionals Think in Action* Burlington: Ashgate Publishing, 1995 and *Educating the Reflective Practitioner: Toward a New Design for Teaching and Learning in the Professions* San Francisco: Jossey-Bass, 1990.

14. J-P Sartre *Existentialism is a Humanism* trans. Philip Mairet, New York, Haskell House, 1948, p. 41.

15. Sartre *Being and Nothingness* p. 565.

16. *Ibid* p. 39.

17. *Ibid* p. 454.

18. J-P Sartre *Search for a Method* trans. Hazel E. Barnes, New York: Alfred A. Knopf, 1963.

19. Sartre *Being and Nothingness* p. 454.

20. Sartre expresses this very clearly in *Being and Nothingness* p. 553, and in *Existentialism is a Humanism* where he writes: "And, when we say that man is responsible for himself, we do not mean that he is responsible only for his own individuality, but that he is responsible for all men." (p. 29); and, "I am thus responsible for myself and for all men, and I am creating a certain image of man as I would have him to be. In fashioning myself I fashion man." (p. 30).

CHAPTER 10
THE SCIENCE OF THE CONCRETE
Claude Levi-Strauss

Note from editor: Here, structural anthropologist Levi Strauss compares two methods of thinking that are grounded in material practice – that of the magical thinker or bricoleur, and that of the scientist or engineer. As he elaborates each, the differences between them become less distinct. In earlier pages of The Savage Mind, *from which this extract is taken, he takes magic and science "as two parallel modes of acquiring knowledge." (13) That many traditional medicinal practices have little practical effect is not the point, he says. Taking the example of the belief that the touch of a woodpecker's beak cures toothache, he asks whether there is a point of view from which the two things (woodpecker/tooth) can be seen as "going together" and whether some initial order can be introduced into the universe by means of such groupings. Classifying, as opposed to not classifying, has a value of its own, whatever form the classification may take (9) and "the thought we call primitive is founded on this demand for order."*

.... And in or own time the 'bricoleur' is still someone who works with his hands and uses devious means compared to those of a craftsman.[1]

The characteristic feature of mythical thought is that it expresses itself by means of a heterogeneous repertoire which, even if extensive, is nevertheless limited. It has to use this repertoire, however, whatever the task in hand because it has nothing else at its disposal. Mythical thought is therefore a kind of intellectual 'bricolage' — which explains the relation which can be perceived between the two.

Like 'bricolage' on the technical plane, mythical reflection can reach brilliant unforeseen results on the intellectual plane. Conversely, attention has often been drawn to the mytho-poetical nature of 'bricolage' on the plane of so-called 'raw' or 'naive' art, in architectural follies like the villa of Cheval the postman or the stage sets of Georges Méliès, or, again, in the case immortalized by Dickens in *Great Expectations* but no doubt originally inspired by observation, of Mr Wemmick's suburban 'castle' with its miniature drawbridge, its cannon firing at nine o'clock, its bed of salad and cucumbers, thanks to which its occupants could withstand a siege if necessary.

The analogy is worth pursuing since it helps us to see the real relations between the two types of scientific knowledge we have distinguished. The 'bricoleur' is adept at performing a large number of diverse tasks; but, unlike the engineer, he does not subordinate each of them to the availability of raw materials and tools conceived and procured for the purpose of the project. His universe of instruments is closed and the rules of his game are always to make do with 'whatever is at hand', that is to say with a set of tools and materials which is always finite and is also heterogeneous because what it contains bears no relation to the current project, or indeed to any particular project, but is the contingent result of all the occasions there have been to renew or enrich the stock or to maintain it with the remains of previous constructions or destructions. The set of the 'bricoleur's' means cannot therefore be defined in terms of a project (which would presuppose besides, that, as in the case of the engineer, there were, at least in theory, as many sets of tools and materials or 'instrumental sets' as there are different kinds of projects). It is to be defined only by its potential use or, putting this another way and in the language of the 'bricoleur' himself, because the elements are collected or retained on the principle that 'they may always come in handy'. Such elements are specialized up to a point, sufficiently for the 'bricoleur' not to need the equipment and knowledge of all trades and professions, but not enough for each of them to have only one definite and determinate use. They each represent a set of actual and possible relations; they are 'operators' but they can be used for any operations of the same type.

The elements of mythical thought similarly lie half-way between percepts and concepts. It would be impossible to separate percepts from the concrete situations in which they appeared, while recourse to concepts would require that thought could, at least provisionally, put its projects (to use Husserl's expression) 'in brackets'. Now, there is an intermediary between images and concepts, namely signs. For signs can always be defined in the way introduced by Saussure in the case of the particular category of linguistic signs, that is, as a link between images and concepts. In the union thus brought about, images and concepts play the part of the signifying and signified respectively.

Signs resemble images in being concrete entities but they resemble concepts in their powers of reference. Neither concepts nor signs relate exclusively to themselves; either may be substituted for something else. Concepts, however, have an unlimited capacity in this respect, while signs have not. The example of the 'bricoleur' helps to bring out the differences and similarities. Consider him at work and excited by his project. His first practical step is retrospective. He has to turn back to an already existent set made up of tools and materials, to consider or reconsider what it contains and, finally and above all, to engage in a sort of dialogue with it and, before choosing between them, to index the possible answers which the whole set can offer to his problem. He interrogates all the heterogeneous objects of which his treasury [2] is composed to discover what each of them could 'signify' and so contribute to the definition of a set which has yet to materialize but which will ultimately differ from the instrumental set only in the internal disposition of its parts. A particular cube of oak could be a wedge to make up for the inadequate length of a plank of pine or it could be a pedestal — which would allow the grain and polish of the old wood show to advantage. In one case it will serve as extension, in the other as material. But the possibilities always remain limited by the particular history of each piece and by those of its features which are already determined by the use for which it was originally intended or the modifications it has undergone for other purposes. The elements which the bricoleur' collects and uses are 'pre-con-strained' like the constitutive units of myth, the possible combinations of which are restricted by the fact that they are drawn from the language where they already possess a sense which sets a limit on their freedom of manoeuvre. And the decision as to what to put in each place also depends on the possibility of putting a different element there instead, so that each choice which is made will involve a complete reorganization of the structure, which will never be the same as one vaguely imagined nor as some other which might have been preferred to it.

The engineer no doubt also cross-examines his resources. The existence of an 'interlocutor' is in his case due to the fact that his means, power and knowledge are never unlimited and that in this negative form he meets resistance with which he has to come to terms. It might be said that the engineer questions the universe, while the 'bricoleur addresses himself to a collection of oddments left over from human endeavours, that is, only a sub-set of the culture. Again, Information Theory shows that it is possible, and often useful, to reduce the physicists' approaches to a sort of dialogue with nature. This would make the distinction we are trying to draw less clear-cut. There remains however a difference even if one takes into account the fact that the scientist never carries on a dialogue with nature pure and simple but rather with a particular relationship between nature and culture definable in terms of his particular period and civilization and the material means at his disposal. He is no more able than the 'bricoleur to do whatever he wishes when he is presented with a given task. He too has to begin by making a catalogue of a previously determined set consisting of theoretical and practical knowledge, of technical means, which restrict the possible solutions.

The difference is therefore less absolute than it might appear. It remains a real one, however, in that the engineer is always trying to make his way out of and go beyond the constraints imposed by a particular state of civilization while the 'bricoleur' by inclination or necessity always remains within them. This is another way of saying that the engineer works by means of concepts and the 'bricoleur' by means of signs. The sets which each employs are at different distances from the poles on the axis of opposition between nature and culture. One way indeed in which signs can be opposed to concepts is that whereas concepts aim to be wholly transparent with respect to reality, signs allow and even require the interposing and incorporation of a certain amount of human culture into reality. Signs, in Peirce's vigorous phrase 'address somebody'.

Both the scientist and 'bricoleur' might therefore be said to be constantly on the look out for 'messages'. Those which the 'bricoleur' collects are, however, ones which have to some extent been transmitted in advance — like the commercial codes which are summaries of the past experience of the trade and so allow any new situation to be met economically, provided that it belongs to the same class as some earlier one. The scientist, on the other hand, whether he is an engineer or a physicist, is always on the look out for that other message which might be wrested from an interlocutor in spite of his reticence in pronouncing on questions whose answers have not been rehearsed. Concepts thus appear like operators opening up the set being worked with and signification like the operator of its reorganization, which neither extends nor renews it and limits itself to obtaining the group of its transformations.

Images cannot be ideas but they can play the part of signs or, to be more precise, co-exist with ideas in signs and, if ideas are not yet present, they can keep their future place open for them and make its contours apparent negatively. Images are fixed, linked in a single way to the mental act which accompanies them. Signs, and images which have acquired significance, may still lack comprehension; unlike concepts, they do not yet possess simultaneous and theoretically unlimited relations with other entities of the same kind. They are however already permutable, that is, capable of standing in successive relations with other entities — although with only a limited number and, as we have seen, only on the condition that they always form a system in which an alteration which affects one element automatically affects all the others. On this plane logicians' 'extension' and 'intension' are not two distinct and complementary aspects but one and the same thing. One understands then how mythical thought can be capable of generalizing and so be scientific, even though it is still entangled in imagery. It too works by analogies and comparisons even though its creations, like those of the 'bricoleur', always really consist of a new arrangement of elements, the nature of which is unaffected by whether they figure in the instrumental set or in the final arrangement (these being the same, apart from the internal disposition of their parts): 'it would seem that mythological worlds have been built up, only to be shattered again, and that new worlds were built from the fragments.'[3] Penetrating as this comment is, it nevertheless fails to take into account that in the continual reconstruction from the same materials, it is always earlier ends which are called upon to play the part of means: the signified changes into the signifying and vice versa.

This formula, which could serve as a definition of 'bricolage', explains how an implicit inventory or conception of the total means available must be made in the case of mythical thought also, so that a result can be defined which will always be a compromise between the structure of the instrumental set and that of the project. Once it materializes the project will therefore inevitably be at a remove from the initial aim (which was moreover a mere sketch), a phenomenon which the surrealists have felicitously called 'objective hazard'. Further, the 'bricoleur' also, and indeed principally, derives his poetry from the fact that he does not confine himself to accomplishment and execution: he 'speaks' not only with things, as we have already seen, but also through the medium of things: giving an account of his personality and life by the choices he makes between the limited possibilities. The 'bricoleur' may not ever complete his purpose but he always puts something of himself into it.

Mythical thought appears to be an intellectual form of 'bricolage' in this sense also. Science as a whole is based on the distinction between the contingent and the necessary, this being also what distinguishes event and structure. The qualities it claimed at its outset as peculiarly scientific were precisely those which formed no part of living experience and remained outside and, as it were, unrelated to events. This is the significance of the notion of primary qualities. Now, 'the characteristic feature of mythical thought, as of 'bricolage' on the practical plane, is that it builds up structured sets, not directly with other structured sets[4] but by using the remains and debris of events in French 'des bribes et des morceaux', or odds and ends in English, fossilized evidence of the history of an individual or a society. The relation between the diachronic and the synchronic is therefore in a sense reversed. Mythical thought, that 'bricoleur', builds up structures by fitting together events, or rather the remains of events,[5] while science, 'in operation' simply by virtue of coming into being, creates its means and results in the form of events, thanks to the structures which it is constantly elaborating and which are its hypotheses and theories. But it is important not to make the mistake of thinking that these are two stages or phases in the evolution of knowledge. Both approaches are equally valid. Physics and chemistry are already striving to become qualitative again, that is, to account also for secondary qualities which when they have been explained will in their turn become means of explanation. And biology may perhaps be marking time waiting for this before it can itself explain life. Mythical thought for its part is imprisoned in the events and experiences which it never tires of ordering and re-ordering in its search to find them a meaning. But it also acts as a liberator by its protest against the idea that anything can be meaningless with which science at first resigned itself to a compromise.

Source: Claude Levi-Strauss *The Savage Mind* trans. George Weidenfeld and Nicolson, London: Weidenfeld and Nicolson, 1976, pp. 17–22.

Notes

1. The 'bricoleur' has no precise equivalent in English. He is a man who undertakes odd jobs and is a Jack of all trades or a kind of professional do-it-yourself man, but, as the text makes clear, he is of a different standing from, for instance, the English 'odd job man' or handyman (trans. note).

2. Cf. 'Treasury of ideas as Hubert and Mauss so aptly describe magic (in Hubert, R. and Mauss, M. 'Esquisse d'une théorie générale de la magie', L'Année Sociologique, tome VII, 1902-3, in Mauss, M., Sociologie et Anthropologie, Paris 1950.

3. Boas, F., Introduction to: James Teit, 'Traditions of the Thompson River Indians of British Columbia', *Memoirs of the American Folklore Society*, vol. 6, 1898, p. 18

4. Mythical thought builds structured sets by means of a structured set, namely, language. But it is not at the structural level that it makes use of it: it builds ideological castles out of the debris of what was once a social discourse.

5. 'Bricolage' also works with 'secondary' qualities, i.e. 'second hand'.

CHAPTER 11
THE TEXTILITY OF MAKING
Tim Ingold

Note from editor: The process of making, according to Ingold is one of giving form, but this does not mean imposing a pre-conceived form on inert and compliant matter, as in Aristotle's concept of hylomorphism. Rather, making is a process of working with forces and the variability of materials. In developing his argument he draws on Paul Klee, Leon Battista Alberti, Gilbert Simondon, Bruno Latour Gilles Deleuze and Félix Guattari. Other connections could be made with Donald Schön's idea of 'back-talk' in design and making, and of shi and the 'force of form' in early Chinese aesthetics as elaborated by Francois Jullien (see Part IV).

In his notebooks, the painter Paul Klee repeatedly insisted that the processes of genesis and growth that give rise to forms in the world we inhabit are more important than the forms themselves. 'Form is the end, death', he wrote. 'Form-giving is life'[1]. This, in turn, lay at the heart of his celebrated Creative Credo of 1920: 'Art does not reproduce the visible but makes visible.'[2] It does not, in other words, seek to replicate finished forms that are already settled, whether as images in the mind or as objects in the world. It seeks, rather, to join with those very forces that bring form into being. Thus the line grows from a point that has been set in motion, as the plant grows from its seed. Taking their cue from Klee, philosophers Gilles Deleuze and Félix Guattari argue that the essential relation, in a world of life, is not between matter and form but between materials and forces.[3] It is about the way in which heterogeneous materials, enlivened by forces of tension and compression and with variable properties, mix and meld with one another in the generation of things. And what they seek to overcome in their rhetoric is the lingering influence of a way of thinking about things, and about how they are made and used, that has been around in the western world for the past two millennia and more. It goes back to Aristotle.

To create anything, Aristotle reasoned, you have to bring together form (morphe) and matter (hyle). In the subsequent history of western thought, this hylomorphic model of creation became ever more deeply embedded. But it also became increasingly unbalanced. Form came to be seen as imposed by an agent with a particular design in mind, while matter, thus rendered passive and inert, became that which was imposed upon. My critical argument in this chapter is that contemporary discussions of art and technology, and of what it means to make things, continue to reproduce the underlying assumptions of the hylomorphic model, even as they seek to restore the balance between its terms. My ultimate aim, however, is more radical: with Deleuze and Guattari, it is to overthrow the model itself, and to replace it with an ontology that assigns primacy to the processes of formation as against their final products, and to the flows and transformations of materials as against states of matter. Form, to recall Klee's words, is death; form-giving is life. I want to argue that what Klee said of art is true of skilled practice in general, namely that it is a question not of imposing preconceived forms on inert matter but of intervening in the fields of force and currents of material wherein forms are generated. Practitioners, I contend, are wanderers, wayfarers, whose skill lies in their ability to find the grain of the world's becoming and to follow its course while bending it to their evolving purpose.

Consider, for example, the operation of splitting timber with an axe. The practised woodsman brings down the axe so that its blade enters the grain and follows a line already incorporated into the timber through its previous history of growth, when it was part of a living tree. 'It is a question', write Deleuze and Guattari, 'of surrendering to the wood, and following where it leads.'[4] Perhaps it is no accident that the word used in Greek Antiquity to describe the skill of the practitioner, tekhne, is derived from the Sanskrit words for axe, *tasha*, and the carpenter, *taksan*. The carpenter is 'one who fashions' (Sanskrit, *taksati*), a shaper or maker. Yet the Latin verb for 'to weave', texere, comes from precisely the same root.[5] The carpenter, it seems, was as much a weaver as a maker. Or more precisely, his making was itself a practice of weaving: not the imposition of form on pliant substance but the slicing and binding of fibrous material.[6] His axe, as it finds its way through the wood, splitting it as it goes, is guided – as Deleuze and Guattari say – by 'the variable undulations and torsions of the fibres.'[7] As for the axe itself, let us suppose that the blade has been knapped from stone. The skilled knapper works by detaching long, thin flakes from a core, exploiting the property of conchoidal fracture taken on by the lithic material through its history of geological compression.[8] Before each blow of the hammer, he locates or prepares a suitable striking platform, whence, on impact, the line of fracture ripples through the material like a wave. The wrought surface of knapped stone, at least until it has been ground smooth, bears the scars of multiple, overlapping fractures.[9]

In the history of the western world, however, the tactile and sensuous knowledge of line and surface that had guided practitioners through their varied and heterogeneous materials, like wayfarers through the terrain, gave way to an eye for geometrical form, conceived in the abstract in advance of its realisation in a now homogenised material medium. What we could call the textility of making has been progressively devalued, while the hylomorphic model has gained in strength.[10] The architectural writings of Leon Battista Alberti, in the mid-fifteenth century, mark a turning point in this development. Until then, as David Turnbull[11] has shown in the case of the great medieval cathedral of Chartres, the architect was literally a master among builders, who worked on site, coordinating teams of masons whose task was to cut stones by following the curves of wooden templates and to lay the blocks along lines marked out with string. There was no plan, and the outcome – far from conforming to the dictates of a prior design – better resembled a patchwork quilt.[12]

For Alberti, to the contrary, architecture was a concern of the mind. 'It is quite possible', he wrote, 'to project whole forms in the mind without any recourse to the material, by designating and determining a fixed orientation and conjunction for the various lines and angles.'[13] Such lines and angles together comprise what Alberti called the 'lineaments' of the building. These lineaments have a quite different status from the lines that masons cut from templates or laid with string. They comprise a precise and complete specification for the form and appearance of the building, as conceived by the intellect, independently and in advance of the work of construction. On paper, the lineaments would have been inscribed as drawn lines, which could be either straight or curved. Indeed, Alberti's lines have their source in the formal geometry of Euclid. 'The straight line', he explains, 'is the shortest possible line that may be drawn between two points', while 'the curved line is part of a circle.'[14] What art historian Jean-François Billeter writes of the line of Euclidean geometry applies with equal force to the Albertian lineament: it 'has neither body nor colour nor texture, nor any other tangible quality: its nature is abstract, conceptual, rational'[15]

Following materials

Thus the textility of building gave way to an architectonics of pure form. And from that point on, despite their common etymological origin, the technical and the textilic were set on radically divergent paths. While the former was elevated into a system of operational principles, a technology, the latter was debased as mere craft, revealing the almost residual or interstitial 'feel' of a world engineered in the light of reason. Embodied within the very concept of technology was an ontological claim, namely, that things are constituted in the rational and rule-governed transposition of preconceived form onto inert substance, rather than in a weaving of, and through, active materials.[16] 'Technology', in other words, is one answer to the question, 'What does it mean to make things?' It is an answer, however, that does not readily stand up in the theatre of practice. For makers have to work in a world that does not keep still until the job is completed, and with materials that have properties of their own and are not necessarily predisposed to fall into the shapes required of them, let alone to stay in them indefinitely.[17] Building contractors, tasked with the implementation of architectural design, know this all too well – as Matisse Enzer, a contractor with long experience of working with architects, explains:

> Architects think of a building as a complete thing, while builders think of it and know it as a sequence – hole, then foundation, framing, roof, etc. The separation of design from making has resulted in a built environment that has no 'flow' to it. You simply cannot design an improvisation or an adaptation. It's dead.[18]

Or as Stewart Brand puts it, there is a kink between the world and the architect's idea of it: 'The idea is crystalline, the fact fluid.' Builders inhabit that kink. Contemporary architecture is not, however, universally blind to the disjunction between theory and practice. The distinguished Portuguese architect Alvaro Siza, for example, admits that while he can build and design houses, he has never been able to build a real house, by which he means 'a complicated machine in which every day something breaks down.'[19] Besides builders and repairmen of diverse trades – bricklayers, joiners, slaters, plasterers, plumbers and so on – the real heroes of house building, according to Siza, are the people who live in them who, through unremitting effort, shore them up and maintain their integrity in the face of sunshine, wind and rain, the wear and tear inflicted by human occupancy, and the invasions of birds, rodents, insects, arachnids and fungi.[20] Like life itself, a real house is always work in progress, and the best that inhabitants can do is to steer it in the desired direction. Likewise the gardener, armed with spade, fork and trowel, has to struggle to prevent the garden from turning into a jungle. More generally, whenever we encounter matter, as Deleuze and Guattari insist, 'it is matter in movement, in flux, in variation'. And the consequence, they go on to assert, is that 'this matter-flow can only be followed. [21]What Deleuze and Guattari call 'matter-flow', I would call material. Accordingly, I recast the assertion as a simple rule of thumb: to *follow the materials*.[22]

To apply this rule is to intervene in a world that is continually 'on the boil'. Perhaps it could be compared to a huge kitchen. In the kitchen, stuff is mixed in various combinations, generating new materials in the process that will in turn become mixed with other ingredients in an endless process of transformation. To cook, containers have to be opened, and their contents poured out. We have to take the lids off things. Faced with the anarchic proclivities of his or her materials, the cook has to struggle to retain some semblance of control over what is going on. An even closer parallel might be drawn with the laboratory of the alchemist. The world according to alchemy, as art historian James Elkins explains, was not one of matter that might be described in terms of its molecular composition, but one of substances that were known by what they look and feel like, and by following what happens to them as they are mixed, heated or cooled. Alchemy, writes Elkins, 'is the old science of struggling with materials, and not quite understanding what is happening.'[23] His point is that this, too, is what painters have always done. Their knowledge was also of substances, and these were often little different from those of the alchemical laboratory. As practitioners, the builder, the gardener, the cook, the alchemist and the painter are not so much imposing form on matter as bringing together diverse materials and combining or redirecting their flow in the anticipation of what might emerge. In their attempts to rebalance the hylomorphic model, theorists have insisted that the material world is not passively subservient to human designs. They have expressed this, however, by appeal not to the vitality of materials but to the agency of objects. If persons can act on objects in their vicinity, so, it is argued, can objects 'act back', leading persons to act differently from how they might otherwise have done. The speed bump on the road, to take a familiar example adduced by Bruno Latour, causes the driver to slow down, its agency here substituting for that of the traffic policeman.[24] We may stare at an object, explains Elkins (with acknowledgement to the psychoanalysis of Jacques Lacan), but the object also stares back at us, so that our vision is caught in a 'cat's cradle of crossing lines of sight'.[25] And in a precise reversal of the conventional subject–object relations of hylomorphism, archaeologist Chris Gosden suggests that, in many cases, it is not the mind that imposes its forms on material objects, but rather the latter that give shape to the forms of thought.[26] In this endless shuttling back and forth between the mind and the material world, it seems that objects can act like subjects and that subjects can be acted upon like objects. Instead of subjects and objects there are 'quasi-objects' and 'quasi-subjects', connected in relational networks.[27]

Yet paradoxically, these attempts to move beyond the modernist polarisation of subject and object remain trapped within a language of causation that is founded on the very same grammatical categories and that can conceive of action only as an effect set in train by an agent. 'Agents', according to anthropologist Alfred Gell, 'initiate "actions" which are "caused" by themselves, by their intentions, not by the physical laws of the cosmos.'[28] The intention is the cause, the action the effect. Assuming that human beings alone are capable of initiating actions in this sense, Gell nevertheless allows that their agency may be distributed around a host of artefacts enrolled in the realisation of their original intentions. These artefacts then become 'secondary agents' to the 'primary agency' of the human initiators.[29] Not all would concur with Gell that actions are the effects of prior intentions, let alone with the identification of the latter with mental states. Intentionality and agency, as archaeologist Carl Knappett argues, are not quite the same: 'artifacts such as traffic lights, sleeping policemen, or catflaps might be described as possessing a kind of agency, yet it would be much harder to argue that they manifest intentionality.'[30] It would indeed be foolish to attribute intentions to catflaps. But is it any less so to suggest that they 'possess agency'? Rather that attributing the action to the agency of the flap (in cohort with that of the cat, and of the cat's owner who installed the flap in the door to save her from having to open it herself), would it not make more sense to attribute the operation of the flap to the action into which it was enlisted, of the cat's making its way in or out of doors? Surely, neither the cat nor the flap possess agency; they are rather possessed by the action. Like everything else, as I shall now show, they are swept up in the generative currents of the world.

Source: Tim Ingold *Being Alive: Essays on movement, knowledge and description* Routledge: New York, 2011, pp. 229–35. The Textility of Making, Tim Ingold, © 2018, reproduced by permission of Taylor & Francis Books UK.

Notes

1. P. Klee *Notebooks, Volume 2: The Nature of Nature* (ed. J. Spiller, trans. H. Norden) London: Lund Humphries, Klee 1973, p. 269.

2. P. Klee *Notebooks, Volume 1: The Thinking Eye* (ed. J. Spiller, trans. R. Manheim) London: Lund Humphries, Klee 1961, p. 76.

3. G. Deleuze and F. Guattari *A Thousand Plateaus: Capitalism and Schizophrenia* (trans. B. Massumi) London: Continuum [originally published as *Mille Plateaux*, vol. 2 of *Capitalisme et Schizophrénie*, Paris: Minuit, 1980], p. 377.

4. ibid., p. 451.

5. V. Mitchell 'Textiles, text and techne' in T. Harrod (ed.) *Obscure Objects of Desire: Reviewing the Crafts in the Twentieth Century* London: Crafts Council, 1997, pp. 324–32, 330.

6. T. Ingold 'Making culture and weaving the world' in P-M Graves-Brown (ed.) *Matter, Materiality and Modern Culture*, London: Routledge, 2000, pp. 50–71, 64–5.

7. Deleuze 2004, p. 450.

8. J. Pelegrin 'Remarks about archaeological techniques and methods of knapping: elements of a cognitive approach to stone knapping' in V. Roux and B. Bril (eds) *Stone Knapping: The Necessary Conditions for a Uniquely Hominin Behaviour* Cambridge: McDonald Institute for Archaeological Research, 2005, pp. 23–33, 25.

9. In his essay On the Mode of Existence of Technical Objects, the philosopher Gilbert Simondon advanced much the same argument with the example of another woodworking tool, the adze. 'This tool', he writes, 'is not merely a block of homogeneous metal shaped to a particular form. It has been forged, which means that the molecular chains in the metal have a certain orientation that varies in different places, like a wood with fibres so disposed as to give the greatest solidarity and the greatest elasticity' (Simondon 1980: 83–84). G. Simondon *On the Mode of Existence of Technical Objects* (ed. J. Hart, trans. N. Mellamphy) Unpublished manuscript, University of Western Ontario, 1980 [translation of *Du Mode d'existence des Objects Techniques*. Paris: Aubier Montaigne, 1958]

10. Protevi comments likewise on how the 'tenaciously deep-rooted' philosophical prejudices of hylomorphism have led to 'the privilege of the architect's vision and the invisibility or denigration of artisanal sensitivity'. J. Protevi *Political Physics: Deleuze, Derrida and the Body Politic* London: Athlone Press, 2001, p. 169.

11. D. Turnbull *Masons, Tricksters and Cartographers* Amsterdam: Harwood Academic, 2000, pp. 53–87.

12. Harvey 1974, p. 33.

13. L. B. Alberti *On the Art of Building in Ten Books* (trans. J. Rykwert, N. Leach and R. Tavernor) Cambridge, MA: MIT Press, 1988, p. 7.

14. ibid., p. 19.

15. J. F. Billeter *The Chinese Art of Writing* (trans. J.-M. Clarke and M. Taylor) New York: Rizzoli International, 1990, p. 47.

16. Precisely because 'technology' is an ontological claim, it makes no sense to treat technology as a subject about which ontological claims can be made. If the claim embodied in the concept is without foundation, then so is the concept itself. *The Perception of the Environment: Essays on Livelihood, Dwelling and Skill*, London: Routledge, 2000, p. 312.

17. T. Ingold and E. Hallam *Creativity and cultural improvisation: An introduction*, Oxford: Berg, 2007, p. 3–4.

18. S. Brand *How Buildings Learn: What Happens to Them After They're Built*. Harmondsworth: Penguin, 1994, p. 64.

19. A. Siza *Architecture Writings* (ed. A. Angelillo) Milan: Skira Editore, 1997, p. 47.

20. ibid.. p. 48.

21. Deleuze and Guattari 2004, p. 451.

22. *follow the materials*. I mean following to be understood here in an active rather than passive sense. It is not blind. The hunter following a trail must remain ever alert to visual and other sensory cues in an ever-changing environment and must adjust his course accordingly. In following materials the practitioner does the same. The consequence of failure would be that the work goes off track and cannot be carried on.

23. J. Elkins *What Painting Is* London: Routledge, 2000, p. 19.

24. B. Latour *Pandora's Hope: Essays on the Reality of Science Studies* Cambridge, MA: Harvard University Press, 1999, pp. 186–90.

25. J. Elkins *The Object Stares Back: On the Nature of Seeing* New York: Simon & Schuster, 1996, p. 70.

26. C. Gosden 'What do objects want?' *Journal of Archaeological Method and Theory* vol 12, no 3, 2005, pp. 193–211, 196.

27. B. Latour *We Have Never Been Modern* (trans. C. Porter) Hemel Hempstead: Harvester Wheatsheaf, 1993, p. 89.

28. A. Gell *Art and Agency: An Anthropological Theory* Oxford: Clarendon, 1998, p. 16.

29. Gell ibid., pp. 20–1.

30. C. Knappett *Thinking Through Material Culture: An Interdisciplinary Perspective* Philadelphia, PA: University of Pennsylvania Press, 2005, p. 22.

See entries in *Bloomsbury Encyclopedia of Design* (ed. Clive Edwards): Form (Abby Mellick Lopes); Michel De Certeau (Katie Hepworth); Intuition (Cameron Tonkinwise); Improvisation (Cameron Tonkinwise); Poiesis (Eleni Kalantidou); Practice Theory (Jacqueline Lorber Kasunic); Praxis (Eleni Kalantidou). On *technê*, *epistêmê*, *phronêsis*, *sophia*, and *nous* see Richard Parry, "*Episteme* and *Techne*" (2014). Hannah Arendt's *The Human Condition* (1958) makes important distinctions between work, making, and action, extending Greek thinking to the modern age. On practice theory see E. Shove et al. *The Dynamics of Social Practice: Everyday Life and How it Changes* (2013); David Nicolini, *Practice Theory, Work & Organization: An Introduction* (2012); Pierre Bourdieu, *Outline of A Theory of Practice* (1977) especially chapter on structures, habitus, and practices; Michel de Certeau, *The Practices of Everyday Life* (1988), especially section on Strategies and Tactics; A. Reckwitz, "Toward a Theory of Social Practices: A Development in Culturalist Theorising" (2002); T. Schatzi et al., *The Practice Turn in Contemporary Theory* (2001). As discussed in the Introduction and Part I, design practice has mainly been theorized in terms of design methods and process, see texts by Schön, Cross, Nelson, and Stolterman in Part I Further Reading. On design practice related to philosophy see Carl Mitcham, "Dasein versus Design: The Problematics of Turning Making into Thinking" (2001); Marcus Jahnke, "Revisiting Design as a Hermeneutic Practice" (2012); and James Wang, "The Importance of Aristotle to Design Thinking" (2013) which takes Aristotle's distinction between making and doing as an argument for designers as makers. On design practice in relation to the subject/object split see Richard Coyne and Adrian Snodgrass, "Is Designing Mysterious? Challenging the Dual Knowledge Thesis" (1991).

PART III
THE ETHOS OF DESIGN

INTRODUCTION

The texts in this section deal with, or can be brought, to the question of design and ethics. They traverse: *ethics* as currently understood; *design ethics* as currently understood; ethics as it has come to us through philosophy; and what an expanded ethical field might be in the context of the pervasiveness of design.

While *ethics*, as a formal idea, has come down to us via the early Greeks, all cultures have an *ethos* inscribed in their social institutions and expressed in how people relate to each other, the latter usually referred to as morality.

What usually comes to mind when ethics is invoked are questions of individual behavior and professional conduct. Law, medicine, and engineering have codes of ethics, as do other service professions including design. These are facilitated by the provision of guidelines on the ethical conduct toward clients and customers: truth in advertising, due diligence, confidentiality, copyright, honesty in financial dealings, complying with legal requirements especially regarding health and safety.

Within design practice, there is an ethical tradition that goes beyond mere compliance to professional codes of conduct; it is expressed as a demand that designers should "do good," exemplified in the classic book by Victor Papanek, *Design for the Real World*, and in more recent times by humanitarian design organizations and projects, design activism, and various appeals for design to be "environmentally friendly." These are obvious examples of ethical conduct in design ("help those who are in dire need" and "do not promote products that are damaging to health"). And sometimes they are gesturally echoed in guidelines, such as when the American Institute of Graphic Designers states: "A professional designer shall take a responsible role in the visual portrayal of people, the consumption of natural resources, and the protection of animals and the environment."[1]

The focus on ethical principles to guide individual conduct obscures the fact that ethics (and the unethical) are pervasively and invisibly inscribed into the design and designed operation of our entire techno-material-symbolic cultures, thus it is not possible in most situations for individual designers to "protect animals and the environment." For example, almost everything we ingest or use on an everyday basis, we do so on the basis of an assumption, a rarely articulated trust, that we will not be harmed—a trust which is sometimes broken. Instruments have been developed—laws, product standards, safety procedures, health warnings, labeling, and the like—to minimize risk of harm.

The interwoven layers of responsibility for providing products, services, and infrastructures based on known parameters as well as minimal levels of safety and well-being, shift ethical behavior, and "duty of care" from individual behavior to the operation of systems, and thus become invisible; except when something fails: a bridge collapses, a plane crashes, people suddenly become ill after eating a food product. As discussed by Elaine Scarry, these failures and the legal actions surrounding them demonstrate the expectation that the world of artifice must take care of us. This can be connected to Heidegger's concept of care as existentially fundamental to human being, noting that care here is a fundamental condition not an emotional state, care as "being ahead of oneself," care as in every day actions to avoid harm. Our lives are so thoroughly lived within the milieu of *the designed* (environments, objects, technologies, and processes) that *the designed* has become a powerful designing agency of human behavior in its own right. Thereby, ethical questions, whether this is "designing for the good or for the bad," become hard to avoid. Yet the potential of a design ethics goes much further. Oftentimes, designed things take care of us, relieving us of the need to take care but also relieving us of the need to notice, to respond, to move our bodies, to think. The extent to which technologies of automaticity render irrelevant the taking of responsibility by human actors is an ethical issue.

Another definition of ethos is the essential nature or disposition of a group of people; in that sense ethics are inevitably *situated*. Therefore to pose the question of design ethics means gaining an understanding of the situated activity of designing—both the concrete situations and the more general context. The latter could be characterized as a global system of economic production and exchange that is clearly not ethically driven: a system geared toward creating and proliferating via innovation and incremental variation, those material and immaterial products and services that promise to deliver happiness in one form or another. Furthermore, this system in its ever expanding global reach to acquire resources and markets has wrought extensive damage on other systems of production and exchange, on nonhuman species, and on that upon which they and we depend, the very atmosphere itself and the climate conditions. The unethical has become a structural condition; thus "ethical design" is only able to skirt around the edges. Its familiar forms and slogans such as human-centered design, humanitarian design, and universal design seem weak and gestural; they are underpinned by an uncritical humanist ethics which fails to see the depth of anthropocentrism and ethnocentrism (this is further discussed in Part IV and Part VIII). A viable design ethics for now, a design ethics that "futures," cannot just be human-centered, it must not "sustain the unsustainable" (Fry), it must take account of nonhuman others as they exist in a web of interdependent relations of the sustainment of that which sustains.

If this is a bleak picture of the possibility of ethical design, we need to return to the point made before about the ways in which ethics as ethos are invisibly inscribed into the operation of systems and structures, and work on ways to significantly amplify this beyond base-level ethics, that is, minimal standards of safety and well-being. Given the extent to which modern life is inextricably bound up with the designed, of how "we can't live without it" in its provision of shelter, clothing, food, mobility, the more relevant question to pose is "how can ethics be inscribed into the designed?". There are everyday examples that can be built upon. Elaine Scarry explains how a chair, any ordinary chair, embodies and performs an ethos of care, as if it is saying "take the weight off your feet." Scarry and the other contributors to this section discuss many examples of ethical (or potentially ethical) designed things: door, bandage, boat, blanket, light bulb, coat, speed bump, dual flush toilet, pill bottle.

To what extent can a design ethics appeal to fundamental categories of philosophical ethics such as "the good," happiness, justice, or equality? The difficulty is not only to have the meanings of the words changed over time, but also the contexts of their application. So, when Aristotle claims that the ultimate aim of human life is happiness (*eudaimonia*), this does not refer to a mood, feeling, or psychological state (nor the commodified forms that allegedly deliver it) but to "living and acting" well; the concern of his *Nicomachean Ethics* is not to make us morally good people "but expert or successful human beings."[2] On the other hand, there are fundamental categories that get overlooked among the distractions and contradictions of contemporary life, such as the irreducibility of the I-Thou relation, the simple presence of another human being as a call, a command to take account—this is the basis of the ethical philosophy of Emmanuel Levinas. As with Heidegger's care and Aristotle's *eudemonia*, this is neither about emotions ("liking" or "pitying") nor morally correct behavior ("being polite"). Grasped or enacted, if it is felt at all, it is on an altogether different plane.

Notes

1. AIGA, Design Business and Ethics series "Client's Guide to Design" AIGA New York, 2009.

2. Aristotle, *The Nicomachean Ethics* (Ethics, Book 1) trans. J. A. K. Thomson, revised Hugh Tredennick, introduction by Jonathan Barnes, London: Penguin, 1976, pp. 27, 29, 34.

CHAPTER 12
ARTIFACTS: THE MAKING SENTIENT OF THE EXTERNAL WORLD
Elaine Scarry

Note from editor: Torture is a major subject of Scarry's acclaimed book, The Body in Pain: The Making and Unmaking of the World, *but her wider concern is the philosophy of justice. This is not approached as abstract principles; rather it is grounded in wide-ranging enquiry into the ways in which artifacts and works of the imagination (like poetry), as integral to human civilization, become actors in an ethical landscape. The author draws on many sources including philosophy, classical literature, legal history and the history of religion. The following extracts from chapter 5 'The Interior Structure of the Artifact' have been selected to emphasize Scarry's insightful explorations into the ethical dimensions of designed materiality.*

..... Artifacts are (in spite of their inertness) perhaps most accurately perceived as "a-making sentient of the external world." While there is no part of making that is empty of ethical content, this particular attribute carries within it a very special kind of moral pressure.

(.....)

The recognition that a made object is a projection of the human body has been formulated throughout these pages in three different ways. The first of the three makes the relation between sentience and its objectifications compellingly visible by describing the phenomenon of projection in terms of specifiable body parts. When, for example, the woven gauze of a bandage is placed over an open wound, it is immediately apparent that its delicate fibers mime and substitute for the missing skin, just as, in less drastic circumstances the same weave of threads (called now "clothing" rather than "bandage," though their kinship is verbally registered in the words "dress" and "dressing") will continue to duplicate and magnify the protective work of the skin, extending even its secondary and tertiary attributes.

(.....)

The second way of formulating the phenomenon of projection is to identify in the made object bodily capacities and needs rather than the concrete shape or mechanism of a specifiable body part. ... The printing press, the institutionalized convention of written history, photographs, libraries, films, tape recordings, and Xerox machines are all materializations of the elusive embodied capacity for memory, rather than materializations of, for example, one cubic inch of brain matter located above the left ear. They together make a relatively ahistorical creature into an historical one, one whose memory extends far back beyond the opening of its own individual lived experience, one who anticipates being itself remembered far beyond the close of its own individual lived experience, and one who accomplishes all this without each day devoting its awakened brain to rehearsals and recitations of all information it needs to keep available to itself. .... many inventions exist that have no specifiable precedent in the body: perhaps the wheel astonishes us in part because we do not "recognize" it—that is, because we intuitively sense that it has no prior existence within the boundaries of our own sentient matter (the ball and socket joint and the rotary mechanism of some insect wings notwithstanding). Although machine tools have been widely described as taking over the work of the muscles, any one-to-one equation is often impossible. The work of the steam engine in magnifying the bodily capacity for movement does not require a mechanistic equivalent in the body; it is perhaps enough simply to know that, for example, at the moment the steam engine first burst forth into John Fitch's imagination, he was, by his own account, limping.' Third and most important, even if every made object did have a bodily counterpart (an improbable proposition given the fragile dimensions of the human body and the robust dimensions of culture), it would even then be more accurate to formulate the projection in terms of "attributes" rather than "parts," since creating is undertaken to assist, amplify, or alter the felt-experience of sentience rather than merely to populate the external world with shapes and mechanisms already dwelling within us.

Even when a given artifact bears an obvious kinship to a bodily part, it will usually be more productive to articulate that kinship in terms of sentient attributes. So, for example, all of the artifacts invoked a moment ago as mimetic of "parts" can now be reinvoked as mimetic of "attributes."

(…..)

… it is part of the work of creating to deprive the external world of the privilege of being inanimate— of, in other words, its privilege of being irresponsible to its sentient inhabitants on the basis that it is itself nonsentient. To say that the "inanimateness" of the external world is diminished, is almost to say (but is not to say) that the external world is made animate. The rest of this section will try to define that "almost" with more precision. As one moves through the three ways of formulating the phenomenon of projection, the "body" becomes progressively more interior in its conceptualization. To conceive of the body as parts, shapes, and mechanisms is to conceive of it from the outside: though the body contains pump and lens, "plumpness" and "lensness" are not part of the felt-experience of being a sentient being. To instead conceive of the body in terms of capacities and needs (not now "lens" but "seeing," not now "pump" but "having a beating heart" or, more specifically, "desiring" or "fearing") is to move further in toward the interior of felt-experience. To, finally, conceive of the body as "aliveness" or "awareness of aliveness" is to reside at last within the felt-experience of sentience; and it is this most interior phenomenon that will now be considered. "Aliveness" or "awareness of aliveness," it will be argued, is in some very qualified sense projected out onto the object world.

When, as in old mythologies or religions, nonsentient objects such as rocks or rivers or statues or images of gods are themselves spoken about as though they were sentient (or alternatively, themselves endowed with the power of sentient speech) this is called "animism." Again, when poets or painters perform the same act of animation, it is called "pathetic fallacy." But as will very gradually become apparent here, to dismiss this phenomenon as mistake or fallacy is very possibly to miss the important revelation about creation exposed there. The habit of poets and ancient dreamers to project their own aliveness onto nonalive things itself suggests that it is the basic work of creation to bring about this very projection of aliveness; in other words, while the poet pretends or wishes that the inert external world had his or her own capacity for sentient awareness, civilization works to make this so. What in the poet is recognizable as a fiction is in civilization unrecognizable because it has come true.

(….)

… it is the benign, almost certainly heroic, and in any case absolute intention of all human making to distribute the facts of sentience outward onto the created realm of artifice, and it is only by doing so that men and women are themselves relieved of the privacy and problems of that sentience. This intention was surely present in the initial apprehension, invention, of "a God" capable of rescuing them from their own sentience (capable, that is, of existing as a metaphysical referent to which their individual sentient experiences could be referred and thus reread in terms of a collective or communally shared objectification), and then again present in the introduction of graven images which bring forth an intensification of that projected sentience in order to bring about in him a more compassionate accommodation of their own sentience.

The story that is told provides the language in which the story of the making of all the artifacts of civilization can be retold. A chair, as though it were itself put in pain, as though it knew from the inside the problem of body weight, will only then accommodate and eliminate the problem. A woven blanket or solid wall internalize within their design the recognition of the instability of body temperature and the precariousness of nakedness, and only by absorbing the knowledge of these conditions into themselves (by, as it were, being themselves subject to these forms of distress), absorb them out of the human body. A city, as though it incorporates into its unbroken surfaces of sand and stone a sentient uneasiness in the presence of organic growth and decay (the tyranny of green things that has more than once led people to the desert whose mineral expanse is now mimed in every modern urban oasis) will only then divest human beings of that uneasiness, divest them to such an extent that they may even come to celebrate and champion that green world, reintroducing it into their midst in the delicate spray of an asparagus fern or in a breathtaking framed photograph of the Andes. A clock or watch, as though it were itself sentient, as though it knew from the inside the tendency of individual sentient creatures to become engulfed in their own private bodily rhythms, and simultaneously knew of their acute and frustrated desire to be on a shared rhythm with other sentient creatures, will only then empower them to coordinate their activities, to meet for a meal, to meet to be schooled, to meet to be healed, after which the clock can be turned to the wall and the watch can be taken off, for these objects also incorporate into their (set-asidable) designs an awareness of sentient distress at having to live exclusively on shared time.

The naturally existing external world—whose staggering powers and beauty need not be rehearsed here—is wholly ignorant of the "hurtability" of human beings. Immune, inanimate, inhuman, it indifferently manifests itself in the thunderbolt and hailstorm, rabid bat, smallpox microbe, and ice crystal. The human imagination reconceives the external world, divesting it of its immunity and irresponsibility not by literally putting it in pain or making it animate but by, quite literally, "making it" as knowledgeable about human pain as if it were itself animate and in pain. When the roar of the flood waters comes, water and rocks and trees are mutely indifferent, but when the mythmaker recounts the story of the flood, the tree is invested with the capacity of compassionate speech: "I too feel the waters rising, and see that you will drown; take hold of this branch." His fiction of object-responsiveness anticipates the actuality of object-responsibility, for though the tree does not speak, when it is itself remade into raft or boat (as when the indifferent rocks are rearranged into a dam), the world outside the body is made as compassionately effective as if every line and nuance of its materialized design were speaking those words. We come to expect this of the world.

(…..)

A material or verbal artifact is not an alive, sentient, percipient creature, and thus can neither itself experience discomfort nor recognize discomfort in others. But though it cannot be sentiently aware of pain, it is in the essential fact of itself the objectification of that awareness; itself incapable of the act of perceiving, its design, its structure, is the structure of a perception. So, for example, the chair encountered so often in the previous chapter, can—if projection is being formulated in terms of body part—be recognized as mimetic of the spine; it can instead—if projection is being formulated in terms of physical attributes—be recognized as mimetic of body weight; it can finally and most accurately, however, be recognized as mimetic of sentient awareness, as will be elaborated below.

If one imagines one human being seeing another human being in pain, one human being perceiving in another discomfort and in the same moment wishing the other to be relieved of the discomfort, something in that fraction of a second is occurring inside the first person's brain involving the complex action of many neurons that is, importantly, not just a perception of an actuality (the second person's pain) but an alteration of that actuality (for embedded in the perception is the sorrow that it is so, the wish that it were otherwise). Though this interior event must be expressed as a conjunctive duality, "seeing the pain and wishing it gone," it is a single percipient event in which the reality of pain and the unreality of imagining are already conflated. Neither can occur without the other: if the person does not perceive the distress, neither will he wish it gone; conversely, if he does not wish it gone, he cannot have perceived the pain itself (he may at that moment be experiencing something else, such as his own physical advantage, or his own resistance to having to attend to another person, but he cannot be perceiving the pain, for pain is in its essential nature "aversiveness," and thus even within technical medical definitions is recognized as something which cannot be felt without being wished unfelt"). If this complex, mysterious, invisible percipient event, happening somewhere between the eyes and the brain and engaging the entire psyche, could be made visible, could be lifted out of the body and endowed with an external shape, that shape would be the shape of a chair (or, depending on the circumstance, a light bulb, a coat, an ingestible form of willow bark). The shape of the chair is not the shape of the skeleton, the shape of body weight, nor even the shape of pain-perceived, but the shape of perceived-pain-wished-gone.

The chair is therefore the materialized structure of a perception; it is sentient awareness materialized into a freestanding design. If one pictures the person in the action of making a chair—standing in one place, moving away, coming back, lifting then letting fall his arm, kneeling then standing; kneeling, half-kneeling, stooping, looking, extending his arm, pulling it back—and if one pictures all these actions as occurring without a tool or block of wood before him, that is, if one pictures only the man and his embodied actions, what one at that moment has before one is not the act of perception (his seeing of another's discomfort and wishing it gone) but the structure of the act of perception visibly enacted. What was originally an invisible aspect of consciousness (compassion) has now been translated into the realm of visible but disappearing action. The interior moment of perceiving has been translated into a willed series of successive actions, as if it were a dance, a dance entitled "body weight begone." Perhaps as he dances, his continual bodily readjustments relieve him of his awareness of his own weight; or perhaps as he dances before his pregnant wife, he (by his expression of concern) half relieves her own problem of body weight, assuring her that she is not alone, engulfed, in her adversity. In any event, the dance is not the original percipient event but that percipient event endowed with a communicable form.

If, now, the tool is placed back in his hand and the wood placed beneath that tool, a second translation occurs, for the action, direction, and pressure of his dance move down across the tool and are recorded in the surface of the wood. The two levels of projection are transformations: first from an invisible aspect of consciousness to a visible but disappearing action; second, from a disappearing action to an enduring material form. Thus in work, a perception is danced; in the chair, a danced-perception is sculpted.

Each stage of transformation sustains and amplifies the artifice that was present at the beginning. Even in the interior of consciousness, pain is "remade" by being wished away; in the external action, the private wish is made sharable; finally in the artifact, the shared wish comes true. With each successive recreation, compassion is itself recreated to be more powerful: in the end, it has made real what it at first only passively wanted to be so. For if the chair is a "successful" object, it will relieve her of the 'distress of her weight far better than did the dance (or alternatively, far better than a verbalized expression of sympathy). Even if, however, it relieves her distress only to the same degree as the expressive dance, it has two striking advantages over its antecedent action. First, the chair itself memorializes the dance, endures through time: to produce the same outcome, the dance would have to be repeated each day, thus requiring that the man enter and sustain the aversive intensity of labor (his sharing of the pain) without cessation, and thereby only redistributing, rather than diminishing, the pain itself. This does not mean that "active sentient compassion" (live human caring) and "compassion made effective" (the freestanding artifact) are at odds with one another, that we are in any sense asked to choose between friendly human presences or instead the companionship of objects. The existence of the second merely extends the range of subjects that can be entered into by the first: when both persons are free of the problem of her weight, they share endless other concerns, work to eliminate other pains, so that increasingly the pleasure of world-building rather than pain is the occasion of their union.

The second advantage of chair over sympathetic expression is that once it is in existence, the diminution of the woman's problem no longer depends on the goodwill of whatever other human being co-inhabits her world. She may have the good fortune to have a compassionate mate; she may instead have an indifferent one; it is also not impossible that she may have one who wishes her ill. The general distribution of material objects to a population means that a certain minimum level of objectified human compassion is built into the revised structure of the external world, and does not depend on the day-by-day generosity of other inhabitants which itself cannot be legislated. …. This is also why a woman imprisoned under a hostile regime in Chile once clung passionately to a' white linen handkerchief slipped to her from another country, for she recognized within the object the collective human salute that is implicit in the very manufacture of such objects;" just as this same salute has been recognized by many prisoners of torture who mention (often with an intensity of gratitude that may at first sound puzzling) the solitary blanket or freshly white-washed walls one day introduced into their midst by the quiet machinations of the International Red Cross." It is almost universally the case in everyday life that the most cherished object is one that has been hand-made by a friend: there is no mystery about this, for the object's material attributes themselves record and memorialize the intensely personal, extraordinary because exclusive, interior feelings of the maker for just this person—This is for you. But anonymous, mass-produced objects contain a collective and equally extraordinary message: Whoever you are, and whether or not I personally like or even know you, in at least this small way, be well. Thus, within the realm of objects, objects-made-for-anyone bear the same relation to objects-made-for-someone that, within the human realm, caritas bears to eros. Whether they reach someone in the extreme conditions of imprisonment or in the benign and ordinary conditions of everyday life, the handkerchief, blanket, and bucket of white paint contain within them the wish for well-being: "Don't cry; be warm; watch now, in a few minutes even these constricting walls will look more spacious."

(…..)

A light bulb transforms the human being from a creature who would spend approximately a third of each day groping in the dark, to one who sees simply by wanting to see: its impossibly fragile, milky-white globe curved protectively around an even more fragile, upright-then-folding filament of wire is the materialization of neither retina, nor pupil, nor day-seeing, nor night-seeing; it is the materialization of a counterfactual perception about the dependence of human sight on the rhythm of the earth's rotation; no wonder it is in its form so beautiful. There would be no need to introduce this example into the expansive company of all the preceding examples except that in this one instance we overtly reveal our recognition that the artifact is a materialization of perception by the 'widely shared convention of inserting it back inside a drawing of the human head where it stands for the moment when a problem is reconceived in terms of its solution. Itself a materialized projection of an instance of that form of perception, it is now, iconographically, pushed back into its original location, where it comes to stand for the generic event of problem-solving.

(…..)

This habit of *taking object-awareness as the norm and object-unawareness as an aberrant and unacceptable occurrence* (author's emphasis) reveals the depth of our expectations more eloquently than would any overt celebration. Though this expectation has many manifestations, it is nowhere so clear as in the law. The "statutes of homicide" in Plato's Laws begin by requiring that a person convicted of murder be put to death: his body will be taken outside the city and stoned, and then carried to the frontier (873). This same course of action is then extended to animals which, upon conviction of having killed a person, "shall be put to death and cast out beyond the frontier" (873e). The same action is then extended to inanimate objects:

If an inanimate thing cause the loss of a human life—an exception being made for lightning or other such visitation of God—any object which causes death by its falling upon a man or his falling against it shall be sat upon in judgment by the nearest neighbor, at the invitation of the next of kin, who shall hereby acquit himself and the whole family of their obligation—on conviction the guilty object to be cast beyond the frontier, as was directed in the case of a beast [as well as of a person]. (873e, 874a)

Two observations are immediately relevant to the present discussion. First, when Plato exempts certain objects from this statute ("an exception being made for lightning and other such visitation of God"), he might have said, "an exception being made for those aspects of the naturally given world that are beyond the reach of civilization." That is, "lightning and other such visitation of God" are privileged not because they are unpunishable (though they are, of course, un-punishable: the lightning cannot be carried beyond the edge of the city) but because of the prior fact that, unlike most aspects of the external world, they are unsusceptible to being reconceived and remade by the human imagination, and thus, unlike most aspects of the external world, cannot be held responsible for their ignorance about and thus harm done to human tissue: that they are unpunishable (i.e., unregenerate) is itself only one form of the larger fact of their being unreconstructable (i.e., unregenerate in the wider sense). Second, it may seem that the sequence in the statutes from persons, to beasts, to objects would permit one to dismiss the inclusion of objects by some version of the following argument: Plato's expectations about the responsibilities of living presences (human animals and other animals) at the last minute spill over into the realm of the nonliving. It is therefore worth noticing that Plato might have, with equal intelligence, presented the sequence in the reverse order. Thus the statutes might have read as follows:

> In civilization, the inanimate external world is reconceived and invested with the responsibility of existing as though it had sentient awareness. Any object, therefore, which exposes its absence of sentient awareness (announces its inanimate objecthood or its object stupidity) by lethally hurting a human being will not be permitted to continue dwelling within civilization and will be carried to the frontier. Further, should a sentient animal lapse into this same object stupidity and kill someone, it will, upon conviction, be deprived of the sentience it has already been guilty of lacking and will be removed from civilization. Finally, as unlikely as it is that any human being should ever lapse into this object stupidity, should this happen, the person will, upon conviction, be similarly deprived and removed.

It should be recalled here, as at a very early point in this book, that the word "stupidity" is not being used as a term of rhetorical contempt for those who willfully hurt others but as a descriptive term for the "nonsentience" or "the lack of sentient awareness," or most precisely, the "inability to sense the sentience of other persons" that is incontestably present in the act of hurting another person. Maximum expectations (e.g., aliveness) begin with persons and may be extended to objects, but minimum expectations begin with objects and may be extended to persons. The sequence of the statutes can be inverted because, in some very real way, the logic underlying civilization's prohibition of homicide proceeds from objects to persons: if this most minimal expectation (not to kill a person) can be required of even the only animate-like, inanimate world, how much more reasonable is it to require this minimal expectation of things that are actually animate (beasts) and finally of persons themselves. In other words, if civilization can ask an object not to act like an object, surely it can ask a person not to act like an object. ...

(.....)

Damage suits usually arise when someone has been killed, paralyzed, or caused prolonged pain, yet the revenge impulse is visible even when one has been only very modestly hurt and is more familiar to us in this form: it is present in the "hatred for anything giving us pain, which wreaks itself on the manifest cause, and which leads even civilized man to kick a door when it pinches his finger."[1] The problem with the revenge vocabulary is that it may mislead us into thinking that it is only at the instant of being hurt that the person projects sentient awareness onto the object, that the act of animism arises within, and is carried outward by, the retaliatory act of revenge: the man is pinched and in the next split-second he projects aliveness onto the door and assumes it will suffer as much by being kicked as he just suffered by being pinched. But it seems instead the case that the act of revenge is itself premised on the prior assumption of animism and must be seen within a much wider frame. Our behavior toward objects at the exceptional moment when they hurt us must be seen within the context of our normal relations with them. The ongoing, day-to-day norm is that an object is mimetic of sentient awareness: the chair routinely relieves the problem of weight. Should the object prove insufficiently mimetic of awareness, insufficiently capable of accommodating the problem of weight (i.e., if the chair is uncomfortable—an animistic phrase we use to mean if "the person is uncomfortable in the chair"), the object will be discarded or set aside. Only now do we reach the third and most atypical occurrence in which the object neither eliminates the problem of sentience, nor even simply passively fails to eliminate the problem of sentience, but instead actually amplifies the problem of sentience by inflicting hurt: the legs of the chair suddenly break beneath the weight of the person and he is hurt. The very reason the chair's object-stupidity strikes all who witness its collapse as a surprise, an outrage, is that it has normally been wholly innocent of such object-stupidity. In fact, it is crucial to notice that if the person now picks up a fragment of that object and hurls it against the wall (as though it could be made to feel the hurt it just inflicted), the person is actually continuing to act out of the context of the normal situation (in which the chair indeed has the mimetic attributes of sentient awareness) rather than out of the immediate moment (in which the chair has just exposed its object-obliviousness).

Thus the moment of revenge merely occasions the dramatization of the ongoing assumption of animism rather than occasioning the animism itself. The retaliatory drama that takes place between Holmes's man-pinching door and door-kicking man must be seen within the wider frame of the fact that nine times out of ten (or, if the man is skilled at opening doors, nine hundred and ninety-nine times out of a thousand), the door has acted as though it were percipiently aware, and has done so because its design is a material registration of the awareness that human beings both need the protection of solid walls and need to walk through solid walls at will. The door not only seems capable of transforming itself back and forth between the two states of wallness and nonwallness but, more remarkably, seems capable of understanding which of the two states the man wants it to be at any given moment—it recognizes what he wants not by requiring from him elaborate paragraphs of self-revelation but only a minimal signal, the turning of his wrist. If the door exists in a realm where people can be anticipated to be incapable of performing this signal (such as when they are carrying groceries), the door may be free of even this small form of communication: it may "sense" that the person wants it to disappear merely by "noticing" that the person is walking in its direction.

The fact that object-awareness is the acceptable, expectable, and uncelebrated condition of civilization, while object-unawareness is the unusual and unacceptable condition is stressed here because it is possible to forget that when one encounters an object in a legal proceeding, one will be encountering it only in its aberrant condition. The brass-knobbed door whose magically correct sense of timing seems "sensitive" to human sentience will never turn up in court; the door that merely fails to be fully sensitive to sentience (e.g. , blows open whenever it rains) will never turn up in court but will instead be endured, repaired, or replaced; it is only the door that by pinching produced blood-poisoning, or the door that let a three-year-old walk into a dangerous boiler room, that may end up there, and if it ends up there, the jury may decide that the door should have known better or, alternatively, that the manufacturer should have made the object to be an object that *knew better*.

(…..)

Everyday artifacts (which may never have been the subject of litigation nor even consumer pressure) are themselves usually characterized by forms of materialized awareness that go far beyond their most immediate use: the door to the boiler room that includes in its design a childproof latch is not only able to "understand" and accommodate the timing of the person's erratic wish that it be now-a-wall-now-not-a-wall, but is also able to "differentiate" small persons from persons in general, and "knows" that the former is a special subcategory of the latter whose wishes should not be accommodated. ….. . What is it that this aspirin bottle—with its long history in the bark of the willow tree and the bowl of the Indian peacepipe—"knows" about the human world? It knows about the chemical and neuronal structure of small aches and pains, and about the human desire to be free of those aches and pains. It knows the size of the hand that will reach out to relieve those aches and pains. It knows that it is itself dangerous to those human beings if taken in large doses. It knows that these human beings know how to read and communicates with them on the subject of amounts through language. It also knows that some human beings do not yet know how to read or read only a different language. It deals with this problem by further knowing how human beings intuitively and habitually take caps off bottles, and by being itself counterintuitive in its own cap. Thus only someone who knows how to read (or who knows someone else who knows how to read) can take off the cap and successfully reach the aspirin which, because the person not only knows how to read but has been made to stop and be reminded to read, will be taken in the right dosage. It contains within its design a test for helping to ensure responsible usage that has all the elegance of a simple three-step mathematical proof. Civilization restructures the naturally existing external environment to be laden with humane awareness, and when a given object is empty of such awareness, we routinely request that the garbage collector (himself a direct emissary of the platonic realm of ideal civilization) carry it away to the frontier, beyond the gates of the beloved city.

The aspirin bottle with its counterintuitive lid has been chosen as a final representative artifact in order to recall and underscore the fact that it is the work of the object realm to diminish the aversiveness of sentience, not to diminish sentience itself. The mental, verbal, and material objects of civilization collectively work to vastly extend the powers of sentience, not only by magnifying the range and acuity of the senses but by endowing consciousness with a complexity and large-mindedness that would be impossible if persons were forever engulfed in problematic contingencies of the body.

It is not objects but human beings who require champions, but the realm of objects has been briefly celebrated here because they are themselves, however modestly, the champions of human beings. The interior structure of the artifact is being attended to in this discussion for two reasons. First, human indifference to other persons is often explained and implicitly excused by pointing out that those who are indifferent are absorbed by their material wealth. But it is a deconstruction of the very nature of material wealth to permit, let alone excuse, this inattention. We sustain this deconstruction by simultaneously surrounding ourselves with material objects in everyday life while philosophically divesting ourselves of them, verbally dismissing and discrediting the importance of the material realm. This act of philosophic divestiture does not work to diminish or even regulate our own desire for objects but only works to permit us to be free of worrying about the objectlessness of other persons. If we cling to objects, we should trust our own clinging impulse; and once we trust that impulse we will acknowledge that such objects are precious; and once we confess that they are precious we will begin to articulate why they are precious; and once we articulate why they are precious, it will be self-evident why our desire for them must be regulated and why their benefits must be equitably distributed throughout the world. It is by crediting them that we will reach the insight that we only pretend to reach when we discredit them. .....

Source: Elaine Scarry *The Body in Pain: The Making and Unmaking of the World* Oxford University Press, 1985, pp. 281–306.

Note

1. Oliver Wendell Holmes, *The Common Law* ed. Mark de Wolfe Howe, Boston: Little, Brown, 1881, 1963, p. 13.

CHAPTER 13
ETHICS BY DESIGN OR THE ETHOS OF THINGS
Cameron Tonkinwise

Note from editor: It is argued here that we do not need to ask 'how can design become ethical?' because it is already ethical, in the way that designed things act in certain ways and incline their users to behave in certain ways. Via an exposition of Bruno Latour's theory of the delegated morality of artefacts as 'actants' and Elaine Scarry's uncovering of the ethos of care that underpins designed materiality, Tonkinwise considers the limits, possibilities and ethical dilemmas of designing to script sustainable behaviour.

"Now say 'thank you.'"

"Thaaank yooooou."

"No, come back here! Now say it like you mean it."

There is something painful about the experience of civilizing children into moral beings. This is not because, in the usual romantic sense, it imposes orthopaedic strictures on their 'natural free spirits.' It is rather that their having to be taught how to show the least respect to others, repeatedly and in the most mechanistic fashion, reveals the fragility and artificiality of what we take to be best about human beings. Listening to children poorly ape the mere signifiers of civility, you cannot not have a Nietzschean moment, seeing the extent to which morality is just a bad habit, a well-rehearsed melodramatic script replayed naturalistically night after night.

In many ways, this gap between act and actuality exposed by children whining 'thank you', that one hopes is merely a 'developmental' evil on the way to the good, is the space between morality and ethics.

The presence of moral conduct does not necessarily mean the presence of ethical being; the former might just be a set of imitated character traits. Ethicalness then must only be a way of being, not a knowledge about that way of being. This is the basis of Levinas' Hebraic ethics: do before you know; ethics comes with being always already hostage to the otherness of the other such that you are, before all else, for the other in all you do.[1] It might suffice to use the Greek version of these formulae: ethics only ever are as an ethos, an essentially lived culture. As 'lived' rather than professed, ethics only ever appear from the outside; they are what anthropologists (or originally, theorists)[2] call the mores or rituals particularly to the nature of a people. The people themselves do not notice their ethics but quite properly take them for granted. At most, a culture might notice lapses in their ethos, incidents that are improper or foreign to their way of life that must consequently be removed. But otherwise, they are moral without having a morality; which is to say, they interrelate in sustainable ways, in ways that sustain their sociality, rather than risk damaging it in irreparable ways.

If this is the nature of ethics, to be embedded in the very nature of interactions beyond knowing, then a culture that has the notion of ethics consciously at issue, a culture that is trying to know what its ethics is or at least codify what it is that would count as being ethical, is in trouble. If we need to explicate for our children the rules of moral behavior and then inculcate them into those artificial modes because they can no longer learn to be ethical merely by participating in a culture, if ethics are not learnable in an apprentice-like manner, osmotically through immersion in exemplary behavior, then we have a very unsustainable society. It is unsustainable not because it is destroying nature, but because it has no nature. Its unsustainability is its lack of an ethics, not because some within it behave unethically. And the absence of the 'naturalized artificial' that is ethics is unsustainable, as without it no authentic moral education can take place to repair such a lacuna.

Aristotle called this learning gap between morals and ethics *akrasia*: knowing the right thing to do and yet not doing it.[3] The icon of modern *akrasia* is perhaps what UNEP calls the 'Global Consumer', actively concerned about sustainability whilst shopping avidly.[4] Such a bipolar figure is not so much unethical as without ethos, without a way of learning to align their ethics with their life. He or she is small child forever espousing sustainability without the ability to transition to being sustainable. And to this extent, our cultures' explicit interest in sustainability is symptomatic of our unsustainability, of the fact that we are culture without the ability to acculturate, a non-culture with an irreparable lack of ethos.

The ethics of things

Ethics has always been associated with human-to-human relations. Products, artefacts, built environments, communications, have only entered the ethical domain as tangential, and therefore neutral means, used by humans in their relations to other humans. To date, things, designed things, have not assumed a central or at least symmetrical, role with humans when it comes to ethics.

The debates of anthropological discourse have drawn attention to the extent to which cultures comprises not only social relations, but also material relations, shared products and environments that are not only the instruments of social relations or the bearers of symbolic meanings, but also essential aspects of that culture in their own right. A viable ethos is not only sustained by a material culture, but exists in that materiality; an immaterial culture is an impossibility.

In this case, it is crucial to understand the role of the design of things in ethics. Beyond the ethicality of the designer and his or her clients, users and stakeholders, is the ethicality, that is, the materialised ethics, of designed products, environments, and communications themselves. Without taking account of the ethics perpetrated by things, one risks being left, suspecting that we live in an 'asociety'. While ethics is now a discursive issue for us, and therefore evidently lacking as integral to our human-to-human relations, that we do nonetheless live in some sort of society, with a continued optimism about change by social learning, must mean that there is an ethos somewhere in how we live, a non-discursive sociality that is preserving the possibility of discourse and thereby the transformative regeneration of an ethics.

I am here paraphrasing what Bruno Latour has cleverly called 'the missing masses'.[5] Theoretical physicists find that the universe is imbalanced when one only takes stock of all the material things in it. They have therefore been forced to theorise that there is a hidden mass somewhere other than in what we currently call matter that holds the universe together. For Latour the converse is true in relation to modern societies. If we only take stock of what we currently understand by 'sociality', it does not add up; our societies should have long since collapsed into irretrievable immorality. There must therefore be an ethical force hidden beyond what we now call 'the social', in other words, in things. Things must be acculturating or ethos-generating. What things design, that is to say, the intentions, actions, understandings and relations that things are designed to design, that they design beyond what their designers intended, and that they are redesigned to design by those who use them, must be a vital part of any ethos with a future.

With this in mind, the question is not, 'what can material design learn from the philosophy of ethics?', but, 'what must the philosophy of ethics learn about design and the axial role of designed things in conserving, promoting and altering what is ethical?' Not, 'how can design become ethical?', but, 'how can design be understood as already ethical, as making things ethical?'

Rude things

To access the ethics of or in design, Latour works backwards, starting from things that are unethical, or at least impolite.[6] He finds an example of a door that rudely will not shut itself after we have moved through, inconveniently remaining an opening when, having served that function, we now have need of a wall once again (for example, to keep the warmth in, a gesture that honours us in the room and dishonours all those outside whose resources we are destroying to keep warm). At a hotel, that bastion of imperial civility, etiquette dictates that there be a doorman, showing respect to those who pass in or out by shutting the door behind them. As Latour points out, this is a clearly moral solution, that is, a particular historico-cultural evaluation of the relevant stakeholders: the value of a door returning to its shut position plus the value of the time and effort of the person passing through the door exceeds the value of the doormen. Such an econo-moral solution is in no way ethical, at least with respect to the doorman's workplace satisfaction, and, in typical fashion, Latour remarks that the original problem returns when the unionised doorman decides to strike for a more rewarding job. It is at this point that the designer is called in. The brief – to devise a mechanism that shuts the door automatically after it is opened – appears neutral enough, though in the context of Latour's tale, the ethico-politico truth is clear — break the strike, render someone unemployed.

The ethicality of the resulting design does not only lie at its origin, withdrawing after the design's implementation, but continues into its use life as becomes clear when we assess the politeness of the resulting design – let's say a spring, that clever way of capturing the energy of those who open the door so that it can be used to shut the door. For most people, the spring shuts the door politely, efficiently, and reliably. But, depending on the specification of the spring, for some people, the door shuts too quickly (e.g., for those carrying bulky items), for others too slowly (e.g., for those trying to keep a wet wind out), and for others still the door refuses to open, so much effort is required to compress the spring (e.g., for the elderly).

By convention, we judge a design by its functionality, and in these cases would find the spring to be under-optimised. This judgment however is not a particularly strong motivation for undertaking the task of redesigning the spring: maybe someday someone will be interested in the intellectual challenge of enhancing the performance of the spring. What would prompt a quicker redesign is judging the performance of the spring in terms of its human equivalent, the person it made redundant: in other words, if this spring were a doorman, it would be a very rude one, selecting who gets to proceed through and at what rate, and outrightly discriminating against many types of people — children, pregnant women, the infirm, etc. Exposing the immoral nature of the spring in this way would motivate the immediate recall of the designer, that expert in making things 'right', that is, morally better.

So we begin to glimpse the ethics in things, the ethos that things enact.

What things know and feel

A more poetic and less cynical account of the ethics in the design of things is provided by Elaine Scarry's stunning *The Body in Pain: The Making and Unmaking of the World*.[7] .... Intriguingly, it is Scarry's interrogations of torture techniques, as exemplars of utterly unethical 'unmaking,' that allow her to understand the making of ethics. Scarry demonstrates, in many ways, that making can only be understood as ethical through and through. What initiates making, and sees making through to the made, and what the actual process of making involves, is ethics.

Her massive argument, violently schematised here, is something like: humans are fundamentally empathetic, so that to acknowledge pain in another is to wish it gone — hence the torturer is fundamentally inhuman; to wish strongly pain were gone for another in a permanent way, covering whenever you cannot be there in person for the one in pain, is to dream of a world that would care for the one in pain itself; focusing this dream leads to a projection of some particular thing that could be made that would take that particular pain away. Making is therefore inspired by the ethical desire to enduringly relieve another's pain …

Things as moral educators

… In a most beautiful way that I cannot go into here, Scarry also demonstrates how the act of making itself can be understood as essentially the act of being ethical materialised

Scarry follows this argument through in numerous ways, but of particular pertinence here is her ability to capture phenomenologically how in everyday life, even non-designers experience and expect things to be moral. When we move through nature and are hurt, tripping on a rock, we are struck by how inert the material world is, how insensitive things are to our fragility, our susceptibility to being hurt … In reaction, the project of making, of remaking the natural world, replacing it with built environments, is an attempt to make the world more respectful of our human condition. Design is the process of trying to make the world friendlier to us clumsy humans; it is the effort to make the world more caring toward us, more accepting of us and so more morally acceptable to us. Just as Latour sees design as the means for making things less rude, Scarry reveals creation to be the process of investing the world with an emotional intelligence, a knowledge of our feelings. To the non-designer, the surprising pleasure that comes from something well-designed lies with the fact that such an artefact seems to know exactly what it is that we feel; it even seems to know our feelings better than we have ever been able to articulate. At these moments, we are judging the outcomes of human making by how sensitive they are to our needs, how attentive they are to what is particular to us.[89] What we are judging is the extent to which that designed thing has realised this ethicality in how it is, as opposed to its merely appearing to; we are assessing whether it has that empathic quality in its ethos, or whether it is merely reiterating what makes it look like it might be moral.

Scarry's evidence for this materialised ethics by design is the scorn with which we punish designed things when they lapse from this ethos. When a product inadvertently hurts us, our naturalised reaction is to hurt it back. For Scarry, this response is not childish, but evidence of the extent to which we take for granted the ethicality that design puts into the world. We hit the door that pinches our fingers in an attempt to re-sensitise what has suddenly emerged as being inertly insensitive or dumb. A more sophisticated version of this animism is the product liability court case, which attempts to establish how perceptive a product needs to be about the range of uses to which it might be subject: the product that does not manifest as warnings or safety features the awareness of certain scenarios that we believe that 'the average person in the street' would foresee, is expelled from our society (i.e., recalled by the manufacture for disposal), just as any person unfamiliar with our manners is.

….. If in the process of taking care of us, a product risks harming us in other ways, then, for it to be ethical, for it to be 'forethoughtful', the product must limit our ability to so harm ourselves. In this case, it is not only passively ethical, receiving and thereby taking our pain away, but actively ethical, orienting us away from harm's way. In fact, invariably for a product to do what it is designed to do it must direct us to use it in the particular ways that allow it to do what it is supposed to. It is animate not only in being ethically sensitive to human fragility, but also in interacting with humans, influencing them into the relationship needed for it to be ethically sensitive. Latour refers to these interactions between things and people as hybrids.

For rhetorical reasons, Latour focuses on these more active examples, where things are not merely ethical, but moralising. Since he is arguing that ethics is not merely a matter of and for humans, but a matter that involves a wide continuum of actors from the human to the non-human, he foregrounds cases where non-human things are strong ethical actors. In these situations, humans, rather than convincing each other in human-to-human ways (e.g., an education campaign about the evil consequences of speeding), delegate agency to things through designs that either make easier what should done and more difficult what should not (e.g., speed humps), or do not allow what should not be done and force what should (e.g., an acceleration pedal that disconnects from the engine when one is exceeding the speed limit). Designing then not only inscribes into things a description of human being, but also an ability for things to prescribe to humans how to be. It precisely because the things we vivify by design have this ongoing force that we from time to time get concerned about the controlling of technology. Having animated such things to make us ethical, we often find it difficult to halt these golems.

An intriguing extrapolation of Latour's argument about ethical delegation to designed things has recently been developed in the context of sustainability by Jaap Jelsma.[10] Jelsma begins with the recognition that at least a decade of information and education by governments and non-government organisations about more sustainable behaviour, no matter how well researched in terms of behaviour change models, has on the whole failed to lead to significant improvements of the sustainability of developed nations. He notes that the return to the focus of policy initiatives of merely technological solutions — i.e., research into breakthrough technical efficiency gains — is evidence of governments, or at least the EU, giving up on moral education in the face of widespread *akrasia*. However, rebound effects such as increased volumes and use of more efficient devices to the point of outstripping the initial per unit efficiency gains, already represent the return of the repressed issue of 'ethos'.

In response, Jelsma takes Latour's descriptions of moral things as a prescriptive design brief. It is not a matter of either behaviour change or built environment/technology change, but behaviour change through built environment/technology change. If the latter can be designed to be ethical in terms of accessibility or safety by dictating appropriate use, why can the latter not also be designed to be a source of ethicality in terms of sustainability? To this end, Jelsma presents a series of examples of devices that 'script' certain types of sustainable behaviour, in this case, water conservation with toilets. The first way of establishing the ethos of ethical water use is by prompting toilet users consciously via a semiotic design strategy — e.g., the dual flush toilet with the two buttons signed in some way. The second influences toilet users in pre-conscious ways via affordances for usability — e.g., the dual flush toilet that assigns the conventional 'press' to the half-flush, requiring you to counter-intuitively 'lift' the button for a full flush, or 'continue to hold down' the button if out of habit you mistakenly press when one in fact you need a full flush.[11] The third influences the toilet users in unconscious ways via system design — e.g., grey and black water recycling systems.

Jelsma recognises that the way these designs design behaviours, moulding users into moral actions, is not deterministic. It is less behaviourism, than ecologism in Bateson's sense. It is less a type of planning, than a situated enabling.[12] The scripts are more or less 'open,' only ever making an ethical outcome easier or harder; they are always able to be tactically subverted by the user. In fact, Jelsma recognises that the less open the script, the more likely it is to provoke counter-moral 'work arounds' in reaction to its impolite impositions. Nevertheless, the point is that by embodying certain ethical positions, these sorts of designs educe ethical ways of living — which, as sustained new ways of living, have greater consequence than mere eco-impact reduction of the production of the product — without the futile didacticism of moralising about sustainability. The ethics in designed things manage to form ethical beings more effectively than any information. By corollary, every designed outcome can be assessed in terms of how ethical it is, that is to say, how effective it is in facilitating and promoting more ethical, or in this case, more water-respecting, ways of being.

Importantly — and in ways that surpass Latour's analysis — Jelsma's shift into the realm of more designerly applications shows that increased levels of moral devolvement to designed things is not merely a matter of efficiency or expediency. It is not that ethics by design/in designs is just better at educating people to be more ethical than education alone. What is significant is that ethics by design/in designs is more of an ethos. It is not a short-cut but an identity, creating ethical ways of living through the inseparability of material things and the things that are done with them.[13] By being embedded in material culture, in the only ever semi-conscious everyday rituals of making use of designed products, environments and communications, ethics by/in design is the only sustainable form of ethics, the only form of ethics that can sustain itself. If we are dependent upon what we design to live, and what we have designed is ethical, that is, designs ethical ways of being, then we are consequently ethical in how we live, irrespective of whatever platitudes we are trained to mouth.

Ethical difficulties

There are clearly dangers in what Jelsma outlines. To an extent he is embracing the way user-centred design only manages to service the user by unethically caricaturing the user.[14] There are limits to the anthropomorphising of things — they have limited capacity for understanding us, particularly in relation to our habit of changing — and this bites back as reductive projections onto us of who and how we are. Whilst aiming at a dispositional ethics, open yet embedded, a certain instrumentalism risks returning the result to moral conventionalism. Nevertheless, his proactive adoption of Latour's idea of delegated morality, further substantiates Scarry's reading of the designed world as a sustaining source of ethics.

The danger within what Jelsma advocates is in fact a wider danger with the way I have presented ethics as ethos. Ethics becomes a hypocritical or *'akrasiatic'* morality, that is to say, it becomes mere displays of the appearance of ethicality rather than being ethical, when it becomes automatic. The child whining 'thank you' has effectively become a machine, a product following the design of a program. In these cases, ethics is being pursued as an explicit intention, a goal in itself, rather than for the other, out of respect for the otherness of the other. For this reason we should be hoping for a more ingrained ethics. However, such an organic ethics itself risks the same automaticity. And when ethics becomes a naturalised artificial, its habitual accomplishment risks being unethical should things change. It does not matter that the ethical is done intuitively, 'without thinking,' so long as it is done; but when situations change, such an unthinking ethics becomes immoral.

The traditional way to avoid this danger is to focus entirely on ethics as thoroughly conscious deliberation. I have not dealt with this aspect of ethics at all because, in the context of this paper and its desire to foreground the materialised aspects of design ethics, it is too anthropocentric. What is needed next is an account of such deliberations that involve non-human actors, where the prescriptions that things make are given voice as constraints and variables in those ethical conversations.[15]

By way of conclusion though, I would like to indicate a different yet related critique, culminating in Jelsma's 'moralising machines'. For Albert Borgmann, the ethics of designed things lies in the extent to which they foster the best in us.[16] Borgmann calls things that enable and promote activities that require our sustained yet bodily active attention to diversely creative outcomes 'engaging.'[17] He contrasts these with 'disburdening' things, things designed to relieve us of the need for activity or attention by delivering predetermined outcomes. In Borgmann's philosophy of technology, the latter risks reducing us to receptive machines, no longer challenged into being more adept humans. Importantly, this unethical outcome is the result of a zealous designing in Latour's and Scarry's sense. Designers, ethically motivated to take others' pain away, invest things with the sensitivity to intelligently direct humans into use patterns that maximise disburdenment. For Borgmann, the most ethical designer, best attuned to the needs of others, will generate the least ethical outcome, the one that most fully services others needs, thereby disabling them. The more ethical outcome is the thing that is perhaps not the most transparently usable: it is the thing that still involves some pain to use, some work. By being less than completely polite, somewhat drawing attention to itself, its materiality and its design, such a thing would enable ethical ways of being, that is to say, ways of being that remain available for case-by-case deliberation by not withdrawing beneath immediate satisfaction.

Borgmann's perspective prevents the sort of materialised ethics explicated by Latour, Scarry and Jelsma from sliding into an unethical total moral design. But it does so by reasserting the materiality of that ethics, the material resistance such an embodied ethics can have, which therefore preserves our human need to continue to work at being ethical, a labour that no technology can replace.

Source: *Design Philosophy Papers Collection Two,* ed. A.M. Willis, 2005, pp. 49–58.

Notes

1. One of the clearest accounts of this is by Jean-Francois Lyotard: 'Levinas' Logic' in A. Benjamin (ed) *Lyotard Reader* Oxford: Blackwell, 1989. Levinas' most accessible self-summaries are in his interviews, see for example, *Ethics and Infinity* Pittsburgh: Duquesne University Press, 1985.

2. *Theoria* referred originally to the activity of Solonists who would travel to other lands to witness significant rites and report back on what they had seen, attesting to their having taken place. See Wlad Godzich by Gregory Ulmer *Heuretics: The Logic of Invention* Baltimore: Johns Hopkins University Press, 1994, 120–1.

3. Aristotle's discussion of akrasia, traditionally translated as 'incontinence', occurs in Book VII of the Nicomachean Ethics 1145a 15-1154b 33: *The Complete Works of Aristotle* Princeton: Princeton University Press, 1984, Vol 2.

4. McCann-Erikson conducted some market research for UNEP's sustainable advertising project that was summarised in the 2002 publication, Can Sustainability Sell?, available at: http://www.uneptie.org/pc/sustain/advertising/publications.htm (last accessed 1 July 2004): "It is clear that young people today have strong concerns about the principles that sustainability highlights. These fall into three key areas: the protection of the environment, animal testing and human exploitation in developing countries. With such strong and consistent views from across the globe, why aren't today's youth doing more? One of the main reasons for inactivity is the contradiction in the minds of these consumers. They are both hedonists and idealists. They want to 'Have it All': a sustainable planet and their favourite brands. This is the 'use and throw' generation, but at the same time, they have dreams of a private and wonderful world. Most importantly they are not aware of the consequences of their own shopping behaviour. There is a feeling that they are 'unable to change the world'. Yet they want the world to change." (10)

5. Where are the Missing Masses?: The Sociology of a Few Mundane Artifacts' in W. Bijker and J.Law (eds) *Shaping Technology /Building Society* Cambridge: MIT Press, 1992; also at http://www.ensmp.fr/~latour/articles/1992.html (last accessed 30 November 2005).

6. I am here paraphrasing the first half of 'Where are the Missing Masses?'

7. Oxford: Oxford University Press, 1985. In what follows, I am closely paraphrasing much of the last chapter, 'The Interior Structure of the Artifact'. (The text by Scarry under discussion is published in this volume – ed.)

8. Harold Nelson and Eric Stolterman usefully characterise this as 'the expected unexpected' or the 'the surprise of self-recognition' in relation to designed outcomes in *The Design Way: intentional change in an unpredictable world* Englewood Cliffs, NJ: Educational Technology Publications, 2003.

9. Scarry's strong humanism at times risks essentialising individualism. Whilst on the one hand what is intriguing about designed products are the way they do manage to be perceived by people as 'custom-made' even though 'mass produced', it is important to acknowledge that it is precisely people's inabilities to balance their own individual perceived needs with the wider needs of others, including non-humans, that leads to unsustainability: a device that services my needs perfectly is inevitably going to be unethically unsustainable in the resources it consumes to do so.

10. See 'Innovating for Sustainability: Involving Users, Politics and Technology' in *Innovation* vol.16 no.2, 2003. Other versions are available online: 'Design of Behaviour Steering Technology', www.ifz.tu-graz.ac.at/sumacad/sa00_jelsma.pdf (last accessed 1 July 2004); and 'Philosophy Meets Design, or How the Masses are Missed (and Revealed

Again) in Environmental Policy and Ecodesign', http://www.comp.lancs.ac.uk/sociology/esf/philosophy.htm (last accessed 1 July 2004).

11. Jelsma uses Latourian terminology and so remains at the level of 'product semantics.' I am supplementing this with Donald Norman's work on 'afforded usability': see *The Design of Everyday Things* New York: Basic Books, 2002. This second example is also not directly discussed by Jelsma.

12. On this distinction see Lucy Suchman's *Plans and Situated Actions* Cambridge: Cambridge University Press, 1987.

13. Following Francois Jullien way of translating Confucian and Daoist notion of shi, a designed ethos is best termed *The Propensity of Things* [the title of his book: New York, Zone, 1995].

14. Jelsma cites favourably Steven Woolgar's famous critique of the way usability testing is not only about modifying the product, but also about 'enrolling' users: 'Configuring the User: The Case of Usability Trials' in John Law (ed) *A Sociology of Monsters* London: Routledge, 1991.

15. This is in fact one of Latour's projects. Though see Tony Fry's review of his latest book in *Design Philosophy Papers* no 1, 2004.

16. I am here paraphrasing Borgmann's 'The Depth of Design' in R. Buchanan and V.Margolin (eds) *Discovering Design*, though the argument is made more fully in *Technology and the Character of Contemporary Life* Chicago: University of Chicago Press, 1984.

17. Mihalyi Czikzentmihalyi calls this zone of challenging creative action, 'flow'. See *Flow: The Psychology of Happiness* London: Rider, 1992.

CHAPTER 14
PRECARIOUSNESS AND GRIEVABILITY
Judith Butler

Note from editor: Here is an argument for the inherent fragility of life as the basis of an ethic. Butler's exploration in this extract and the book from which it is drawn, exposes precariousness and grievability as underpinning the social and material supports necessary for life to flourish. Grief is for the dead, grievability is for the living, and thus it initiates an ethic.

We read about lives lost and are often given the numbers, but these stories are repeated every day, and the repetition appears endless, irremediable. And so, we have to ask, what would it take not only to apprehend the precarious character of lives lost in war, but to have that apprehension coincide with an ethical and political opposition to the losses war entails? Among the questions that follow from this situation are: How is affect produced by this structure of the frame? And what is the relation of affect to ethical and political judgment and practice?

To say that a life is precarious requires not only that a life be apprehended as a life, but also that precariousness be an aspect of what is apprehended in what is living. Normatively construed, I am arguing that there ought to be a more inclusive and egalitarian way of recognizing precariousness, and that this should take form as concrete social policy regarding such issues as shelter, work, food, medical care, and legal status. And yet, I am also insisting, in a way that might seem initially paradoxical, that precariousness itself cannot be properly *recognized*. It can be apprehended, taken in, encountered, and it can be presupposed by certain norms of recognition just as it can be refused by such norms. Indeed, there ought to be recognition of precariousness as a shared condition of human life (indeed, as a condition that links human and non-human animals), but we ought not to think that the recognition of precariousness masters or captures or even fully cognizes what it recognizes. So although I would (and will) argue that norms of recognition ought to be based on an apprehension of precariousness, I do not think that precariousness is a function or effect of recognition, nor that recognition is the only or the best way to register precariousness.

To say that a life is injurable, for instance, or that it can be lost, destroyed, or systematically neglected to the point of death, is to underscore not only the finitude of a life (that death is certain) but also its precariousness (that life requires various social and economic conditions to be met in order to be sustained as a life). Precariousness implies living socially, that is, the fact that one's life is always in some sense in the hands of the other. It implies exposure both to those we know and to those we do not know; a dependency on people we know, or barely know, or know not at all. Reciprocally, it implies being impinged upon by the exposure and dependency of others, most of whom remain anonymous. These are not necessarily relations of love or even of care, but constitute obligations toward others, most of whom we cannot name and do not know, and who may or may not bear traits of familiarity to an established sense of who "we" are. In the interest of speaking in common parlance, we could say that "we" have such obligations to "others" and presume that we know who "we" are in such an instance. The social implication of this view, however, is precisely that the "we" does not, and cannot, recognize itself, that it is riven from the start, interrupted by alterity, as Levinas has said, and the obligations "we" have are precisely those that disrupt any established notion of the "we."

Over and against an existential concept of finitude that singularizes our relation to death and to life, precariousness underscores our radical substitutability and anonymity in relation both to certain socially facilitated modes of dying and death and to other socially conditioned modes of persisting and flourishing. It is not that we are born and then later become precarious, but rather that precariousness is coextensive with birth itself (birth is, by definition, precarious), which means that it matters whether or not this infant being survives, and that its survival is dependent on what we might call a social network of hands. Precisely because a living being may die, it is necessary to care for that being so that it may live. Only under conditions in which the loss would matter does the value of the life appear. Thus, grievability is a presupposition for the life that matters. For the most part, we imagine that an infant comes into the world, is sustained in and by that world through to adulthood and old age, and finally dies. We imagine that when the child is wanted, there is celebration at the beginning of life. But there can be no celebration without an implicit understanding that the life is grievable, that it would be grieved if it were lost, and that this future anterior is installed as the condition of its life. In ordinary language, grief attends the life that has already been lived, and presupposes that life as having ended. But, according to the future anterior (which is also part of ordinary language), grievability is a condition of a life's emergence and sustenance.[1] The future anterior, "a life has been lived," is presupposed at the beginning of a life that has only begun to be lived. In other words, "this will be a life that will have been lived" is the presupposition of a grievable life, which means that this will be a life that can be regarded as a life, and be sustained by that regard. Without grievability, there is no life, or, rather, there is something living that is other than life. Instead, "there is a life that will never have been lived," sustained by no regard, no testimony, and ungrieved when lost. The apprehension of grievability precedes and makes possible the apprehension of precarious life. Grievability precedes and makes possible the apprehension of the living being as living, exposed to non-life from the start.

Source: Judith Butler, *Frames of War: When is Life Grievable?* London: Verso, 2009, pp 13–15.

Note

1. See Roland Barthes *Camera Lucida: Reflections on Photography* trans. Richard Howard, New York: Hill and Wang, 1982; and Jacques Derrida *The Work of Mourning* Pascale-Anne Brault and Michael Naas, eds., Chicago: University of Chicago Press, 2001.

CHAPTER 15
THE ONE FOR THE OTHER
Adriaan Peperzak

Note from editor: The author explains, with admirable clarity that does not oversimplify, the ethics of Emmanuel Levinas which is based on the I-thou relation, not as a code of behavior or set of moralistic norms, but on the 'I' that every person is as it confronts the sheer fact of the existence of the (human) Other as 'that which is not I' yet is not reducible to a phenomenal thing outside myself that I grasp for my own purposes; for the Other has a face, as s/he faces me.

….. Against the thesis that all truths and values can ultimately be reduced to the transcendental activity of an autonomous subject, Levinas insists forcefully on the irreducible moments of heteronomy. Instead of seeing all realities as unfolding or surrounding elements of one basic and central instance called "the Same," which realizes itself by appropriating them, the irreducibility of all Otherness must be recognized. This recognition supplants the overt or hidden monism of ontology by a pluralism whose basic ground model is the relation of the Same *(le Même)* and the Other *(l'Autre)*.

The otherness of the Other is concretized in the face of another human. The proof for Levinas's basic "principle" lies in the most ordinary, simple, and everyday fact of another facing me. I can see another as someone I need in order to realize certain wants of mine. She or he is then a useful or enjoyable part of my world, with a specific role and function. We all belong to different communities, in which we function more or less well on the basis of reciprocal needs. I *can* also observe another from an aesthetic perspective, for example, by looking at the color of her eyes, the proportions of his face, and so on. But none of these ways of perception allows the otherness of the other to reveal itself. All aspects manifested by a phenomenological description that starts from these perspectives are immediately integrated by my self-centered, interested, and dominating consciousness. These ways of looking at them transform the phenomena into moments of my material or spiritual property. The sort of phenomenology based on these and similar observations is a form of *egology*.

Another comes to the fore *as other* if and only if his or her "appearance" breaks, pierces, destroys the horizon of my egocentric monism, that is, when the other's invasion of my world destroys the empire in which all phenomena are, from the outset, a priori, condemned to function as moments of my universe. The other's face (i.e., any other's facing me) or the other's speech (i.e., any other's speaking to me) interrupts and disturbs the order of my, ego's, world; it makes a hole in it by disarraying my arrangements without ever permitting me to restore the previous order. For even if I kill the other or chase the other away in order to be safe from the intrusion, nothing will ever be the same as before.

When Levinas meditates on the significance of the face, he does not describe the complex figure that could be portrayed by a picture or painting; rather, he tries to make us "experience" or "realize" what we see, feel, "know" when another, by looking at me, "touches" me: *antrui me vise*; the other's visage looks at me, "regards" me. Similarly, the word "language" often used in this context, evokes the speech addressed to me by some living man or woman and not the linguistic structures or anonymous meanings that can be studied objectively or practiced by a style-conscious author. *Autrui me parle*: primordially, it is not important *what* is said; even if the words are nonsensical, there is still their being addressed. Neither is it relevant *who* speaks to me; any other is the revelation of *the* Other, and peculiar features deserving special attention would only lead me away from the "absolute otherness" that is at stake. In order to concentrate on the other's otherness, Levinas often stresses the *nakedness* of the other's face: if I am touched, if I am conscious of being concerned, it is not because of the other's beauty, talents, performances, roles, or functions but only by the other's (human) otherness.

As disrupting the horizon of my egological—and thus ontological—ways of handling and seeing the world, the others resist a description that would present them as a particular sort of phenomenon among other phenomena within a universal order of beings. Since they "show" and "present" precisely those realities that do not fit into the universal openness of consciousness, they cannot be seized by the usual categories and models of phenomenology. The other transcends the limits of (self-) consciousness and its horizon; the look and the voice that surprise me are "too much" for my capacity of assimilation. In this sense, the other comes toward me as a total stranger and from a dimension that surpasses me. The otherness of the other reveals a dimension of "height" *(hauteur):* he/she comes from on high."

Husserl's theory of intentionality, based on an adequate and symmetric correlation between noesis and noema, no longer fits. A forgotten element of Descartes's analysis of consciousness, however, offers a formal structure much closer to the relation meant by Levinas. According to Descartes's third *Metaphysical Meditation,* all human consciousness contains not only and not primarily the idea of itself but also and precedingly the irreducible "idea of the infinite," that is, an immediate and a priori given relation of the conscious subject to a reality that can neither be constituted nor embraced by this subject. This means that the cogito from the outset is structured by a bipolarity other than the bipolarity of the noetico-noematic relation of phenomenology, in which an idea and its *ideatum* fit one another adequately. Descartes still knew (as all great metaphysicians before him) that consciousness "thinks more than [or beyond] that which it can think." The infinite is different from any noema or *cogitatum,* for it essentially surpasses our capacity for conception and embracing. Although Descartes identifies the infinite" with "God" (i.e., the God of the traditional, late scholastic philosophy), we can consider the formal structure he discovers to be the structure of my relation to the other in the form of another human being. When I am confronted with another, I experience myself as an instance that tries to appropriate the world by labor, language, and experience, whereas this other instance does not permit me to monopolize the world because the Other's greatness does not fit into any enclosure— not even that of theoretical comprehension. This resistance to all integration is not founded on the other's *will; before* any possibility of choice and *before* all psychological considerations, the mere fact of another's *existence* is a "surplus" that cannot be reduced to becoming a part or moment of the Same. The Other cannot be captured or grasped and is therefore, in the strictest sense of the word, incomprehensible.

In all his works, Levinas has endeavored to show that the (human) other radically differs from all other beings in the world. The other's coming to the fore cannot be seen as a variation of the general way of appearance by which all other beings are phenomenal. This is the reason why Levinas reserves the word "phenomenon" for realities that fit into the totality of beings ruled by egological understanding. Since the other cannot become a moment of such a totality, it is not a phenomenon but rather an *"enigma"* not to be defined in phenomenological terms. If visibility, in a broad and metaphorical sense, is a feature of every being that can become a phenomenon, Levinas may even call the other "invisible!'"

The way the other imposes its enigmatic irreducibility and nonrelativity or absoluteness is by means of a command and a prohibition: You are not allowed to kill me; you must accord me a place under the sun and everything that is necessary to live a truly human life. This demands not only the omission of criminal behavior but simultaneously a positive dedication: the other's facing me makes me responsible for him/her, and this responsibility has no limits.

We meet here with an exceptional or extraordinary *fact*: a fact that is at once and necessarily a *command* and a *norm*. By seeing another looking at me, or by hearing a voice, I "know" myself to be *obliged*. The scission between factuality *(be)* and normativity *(ought)-a* scission many philosophers since Hume have believed in— has not yet had the time to emerge here. The immediate experience of another's emergence contains the root of all possible ethics as well as the source from which all insights of theoretical philosophy should start. The other's existence as such reveals to me the basis and the primary sense of my obligations.

The abstract structure that was opposed to the tautology of egocentric monism has now been concretized into a relation between the selfhood of an ego and the otherness of the other person who comes toward this ego. This relation posits a certain connection, still to be qualified and a separation. The latter is necessary in order to avoid the consequence that the independence and difference of both the other and me are drowned in a fusion. The connection lies in the fact that the other's emergence answers the deepest desire motivating me. This *desire* differs radically from all forms of *need*. A need can be satisfied. The radical human desire is, however, too "deep" or "great" to be fulfilled; it wants the absolute and infinite, which does not fit into the "comprehension" and capacity of the desiring subject. The answer given by the absolute in the form of the "invisible" other is not a species of satisfaction but rather an infinite task: the task of my responsibility toward everybody I shall meet.

Source: Adriaan Peperzak, 'Otherness' in *To the Other: An Introduction to the Philosophy of Emmanuel Levinas*, West Lafayette, Indiana: Purdue Uni Press, 1993, pp. 19–22.

CHAPTER 16
ETHICS IN THE MAKING
Bodil Jönsson, Peter Anderberg, Eva Flodin, Lone Malmborg, Camilla Nordgren and Arne Svensk

Note from editor: The authors, who are rehabilitation designers and an interaction designer, present a case for the value of a phenomenological approach that is attuned to the lived body as defined by philosopher Maurice Merleau-Ponty. Through discussion of examples they advocate a situated design ethics which goes beyond abstract principles.

…. The more ethically grounded a given area of research is, the greater the chance it can contribute to long-term, meaningful breakthroughs in knowledge. An improved *ethics in design* can enable a critical questioning that in turn leads to entirely new research questions.

The mere involvement of human subjects and the application of safety provisions in design research do not guarantee it will meet ethical considerations, best practices or standards. The entire complex interaction with users offers intriguing possibilities and risks, or can result in mediocrity in areas such as: preparation and implementation that is worth the research person's time; respect for users' contributions; dignified treatment; feedback in an iterative and interactive process with mutual information and inspiration; and products and processes that are truly influenced by the users. This reasoning applies to all, but with special distinction to people who are disabled and elderly. Starting with specific needs as opposed to more general ones (the latter of which result in the necessity for more abstract specifications for the multitudes) can, above and beyond the ethical dimension, result in increased innovation and effectiveness for society on the whole. Proceeding from the particular to the general is of considerable value, for ethical reasons as well as for sheer effectiveness.

Involving persons with a variety of disabilities in product development helps to ensure innovative and use worthy products.[1] One of many prerequisites for ethically sound user involvement is that all participants are aware of the interference taking place in an iterative design process.

(…..)

Ethical guidelines versus situated ethics

Traditionally, medical research and clinically practicing professionals have been in the vanguard of creating ethical guidelines, with other research fields involving human subjects and human well-being close behind. Today, the medical disciplines are also front runners in combining their work on general ethical principles (autonomy, justice, and beneficence, for instance) with research on situated ethics, which is less mechanistic and closer to the context of real people in actual situations and work practices.

Situatedness urges different approaches for different disciplines. The engineering and design sciences, having safety, accessibility and 'universal design' of artefacts and the built environment on their agenda, cannot lean towards medical exemplars. They need to develop their own. An initial difficulty is that the existing key ethical principles, however 'universal' they appear to be, originate from medicine. The spirit of the *Nuremberg*

Code, the *Helsinki Declaration* and *The European Convention* (with its explanatory report) is not particularly vitalised in design, to say the least.[2] The reason is obvious: none of them have been formulated based on experiences from design of civil products for everyday life. Nonetheless, ethical aspects are definitely present in test usages as well as in the influence of the resulting technology in later, everyday use. Ethical design perspectives can also be deduced from *The Charter of Fundamental Rights of the EU* ('the right to freedom of expression and information'),[3] the *Convention on the Rights of the Child*,[4] and from *Citizens Rights and New Technologies: A European Challenge* in which the European Group on Ethics in Science and Technologies (EGE) stresses the two basic concepts of *dignity* and *freedom*.[5] Accessibility and 'design for all' are such fundamental perspectives that they should not be treated separately. They have societal implications for education, information and participation in social and political processes. *The Principles of Universal Design*, with its approach that environments, services and products should be designed for use by as many people as possible regardless of situation or ability, is an example of this perspective.[6]

Creating common guidelines for rehabilitation design is a challenge, as is the possibility of working the other way round: to open up for a mainly *situated ethics,* based on the spirit of existing codes and declarations rather than being deduced from them. The core of situated design ethics is made up of means and methods that (using the main declarations as guidance) reveal the most important ethical aspects in a given situation, elaborate these, document the thoughts, their implementations and outcomes and make them openly available with the goal of yielding exemplars and inspiring a vital and on-going discussion.

Exemplar 1: you have to have options to make a choice

Hanna was born with a nerve-muscle disease that severely restricts her mobility. At 1½ years of age, she received her first standing support device in order to exercise her muscles and put pressure on her skeleton. In the process of standing, however, she discovered that there was a lot to see from this upright vantage point. Objects in other parts of the room caught her attention. Without the support of her mother's arms she was suddenly on her own in the world. She wanted to come closer to the objects that she could see at the edge of her upright horizon. Her mother had to move the stationary supporter to the thing that attracted Hanna's attention. 'There! There!' she said and pointed. She quickly focused on something else and wanted to move on to it and then the next object and the next. Her mother soon realised that this was not so much about Hanna's wish to interact with different objects: what she actually was after was the enjoyable feeling of moving around in an upright position. This resulted in the construction of a motorised standing support device that offered Hanna the opportunity to move around in an upright position on her own.

One such device after the other has seen the light of day and enabled Hanna, now a young adult, to gain the identity of a standing — not a sitting — person, including all the existential, physical and practical effects and side effects involved. One such side effect (that was foreseen) is that Hanna will never master the ability to sit — she will remain a standing or a lying person for the rest of her life. The critical moment is to be found in her early childhood when the people in her surroundings were open-minded enough to start questioning whether a future position as a seated person would be right for Hanna with her 'stand-up' ambitions.[7]

This exemplar might serve as a revelation: what are the ethics (if any) behind the dominating 'wheel-chair-for-all' attitude that in no way questions the underlying assumption that somebody who cannot stand up and walk on her own has to live her life primarily as a seated person? In design terms: what are the ethical issues involved in not offering motorised standing supports as an option for mobility injured people? It is easy to understand that an aid in the best of cases does not only fulfil the function it is meant to (to stand up in the example of Hanna); it can also reshape the person's existence and existential terms (Hanna achieved an autonomous, upright mobility). This aspect should be involved in future body technology.[8]

In design, the focus might be on 'that-which-ought-to-be' (*desiderata*) versus 'that-which-is' (description and explanation).[9] The concept of *desiderata* is an inclusive whole of aesthetics, ethics and reason. *Desiderata* is about what we intend the world to be, which is more or less the voice of design. The greater the difference between the designer's and the user's worlds of concepts, the greater is the need for a user-adjoining and situated design process. You need to immerse yourself in concrete experiences – not only base your understanding on abstract ones. You need to accept and acknowledge the existence of different communities of practice.[10] You need to accept desire as an initiator of change. You need to allow disturbances and not only inform and be informed, but also inspire and be inspired. Designers may be informed and inspired by the users, at the same time as the users are informed and inspired by the designers. Utilising this two-way information and inspiration in both groups to its full extent has profound ethical implications, while at the same time making the process more efficient and situated. Cf. the framework by Kensing and Munk-Madsen.[11]

(.....)

Design ethics and the human sector

.... Addressing ethics makes it possible to discuss what design does, what it contributes and what designers may affect in their work.[12] As Tonkinwise puts it, ethics has always been associated with human-to-human relations.[13] But, according to Latour, artefacts are society and culture made sustainable.[14] Products, artefacts, built environments and communication are also 'actants' themselves and therefore enter the ethical domain not only as neutral means used by humans in their relations to other humans. Using an analogy from physics, Bruno Latour finds in designed activities what he labels 'the missing masses', which is to say that if we only take into account what we currently understand by 'sociality', our cultures should have long since collapsed into irretrievable immorality. The 'missing masses' names an ethical force hidden beyond what we now call 'the social', and the force is in the things *per se*. Things are acculturating or ethos-generating and a vital part of any ethos with a future.

In the *human sector* people work with and for other people. In addition to healthcare, schools and social services, this sector comprises people-to-people operations in business, the rest of society and the large, informal sector/economy in which people help people because they are relatives or friends. Awareness of the role of artefacts and design of new artefacts requires design processes that proceed from the *logic of the human sector*, not the technical one as is the case in the electronic, manufacturing and forest industries. With another approach to humans in design, the opportunities for real participation of people with disabilities increase, as do their opportunities to make decisions on their own. The design of a new technology can have a strong impact on the human sector and help improve it.

Exemplar 2: being there

The following excerpts from Peter Anderberg's study elaborate how people who have significant mobility/ physical impairments *and* who are accustomed to using computers experience the internet:

For the individual, the bodiless presence on the internet has many advantages. Why waste energy trying to convince your banking establishment to rebuild its entrance, when internet banking is so much easier? Why risk the danger of being dragged up the stairs to the local pub when it is so much easier to go to an online forum for company, where you do not have to worry about physical safety, accessible restrooms or deal with the attitudes of others? This ease and convenience, however, can easily lead to self-imposed restrictions, where what is experienced as choice becomes a restraint instead. The choice is very understandable on the individual level, but for the political endeavours of disabled people as a group, the picture becomes somewhat more complicated. The invisibility of the body can undermine the understanding of how disability is created in society, and be used against the community of disabled people. Why should a university adapt its buildings when most classes are available as online and distance studies?

There was a sense that the world was moving in their direction, with increasingly more societal functions being moved to the internet. An online identity is becoming a more 'normal' one for all. If everybody else finds their information or does their banking over the internet, *being there* is the most important.[15]

This exemplar not only illustrates the influence of design and technology on human individuals and groups/mankind as a whole but also pinpoints some reflections with special significance for the human sector. If a successful innovation system is to be achieved in the human sector, it should be based on how people live and act rather than how machines function. A methodology can be initiated that deals not so much with 'running faster' but with 'running differently' and with a clear sense of purpose.

Design science in relation to other sciences

… Human needs, wishes and dreams are the starting points for design research in rehabilitation engineering. The design of technical solutions represents in itself an interpretation of problems in a language of its own, different from the word-based analyses of observations, interviews, questionnaires and the like.

A design process in a disability context has to start with the person, end with the person and interact with her throughout the process if the results are to have any success. The situated is a necessary but not sufficient condition. … The solutions that grow out of the situated processes represent in themselves an interpretation of the actual problem and illuminate them in an implemented form and in their own 'languages', based less on words and interpretation and more on that we humans, in action, can show one another what we mean. This was already pinpointed and analysed by Vygotsky in the 1930s.[16] Paul Dourish discerns similar perspectives from a phenomenological interactive design perspective.[17]

Exemplar 3: pictures as a language

Sometimes virtual reality can be experienced as more real than actual reality. This can only be revealed through artefacts. For some people with autism, communication with other people isn't sufficient, not even that which includes pointing at the real object. It may require a detour by means of artefacts so that the concrete can be made real for the person involved. During an outing in the woods, a special education teacher placed her hand on a stone at the same time as she asked a pupil with autism to sit on it. The pupil did not seem to understand at all what she meant. She then took a photo of the stone with a digital camera and showed the display screen to the pupil while at the same time asking him to sit down on the stone. He did so immediately.[18]

Case studies compared to statistically based studies

Case studies should not be considered merely pathfinders for later statistically based studies.[19] They have significant advantages that cannot be found in statistical studies and vice versa. The field of rehabilitation engineering and design is based largely on case studies. This is not only because of the difficulties in finding enough subjects in the same 'category'; it is also (mainly) connected to the situated: it is the human being in her environment together with those around her that is the focal point. To pretend that one's own everyday environment can be replaced by a laboratory environment without considerably influencing usability tests is not only naïve but unethical in its approach.

Exemplar 4: relational usability

When designing a friendly restroom for elderly or disabled persons, interactions with the future users play an important role. To replace authentic users with young people loaded with weights and knee-joint movement restrictors reveals a misunderstanding of the situation as well as an absence of respect. Our experience tells us that research persons from the actual groups are happy to commit their time, share experiences and take part in testing. But it is pointless not to take into account outside influencing factors such as how much sleep the person got the night before, time of the day, season, increased or decreased weight, temperature, etc. Average percentages in usability tests that disregard the influences of these factors are misleading and of much less importance than relevant situated descriptions of individual cases and processes out of which later important patterns of needs and wishes can be detected.

Most often, the design of doors, locks, alarms, toilet seats, lighting, etc. are carried out separately. For the target groups, the margins are so small that a failure in one can result in a failure of all that follows – it is the entire chain of artefacts and the complete process that ought to be tested. …

Design and action research versus phenomenology and grounded theory

In rehabilitation engineering and design, the researcher is supposed to lean forward rather than lean backward, to be a practitioner but a reflective one.[20] Although seldom mentioned or brought up to a conscious level, technology and design involve action research. Action research is sometimes considered questionable in social sciences. There is a fear that the researcher might be involved to such a degree that he or she is no longer 'objective', and that the situation is so biased that it can no longer be scientifically studied. However, *not* being an action researcher in rehabilitation engineering and design, *not* aiming to improve situations, solve problems, strengthen capabilities, enable functioning – at least in the long run – is unethical in the context discussed here.

The quality criteria of design in a disability context are linked to interaction with the user, through cultural probes, sketches, mock-ups, prototypes, material or immaterial artefacts; and observing and intervening in actual usage. It is possible to use emerging technology early in the design phase to reveal new knowledge about the user. Of course, a process of this kind influences the persons involved, but that is not to be considered a drawback. On the contrary, it is a built-in part of the process and a cornerstone of the research. It is part of the aim of the iterative design process. Including the user with the designer and researcher in the design process is 'a goal, not a foul.'

Let's take a look at two of the fundamental concepts in phenomenology: *phenomenon* and *lifeworld*. Phenomenon in this context does not stand for the occurrence in and of itself, but for the occurrence experienced by someone. The word 'phenomenon' means 'that which shows itself' and it is implicit in the definition that there is someone to whom it is shown. Our focus on the experienced person – the individual with the disability – thus becomes obvious from a phenomenological perspective. It is the phenomenon as it appears to her that we want to call attention to; how she experiences her world and the special conditions that we, if we understand them, can help to improve and enhance with an assistive aid. 'We want to go back to the things themselves,' says Edmund Husserl, phenomenology's founder, in his 1901 publication *Logische Untersuchungen*.[21]

The *lifeworld*, the lived world, is the other indispensable concept and is strongly associated with that of phenomenon. The lifeworld is the world we already find ourselves in, are familiar with and take for granted. It is pre-reflexive and pre-scientific and it both influences us and is influenced by us. We exist in this world with our bodies, which, in the philosophy of the French phenomenologist Maurice Merleau-Ponty, is an integrated whole that he calls 'the lived body'. 'The body is the vehicle of being in the world'. 'The body is the general medium for having a world'.[22]

Phenomenology's desire to allow phenomena, the things that appear, to be the controlling factors, in our opinion is close to Norman's affordance, a concept that surfaced 80 years later.[23] A significant difference is that phenomenology does not just indicate the phenomena, the individual things and how they emerge, but also the lifeworld as the point of departure. Affordance is a concept that originally was used in psychology to describe how objects, people, situations and so forth, offer or afford opportunities for possible interactions to an observer. It is these offerings in the first place that we perceive when we are confronted with phenomena.

The designer in a rehabilitation context has quite a different task than a researcher in a grounded theory context, where the task is mainly to understand what is happening and how the players manage their roles. The researcher gains understanding through observations, conversations and interviews. Data collection, note taking, coding and sorting are all part of the work before writing; categories and theories are supposed to emerge during the process. Grounded theory is distinguished in that it is explicitly emergent and does not test hypotheses. The aim, as Glaser explains, is to discover the theory implicit in the data.[24]

Design versus the medical or social model

Of course, there are many models in disability sciences, but none that is satisfactory for design. *The medical model* oversimplifies disability as an individual characteristic and directs awareness towards individual adjustments and means. *The social model*, on the other hand, directs awareness towards ideological and political analysis, not towards practical everyday solutions for experienced functioning. In 'Making both ends meet', Peter Anderberg introduces what might be the beginning of a relevant model, *FACE,* in which Function is analysed from three different factors: Attitude, Control and Enabling.[25] One of the advantages with the FACE model is that it necessitates the consideration of ethical aspects.

(.......)

To sum up

In rehabilitation engineering and design, there is a need for concrete experiences, acknowledgement of different communities of practice, acceptance of desire as an initiator of change, and an openness for the value of two-way inspiration and information. This all implies an ethics that is dual: operationally situated but with its exemplars continuously questioned and examined in the spirit of international ethical codes, charters and declarations. Induction, deduction, and abduction in between the generalised ethical level and the situated one would vitalise ethics in the design research community. The processes can be strongly facilitated if the confusion and overlaps of design concepts could be replaced by more standardised and agreed-upon core concepts.

Source: *Design Philosophy Papers Collection Three*, ed. A.M. Willis, 2008, pp. 29–39.

Notes

1. Håkan Eftring 'The Useworthiness of Robots for People with Physical Disabilities' Doctoral thesis, Lund, Sweden: Certec, LTH, Lund University, 1999. Available at: http://www.english.certec.lth.se/doc/useworthiness/useworthiness.pdf

2. *Nuremberg Code* Washington, D.C., USA, 1949-1953. Available at: www.ushmm.org/research/doctors/Nuremberg_Code.htm; *Helsinki Declaration* Helsinki, Finland: 18th World Medical Assembly, June 1964, amended 1975, 1983, 1989. Available: http://onlineethics.org/reseth/helsinki.html; *The European Convention 2003*. Available: http://european-convention.eu.int/

3. *The Charter of Fundamental Rights of the European Union* Nice, France, Dec. 2000. Available at: http://www.europarl.eu.int/charter/default_en.htm

4. *Convention on the Rights of the Child* UNICEF, 2002. Available at: www.unicef.org/crc/crc.htm

5. *Citizens Rights and New Technologies: A European Challenge* Brussels, May, 2000. Available at: http://europa.eu.int/comm/european_group_ethics/docs/prodi_en.pdf

6. Bettye R. Connell, Mike Jones, Ron Mace, Jim Mueller, Abir Mullick, Elaine Ostroff, Jon Sanford, Ed Steinfeld, Molly Story, and Gregg Vanderheiden *The Principles of Universal Design* NC, USA: NC State University, The Center for Universal Design, Version 2.0, 1997. Available at: http://www.design.ncsu.edu/cud/univ_design/principles/udprinciples.htm

7. Eva Flodin 'Assistenter i min livsvärld (Assistents in my lifeworld)' Praktiskt-Pedagogiska Problem (Practical-Pedagogical Problems) Halmstad, Sweden: Halmstad University, no 12, 2000 and Eva Flodin 'Jakten på Instinktivspelaren' (Hunt for the Instinctive Player) Master thesis, Halmstad, Sweden: Halmstad University, 2000.

8. Edward Tenner *Our Own Devices – The Past and the Future of Body Technology* New York: Random House, 2003.

9. Harold G. Nelson and Erik Stolterman *The Design Way: intentional change in an unpredictable world* Englewood Cliffs (NJ, USA): Educational Technology Publications, 2003.

10. Jean Lave and Etienne Wenger *Situated Learning: Legitimate Peripheral Participation* New York, USA: Cambridge University Press, 1991.

11. Finn Kensing and Andreas Munk-Madsen 'PD: structure in the Toolbox' Communication of the ACM vol 36, issue 6, New York, USA: ACM Press, 1993, 78–85. Available at: http://doi.acm.org/10.1145/15371.163278

12. State-of-the-art in design ethics has been well elaborated in other issues of *Design Philosophy Papers*. See in particular, Sean Donahue 'Discipline Specific Ethics' *Design Philosophy Papers* no 2, 2004 and *Design Philosophy Papers Collection Two* 2005; Tony Fry 'Design Ethics as Futuring' *Design Philosophy Papers* no 2, 2004.

13. Cameron Tonkinwise 'Ethics by Design, or the Ethos of Things' *Design Philosophy Papers*, no 2, 2004 and *Design Philosophy Papers Collection Two* 2005.

14. Bruno Latour 'Technology is Society Made Durable' in J. Law (ed) *A Sociology of Monsters. Essays on Power, Technology and Domination* (Sociological Review Monograph) New York and London: Routledge, 1991, 103–131.

15. Peter Anderberg 'Being there' *Disability and Society* vol 20, no 7, 2005, 721–735.

16. Lev S. Vygotsky *Mind in Society* Cambridge, MA, USA: Harvard University Press, 1930.

17. Paul Dourish *Where the Action Is. The Foundations of Embodied Interaction* Cambridge, MA, USA: MIT Press, 2001.

18. Bodil Jönsson 'Enabling communication: pictures as language' in Malcolm MacLachlan and Pamela Gallagher (eds) *Enabling Technologies. Body Image and Body Function* Edinburgh, UK: Churchill Livingstone, 2004, 33–57.

19. Vilayanur S. Ramachandran and Sandra Blakeslee *Phantoms in the Brain. Probing the Mysteries of the Human Mind* New York: William Morrow & Company, 1998.

20. Donald Schön *The Reflective Practitioner. How Professionals Think in Action* New York: Basic Books, 1983.

21. Edmund Husserl *Logische Untersuchungen (Logical Investigations) vol II*, 1901, p.7. Available online in German at: http://www.princeton.edu/~batke/phph/husserl/lu/

22. Maurice Merleau-Ponty *Phenomenology of Perception* New York and London: Routledge, 1962, 82 and 146.

23. Donald Norman *The Psychology of Everyday Things* New York: Basic Books, 1988.

24. Barney G. Glaser 'Naturalist Inquiry and Grounded Theory' *Forum: Qualitative Social Research* Jan., 2004. On-line Journal, vol 5, no 1, art 7. Available: http://www.qualitative-research.net/fqs-texte/1-04/1-04glaser-e.htm

25. Peter Anderberg 'Making both ends meet' *Disability Studies Quarterly* vol 25, no 3, 2005.

GUIDE TO FURTHER READING

For general works on ethics see Robert Doran, *The Ethics of Theory: Philosophy, History, Literature* (2016); Peter Singer, *Ethics in the Real World* (2016); Alistair Macintyre, *After Virtue* (2007 edition); Simon Blackburn, *Ethics* (2001). On feminist ethics see Joan Copjec, *Imagine There's No Woman: Ethics and Sublimation* (2002) and Claudia Card, *On Feminist Ethics and Politics* (1999). On design ethics see the classics by Victor Papanek, *Design for the Real World* (1972) and E. F. Schumacher, *Small is Beautiful* (1973); also Tony Fry, *Design Futuring: Sustainability, Ethics & New Practice* (2009); D. G. Berman, *Do Good Design* (2009); Clive Dilnot, "Ethics? Design?" (2005); Peter-Paul Verbeek, "Design Ethics and the Morality of Technological Artifacts" (2008) in P. E. Vermaas et al. (eds.), *Philosophy and Design*; and in the journal *Design Philosophy Papers*, Sean Donahue "Discipline Specific Ethics" (2004); Tony Fry "Design Ethics as Futuring" (2004). See also, Albert Borgmann, "The Moral Significance of Material Culture" (1995); Bodil Jönsson et al., *Mobility and Learning Environments: Engaging People in Design of their Everyday Environments* (2002). Consideration of design ethics is extended in Part IV, with Emmanuel Levinas "Metaphysics and Transcendence" forming a bridge. Part IV considers the question of the same-other relation whereby in Eurocentric discourse, the other is constituted as a negative other (excluded, eliminated) or sought to be made the same (assimilated), see in particular contributions by Madina V. Tlostanov, Mahmoud Keshavarz, and Timothy Mitchell, as well as the Part IV Further Readings on humanitarian design. In Part VIII, Rosi Braidotti, Isabelle Stengers, Claire Colebrook, Vinciane Despret, and Michel Meuret implicitly or explicitly address ethics in their critiques of anthropocentrism.

PART IV
DESIGN AND THE OTHER

INTRODUCTION

The texts in this section build on the question of Otherness raised in Part III in the philosophy of Emmanuel Levinas (as explained by Adriaan Peperzak), bringing it to the specificity of culture, history, political and economic power. Terms we will encounter like ethnocentrism, ethnocide, Eurocentrism, orientalism, colonialism, coloniality, and decoloniality all of which have been coined by thinkers trying to grasp the complexity and engage the fraught, often de-humanizing and unequal relations between peoples of different parts of the world over the past four hundred years and the continuing effects. At first, these debates may seem a long way from design, until it is realized that what is under discussion is the underside of the making of the modern world and modern(ized) peoples—the very same project that also created design as a distinct form of practice and "the designer" as a professional identity.

We need to start with properly acknowledging the historically longstanding, violent relation between Same and Other that was produced by colonialism and its after-effects.

While empires and the subjugation of one people by another existed in earlier periods of history, European colonization of Africa, the Middle East, North and South America, and a good part of Asia was of an unprecedented scale. Its effects are still felt, seen, and act as determinates of many of the world's geopolitical problems. Colonizer-imposed boundaries paid no heed to people, place, or natural resources beyond the interests of, and competitive relations between, the imperial powers: England, Spain, France, Belgium, Germany, and Portugal. The loss or gains of imposed territorial divisions, the forcing together or apart of cultural groups, the loss or gain of natural resources continue to fuel conflicts of the present. Beyond the taking of land, exploitation of resources, the enslavement and killing of people, colonialism also enacted cultural destruction, known as ethnocide[1] with ongoing psycho-social consequences.[2] Of this Pierre Clastres said, "Ethnocide is based on the assumption that the colonized subject is not simply a threatening other to repress by physical force, but a creature that can be reformed and 'made like us' through education, religious conversion via missionaries, and the like."[3]

Ethnocide is systematic devaluation of the other's culture while holding up the colonizer's own culture as the model to follow, this producing a sense of inferiority in the colonized population. It involves such actions as banning, persecuting, and belittling indigenous customs, languages, spiritual practices, modes of dress, and so on. This was not just a pragmatic strategy of colonizers occupying land and seeking to create a compliant native workforce, it also involved the production of knowledge—religious pronouncements and scientific studies that designated the native subject as less-than-human—as lacking a soul, as savage, as primitive, thereby justifying the brutal actions of colonizers.[4]

As Pierre Clastres shows, there is an inevitability in the way a collective group defines itself against others beyond the group. Drawing on anthropological evidence on the ways that tribal societies name themselves, tells that

all cultures thus create division of humanity between themselves on the one hand, a representative par excellence of the human, and the others, which only participate in humanity to a lesser degree.[5]

But, he argues, it is only the West that is ethnocidal because of the combined power of their powerful homogenizing institutions of the state and capitalism. Historically, what this *power enabled* was that European nations were able to extend their mechanisms of militarized control and administration well beyond their own borders *so as* to facilitate the exploitation of resources of *colonized nations* such as precious minerals or land and labor to grow crops (like cotton) to be shipped to centers of industrial production in Europe to be processed into profitable commodities. European colonialism was thus indivisible from economic modernity. The homogenization Clastres speaks of is cultural and psychological, as well as economic. The latter compelling colonized peoples to shift from being subsistence producers to being indentured wage laborers, this entailing the destruction of ways of dwelling, sense-making, cultural practices, and beliefs with shattering effects across many generations.

There are "softer" forms of Eurocentric colonialism such as education which displaces languages and knowledge in the name of "progress." Critical of this homogenization strategy, some Western cultural producers and institutions have sought to preserve and celebrate non-Western cultures. Their actions, materialized as scholarship, exhibitions, books, even when claiming to extol difference, reduce otherness to the same, for example by gathering together sacred or practical artifacts and labeling them art. Such appropriations work to silence other readings by others of their own suppressed histories. More overt, are the appropriations of the culture industries in their ceaseless search for innovation, often with little benefits flowing to the originating cultures.

Eurocentrism is flawed at a fundamental level because it is based on a totalizing view of the other that pays no attention to how the others define themselves. Edward Said made this point forcefully in his landmark book *Orientalism* that showed "the Orient" to be a construction of European intellectuals (in art, literature, travelers' tales, popular imagery, political, and scientific discourse) that homogenized the diversity of Arabic cultures into a series of exotic stereotypes that had little to do with those cultures' own versions of themselves. This was "a system of knowledge about the Orient, an accepted grid for filtering through the Orient into western consciousness." The key point is not so much whether this version was right or wrong in an absolute sense; rather that because of the political and economic dominance of Europe over the Middle East from the eighteenth to mid-twentieth century, Orientalist discourse held sway; it was legitimized by the powerful, prestigious centers of learning of the West which became the models of learning and research everywhere, including in "postcolonial" nations, thus "Orientals" studying in such institutions encountered themselves defined as Others deficient in those capacities Western humanism elevated to the highest level, like rationality.

"Postcolonial" studies, of which Said's *Orientalism* was a founding text, in the analysis of the ongoing cultural impacts of colonialism especially in the cultural sphere, revealed implicit Eurocentric and colonialist assumptions in works of literature, visual arts, cinema, and popular media—this is no longer contentious. But Postcoloniality is now being overtaken by the more active figure of decoloniality: a designation preferred by scholars from the global South,[6] because it signals a process that is not yet finished. Decolonial scholars have also introduced the term "epistemological colonialism" which goes to the displacement of non-Western modes of thinking by entire systems of Western thought and belief, imposed directly through education and indirectly through Western economic domination of publishing, media, and culture industries.

Notes

1. Pierre Clastres, "Of Ethnocide," in *Archeology of Violence* trans. Jeanine Herman, New York: Semiotexte, 1994, 46–53.

2. The psychology of the colonized subject was first explored by Martinique-born psychologist Franz Fanon in *Black Skins White Masks* (1952).

3. See "Eurocentrism" *Bloomsbury Encyclopedia of Design*, 2015.

4. Extending from the Valladolid debate of 1550–51 as to whether the indigenous people of Spanish colonies actually had souls, through to the Social Darwinism of the nineteenth and early twentieth centuries wherein a hierarchy of races—with white Europeans at the top—was sought to be scientifically justified. See Matt Kiem, "Race" in *Bloomsbury Encyclopedia of Design*, London: Bloomsbury, 2015.

5. Clastres, "Of Ethnocide" p. 46. He continues: "The discourse that primitive societies use for themselves, a discourse condensed in the names they confer upon themselves, is thus ethnocentric through and through: an affirmation of the superiority of its cultural self, a refusal to recognize others as equals. Ethnocentrism appears, then, to be the most shared thing in the world."

6. Global South is not a geographical description, it is a way of referring to less powerful nations, mostly former colonies, that are in a structurally weaker position, economically and politically, in relation to the North: the United States and major European powers.

CHAPTER 17
WHAT IS COLONIALITY OF KNOWLEDGE?
Madina V. Tlostanova

Note from editor: There have been extensive debates amongst Western scholars on the nature of modernity. When did the modern era begin? What are the characteristics of modernity? What were its causes – were they primarily economic, social, technological or epistemic? Despite the variety of positions and emphases, Western scholars take modernity as given. Madina Tlostanova and her colleagues of the international decolonial collective (Walter Mignolo and Arturo Escobar) do not. They argue that modernity is an idea, a way of describing an historical processes that legitimizes and makes it seem inevitable, and eventually, the destiny of all nations. However, the binaries of colonizer/colonized or western/non-western are too simple to account for the complexity of asymmetric power relations globally, and their effects on knowledge production and on knowledge producers. Therefore in discussing the ambiguous situation of post-Soviet era scholars, Tlostanova deploys new terms such as colonial difference, imperial difference, self-orientalizing and double colonization.

Coloniality of knowledge is a typically modern syndrome, consisting in the fact that all models of cognition and thinking, seeing and interpreting the world and the people, the subject-object relations, the organization of disciplinary divisions, entirely depend on the norms and rules created and imposed by Western modernity since the 16th century, and offered to humankind as universal, delocalized and disembodied. Coloniality of knowledge is a term coined by the international decolonial collective whose main task has been for over two decades to critically analyze modernity and its darker side – coloniality, to trace the genealogy of modernity's violence in relation to its internal and external others, as well as to restore the alternative genealogies of decolonial struggles in order to offer ways of delinking from modernity/coloniality and decolonizing our being, knowledge, perception, gender, and memory.[1] Global coloniality is different from colonialism though its origins go back to the colonization of the New World. Yet colonialism is a historical and descriptive term which does not attempt a deconstruction of epistemic and discursive grounds of the modern/colonial project and seldom ventures into the depths of the philosophy of science in order to manifest its dominant colonialist roots. Global coloniality by contrast continues long after colonialism is over and flourishes in unexpected and not evident spheres of modern disciplines and academic divisions, in the production and distribution of knowledge, as well as in geo-historical and geo-political situations that do not render themselves so obviously to any postcolonial interpretation, which is the case of the post-Soviet spaces and thinkers.

Global coloniality is always manifested in particular local forms and conditions, remaining at the same time a recognizable connecting thread for the wholesome perception and understanding of otherwise often meaningless and cruel dissociated manifestations of modernity. Ontological othering in modernity has epistemic roots because modernity above all is a knowledge generating system and not as much an objective historical process. It is an idea that describes certain historical processes in particular ways and manages to force everyone to believe that it is an objective ontological reality. Once the idea of modernity was created, it legitimized the system of knowledge that created it. Both became instruments for disavowing other systems of knowledge and pushing other historical processes outside modernity. The making of epistemic modernity went hand in hand with epistemic coloniality, that is, with colonization of knowledge by either absorbing its content or by rejecting it.

Enrique Dussel demonstrated that the darker ego conquiro eventually leads to the lighter ego cogito 'subjugating the other, the woman and the conquered male, in an alienating erotics and in a mercantile capitalist economics.'[2] Philosophy and science which habitually focus on relations with and to objects rather than inter-human communications, and particularly, communications with the Other, are only the darker sides of the master morality of female oppression and racial differentiation. Decolonizing knowledge then means destabilizing the usual subject-object relationship from a specific position of those who have been denied subjectivity and rationality and regarded as mere tokens of their culture, religion, sexuality, race, and gender. For such people stressing the subjective specificity of our knowledge would be different from the start, from a mere postmodernist claim at situated knowledges. Becoming epistemic subjects and looking at the world from the position of our own origins, lived experiences, and education, we can then regard as objects of our study the Western imperial formations and thinkers who created institutions of knowledge that became the measure of all possible knowledges.

Zero point epistemology and disciplinary decadence

Most modern disciplines being ideological and epistemic products of the West, are grounded in what Santiago Castro-Gomez called the hubris of the zero-point[3] that is, an arrogant urge to take the vantage point of the observer and occupy a specific secure place exempt from reality (an observer who cannot be observed) and seemingly free from any subjective biases and interests, claiming to be emanating pure and uncompromised Truth. Such an Archimedean position, hiding the interconnection of geo-historical location and epistemology and body-racial and gendered epistemic configurations, is also a view point grounded in certain languages and categories of thought automatically eliminating anyone who writes and thinks in a different language or uses categories and concepts unknown to the West. Castro-Gomez expresses this syndrome in the following way:

> The co-existence of diverse ways of producing and transmitting knowledge is eliminated because now all forms of human knowledge are ordered on an epistemological scale from the traditional to the modern, from barbarism to civilization, from the community to the individual, from the orient to occident (…) By way of this strategy, scientific thought positions itself as the only valid form of producing knowledge, and Europe acquires an epistemological hegemony over all other cultures of the world.[4]

In the post-enlightenment world this zero point epistemology shifted its source and authority from God to Reason (and from theodicea to ratiodicea) making it possible for specific groups to assume such a secure and undisputed locus of enunciation.

This leads to a meaningless proliferation and implosion of disciplines, particularly in the humanities and social sciences. Disciplines are often losing any links with reality and social practices, concentrating on their own, often invented solipsist problems instead. This alarming tendency has already led to many calls for undisciplining the disciplines as a way of their overcoming in order to save them for the future but also to remain faithful to social reality.[5] Lewis Gordon entitled this phenomenon a 'disciplinary decadence', when a 'method facilitates the epistemic rejection of reality'[6] and scholars concentrate on the problems of frozen and de-ontologized disciplines and not human beings in the real world, thus rejecting unpleasant truths and turning to pleasant self-deceptions or deliberate acts of bad faith (a rethought Sartrean'mauvaise foi') instead, as a form of war against social reality and fleeing responsibility and freedom of choice through presenting one's opinion as universally true and one's discipline as a 'rationalization of itself as world' through continued practices or even rituals of the discipline.[7] A way out of this dead-end for Gordon lies in a critical good faith, a teleological suspension of disciplines and a willingness to rediscover anew the ideas and goals that disciplines were based on at their birth and subsequently forgot.

Gordon's opinion is supported by many other non-Western scholars.[8] To cope with disciplinary decadence we must turn to those intersecting fields which are intended to shape political and intellectual coalitions with other others and eventually work for the emergence of coalitional consciousness transversal in relation to both Western and non-Western theorizing and activism.

(....)

The imperial difference and the post-Soviet coloniality of knowledge

The asymmetrical knowledge configuration is no news and a number of non-Western scholars have recently started to discuss the possibilities and tools for going beyond the mere recognition model and elaborating alternative methods, perspectives and optics.[9] However the collapsed Soviet Union and its present remnants, some of which are independent states while others still remain satellites and quasi-colonies of Russia, is a region whose recent local history has affected the global situation yet did not allow its inhabitants to become knowledge producers and has in some cases even withdrawn this privilege if they had it before. In a way this trajectory was the opposite to the usual logic of the non-Western world slowly entering the space of rationality which we find in postcolonial cases. In the post-Soviet case the shift is reversed, from the second world to the global South or to a strange limbo of the poor North which refuses to be equalized with the poor South and which in addition to that has its own South and East of the poor North[10] .... The post-Soviet condition as its part has been determined by external imperial and double colonial difference transparent in the West/East and North/South divisions. Colonial difference refers to the differential between the first class capitalist empires of modernity (the so called heart of Europe) and their colonies, as the absolute others of the first world or the global North today.

Imperial difference refers to various losers which failed to or were prevented by different circumstances and powers from fulfilling their imperial mission in secular modernity taking as result various second-class places. Importantly, they were intellectually, epistemologically and culturally colonized by the winners and developed a catching up logic, an array of psychological hang-ups, schizophrenic collective complexes, ideologies of the besieged camp or alternatively, victory in defeat and consequently lapses into imperial jingoism and revenge.

Imperial difference is not homogeneous as it is further divided into internal and external versions. The former refers to the European losers of the second (secular) modernity which subsequently became the South of Europe, while the latter means the not-quite-Western, not-quite-capitalist empires of modernity, for instance the Ottoman Sultanate or Russia as a paradigmatic case of such a Janus-faced racialized empire which feels itself a colony in the presence of the West and plays the part of a caricature civilizer mimicking European colonization models and missions in its own non-European colonies. The external imperial difference which was coded as colonial in the West, generated Russia's secondary status in European eyes and consequently, an open or hidden orientalization. At the same time within Russia itself there is a specific version of secondary Orientalism as a direct result of secondary Eurocentrism. The imperial difference generated an open or hidden orientalization of Russia by the West. This sensibility can be defined as a balancing between the role of an object and that of the subject in epistemic and existential sense. Western Orientalist discourses have been transmuted in secular modernity as specific ways of representation and interpretation of Russian non-European colonies, which were used as replacements of the missing Orient and coded as such. In the end both mirrors – the one turned in the direction of the colonies and the one turned by Europe in the direction of Russia itself—appear to be distorting mirrors that create a specific unstable sensibility of Russian scholars in the humanities and social sciences.

Russia projected its own inferiority complexes onto its non-European colonies in the Caucasus and Central Asia through its self-proclaimed modernizer and civilizer role.

(.....)

The post-Soviet internal coloniality of knowledge vis-à-vis the global epistemic coloniality

.... As a secondary empire in modernity Russia has never managed to occupy the position of a rational subject and stayed at the level of producing culture (literature, ballet, etc.) and natural resources. The only exceptions were the sporadic attempts to revolt against the Western intellectual dominance through decolonizing impulses of a subalternized empire such as the Slavophile movement in the nineteenth century and later the Eurasianists whose ideas are often trivialized in contemporary Russian neo-imperial reactionary political movements and in the works of their social theorists. These paradoxically dissenting imperial discourses (as opposed to official conservative imperial imaginary and sciences) still applied Western methodological and theoretical tools even if they were aimed at destroying the Western epistemic dictate. This chronic intellectual dependency could not be overcome even in the case of the massive application of religious discourses in what stood for social sciences.

In the second half of the twentieth century even this meager resource of independent knowledge was cut off and the resulting post-Soviet social sciences emerged as pale copies of the long forgotten Western originals. When these copies are further recopied in Central Asia or the Caucasus it becomes a doubly colonized knowledge losing any links with reality and any activist edge. As a result the post-Soviet space emerges as marked with many silences and omissions, unspoken resentments and continued scorns between Russian and non-Russian, secondary European and non-European subjects.

(.....)

An author-critic forum on decolonial theory and gender research in Central Asia published in an area studies journal Central Asian Survey[11] revealed this persisting epistemic power asymmetry when some Western researchers refused to complicate their simple picture of Central Asia with more nuanced and subtle categories and subjectivities ...... (while) Central Asian researchers mostly agreed on the continuing discrimination and Orientalism in relation to themselves in Western dominated academia, yet refused to question the generally accepted Western scientific terminology and approaches defending them, once again, as presumably objective and uncontaminated by locality and/or ideology and silently agreeing that knowledge is always produced in the West.

The latter is a manifestation of mind-colonization which in case of the ex-colonial others has resulted in unhealthy self-orientalising and self-negation or in Duboisean terms – in a peculiar double consciousness which is very hard to resolve. In the Caucasus and Central Asia the Soviet modernity is replaced with either the Western progressive model or the pedaling of official national(ist) discourses. The complex indigenous cosmologies discordant with modernity/coloniality are erased or negatively coded even in the works of local scholars themselves who are forced to buy their way into the academic sphere through conforming to Western mainstream research.

(.....)

Possible ways out?

Real ways out of the complex intersection of internal and external epistemic asymmetries in the case of the post-Soviet space are not in recognition claims – asking the global North to recognize the Russian and post-Soviet presence in knowledge production is ineffective and meaningless. Instead of that we should delink from the losing battle and from the logic of catching up and dependency discourses in the sphere of knowledge production[12] and concentrate on creating a relevant social science which would be well aware of other models, including the latest Western and especially non-Western ones (to which so far Russian scholars condescendingly remain blind because of their old imperial attitudes), but would not simply repeat them or apply them to a different material.

Restoring an essential vital link of any social science with social reality and experience, would lead to attempts to create a serious but still missing critical conceptualization of the history of the Soviet modernity. Instead of that in Russia we find the familiar thoughtless reproduction of the cold war knowledge architecture, disciplinary decadence as an effort to hide the absence of any relevant existential, epistemic or at least political and social projects behind the disciplinary implosion and tightening disciplinary boundaries and restrictions supported by such still existing Soviet bureaucratic institutions as the Higher Attestation Committee which is responsible for inventing and banning disciplines, and strangles any inter-disciplinarity (or trans-disciplinarity) in the bud. ….

The only way out of this frozen bipolarity is a conscious willingness on the part of the few post-Soviet social scientists capable of doing it, to decolonize knowledge and to get rid of the self-colonizing syndrome as well. The value of any independent social approaches then would be linked with their ability to disavow the epistemic grounds of the rhetoric of modernity and it disciplines and methods which in the dominant system are presented as the only legitimate ones and existing forever, and turn to the goals and tasks of academia that have been long forgotten, such as the crucial aim of the university to shape not a submissive and loyal narrow specialist in some applied science but first of all a critically thinking self-reflexive and independent individual, never accepting any ready-made truths at face value, truly and unselfishly interested in the world around in all its diversity and striving to make this world more harmonious and fair for everyone and not only for particular privileged groups. And is this not ultimately the true mission of a vigorous decolonized social theory?

Source: Madina Tlostanova , 'Can the Post-Soviet Think? On Coloniality of Knowledge, External Imperial and Double Colonial Difference' *Intersections: East European Journal of Society and Politics* 1 (2): 38–58.

Notes

1. Mignolo, W. and A. Escobar. (2009) (eds.) *Globalization and the Decolonial Option*. London, UK: Routledge.

2. Dussel, E. (1995) *The Invention of the Americas. Eclipse of "the Other" and the Myth of Modernity*. New York, NY: Continuum, p. 43

3. Castro-Gomez, S. (1995) *La hybris del punto cero: ciencia, raza e ilustración en la Nueva Granada (1750-1816) (The Hubris of the Zero Point: Science, Race and Illustration in New Granada [1750-1816])*. Bogotá: Editorial Pontificia Universidad Javeriana.

4. Castro-Gomez, S. (2007) The Missing Chapter of Empire: Postmodern reorganization of Coloniality and Post-Fordist Capitalism. *Cultural Studies*, 21 (2–3): 433.

5. Castro-Gómez, S. and E. Mendieta (1998) (eds.) *Teorias sin Disciplina (Latinoamericanismo, Postcolonialidad y Globalizacion en Debate)*. México: Miguel Ángel Porrúa.

6. Gordon, L. (2006) *Disciplinary Decadence: Living Through in Trying Times*. Boulder, CO: Paradigm Publishers and Gordon, L. (2010) *Theory in Black: Teleological Suspensions in Philosophy of Culture*. Qui Parle: *Critical Humanities and Social Sciences*, 18 (2): 201

7. Gordon, L. (2010) Philosophy, Science, and the Geography of Africana Reason. *Personality. Culture. Society.* 12 (3): 54.

8. Sandoval, Ch. (2000) *Methodology of the Oppressed*. Minneapolis, MN and London, UK: University of Minnesota Press and Smith, L.T. (1999) *Decolonizing Methodologies: Research and indigenous Peoples*. London, UK: Zed.

9. Mignolo, W. (2014) Spirit out of Bounds Returns to the East: The Closing of the Social Sciences and the Opening of Independent Thoughts. *Current Sociology Monograph*. 62 (4): 584–602.

10. Tlostanova, M. (2011) The South of the Poor North: Caucasus Subjectivity and the Complex of Secondary "Australism". *The Global South*, 5(1): 66–84.

11. Megoran, N., C. Haris, S. Sharapova, M. Kamp, J. Townsend, N. Bagdasarova and M. Tlostanova. (2012) Author-critic forum: decolonial theory and gender research in Central Asia. *Central Asian Survey*, 31 (3): 355–367.

12. Lander, E. (2000) *La Colonialidad del Saber: Eurocentrismo y Ciencias Sociales. Perspectivas Latinoamericanas.* Buenos Aires: Consejo Latinoamericano de Ciencias Sociales. [CLACSO] and UNESCO.

CHAPTER 18
ENFRAMING
Timothy Mitchell

Note from editor: Mitchell's book Colonising Egypt *shows how colonial power in nineteenth century Egypt was exercised through micro-physical disciplinary means aiming to create institutions of order that would produce compliant, governable subjects. From their Eurocentric perspective, administrators, writers, academics and others considered Egypt through an "enframing gaze" finding the cities and ways of life lacking definition and order, by which they meant lack of visually perceptible order based on a plan. So deeply engrained was this representational thinking, that it was unable to see order based on other principles. Were the streets and houses of old Cairo designed? If so, how could this 'non-planned' designing be characterized?*

..... In the Berber and Arabic languages there are several words for this life, in the sense of what builds and flourishes. To indicate some of the larger significance ... I will mention briefly the use of one such term, taken from a relatively well-known historical source, the work of Ibn Khaldun, who lived in North Africa in the fourteenth century. Ibn Khaldun's major work, the Muqaddima, is an extended study of 'umran, a word usually translated in this context as 'civilisation' or 'culture'. The book examines the political and historical conditions under which 'umran appears, flourishes, and declines. Ibn Khaldun discusses such political conditions not in terms of some abstract framework such as 'the state', but in terms of the rise and decline of the built environment. Political life is examined as the building and decay of cities. The word to build, in this context, is 'amar (the ' here refers to the Arabic letter 'ayn), a word which for Ibn Khaldun can mean to live, prosper, flourish, be full, fill with life, inhabit, raise, be in good repair, build, and rebuild. It is from this word that is produced the term 'umran, with the same kinds of meaning: activity, bustling life, fullness (of a market well-stocked with goods, for example, or a harbour frequented by ships and merchants), prosperity, building.[1] Ibn Khaldun's study of 'umran is a study of the conditions that can bring about this building, this fullness, which we awkwardly translate as culture. Building is an active, undetermined process, marked in cycles of abundance and decay, rather than simply the material realisation of a predetermined 'plan'.

Nowhere in the Muqaddima does building, or 'umran, involve the notion of a plan. Consequently in Ibn Khaldun the word 'umran never means culture in the modern senses of the term, which are inseparable from the idea of a plan. The modern term establishes its meaning in contradistinction to an inert 'materiality' of the city, by designating an ideality of shared meanings or social patterns. The meaning of Ibn Khaldun's term, whatever its technical senses, remains rooted in a process of growth and fullness. It does not derive its force from any distinction between materiality versus meaning, the city versus its plan.[2] Without reference to Ibn Khaldun, and in the rather different context of the Berber village, Bourdieu draws attention to a very similar notion of fullness. In the housing he studied, the practices demanded of the peasant follow a pattern of emptying and filling. Analogies are drawn, as we saw, between the fullness of the fields, the fullness of the stomach and the fullness of the pregnant woman. In general, the processes of social and agricultural life seek 'the filling of the house' (la' mmara ukham), where the Berber word for filling corresponds to the Arabic terms 'amar and umran.[3]

The notion of cyclical growth and fullness apprehends the processes of the world without dividing it into a material realm and a conceptual, and is connected to an entire understanding of history and politics in the writing of Ibn Khaldun. A proper discussion of his ideas lies beyond the scope of this work, but it is in these sorts of terms that one might approach the question of order in the pre-colonial Middle Eastern or Mediterranean town. Discussions of the so-called Islamic city have tended to acknowledge none of the peculiarity of the methods of order and meaning that characterise cities since the industrial age, sometimes making do instead with a reference to the 'organic' nature of pre-modern cities and then examining the consequent problem of their 'order'. But there was no problem of order, in our own sense of a framework or plan, in such cities, just as there was no word naming such a thing in Ibn Khaldun. There was instead a cycle of fullness and emptiness, a continuous life which includes death (whereas order can never include disorder), a continuous building and rebuilding amid the forces of decay.

What this amounted to, then, was a way of building and living that refused to resolve itself into the appearance of a frame and what is enframed. A Middle Eastern town never affected a distinction between the `materiality' of building and other practices and the 'ideality' of their structure and representational meaning. A town was not built as a series of structures located in space. The spacing was the building, and such spacing, in the city as much as in the village, was always polarised.

In the case of pre-modern Cairo, for example, building usually involved opening up an enclosure, such as a courtyard enclosed by rooms or columns, polarised in many cases according to the direction of Mecca. This was so not only with mosques, but with ordinary housing as well, at least up until after the Ottoman conquest. In fact it has been shown, for Cairo, that the orientation of building, of worshipping, and of receiving guests, the direction of Mecca, the path of the sun, the forces of the zodiac and the properties of the prevailing winds were all precisely correlated.[4] With larger houses, the interior space carved out as courtyard and rooms was aligned precisely with such 'polar' directions and forces, rather than with the street or with neighbouring buildings.[5] The house, or the shared housing in the case of poorer dwellings, then expanded around this enclosure, in whatever shape and size the presence of neighbouring buildings allowed. Its generally blank and irregular exterior seldom corresponded to the shape, or represented the purpose, of its carefully oriented interior. In this sense there were no exteriors, and the city was never a framework of streets on which structures were placed. As we will see, streets too were enclosures. The city was the spacing of intervals or enclosures forming a continuous materiality. Its order was a question of maintaining, within such enclosures, the proper relationships between directions, forces and movements, not its ability to reveal in material form the determining presence of a non-material plan or meaning. It was an order without frameworks.

The outside

A second, related way of characterising the modern kind of order I have called enframing is that it works by determining a fixed distinction between outside and inside. There appears to be an unambiguous line along which an exterior frames an interior. The new colonial and European cities of the nineteenth century made their clearest principle the fixed divide between the bourgeois interior and the public exterior. There has been no difficulty since then in discovering a similar division in the traditional Middle Eastern town; similar but in fact more rigid, between the interior world of women and the family and the public, male world of the marketplace and mosque.

At first sight the Kabyle village seems to exemplify this fundamental division. The walls of each house certainly separate an inside from an outside, the one corresponding to a female world and the other the male. But if we look at the house more closely, or rather situate ourselves within it (for the method of building provides no place for an outside observer to stand), this fixed division begins to invert itself and collapse. First, as we saw, the female interior is itself composed out of a 'male' upper part and a 'female' lower part. But this, Bourdieu tells us, is really only at night, and especially in the winter when the men sleep indoors. In the summer, when they sleep outside in the courtyard, the house as a whole forms a 'female' interior. During the daytime, however, the courtyard is made temporarily a women's space by the exclusion of the men, who are confined to the gateway, the place of assembly, or the fields. (Women can only be said to be confined to the interior in the sense that men, for example, are also confined to the fields.) So the dividing of male and female space, outside and inside, varies with the time, the season, the work to be done, and other forces and demands. It is such unstable forces and demands that polarise space, and each polarity occurs only as the temporary exclusion or postponement of its own opposite.

If we turn from the village to the town, things at first seem rather different. Andre Raymond's work on the great Arab cities of the eighteenth century stresses the distinction between the public world of the mosques and markets on the main thoroughfares, and the private world enclosed around the courtyards of the houses, which opened not on to the street but on to blind alleyways whose gates to the street were always closed at night. In Ottoman Cairo, these impasses leading to courtyards are said to have formed almost half the total length of the city's streets.[6] The market streets were distinguished from such impasses as public places where strangers to the city could enter and do business. Disputes involving strangers required the intervention of public officials, who would never intervene in the private disputes of the courtyard or alley.

But again the distinction between the public exterior and the domestic enclosure was not some fixed boundary. The market streets were lines of penetration from outside the city, where external routes extended into the urban interior. They too formed only a 'hollow enclosure' like the courtyard, as Roberto Berardi has written, stretched out in linear form to contain the visiting stranger. They too had gates, separating the city into quarters. At night, the gates of the city would close upon the world outside, those of the impasses upon the streets and lanes, of these upon the main thorough-fare, and of the thoroughfare upon the neighbouring quarters. The city, writes Berardi, is 'a network made up of enclosures, of prohibitions and accorded rights. There is no more than a sliding between its moment of permission and its moment of prohibition. It is in fact this sliding between degrees of opening and accessibility, of closure and exclusion, that in everyday practice is lived.[7] Rather than a fixed boundary dividing the city into two parts, public and private, outside and inside, there are degrees of accessibility and exclusion determined variously by the relations between the persons involved, and by the time and the circumstance.

Source: Timothy Mitchell, *Colonising Egypt*, Berkley: University of California Press, 1991 pp. 53–58.

Notes

1. Cf. Mushin Mandi, *Ibn Khaldun's Philosophy of History*, Chicago: University of Chicago Press, 1957; Phoenix ed., 1964, pp. 184–7.

2. This is not to deny, of course, that there were regular, carefully ordered constructions in pre-nineteenth-century Arab cities (often laid out as the core of newly founded dynastic capitals) — just as the Kabyle house can be understood as a carefully ordered construction. The point is not the regularity of the building in modern cities, which in itself is nothing new, but the new distinction between the materiality of the city and its non-material structure. It is interesting to note the remark of al-Jahiz on the circular palace-complex (misleadingly referred to as the 'round city') constructed in the year 762 by the Caliph al-Mansur: 'It is as though it were poured into a mould and cast'. The regularity of the building is evoked by referring to the process of construction, and not in terms of any distinction between the materiality of the city and its 'structure'. Cited J. Lassner, 'The Caliph's personal domain: the city plan

of Baghdad re-examined', in Albert Hourani and S. M. Stern, eds., *The Islamic City*, Oxford: Bruno Cassirer, and Philadelphia: University of Pennsylvania Press, 1970, p. 103.

3. Pierre Bourdieu, *'The Kabyle house or the world reversed' in Algeria 1960*, Cambridge University Press, 1977, p. 145; and *Outline of a Theory of Practice*, Cambridge University Press, 1977, pp. 111, 126.

4. S. D. Goitein, *A Mediterranean Society: The Jewish Communities of the Arab World as Portrayed in the Documents of the Cairo Geniza*, 4 vols. Berkeley: University of California Press, 1967-85, 4: 64–74; David King, 'Architecture and astronomy: the ventilators of Cairo and their secrets', *Journal of the American Oriental Society* 104 (1984): 97–133.

5. King, 'Architecture and astronomy'.

6. Andre Raymond, *Artisans et commercants au Caire au XVIIIe siècle*, 2 vols. Damascus: Institut francais de Damas, 1973, Grandes vines arabes, p. 186.

7. Roberto Berardi, 'Espace et ville en pays d'Islam', in D. Chevallier, ed. *L'Espace sociale de la vine arabe*, Paris: Maissonneuve et Larose, 1979, p. 106.

CHAPTER 19
THE VIOLENCE OF HUMANITARIAN DESIGN
Mahmoud Keshavarz

Note from editor: War, conflict, economic and environmental pressures are prompting mass movements of people from the Global South to Europe, USA and even far-distant Australia. This is being met with increasing efforts to contain, control and exclude them. Borders are sought to be secured by a variety of spatial and non-spatial practices that create virtual borders that are no less real in their effects – thus we can speak of borderwork, bordering and passporting, which Mahmoud Keshavarz does in an extensive study on 'Design-Politics' from which the following is extracted. The focus here is on the problematic role of humanitarian design in the exclusionary and frequently violent borderwork that is re-creating the Mediterranean Sea as European space. A design proposal for a 'life-saving' line of buoys is given particular critical attention.

…. As images of the Mediterranean Sea, broken fishing boats and hundreds of drowning migrants sporadically circulate in the media, the events are referred to as a humanitarian disaster and crisis, which in return demand humanitarian interventions. The drowning of migrants in the Mediterranean Sea has frequently been framed as a crisis. One example was the "Lampedusa Crisis" in October 2013, when 300 irregular border crossers drowned. Another was the April 2015 "Mediterranean Crisis", referring to a period when more than 1800 migrants were found dead or lost at sea. Alison Mountz argues that states generally "develop narratives to explain and perform their day-to-day work" and that they "excel in particular at performing crisis."[1] When such a term is used, the performance of the term tends to mobilise new policies, regulations and security measures such as military interventions against certain populations and groups, with, in this context, migrants and migration brokers being the main target. … Crisis calls for immediate action, ignoring how practices of borderwork or spaces of borders shape and produce such vulnerabilities, precarity and eventually the spectacle of death.[2] When the loss of life in the Mediterranean is framed through crisis, then humanitarian practices of aid rush onto the scene, ignoring the practices and materialities that have made such disasters possible in the first place. Crisis in this context constitutes the humanitarian practices that de-materialise the spaces of borders, thus allowing for more ubiquitous practices of control and border-working that do not actually look like borders. This is why scholars of humanitarianism have been stressing and highlighting the fine line between care and control.[3] Through humanitarianism, the brutality of European border spaces disappears from sight.[4] Humanitarian practices also formulate another narrative, that of emergency action and a military operation against those so-called criminals. This has a number of consequences, as Polly Pallister-Wilkins writes:

It works towards the continuation of such a border control system while failing to take account of the fact that interventions to save lives and secure borders have the same practical effects.

(…..)

Humanitarian interventions in the name of a universal humanity, alongside more routine border policing efforts, work to reproduce the Mediterranean as European space. Humanitarian interventions are strategies of control and a form of border technology designed to stop an emergency and to restore the status quo: the continuation of an external European border regime that makes regular forms of migration for many non-Europeans all but impossible. As such, humanitarianism is an inherently conservative strategy.[5]

Humanitarianism thus re-frames the existing spaces of borders, exercised by European actors, as a space belonging to European decision makers, security companies and private philanthropists who can make decisions about the life or death of migrants in the sea by staging interventions and interceptions into the device, or rather, the space of a boat. This is another aspect of circulatory borderwork. As William Walters argues, we are witnessing a shift from the securitisation of migration to the humanitarianisation of migration.[6] Notwithstanding, the former is still growing stronger, but remains incomplete unless the latter enters the scene of the border spectacle. Frontex not only protects borders from illegalised entry with its specific techniques and practices, but it also searches for and rescues migrants in distress at sea.[7] Frontex, by creating a space for humanitarian practice and letting other non-governmental actors[8] participate in "border play", plays the role of the good border guard, the one who controls but also cares, or the one who cares but also has a great degree of power to control the sea in order to ensure the safety and security of borders.

(.....)

If we move beyond the bureaucratic and technocratic rationalization presented by Frontex ...... Frontex comes to the fore as a particular actor, one that is constantly occupied with designing spaces of operation and security. These designs, due to their continuous use, generate consumption practices in which the most hyper-visible things within these relations are the bodies that get caught in these specific spaces. Frontex operates within three geometries and in a vertical manner: on land, water and air. Rather than merely protecting and regulating the external borders of Europe as it claims to, Frontex in fact regulates and controls the circulation of goods and people well beyond European territories, and within an ambiguous European space that needs to be thought of as a volume. Once a territory and its borders and politics are understood in the form of volume, new geographies of security shaped by the political technologies of territory are revealed.[9]

(.....)

Humanitarian interventions have always been justified as a temporary way of working within an 'immediate' situation, an emergency condition of saving lives and bringing dignity to the universal concept of humanity. However, studies of humanitarianism, particularly in relation to refugee camps, tell a different story: that the majority of humanitarian practices become the norm and prolong the condition of precariousness and misery, making the suffering body into a spectacle and thus, a marketable commodity.[10]

(.....)

Humanitarian design has been advocated for as a way to craft technical solutions to problems in the Global South such as water access, emergency shelter, affordable housing, education, health, etc., by engaging a wide range of actors such as professional design firms, development companies, charities, NGOs and residents of the aid-receiving communities.[11]

As argued by Cedric J. Johnson, humanitarian designers seek to propose technical solutions to problems rooted in imperial and colonial histories, structural inequalities, labour exploitation and the neoliberal restructuring of societies worldwide. In pursuing technical solutions, they neglect the politics and history of the conditions into which they intervene. Consequently, the global poor – as the main users and consumers of humanitarian goods – are constructed as possible sites and design opportunities for the generosity of the elite, rather than as historical subjects with their own worldviews, skills and political formulations of life.[12]

Being justified and moralised on the basis of choosing and favouring the design of "products that save the lives of humans" and "empower[ing] them" instead of giving services to the Global North (Pilloton makes such claims[13]), humanitarian design is associated often unreflectively with "empathy" and what is called "empathic design."[14] In both cases a new market economy is created in which the suffering of the often racialised and gendered bodies of the South and East are subject to commercialisation and new, innovative methods of neoliberal soft power. Consequently, a seemingly emergent and temporary humanitarian situation turns into a permanent site for the consumption of aid products specifically designed for the "humanitarian market".

Even though the turn from temporary to permanent is something that humanitarian and aid workers are reluctant to accept, for humanitarian designers, the opposite is true. The notion of permanence forms the basis of humanitarian design practice.[15]In order to discuss how humanitarian design in practice (despite its best intentions) participates in circulatory borderworks, I will critically discuss a design concept proposed by an architectural firm that aims to save migrants in distress in the Mediterranean Sea.

"47 Buoys: Line of Rescue Buoys to Stop the Slaughter of Illegal Immigrants in the Mediterranean Sea" is the title of a proposal by the French architecture and design firm Mutations Architectes that was sent to the Office of the United Nations High Commissioner for Human Rights (OHCHR). The design concept is based on designing and installing 47 buoys in the Mediterranean Sea, "laying a line of buoys from South to North Mediterranean Sea, each buoy being equipped with an emergency alarm system to activate rescue of endangered travelers."[16]

In a letter attached to their proposal, the designers sought to show their awareness of the two main sources of criticism they might face: "knowing that is not solving the problem at its roots, the premise of this project is that if one disagrees with a system, and that system is hard to frontally transform, then it remains possible to understand its rules, to integrate it and to change it from inside. The output of it is a compromise, which would have his detractors of all sides. Those who think that this is encouraging illegal immigration and those who think it is absurd and cruel to 'save' people just to return them in terrible situation. Nevertheless, us, architects, are having the role to give a shape to the creations of our societies, as strange as they might be. Here is one." (ibid).

In the autumn of 2013, after the death of 300 migrants near the island of Lampedusa, I received an e-mail from a professor of Law who forwarded this proposal to me, thinking I might be interested in the concept. When I replied to clarify my critical standpoint in relation to humanitarian design, we began a long e-mail exchange on the position of these artefacts or "humanitarian goods" and how they might be problematic or helpful:

Dear Mahmoud,

For some reason or other, this proposal by French architects to construct life buoys between Libya and Italy reminded me of (what I remembered of) your project. The U.N. Special Rapporteur on the Human Rights of Migrants presented it briefly at a conference this week, regretting that "it will of course go nowhere" due to lacking backing by states.

Kind regards

I replied at length:

[…] I find this proposal very interesting, not because it delivers a so called solution to the tragedy of the Mediterranean Sea, but because simply and naively it illustrates my critique on the thinking of design practice as a solution, which indeed has become one of the best tools to domesticate technology for bio-political practices. […]

If we look at it closely, I see these life buoys as floating Frontex, reminding me again that borders are not strict and solid, but rather fluctuated. The misleading dichotomy of the inside-outside of borders often does not let us to see that what actually gets bordered are the in betweenness spaces that are the products of border-working. It's not about depriving someone of human rights, of the given […], but it is about deprivation of possibilities to act and to move. This is a "humanitarian Frontex" that does not merely block or deport, but make migrants the spectator of their unworthiness of being part of the European continent. These buoys in the sea, their materialities and their constant presence as part of the sea are constant reminders to unwelcome populations [...]. Beyond the mere simplification of "saving them in order to deport them" which is easy to criticise, the horrible aspect of such thinking, to me, lies in Heidegger's concern on technology: that what kind of world we are producing with these buoys and what kind of world we are losing. Just imagine while taking a touristic cruise on the Mediterranean Sea [as I guess that is the only possible way we as privileged will travel across the Mediterranean], you will see all these floating "devices" every 10 km as inevitable parts of the sea. The sea will not be meaningful anymore without these buoys. What kind of sea are we then making by installing these techniques? [...]

All the best and have a good break over the coming weeks.

Mahmoud

He later replied:

Dear Mahmoud,

[...] You might be right that it is born out of a charitable impulse, in which case I would share your skepticism. But it might also be the case that it is an attempt to manipulate the mainstream discourse with a gesture that seems to say "look, here is a small, life-saving technical proposal, why not adopt it?" The faux naivité of the question may be rather productive, because states are incapable of engaging in a "technical discussion" (on why the buoys after all are impossible to deploy) without revealing that they would rather have people losing their lives at sea than to engage in any discourse that leads away from the primacy of militarized and non-public solutions that Europe is pursuing today. [...]

Obviously, if the self-saving migrants were harvested by Frontex and returned, you would be correct in your analysis. Things might be different if we imagine the buoys being placed out in a completely private initiative. They would open for an unanswerable question. What if a migrant would reach a buoy, call an involved NGO from its telecommunication equipment? Would the NGO need to organize its own, private, resources to save that person? Is that what a thinking beyond the nation state demands of us now? Would they then smuggle her or him into the EU? Or would they call the border guards, speaking in a language of human rights demands, but nonetheless interpolating the state to do the job that only a state can do? These are brutal and necessary thought experiments, forced upon us even before any buoy is placed out.

[...]

Kind regards

In the above-quoted conversation, my deep pessimism about design being understood as a problem-solving task should be obvious. In contrast, his idea is about how this proposal might open up discussion. He is right, but he is only right if the discussion is not determined by strong material practices, the spectacle they make and the space of borders they themselves produce. Only when we dismiss all of these potential outcomes of the line of buoys, might we be able think of this design intervention as a critique. After all, Frontex is present at sea in the form of boats, drones and helicopters, but with buoys, authorities indeed draw a line, remake the map and rearticulate the Mediterranean Sea in unique ways. The buoys are not the innocent lifesavers that they appear to be in the scenarios illustrated by the designers; they are thick, cruel manifestations of our inability as humans to think of the world in a different way. They are the material evidence of how the 'solutions' we generate often forget the history and politics of how our past 'solutions' created the problems we face today. The so-called solution of forming societies based on ethnicity and drawing lines to control and regulate the movement of people and goods defined as others, not belonging to this or that particular territory, created the problem we face today, with the ever-growing number of nation-sates and their ever multiplying borders. Solutions to problems produce a duality, fixing the conditions in time and place, thus reproducing the status quo. As Arturo Escobar asserts, in contrast to the technocentric argument at the heart of humanitarian and development programs, problems created by the modernisation of the world do not necessarily have "modern solutions."[17] This is why design cannot be about problem-solving but needs to be a form of situational recognition. Design needs to act upon that recognition, which is a form of rearticulation and negotiation of the forces involved in a situation, with directions determined by a certain politics.

Humanitarian design should be subject to critique, not only as an instrument of humanitarianism, but also for the lack of recognition it carries in terms of what design has done to the condition into which humanitarian design intervenes, and hopes to solve. As humanitarian design also often comes from a Western-oriented understanding of design as a task of problem-solving, it is completely blind to how, in practice, design as a strong material force that articulates as well as manipulates the possibilities of situations has caused the event or 'the crisis' humanitarians in fact try to address. As designers Helder Pereira and Coral Gillett write in the anthology *Design in the Borderlands*, what is missing from the debate over the necessity or problematic of humanitarian design is "a fundamental rethinking of the structural conditions that create the 'need' for humanitarian design responses in the first place."[18]

As humanitarianism engages, or, at least is supposed to engage only with the present, it refuses to think about the past and the future and concentrates only on the emergency of saving lives right now, therefore forgoing a thorough assessment of long-term considerations. It thus explicitly claims to occupy an apolitical situation. Humanitarian design adopts the same position. There is, however, an issue here. The materiality of design tends to last longer than emergency rescue practices. Design solutions to emergency crises thus move beyond the site and moment of emergency and turn temporary status into a permanent condition. The spectacle and the materialities that design practices offer, reconfigure the exception into the norm and tend to normalise the condition of suffering. While design's materiality and artefactuality informs us about design's instability and reminds us that designed things do not last forever, it also generates certain practices, behaviours and patterns that tend to persuade us that this is the only possible way to work with these situations. It offers actions and activities flowing from the designed work – the designed solution – which tends towards inertia. Ilana Feldman writes that, in the context of Palestinian refugee camps across the Middle East, we need to examine what it means to shift humanitarianism "from crisis response to condition of life", not only thinking about "the politics of life but politics of living."[19] While Feldman is right, she assumes that humanitarianism is about crisis response, while humanitarian design as a way of enacting the ethics and politics of humanitarianism shows very well that humanitarianism is also about designing certain conditions of life. It enters and legitimises itself as a crisis response but nonetheless establishes certain conditions and thus a certain politics of life. Humanitarian design clearly informs us that the claim humanitarianism makes on engaging with saving only in the here-and-now is incorrect. Materialised articulations of rescue practices and systems tell us that humanitarianism always already comes from certain politics and histories and establishes specific politics and futures.

Those advocating these humanitarian designs thus refuse to think with history, to think of how they and their practices are embedded in history. A Mediterranean Sea rearticulated materially with buoys not only monumentalises the suffering of migrants but also reveals the biopolitics that design engages in by offering solutions to problems framed as crises. This is how "humanitarian reason"[20] works: biopolitical welfare policies lead to a certain reasoning for humanitarian practices through various persuasive and moralised means such as (.....) Life Buoys which, in return, depoliticise and de-historicise the conditions with which designers work. What is central to buoys, I argue, is that the body of a migrant is kept biologically alive while deprived of its political rights. As Miriam Ticktin reminds us:

Humanitarianism is about the exception rather than the rule, about generosity rather than entitlement. The regime of humanitarianism is based on engaging other people in relationships of empathy and in this way demonstrating one's common humanity; this is an ethics that, when taken to the extreme, entails selling one's suffering, bartering for membership with one's life and body.[21]

However, because humanitarian goods participate in another economy – a moral economy of sorts – criticising them is difficult in relation to which moral position one occupies when criticising the products that apparently help those who are dying in the Mediterranean Sea. After all, who does not want to save human beings? Critiquing humanitarian design, and specifically the proposed life buoys that will save those who cross the Mediterranean irregularly, is not a simplified call to tear down the materialised articulations of borders. If some of the strong material practices that shape the spaces of borders to be consumed in a circulatory way evaporate, the 'illegality' of border crossing in an irregular way would not disappear. The illegalisation of mobility and bodies will not disappear as long as the laws protecting the politics and economics of what constitute a desirable and undesirable migration or mobility are in place. At the same time, without those material practices of borderwork, we would not be able to consume and believe in the 'illegality' of some and the legality of others, the illegality of certain movements and the legality of others.[22] The role of design becomes important here because of the persuasiveness it implies. It persuades us to believe in a 'factual' duality of legality-illegality through the artefactual mediations and articulations it designs. It directs us to consume such 'facts' discursively and dismisses the materiality and artefactuality behind the very same circulating facts, values and norms. This, in return, opens up new possibilities for shaping the law. Migration policies become the border when they are materialised, and they become effective and taken seriously in productions and consumptions when designed and circulated. These design works do not necessarily need to come from the forces of the law, the sovereign, or the state but also from designers concerned with humanitarian causes. This is another instance of how border-working performs in a circulatory way. These buoys are constitutive of what is often referred to as 'good' borders: those that feature "open communication, formal demarcation agreements, standing boundary commissions, accessible transportation links, and a minimal military or police presence."[23] They thus reconstitute the border along the sea, making us see and believe in the irregularity of moving those bodies that might perish there. The spectacle of the border thus frames events in a certain way so that humanitarian intervention becomes the only possible way to encounter those events. Crisis as a problem and humanitarianism as a solution, sustain local sites of exploitation and coercion as well as reproducing the global circulation of moral sentiments in the service of contemporary economy and politics.

Source: Extract from Mahmoud Keshavarz, 'Design-Politics: An Inquiry into Passports, Camps and Borders' Doctoral Dissertation in Interaction Design, Dissertation Series: New Media, Public Spheres and Forms of Expression, Faculty of Culture and Society, School of Arts and Communication, Malmö University, 2016 ISSN 978-91-7104-683-3 (pdf)

Notes

1. Mountz Mountz, Alison. 2010. *Seeking Asylum: Human Smuggling and Bureaucracy at the Border*. Minneapolis: University of Minnesota Press. (2010, xvi–xvii).

2. Cuttitta, Paolo. "'Borderizing' the Island Setting and Narratives of the Lampedusa 'Border Play'". *ACME: An International E-Journal for Critical Geographies* 13 (2): 196–219, 2014.

3. Fassin, Didier. 2005. "Compassion and Repression: The Moral Economy of Immigration Policies in France". *Cultural Anthropology* 20 (3): 362–87.; Ticktin 2005 Ticktin, Miriam. 2005. "Policing and Humanitarianism in France:

Immigration and the Turn to Law as State of Exception". *Interventions* 7 (3): 346–68; Feldman, Ilana, and Miriam Ticktin. 2010. *In the Name of Humanity: The Government of Threat and Care.* Durham, North Carolina: Duke University Press; Agier, Michel. 2011. *Managing the Undesirables.* Cambridge: Polity.; Weizman 2012; Pallister-Wilkins, 2015a). Weizman, Eyal. 2012. *The Least of all Possible Evils: Humanitarian Violence from Arendt to Gaza.* London: Verso Books.; Pallister-Wilkins, Polly. 2015. "The Humanitarian Politics of European Border Policing: Frontex and Border Police in Evros. *International Political Sociology* 9 (1): 53-69.

4. Tsianos and Karakayali, 2010 Tsianos, Vassilis, and Serhat Karakayali. 2010. "Transnational Migration and the Emergence of the European Border Regime: An Ethnographic Analysis *European Journal of Social Theory* 13 (3): 373–387.)

5. Polly Pallister-Wilkins. 2015b. "The Humanitarian Policing of 'Our Sea'". http://bordercriminologies.law.ox.ac.uk/humanitarian-policing-of-our-sea/ (accessed 5 December 2015). (2015b)

6. Walters, William. 2004. "Secure Borders, safe haven, domopolitics". *Citizenship Studies* 8 (3): 237–60. Also see Walters, William. 2015. "Migration, Vehicles, and Politics: Three Theses on Viapolitics". European Journal of Social Theory 18 (4): 469-488.

7. Frontex is the European Union's border control agency and is tasked with the integrated border security and fortification of the European Union's external border. Established in 2004 and located in Warsaw with financial, administrative and legal autonomy, its main tasks, according to European Council Regulations are: (a) to co-ordinate operational co-operation between member states in the field of external border management, (b) to assist member states in training national border guards, including the establishment of common training standards, (c) to carry out risk analyses, (d) to follow up on the development of research relevant to the control and surveillance of external technical and operational assistance at external borders, and (f) to provide member states with the necessary support for organizing joint return operations.(European Union. 2004. Council Regulation (EC) no. 2007/2004 of 26 October 2004. Establishing a European Agency for the Management of Operational Cooperation at the External Borders of the Member States of the European Union. Public Law 2007/2004. http://frontex.europa.eu/assets/About_Frontex/frontex_regulation_en.pdf (accessed 18 March 2015)).

8. One of these actors is the American philanthropist Christopher Catrambone, with his nonprofit contribution to the scene, Migrant Offshore Aid Station (MOAS). This is the non-profit wing of his company, the rest of which specialises in insurance underwriting, insurance broking and intelligence services offering safety and security information to its clients. He has a website with dozens of photos portraying himself, his family and migrants. Calling himself an entrepreneur, humanitarian and adventurer, the slogan of his philanthropic boat and service is "no one deserves to die at sea". See: http://www.christophercatrambone.com/ (accessed 25 December 2015).

9. Elden, Stuart. 2013. "Secure the Volume: Vertical Geopolitics and the Depth of Power". Political Geography 34 (3): 35-51.

10. Malkki, Liisa H. 1996. "Speechless Emissaries: Refugees, Humanitarianism, and Dehistoricization". *Cultural Anthropology* 11 (3): 377–404.1996; Agier, 2002, 2008 Agier, Michel. 2008. *On the Margins of the World: The Refugee Experience Today.* Cambridge: Polity; Agier, Michel. 2002. "Between War and City Towards an Urban Anthropology of Refugee Camps". *Ethnography* 3 (3): 317–41.; Feldman, 2011 Feldman, Ilana. 2011. "The Humanitarian Circuit: Relief Work, Development Assistance, and Care in Gaza, 1955–67". *In* Forces of Compassion: Humanitarianism Between Ethics and Politics, *edited by Erica Bornstein, and Peter Redfield,* 203-26. *Santa Fe, New Mexico: School of Advanced Research Press.*, Ticktin, Miriam. 2014. "Transnational Humanitarianism". *Annual Review of Anthropology* 43: 273-89,).

11. Cameron and Stohr, 2006; Bell, Bryan, Katie Wakeford, and Thomas Fisher. 2008. *Expanding Architecture: Design as Activism.* New York: Metropolis Books. 2008; Bell, Bryan. 2004. Good Deeds, Good Design: Community Service Through Architecture. New York: Princeton Architectural Press; Heller and Vienne, Heller, Steven, and Veronique Vienne. 2003. *Citizen Designer: Perspectives on Design Responsibility.* New York: Skyhorse Publishing Inc.2003; Pilloton, Emily. 2009. *Design Revolution: 100 Products that are Changing People's Lives.* London: Thames and Hudson. 2009.

12. Johnson, Cedric G. 2011. "The Urban Precariat, Neoliberalization, and the Soft Power of Humanitarian Design". *Journal of Developing Societies* 27 (3-4): 445–75. 2011).

13. Pilloton, Emily. 2009. *Design Revolution: 100 Products that are Changing People's Lives.* London: Thames and Hudson. 2009.

14. Nielsen, Brita Fladvad. 2014. "Out of Context: Ethnographic Interviewing, Empathy, and Humanitarian Design". *Design Philosophy Papers* 12 (1): 51–64 2014) and what is called "empathic design" Mattelmäki et. al, 2014 Mattelmaki, Tuuli, Kirsikka Vaajakallio, and Ilpo Koskinen. 2014. "What Happened to Empathic Design?". *Design Issues* 30 (1): 67–77.).

15. This is evident in Brita Fladvad Nielsen's (2014) definition of humanitarian design: "aimed at filling non food item (NFI) demands in a disaster setting, reaching from the emergency phase to the durable solutions phase" (Nielsen, Brita Fladvad. 2014. "Out of Context: Ethnographic Interviewing, Empathy, and Humanitarian Design". *Design Philosophy Papers* 12 (1): 51-64, p. 51). Criticism and comments against and in support of humanitarian design have been dealt with through discussions of development programmes, empowerment, aid and missionary projects (Change Observer, 2010 "Humanitarian Design vs. Design Imperialism: Debate Summary". Change Observer. 16th July 2010. http://designobserver.com/feature/humanitarian-design-vs-design-imperialism-debate-summary/14498/ (accessed 12 May 2015)), often after the former have been warned against becoming practices of "new imperialism" (Nussbaum, Bruce. 2010. "Is Humanitarian Design the New Imperialism?". Fast Company Design. www.fastcodesign. com/1661859/is-humanitarian-design-the-newimperialism (accessed 17 January 2015).).

16. Mutations Architectes, 2013 http://www.mutations-architectes.com/47-bouees/ (accessed 17 September 2017).

17. Arturo Escobar Escobar, Arturo. 2004. "Development, Violence and the New Imperial Order". *Development* 47 (1): 15-21. 2004

18. Pereira, Helder, and Coral Gillett. 2014. "Africa: Designing as Existence" *Design in the Borderlands*, edited by Eleni Kalantidou, and Tony Fry, 109–132. London: Routledge. .. Helder Pereira and Coral Gillett write in the anthology *Design in the Borderlands* (Kalantidou and Fry, 2014) (2014, p. 118).

19. Ilana Feldman Feldman, Ilana. 2012. "The Humanitarian Condition: Palestinian Refugees and the Politics of Living". *Humanity: An International Journal of Human Rights, Humanitarianism, and Development* 3 (2): 155–72. (2012) (p.157).

20. Didier Fassin, Fassin, Didier. 2012. *Humanitarian Reason: A Moral History of the Present.* Berkeley: University of California Press.2012)

21. Ticktin, Miriam. 2009. "The Violence of Humanitarianism". In *Cultures of Fear: A Critical Reader*, edited by Uli Linke, and Danielle Taana Smith, 132–148. London: Pluto Press 2009, p.147).

22. De Genova, De Genova, Nicholas. 2013. "Spectacles of Migrant 'Illegality': the Scene of Exclusion, the Obscene of Inclusion". *Ethnic and Racial Studies* 36 (7): 1180–1198.2013, p.1190

23. Diener and Hagen, Diener, Alexander C., and Joshua Hagen. 2012. *Borders: A Very Short Intro375duction.* Oxford: Oxford University Press. 2012, p. 66).

CHAPTER 20
THE FORCE OF FORM, THE EFFECT OF GENRE
Francois Jullien

Note from editor: Reading this extract from The Propensity of Things *together with Ledderose's 'Why Not an Alphabet?' gives a sense of an internally coherent style of thinking, a system of rationality, based on a different foundation to that of the West. Jullien explores "the emergence of an autonomous aesthetic mindset" in China at the end of the second century A.D. This would appear to be a point of commonality between East and West, but he shows that this mindset cannot be understood through Western aesthetic categories such as mimesis or style. Underlying this is the difficult-to-translate idea of shi that comes from a very different understanding of nature and of how things come to be.[1]*

…. But from the start this mode of thought never conceived of artistic activity as the West initially did, that is, as mimesis (the reproduction or imitation of a particular kind of "nature" at some level more "ideal" or more "real," either more general or more specific, than nature is normally understood to be.' Rather, artistic activity was seen as a process of actualization, which produced a particular configuration of the dynamism inherent in reality. It operated and was revealed through the calligraphy of an ideogram, through a landscape painting, or a literary composition. The particular disposition that receives form can potentially express the universal dynamism. This potential must be maximally exploited: it lies in the tension that animates the various elements of an ideogram set down in calligraphy, in the force and movement of forms in a painting, in the effect created by a literary text. The ancient strategic model thus also serves as a basis for aesthetic theory; art too can be conceived in terms of *shi*, as a possible setup.

The force of form in calligraphy

The transition between military art and the art of writing is explicit: When they discussed calligraphy, the Ancients stressed the paramount importance of *shi*. … Calligraphy is a study that rests on the configuration [of ideograms]. Now, once there is a configuration, there is a potential stemming from that configuration. Strategists ascribed the greatest importance to the positioning [of the troops on the battlefield] and to the potential 'born of that disposition: as soon as one obtains the advantage constituted by that potential [*shi*], one holds the key to success."

The Chinese art of calligraphy can be considered a prime example of dynamism at work within a configuration because, in the case of each ideogram copied, a particular gesture is converted into a form, just as a particular form is equally converted into a gesture. In this schema the figure produced and the movement producing it are equivalent; one can speak of the *shi*; of the brush that delineates the ideogram just as one speaks of the *shi* of the ideogram that it traces,' The same force is at work, apprehended at two separate stages or, as it were, in two different "states." Thus, *shi* can be defined overall as the force that runs through the form of the written character and animates it aesthetically. "When *shi* comes, do not stop it; when it departs, do not hinder it" we are advised in a treatise believed to be one of the earliest on the theory of calligraphy. On the one hand there is the "configuration" (of the various elements making up the strokes in the ideogram), on the other, the "potential"; on the one hand, one "considers" the "form" of the character from the perspective of its appearance, on the other one "pursues" the *shi* through the lines traced, appreciating the effects of tension produced by the alternation of different strokes. The "body" of the character is seen as evolving: "If the *shi* is harmonious, the body will be well balanced." But the *shi* of the writing is simultaneously distinct from the overall body of characters, each of which is regarded as a particular written form: "One and the same *shi*, whatever the body [form of the writing used." *Shi*, the determining factor in calligraphic art, thus serves to unify the strokes set down, however varied they may be.

However, it would be a mistake to believe that Chinese aesthetic thought developed through careful discrimination between terms, resorting to precise conceptualizations and definitions in the Greek, particularly Aristotelian, manner. Rather, the terms operate through networks of affinities, one constantly implying another through allusion. They interact more through contrast than in terms of the separate fields they denote. Instead of proceeding from pre-established, methodical distinctions (inevitably abstract and also very convenient), they frequently convey their meaning through the interplay of parallelisms and correlations made possible by their infinitely rich evocatory powers. Aesthetic phenomena are expressed more through a series of polarities than through concepts. The *shi* of calligraphy can thus be likened to an ideogram's internal "skeleton" which provides the character's structural consistency, and it is thereby opposed to the enchanting grace of a mere flourish. However, it may be equally opposed to the rigid and fixed structure essential to the nature of writing, and is absorbed in this sense into the delicate form of the line. It is an in-between term, at times relating to the invisible, subjective, and cosmic energy pervading and operating through the activity of calligraphy, at other times relating to the shape or form of the individual ideograms at the definitive stage when each is set down; in the latter case it tends to be fused with that particular configuration.

But even when *shi* is simply understood as the configuration of a written character, it suggests the breath that lives in that character and that makes itself felt through it — here again, the oscillation between two poles. "In default of any other term bequeathed by the tradition *shi* may be explained metaphorically as a leap, a soaring, a bound. For example, a particular specimen of writing on a seal is described as "stretching out its neck and contracting its wings, its *shi* aspiring to reach the clouds." In general, it is *shi* that "gives life" and makes the slightest dot or stroke vibrate, as if we were reliving the moment of its execution. *Shi* thus always enhances what would be mere empty representation without it, for *shi* gives depth to a representation and exceeds its concrete limitations by revealing, within the actualized static form, a dimension of perpetual, soaring flight. *Shi* is not only the internal energy from which that form has proceeded; it is also the effect of the tension this energy produces. The "form" is seized on in all its propensity, which means it should be seen not merely as "form" but also as a continuing process.

But what is the concrete source of this effect of tension forever animating the various elements of the character in calligraphy? In other words, how can this character function efficaciously as a configuration? Zhang Huaiguan tells us that the first rule for handling a brush is that "*shi* must be achieved, both for dots and for strokes, through the creation of tension between top and bottom, lowering-lifting, separating-gathering together." The logic of the dynamism at work depends on contrast and correlation. Each element composing the configuration of the ideogram must either attract or repel another, either "turning to face another" or "turning its back on another." A line at the top bending down-ward is complemented by one at the bottom curving upward; and the tip of the former implicitly prefigures and initiates the latter. In similar fashion, one stroke turns heavily back on itself while another carries on into a free-flowing tip; here the ink is thicker, there thinner. Separation gives rise to closeness, opposition to balance. Polarity engenders reciprocity and conversion. In this way the elements in the painted figure play off each other to an advantage, as if by "mutual reflection." allowing their common pulse to circulate freely among each other with no "bleeding" at any point. This produces the ideogram's *shi*, at once "vigorous in a male fashion and charming in a feminine way." The various elements in the configuration of the written character thus create a magnetic field of maximum intensity and perfect harmony. The ideogram set out in calligraphy becomes a living symbol of the great process of the world, constantly maintaining its equilibrium at the center as a seat of plenitude, yet constantly dynamic because it is self-regulated.

Tension at the heart of configuration in painting

This formula applies equally well to the other art of the brush: in painting as in writing, one must always strive to "obtain" or "achieve" *shi*, since it is easily "missed" or "lost." The two possibilities in these two common pairs of terms echo the ancient Chinese political concept of the efficacy of position, which one either occupies or abandons. When the term *shi* entered the domain of painting theory (an extension of calligraphy theory), so far as the depiction of people and horses was concerned the term still wavered between the interrelated meanings of "disposition" and "impulse." But with respect to the elements composing a landscape, the term truly came into its own for example, describing the mountain that provides the setting for a religious scene (and here, for the first time, the setting matters more than the human subject) the artist shows he is sensitive to the effect produced by a narrow crest of rock snaking up through the surrounding crags: it creates a "dynamic. configuration" (*shi*), thanks to its line "snaking and weaving like a dragon." Facing this first peak, another rises proudly. a bare rock face that merges into a cinnabar escarpment, the foot of which plunges into a ravine. This escarpment must be painted in flaming red, Gu Kaizhi tells us, to heighten the dynamic configuration (*shi*) created by this dangerous precipice). The lines of the painting that depict this vertiginous drop achieve the greatest possible tension. Similarly, the line that runs down to the other edge of the picture, where it then tails off, completes the composition by producing a carefully created effect of suspension.

The mountain is the central element in the Chinese aesthetics of landscape painting and is also the place par excellence for *shi*, for it allows the most diverse tensions to operate together at the heart of its configuration. When painting a mountain, an artist can exploit all the possibilities of height and distance: the pinnacles that rise, sharp and straight, on the horizon produce the effect (*shi*) of the encrusted, comblike spine of a rhinoceros. One need only acid a trail of clouds or mist clinging to the side of one of its slopes to confer on the mountain an effect (*shi*) of measureless height; similarly, by simply blurring the lines a little, greater distance. is imparted to the. *shi* of the mountain. The painter can also exploit the possibilities of alternation and contrast. The curved flank of the mountain, now convex, now concave. "opens" and "closes," spreads out then folds in, making "the mountain's *shi*" "twist" and "undulate" ; the peak rises, then falls, and the mountain "moves" as it stretches. Like the shape of an ideogram, the mountain too is conceived of in all its propensity and the tension is heightened by the contrast between its slopes: one rises, another fails. Meanwhile the animation of a village is countered by expanses of solitude.

Similar contrasts can he found in the overall landscape where water complements mountains and vice versa. Though their natures are fundamentally opposed at the same time the qualities of the two elements discreetly interact: even as the mountain represents stability, it appears "to become animated and to move" through the diversity of its aspects; and even as it flows, water seems "to become compact" through the mass of its waves. To emphasize the *shi* of the water, it should be painted as contained by a deep gorge, rushing straight down or swirling around the rocks. Every drop of water is in motion, thus turning it into "living water." It should not be painted too "soft," for that would diminish its *shi*, or too "stiff," like a plank, or too "dry," like dead wood: if done correctly, the force of the propensity imprinted in its lines will then make it seem to strive "to splash the walls."

This quest to depict tension can be sensed in the other elements of the landscape as well. This is particularly the case with rocks, whose *shi* is conveyed by emphasizing their tendency to pile up at the foot of a mountain, "pressed one against another," as after a rock fall, and in the trees, particularly the pines, in which we detect the same lofty aspiration of the mountain peak. A pine tree should also be painted in isolation, "dangerously" rearing its knotted trunk, like a rippling peak, "up to the Milky Way," while its lower branches droop toward the ground. The same applies even to the light and supple willow, to which *sbi* can be imparted simply by feathering the delicate tips of its branches.

As with the calligraphic ideogram, the logic of this dynamism is one of contrast and reciprocity. The theme of the copse illustrates this best. To confer *shi* on a copse, the most important principle is that of "irregularity," achieved by having the trees spread out in some places and not in others: the branches should not extend from the trunk at even intervals, and they should inter-lace sparsely in one place, with a single dead bough suspended amid the trunks, but in another place more densely and bushily: "It must be assessed with *shi* in mind, if it is to be successful." Such irregularity is dynamic because it is produced by an alternation between straight lines and curved ones (the constant preference for curves, that of common tastes, becomes monotonous), between what is intricate and what is more "coarse" and careless, and between compact, clogily crowded clumps and spaces containing no more than a scattering of trees. The principle behind all these contrasts is the opposition of emptiness and fullness, a principle that is as central to Chinese aesthetics as it is essential to their vision of the world: "To bring into play this opposition between emptiness and fullness will be enough to achieve *shi*." What must be done is group together pines, cedars, old acacias, and old juniper trees in clumps of three or five, in such a way as to emphasize their *shi*: "Then they will begin to dance with heroic and warlike energy, some lowering their heads, others tossing them aloft, now bending low, now stretching straight up, undulating yet balanced." As with the strokes and dots that compose an ideogram, here too the aesthetic configuration, whose opera-tion is achieved by means of attraction, tension. and interchange, is completely efficacious.

The aesthetic setup

We know that the history of Chinese aesthetics as a whole is an evolution from the initial primary concern for external resemblance to a desire to transcend the purely "formal" representation of reality through a "spiritual communion" with it and finally convey the "intimate resonance" that animates it. The effect of tension characterized by *shi* occupies an intermediate stage in this process. While a formal configuration ("round, flat, or square") can be caught by a brush, the effect of tension imparted by the *shi* that imbues it, "through twisting or broken-off movements and by indicating tendency and direction," though possible to capture with a brush, cannot be rendered fully, for "it has to do with mental representation" and "something in it is bound to elude the brush." The effect of tension imparted by *shi* is responsible for ensuring that the aesthetic process progresses from the merely figurative to the spiritual.

Even at the level of artistic method, the distinction can be seen to be fundamental to Chinese pictorial technique, for it is reflected in the different natures of ink and brush. While the ink "spreads out the configuration of the mountains and rivers," the brush "shows their different *shi* in turn"; at the heart of the land-scape, "the ocean of ink surrounds and sustains" the line of the mountain painted by the brush, but this line instead "directs and leads." The ink spreads out and fills the space, but the brush informs and imparts dynamism. Among the elements that make up a landscape, the tension imparted by *shi* can be seen in sym-bolic terms to possess an affinity with wind. Similarly diffused through forms and thereby animating them, it too is a physical reality, but an evanescent one manifested only in its effects. The tension is all the more powerfully conveyed since it is never totally actualized: hence the value of the brush stroke that is all the more forceful when remaining inchoate, barely suggesting a line of eter-nal suspense.

Consider a frail skiff painted in the middle of an expanse of water. Because it is so far away, the sail sheet is not detectable; even so, "if one does not paint it at all, the representation will lack *shi*." The solution is to paint only the bottom corner and not show the precise spot at which the boatman's hand holds it which the distance makes it impossible to see. *Shi* thus creates its effect of tension at the exact boundary between the visible and the invisible, where the explicit nature of the configuration becomes more richly charged with implicit meaning, emptiness becomes allusive," and the finite and the infinite illuminate and reinforce one another *Shi* starts out as a painterly technique; but it also and inevitably provokes emotion. By rendering form in an effective way, it immediately conjures up a lifelike impression. And the effect produced is of crucial importance, for *shi* is responsible for opening up that which is concrete to that which lies beyond it, and for conveying through what is represented the suggestion of something "beyond," an effect essential to art. Through *shi* the visible configuration evokes the infinite: the world of representation accedes to a spiritual dimension and, at the edge furthest from the visible, gestures toward the invisible.

Literary configuration and the propensity for effect

The kinship between calligraphy and painting is obvious in China. But the common model provided by strategy can serve as a basis for developing an analogy between the Chinese art of writing and the more general art of literature. Just as for troops "there is no constant disposition on the battlefield," for the ideograms rendered by calligraphy "there is no single way, always the same, of actualizing their configuration"": as with water and fire, there are multiple potentialities stemming from their disposition (*shi*), and these are "not determined once and for all." Literature benefits from a comparable variability. Because of the diversity of what texts need to express, they are composed in different ways, in each case producing the type of potentiality that stems as a literary effect from the particular form of the composition *Shi*). It is up to the writer to determine (and exploit) this potentiality most effectively." A text should also be regarded as a particular configuration (of words) that can be used to good effect, as seemingly demonstrated by one chapter of the Chinese tradition's finest work of literary thought, the *Wenxin diaolong*, whose exceptional profundity is only today being rediscovered, after more than a millennium of obscurity.

Let us consider the text to be a particular actualization, a literary configuration, and *shi* to be its propensity for effect. Various themes from strategy stress the "natural" character of such a propensity, modeled after the tendency of a bolt projected by a crossbow to fly straight, or water confined to the bottom of a ravine to swirl about: the propensity for the text's effect emanates from its constitution just as a spherical body tends to roll and a cubic one remains still. The propensity can produce both good and bad effects, and in literature these are brought about by both content and form. From a positive perspective, someone taking the canonical texts as a model will "spontaneously" achieve a classical elegance; equally, a writer inspired by works of the imagination (the Limo, as opposed to the Aging) will "necessarily" produce the charm of the unexpected. Negatively, however, if the thoughts are put together superficially or make little impact, the text will lack "implicit richness," and if its style is overlabored or too succinct it will lack "rhetorical abundance." In the same way, water carried swiftly along makes no ripples, and a dead tree casts no shade.

Liu Xie, the Chinese theorist of poetics, shows us that the propensity that leads to effect does not merely stem of its own accord from the constitution of the text. It also intrinsically reflects that constitution, as he explains, drawing an analogy with painting. In painting, the association of different colors produces a particular picture (whether it is a horse or a dog that is represented); similarly, in literature, the interweaving of everything being expressed produces different propensities for effect (which may be elevated or vulgar). The result depends on the specificity of the style employed. Thus, two contrary but complementary principles should guide the writer in managing this propensity for effect: on the one hand, he should combine the most diverse possibilities, so as to confer the maximum efficacy on the text;' on the other hand, he should respect the text's overall unity, so as to present its necessary homogeneity. For example, instead of ruling out "magnificence" to promote nothing but "elegance," the writer should exploit the potentials of both those contrary qualities, just like a general who skillfully combines head-on charges with attacks from the flank. At the same time, though, each text belongs to a certain genre, which leads to a definition of the literary genres stricto sensu, divided by their aims ("classical elegance," "limpidity of emotion," "precision in expression," etc.). This is the source of the table of twenty-two genres, classified according to six applicable literary criteria, five of which cover four genres each and one that includes only two. The most appropriate analogy for a text will thus, in the last analysis, be of a bro-cade fabric that, despite the interweaving of threads of the most varied colors, still retains in each case its own "basic texture."

Liu Xie also suggests, however, that it is quite possible to reverse this perspective and consider a text's propensity for effect in relation to the individual identity of the author rather than the genre to which it belongs. In other words, its propensity depends on his taste and his habits, both of which are personal. From this perspective, such propensity might be likened to the surplus of energy and vigor that can spread "beyond" the text, but that would mean interpreting the propensity for effect too exclusively in terms of the energy that is put into literary creation as breath (qi). There is an interesting distinction between effect and force: "The propensity that supports the text" may tend equally toward gentleness or its opposite, and its expression need not be vigorous and vehement to have *shi*. Nevertheless, and even more subtly, although propensity is distinct from force, it will still be manifested as a tension, which should be made to operate neither too strongly nor too obviously. Hence, the factor of tension needs to be balanced by a contrary factor of diffuse and harmonious saturation that permeates the tension and brings about relaxation and enjoyment.

Since a literary effect is supposed to be natural, in that it emanates from a propensity, it is not hard to imagine what an "artificial" literary effect would be like. Such an effect would not stem from a setup suited to the text and its particular genre, for the text would have been motivated by the decision to strive for novelty. It is normal to aim for originality, concludes Liu Xie, but this should not be confused with eccentricity. Originality comes from the successful use of the inherent potential of the work, but eccentricity results purely from contrariness, contradiction, and a quasi-mechanical subversion of whatever is correct and expected." It produces no more than a false "air of originality" with no effect at all. To cut corners, violence has been done to the shaping of the text instead of the text being left to work on its own.

Difference from the idea of style

As we can see, our starting point of strategic thought also serves as a dominant model in the interpretation of literary composition, since literary composition is also conceived as a way of managing and exploiting natural propensities which stem from the different types of texts suited to the diverse situations in which an author finds himself, and because the aim is always to produce the maximum (artistic) effect. Now what must be understood is how to grasp this Chinese perspective in a specifically literary con-text, beginning from our own concepts.

Applied to the domain of literature, this theory of propensity inevitably overlaps with our Western notion of "style," combining two major concepts that have been formative at different times in our own tradition. When Chinese thought relates *shi* to literary genre, it seems reminiscent of the "teleological" attitude of classical rhetoric, which regards style as a matter of effectiveness in discourse. Equally, when Chinese thought relates *shi* to the personality of the author, it coincides with genetic theories of style that first became influential under romanticism. These replaced the teleological interpretation with a causal one in which style expressed a particular individual or a particular period and was viewed as the "transmutation of a humor," to borrow Roland Barthes's phrase. Under the influence of Western ideas, contemporary Chinese literary critics tend to equate the theorization of *shi* with a Chinese theory of "style" — while recognizing with some embarrassment that there are in fact other ideas in this fifth-century treatise, as well as in other works in the Chinese tradition, that likewise conjure the idea of "style." Is this just a matter of the vagueness of Chinese concepts and the failings of polysemy? Or might it not rather reflect a general difference of perspective on how literature was conceived, one that does not allow us, in the last analysis, to match up their ideas and ours?

The fact is that our own conception of style proceeds from a philosophy of "form" (as testified by the influence in this domain of the Aristotelian school). In Antiquity, this is "the specific form of a work as shaped by its function" (Pierre Guiraud); in the modern period, it is "form without destination" (Barthes, who suggests that the actual "writing" is "the moral of this form". The efficient form is here understood in its relation to the material content. However, in Chinese thought, as in calligraphy, for example, the "form" through which the literary *shi* is realized is that of a particular configuration which itself operates spontaneously to create an effect. Thus, what we customarily translate as "form" in Chinese texts of literary criticism is not the opposite of "content" but the end product of the process of "actualization," *shi* being the potentiality characterizing that actualization.

Source: edited extract from Chapter 4 of Francois Jullien, *The Propensity of Things: Towards a History of Efficacy in China* (trans. Janet Lloyd), New York: Zone Books, 1995, pp. 75–89.

Note

1. The large number of marginal and endnotes in Jullien's book, *The Propensity of Things: Towards a History of Efficacy in China* (trans. Janet Lloyd New York: Urzone, 1995) have been removed from this extract. His first note states: "The aesthetic texts on calligraphy cited in this chapter can be found in the *Lidai shufa lunwenxuan* (Shanghai: Shuhua chubanshe, 1980) (hereafter *Lidai*); those on the aesthetics of painting are in Yu Jianhua, ed., *Zhongguo hualan leibian* (Hong Kong, 1973) (hereafter *Leiban*); finally, in the field of literary "theory," the *Wenxin diaolong* is cited from the edition by Fan Wenlan (Hong Kong: Shangwu yinshuguan)."

CHAPTER 21
WHY NOT AN ALPHABET?
Lothar Ledderose

Note from editor: This is a brief extract from Ledderose's book Ten Thousand Things, *which analyses the common factor across a range of Chinese cultural forms – such as writing, cooking, building, the production of ceramics, bronze, and silk – which is a module system that allows a very large number of variations to be created from combinations of a limited number of interchangeable units. While other cultures used modular systems, the Chinese developed it early to an advanced level and applied it widely, to the extent of it becoming a distinctive pattern of thinking. Modularity, he argues, has been a major factor in the continuity of Chinese civilization over millennia. Modularity is also a powerful example of 'the designing of thinking': that thinking is 'designed by' categories and their inter-relation; and that modularity as an idea, as a product of thinking, has almost limitless capacity for material and immaterial application, and thus for shaping worlds (the designed designing).*

Although much has been said thus far about the advantages of the module system, the question has to be asked whether the Chinese could not have made life more comfortable for themselves by discarding altogether even the nicest of module systems and using an alphabet instead.[1] There can be little doubt that an alphabet is far less cumbersome for the user. You only have to learn some two dozen different graphs. This process requires only a couple of weeks, not the many years that Chinese children have to spend memorizing several thousand graphs. Other than in the Chinese script, you can also immediately understand the meaning of a word when seeing it written for the first time (provided that you have heard it before). With an alphabet, typewriters and computers are easier to use, and newspapers are easier to print—although apparently not faster: like major Western newspapers, the *People's Daily* (*Renmin ribao*) comes out every morning in millions of copies.

Several reasons can be adduced to explain why the Chinese did cling to their system of characters. Characters are graphically more interesting and beautiful than the letters of an alphabet; the system is more compact, as more information is contained on one page of the *People's Daily* than on one page of the *New York Times*. But there is another reason, a single overriding reason: the Chinese did not want to entrust their cherished texts to the fleeting sounds of the spoken language.

This, however, is precisely what the Europeans did. The letters of the alphabet are symbols of sound. Westerners only record in their script the ephemeral sounds of a word, not its meaning. Script in the West is thus linked inextricably to all the phonological changes and diversifications that are bound to occur in any language. Whenever the pronunciation of vowels and consonants changes, whenever there are new developments in grammar and syntax, the script must follow suit. Whenever a group of people speaking a particular dialect achieves political independence, their dialect may become a language in its own right, requiring a separate script and literature. When Latin ceased to be the universal European language after the fall of the Roman Empire, a variety of national languages and literatures evolved. Now Europeans have to learn a new language every time they want to read something written five hundred kilometers away, or five hundred years before.

Not so in China. Characters are symbols of meaning. Because they record the meaning of a word, not its sound, the system of script did not have to follow slavishly all the phonological and other changes that occurred in Chinese, as in every other spoken language. Even the few examples in this chapter demonstrate that an educated Chinese can read most texts written in all parts of the empire at any time in history, be it hundreds, even thousands of years ago. Script in China thus became the most powerful medium for preserving cultural identity and stabilizing political institutions. And if one wonders why the bureaucrats in Brussels have not yet been able to reunite Europe, the answer may be that they use an alphabet.

The Chinese by contrast still use many thousands of characters, with which they are apparently happy. This is possible because they have developed the module system, which allows them to handle this mass. Only with a module system is it feasible to design, to use, and to remember thousands of distinguishable shapes. Only with a module system could the Chinese script fulfill its true function: to guarantee the coherence of China's cultural and political traditions. This awesome unity is unsurpassed in world history.

Source: Why Not an Alphabet? Lothar Ledderose, extract from *Ten Thousand Things: Module and Mass Production in Chinese Art*, Princeton University Press, 2000, pp. 22–3.

Note

1. For a comparative analysis of the major writing systems in world history see Geoffrey Sampson, *Writing Systems: A Linguistic Introduction*, Stanford University Press, 1985.

GUIDE TO FURTHER READING

See entries in *Bloomsbury Encyclopedia of Design* on Colonialism, Cultural Relativism, Culture, Ethnocentrism, Globalization, Humanitarian Design, Power, and Race. On decoloniality and design see Eleni Kalantidou and Tony Fry (eds) *Design in the Borderlands* (2014). On decoloniality see Madina V. Tlostanova and Walter D. Mignolo, *Learning to Unlearn: Decolonial Reflections from Eurasia and the Americas* (2012); W. Mignolo and A. Escobar (eds) *Globalization and the Decolonial Option* (2009); W. Mignolo and M. Tlostanova "The Logic of Coloniality and the Limits of Postcoloniality" (2007); Arturo Escobar "Economics and the Space of Modernity" (2005); on Eurocentrism see Peter K. J. Park, *Africa, Asia, and the History of Philosophy: Racism in the Formation of the Philosophical Canon, 1780–1830* (2013); Boaventura de Sousa Santos, *Epistemologies of the South: Justice Against Epistemicide* (2014); Enrique Dussel "Europe, Modernity and Eurocentrism"; Edward Said, *Orientalism* (1978). On humanitarian design: Cameron Sinclair and Kate Stohr, *Design Like you Give a Damn: Architectural Responses to Humanitarian Crisis* (2006); Emily Pilloton, *Design Revolution: 100 Products that are Changing People's Lives* (2009). For critique of humanitarian design see Cedric G. Johnson "The Urban Precariat, Neoliberalization, and the Soft Power of Humanitarian Design" (2011); Change Observer "Humanitarian Design vs. Design Imperialism: Debate Summary" on Design Observer website (2010). The literature of critique of humanitarianism is much larger, spanning many disciplines, see, for example, Ilana Feldman and Miriam Ticktin, *In the Name of Humanity: The Government of Threat and Care* (2010), and it connects with the critique of developmentalism, see Arturo Escobar, *Encountering Development: The Making and Unmaking of the Third World* (1995) and Farzana Naz, "Arturo Escobar and the Development Discourse" (2006).

PART V
BEING DESIGNED AND THINGS

INTRODUCTION

This section deals with the relational structure of people and things, specifically, the co-constitution of us and the world. Some of the texts address this relation directly while others presuppose it and focus more on things of the world or the thing itself—as object or as matter or "that which is not I." Most of the texts are informed by phenomenology; so first, some brief orientations are needed on two key ideas of phenomenological philosophy: object and world.

"Object" does not necessarily mean physical object, rather it means "object of consciousness" and therefore refers to both material and immaterial things. Speaking of the founder of phenomenology, Edmund Husserl, Graham Harman makes the point that he was focused "on intentionality, which means: on objects lying before the mind. All perception, judgment, love, and hate is perception, judgment, love, or hate *of some object*."[1] The question "what is an object?" goes to the very heart of Western philosophy, linking with other massive questions of "what is real?," "what is being?" the answers to which are so varied and complex that we can't possibly summarize them here. What does need to be registered nevertheless, as a supplement to the critique of Cartesianism in many of the texts in this Reader, is the significance of seventeenth-century philosopher Rene Descartes' "cogito ergo sum" (I think therefore I am), in other words, this is the only thing I know for sure—myself, thinking; it is quite possible that all the objects of my consciousness—everything I register as seen, heard, felt, and so on, could well be no more than projections of my mind.[2]

Let us consider "world." World is not the same as planet earth or environment or habitat; it does not name a physical entity. There is more than one world, no human being is without world, and animals also have worlds which are not just reducible to habitat. World names something that is both grasped and dwelt in, something that has been rendered as a relational totality via the designation of mind, as in descriptions such as "my world" or "the world of mathematics." World is a central concept for phenomenology, and it has nothing to do with scientific naturalism, nor does world come to be known via the methods of empirical science, describing things in terms of their physical and chemical properties. World is where we find ourselves, we are "thrown" into it, not just in the sense of being born, but world is a place in which things are meaningful—they have names and uses and orders of relative significance according to which cultural world a particular "I" finds itself in. The significance here is that "being in a world" is a precondition for knowing anything at all, including scientific knowledge. It is not as if our world is contained within the universe or the planet or nature because "it is always within the world that the universe or nature is disclosed to us."[3]

Phenomenology seeks to understand things in their everyday worldly context. In its take-up within design and architectural theory, a phenomenological approach is attuned to situatedness: "the idea of us and our world being co-constituted in a relational and dynamic unity . . ." as pointed out by Stephen Read in "Technicity and Publicness."

Another way of thinking this co-constitution of us and our world, already encountered in Part I, is the designing of the designed (Fry) or "we design, and what we design, designs us." Yet for most of the time this is not seen: the very process of using things becomes familiar (naturalized) such that the things themselves disappear in their efficacy, they are no longer something to wonder about. This is Heidegger's point in his famous example of the hammer, a piece of equipment that is "ready to hand" and is known in the first instance "pre-reflectively" just in using it (know-how and know-what get conflated); the hammer only becomes an object of reflection if it breaks or cannot be found when needed. To what extent does this apply to the complex networked material and immaterial things among which affluent people live today? We live among designed things that conceal their designedness. Those that declare, that shout out "Look at me, I am designed" are the least significant. They are decoys drawing attention away from the designedness of everything else.

Designed things are designed to disappear: convenience, automaticity, and minimization of user effort were the founding principles of industrial design. In the 1920s and 1930s this focused on cars, trains, and aircraft as well as the introduction of domestic labor-saving appliances such as toasters, the electric cooker, and the washing machine, products marketed with the promise they would create more leisure time, yet their effects were not so simple. The automatic washing machine eliminated the physical labor of clothes-washing, traditionally done once a week, but its convenience prompted more frequent washing, thus not necessarily "saving time," this also increased water use, and the generation of wastewater laden with phosphates, which had negative effects on biophysical environments such as riverine ecosystems.

New devices and technologies can configure to create new practices with big effects. To take one example: the remote control, which eliminates the need to interact directly with a TV to switch channels. The remote control combined with the introduction of cable TV which vastly increased the number of programs available at any one moment *afforded* the new practice of channel surfing. Now, affordance is an idea familiar to product designers that claims that there should be an appropriate "fit" between object and use, particularly in relation to the capacities of the human body, and that the designed object should communicate directly how it should be used without mediation of signage and instructions. Michael May in "Beyond Affordances" critiques the naturalism and universalism of the theory of affordance. To this could be added the problem of the anthropocentrism of affordance, even when examples of animal behavior are cited. There is yet another way to think affordance, which is to decenter the human being and to see affordance systemically whereby certain elements configure in particular ways to produce effects. Returning to the TV remote control: it is a device that affords staying seated for long periods of time. It doesn't do this alone, but systemically, and this has further effects: a TV remote control plus a vast choice of video content plus a comfortable chair plus readily available snack food with high sugar and fat content all add up to a system (or sub-system depending on the perspective[4]) that produces excess calories stored as fat in human bodies, and thereby contributes to the larger system that produces the "obesity epidemic." There is a parallel here with Christopher Alexander's example of traffic light, newspaper-vending machine, and pedestrian forming a dynamic subsystem of economic exchange within the larger system of a city.[5]

Notes

1. Graham Harman, "The Road to Objects," *continent* Volume 3, Issue 1, 2011, 171–79, 171.

2. For further explanation see Lex Newman, "Descartes' Epistemology" in *The Stanford Encyclopedia of Philosophy* ed. Edward N. Zalta, Winter 2014 Edition. http://plato.stanford.edu/archives/win2014/entries/descartes-epistemology/

3. "When we think scientifically of the universe or nature as containing our world, we are not thinking of the world in the proper philosophical sense as the space of meaning in which anything is intelligible. When we think of the world in this philosophical way, however, then we have to reverse the formulation and say that the universe or nature is within the world (Heidegger 1982, p. 165), for it is always within the world that the universe or nature is disclosed to us. In this way, the world as the space of meaning has priority in the order of philosophical inquiry and understanding over the universe as represented by empirical science . . . whereas naturalism takes objectivity as its point of departure, phenomenology asks how objectivity is constituted in the first place." Review by Evan Thompson of Havi Carel and Darian Meacham (eds.) *Phenomenology and Naturalism: Examining the Relationship between Human Experience and Nature* Cambridge University Press, 2013 in *Notre Dame Philosophical Review* 10/7/2014, http://ndpr.nd.edu/news/49272-phenomenology-and-naturalism-examining-the-relationship-between-human-experience-and-nature/

4. On system and observer see Niklas Luhmann, *Social Systems* Stanford: Stanford University Press, 1995.

5. Christopher Alexander, "A City is not a Tree," *Architectural Forum* 172, April–May, 1965.

CHAPTER 22
THE THING
Martin Heidegger

Note from editor: Heidegger begins this essay by evoking the new technologies of his era that appear to abolish distance; yet, he says, they do not actually bring things near. This leads him to think on nearness, and ordinary things that are close but overlooked, that we do not really know in themselves. He takes the example of a jug, explaining it as a "thing that things". While his examples are no longer new (airplane, TV) or in the case of the jug, old fashioned, his idea of 'thinging' could be brought to a more recent technological thing like a mobile phone which is both a familiar object and a technology, and which reconfigures 'near and far'.

All distances in time and space are shrinking. Man now reaches overnight, by plane, places which formerly took weeks and months of travel. He now receives instant information, by radio, of events which he formerly learned about only years later, if at all. The germination and growth of plants, which remained hidden throughout the seasons, is now exhibited publicly in a minute, on film. Distant sites of the most ancient cultures are shown on film as if they stood this very moment amidst today's street traffic. Moreover, the film attests to what it shows by presenting also the camera and its operators at work. The peak of this abolition of every possibility of remoteness is reached by television, which will soon pervade and dominate the whole machinery of communication.

Man puts the longest distances behind him in the shortest time. He puts the greatest distances behind himself and thus puts everything before himself at the shortest range.

Yet the frantic abolition of all distances brings no nearness; for nearness does not consist in shortness of distance. What is least remote from us in point of distance, by virtue of its picture on film or its sound on the radio, can remain far from us. What is incalculably far from us in point of distance can be near to us. Short distance is not in itself nearness. Nor is great distance remoteness.

What is nearness if it fails to come about despite the reduction of the longest distances to the shortest intervals? What is nearness if it is even repelled by the restless abolition of distances? What is nearness if, along with its failure to appear, remoteness also remains absent?

What is happening here when, as a result of the abolition of great distances, everything is equally far and equally near? What is this uniformity in which everything is neither far nor near— is, as it were, without distance?

Everything gets lumped together into uniform distancelessness. How? Is not this merging of everything into the distance- less more unearthly than everything bursting apart?

Man stares at what the explosion of the atom bomb could bring with it. He does not see that the atom bomb and its explosion are the mere final emission of what has long since taken place, has already happened. Not to mention the single hydrogen bomb, whose triggering, thought through to its utmost potential, might be enough to snuff out all life on earth. What is this helpless anxiety still waiting for, if the terrible has already happened?

The terrifying is unsettling; it places everything outside its own nature. What is it that unsettles and thus terrifies? It shows itself and hides itself in the way in which everything presences, namely, in the fact that despite all conquest of distances the nearness of things remains absent.

What about nearness? How can we come to know its nature? Nearness, it seems, cannot be encountered directly. We succeed in reaching it rather by attending to what is near. Near to us are what we usually call things. But what is a thing? Man has so far given no more thought to the thing as a thing than he has to nearness. The jug is a thing. What is the jug? We say: a vessel, something of the kind that holds something else within it. The jug's holding is done by its base and sides. This container itself can again be held by the handle. As a vessel the jug is something self-sustained, something that stands on its own. This standing on its own characterizes the jug as something that is self-supporting, or independent. As the self-supporting independence of something independent, the jug differs from an object. An independent, self-supporting thing may become an object if we place it before us, whether in immediate perception or by bringing it to mind in a recollective re-presentation. However, the thingly character of the thing does not consist in its being a represented object, nor can it be defined in any way in terms of the objectness, the over-againstness, of the object.

The jug remains a vessel whether we represent it in our minds or not. As a vessel the jug stands on its own as self- supporting. But what does it mean to say that the container stands on its own? Does the vessel's self-support alone define the jug as a thing? Clearly the jug stands as a vessel only because it has been brought to a stand. This happened during, and happens by means of, a process of setting, of setting forth, namely, by producing the jug. The potter makes the earthen jug out of earth that he has specially chosen and prepared for it. The jug consists of that earth. By virtue of what the jug consists of, it too can stand on the earth, either immediately or through the mediation of table and bench. What exists by such producing is what stands on its own, is self-supporting. When we take the jug as a made vessel, then surely we are apprehending it—so it seems—as a thing and never as a mere object.

Or do we even now still take the jug as an object? Indeed. It is, to be sure, no longer considered only an object of a mere act of representation, but in return it is an object which a process of making has set up before and against us. Its self-support seems to mark the jug as a thing. But in truth we are thinking of this self-support in terms of the making process. Self-support is what the making aims at. But even so, the self-support is still thought of in terms of objectness, even though the overagainstness of what has been put forth is no longer grounded in mere representation in the mere putting it before our minds. But from the objectness of the object, and from the product's self-support, there is no way that leads to the thingness of the thing.

What in the thing is thingly? What is the thing in itself? We shall not reach the thing in itself until our thinking has first reached the thing as a thing.

The jug is a thing as a vessel—it can hold something. To be sure, this container has to be made. But its being made by the potter in no way constitutes what is peculiar and proper to the jug insofar as it is qua jug. The jug is not a vessel because it was made; rather, the jug had to be made because it is this holding vessel.

The making, it is true, lets the jug come into its own. But that which in the jug's nature is its own is never brought about by its making. Now released from the making process, the' self-supporting jug has to gather itself for the task of containing. In the process of its making, of course, the jug must first show its outward appearance to the maker. But what shows itself here, the aspect (the eidos, the idea), characterizes the jug solely in the respect in which the vessel stands over against the maker as something to be made.

But what the vessel of this aspect is as this jug, what and how the jug is as this jug-thing, is something we can never learn—let alone think properly—by looking at the outward appearance, the idea. That is why Plato, who conceives of the presence of what is present in terms of the outward appearance, had no more understanding of the nature of the thing than did Aristotle and all subsequent thinkers. Rather, Plato experienced (decisively, indeed, for the sequel) everything present as an object of making. Instead of "object"—as that which stands before, over against, opposite us—we use the more precise expression "what stands forth." In the full nature of what stands forth, a twofold standing prevails. First, standing forth has the sense of stemming from somewhere, whether this be a process of self-making or of being made by another. Secondly, standing forth has the sense of the made thing's standing forth into the unconcealedness of what is already present.

Nevertheless, no representation of what is present, in the sense of what stands forth and of what stands over against as an object, ever reaches to the thing qua thing. The jug's thingness resides in its being qua vessel. We become aware of the vessel's holding nature when we fill the jug. The jug's bottom and sides obviously take on the task of holding. But not so fast! When we fill the jug with wine, do we pour the wine into the sides and bottom? At most, we pour the wine between the sides and over the bottom. Sides and bottom are, to be sure, what is impermeable in the vessel. But what is impermeable is not yet what does the holding. When we fill the jug, the pouring that fills it flows into the empty jug. The emptiness, the voids is what does the vessel's holding. The empty space, this nothing of the jug, is what the jug is as the holding vessel.

But the jug does consist of sides and bottom. By that of which the jug consists, it stands. What would a jug be that did not stand? At least a jug manqué, hence a jug still—namely, one that would indeed hold but that, constantly falling over, would empty itself of what it holds. Only a vessel, however, can empty itself.

Sides and bottom, of which the jug consists and by which it stands, are not really what does the holding. But if the holding is done by the jug's void, then the potter who forms sides and bottom on his wheel does not, strictly speaking, make the jug. He only shapes the clay. No—he shapes the void. For it, in it, and out of it, he forms the clay into the form. From start to finish the potter takes hold of the impalpable void and brings it forth as the container in the shape of a containing vessel. The jug's void determines all the handling in the process of making the vessel. The vessel's thingness does not lie at all in the material of which it consists, but in the void that holds.

And yet, is the jug really empty?

Physical science assures us that the jug is filled with air and with everything that goes to make up the air's mixture. We allowed ourselves to be misled by a semipoetic way of looking at things when we pointed to the void of the jug in order to define its acting as a container.

But as soon as we agree to study the actual jug scientifically, in regard to its reality, the facts turn out differently. When we pour wine into the jug, the air that already fills the jug is simply displaced by a liquid. Considered scientifically, to fill a jug means to exchange one filling for another.

These statements of physics are correct. By means of them, science represents something real, by which it is objectively controlled. But—is this reality the jug? No. Science always encounters only what its kind of representation has admitted beforehand as an object possible for science.

It is said that scientific knowledge is compelling. Certainly But what does its compulsion consist in? In our instance it consists in the compulsion to relinquish the wine-filled jug and to put in its place a hollow within which a liquid spreads. Science makes the jug-thing into a nonentity in not permitting things to be the standard for what is real.

Science's knowledge, which is compelling within its own sphere, the sphere of objects, already had annihilated things as things long before the atom bomb exploded. The bomb's explosion is only the grossest of all gross confirmations of the long-since-accomplished annihilation of the thing: the confirmation that the thing as a thing remains nil. The thingness of the thing remains concealed, forgotten. The nature of the thing never comes to light, that is, it never gets a hearing. This is the meaning of our talk about the annihilation of the thing. That annihilation is so weird because it carries before it a twofold delusion: first, the notion that science is superior to all other experience in reaching the real in its reality, and second, the illusion that, notwithstanding the scientific investigation of reality, things could still be things, which would presuppose that they had once been in full possession of their thinghood. But if things ever had already shown themselves qua things in their thingness, then the thing's thingness would have become manifest and would have laid claim to thought. In truth, however, the thing as thing remains proscribed, nil, and in that sense annihilated.

This has happened and continues to happen so essentially that not only are things no longer admitted as things, but they have never yet at all been able to appear to thinking as things.

To what is the nonappearance of the thing as thing due? Is it simply that man has neglected to represent the thing as thing to himself? Man can neglect only what has already been assigned to him. Man can represent, no matter how, only what has previously come to light of its own accord and has shown itself to him in the light it brought with it.

What, then, is the thing as thing, that its essential nature has never yet been able to appear?

Has the thing never yet come near enough for man to learn how to attend sufficiently to the thing as thing? What is nearness? We have already asked this question before. To learn what nearness is, we examined the jug near by.

In what does the jug-character of the jug consist? We suddenly lost sight of it—at the moment, in fact, when the illusion intruded itself that science could reveal to us the reality of the jug. We represented the effective feature of the vessel, that which does its holding, the void, as a hollow filled with air. Conceived in terms of physical science, that is what the void really is; but it is not the jug's void. We did not let the jug's void be its own void. We paid no heed to that in the vessel which does the containing. We have given no thought to how the containing itself goes on. Accordingly, even what the jug contains was bound to escape us. In the scientific view, the wine became a liquid, and liquidity in turn became one of the states of aggregation of matter, possible everywhere. We failed to give thought to what the jug holds and how it holds.

How does the jug's void hold? It holds by taking what is poured in. It holds by keeping and retaining what it took in. The void holds in a twofold manner: taking and keeping. The word "hold" is therefore ambiguous. Nevertheless, the taking of what is poured in and the keeping of what was poured belong together. But their unity is determined by the outpouring for which the jug is fitted as a jug. The twofold holding of the void rests on the outpouring. In the outpouring, the holding is authentically how it is. To pour from the jug is to give. The holding of the vessel occurs in the giving of the outpouring. Holding needs the void as that which holds. The nature of the holding void is gathered in the giving. But giving is richer than a mere pouring out. The giving, whereby the jug is a jug, gathers in the twofold holding—in the outpouring. We call the gathering of the twofold holding into the outpouring, which, as a being together, first constitutes the full presence of giving: the poured gift. The jug's jug-character consists in the poured gift of the pouring out. Even the empty jug retains its nature by virtue of the poured gift, even though the empty jug does not admit of a giving out. But this nonadmission belongs to the jug and to it alone. A scythe, by contrast, or a hammer is incapable of a nonadmission of this giving.

The giving of the outpouring can be a drink. The outpouring gives water, it gives wine to drink.

The spring stays on in the water of the gift. In the spring the rock dwells, and in the rock dwells the dark slumber of the earth, which receives the rain and dew of the sky. In the water of the spring dwells the marriage of sky and earth. It stays in the wine given by the fruit of the vine, the fruit in which the earth's nourishment and the sky's sun are betrothed to one another. In the gift of water, in the gift of wine, sky and earth dwell. But the gift of the outpouring is what makes the jug a jug. In the jügness of the jug, sky and earth dwell.

The gift of the pouring out is drink for mortals. It quenches their thirst. It refreshes their leisure. It enlivens their conviviality. But the jug's gift is at times also given for consecration. If the pouring is for consecration, then it does not still a thirst. It stills and elevates the celebration of the feast. The gift of the pouring now is neither given in an inn nor is the poured gift a drink for mortals. The outpouring is the libation poured out for the immortal gods. The gift of the outpouring as libation is the authentic gift. In giving the consecrated libation, the pouring jug occurs as the giving gift. The consecrated libation is what our word for a strong outpouring flow, "gush," really designates: gift and sacrifice. "Gush," Middle English guschen, gosshen—cf. German Guss, giessen—is the Greek cheein, the Indo-european ghu. It means to offer in sacrifice. To pour a gush, when it is achieved in its essence, thought through with sufficient generosity, and genuinely uttered, is to donate, to offer in sacrifice, and hence to give. It is only for this reason that the pouring of the gush, once its nature withers, can become a mere pouring in and pouring out, until it finally decays into the dispensing of liquor at the bar. Pouring the outpour is not a mere filling and decanting.

In the gift of the outpouring that is drink, mortals stay in their own way. In the gift of the outpouring that is a libation, the divinities stay in their own way, they who receive back the gift of giving as the gift of the donation. In the gift of the outpouring, mortals and divinities each dwell in their different ways. Earth and sky dwell in the gift of the outpouring. In the gift of the outpouring earth and sky, divinities and mortals dwell together all at once. These four, at one because of what they themselves are, belong together. Preceding everything that is present, they are enfolded into a single fourfold.

In the gift of the outpouring dwells the simple single foldness of the four.[1]

The gift of the outpouring is a gift because it stays earth and sky, divinities and mortals. Yet staying is now no longer the mere persisting of something that is here. Staying appropriates. It brings the four into the light of their mutual belonging. From out of staying's simple onefoldness they are betrothed, entrusted to one another. At one in thus being entrusted to one another, they are unconcealed. The gift of the outpouring stays the onefold of the fourfold of the four. And in the poured gift the jug presences as jug. The gift gathers what belongs to giving: the twofold containing, the container, the void, and the outpouring as donation. What is gathered in the gift gathers itself in appropriatively staying the fourfold. This manifold- simple gathering is the jug's presencing. Our language denotes what a gathering is by an ancient word. That word is: thing. The jug's presencing is the pure, giving gathering of the one- fold fourfold into a single time-space, a single stay. The jug presences as a thing. The jug is the jug as a thing. But how does the thing presence? The thing things. Thinging gathers. Appropriating the fourfold, it gathers the fourfold's stay, its while, into something that stays for a while: into this thing, that thing.

The jug's essential nature, its presencing, so experienced and thought of in these terms, is what we call thing. We are now thinking this word by way of the gathering-appropriating staying of the fourfold. At the same time we recall the Old High German word *thing*. (......) *thing* means a gathering, and specifically a gathering to deliberate on a matter under discussion, a contested matter. In consequence, the Old German words thing and dinc become the names for an affair or matter of pertinence. They denote anything that in any way bears upon men, concerns them, and that accordingly is a matter for discourse. The Romans called a matter for discourse *res*.(......)

Conversely, in later times, especially in the Middle Ages, the term res serves to designate every ens qua ens, that is, everything present in any way whatever, even if it stands forth and presences only in mental representation as an *ens rationis*. The same happens with the corresponding term thing or dinc; for these words denote anything whatever that is in any way. Accordingly Meister Eckhart uses the word thing (*dinc*) for God as well as for the soul. God is for him the "highest and uppermost thing." The soul is a "great thing." This master of thinking in no way means to say that God and the soul are something like a rock: a material object. ......

Because the word thing as used in Western metaphysics denotes that which is at all and is something in some way or other, the meaning of the name "thing" varies with the interpretation of that which is—of entities. Kant talks about things in the same way as Meister Eckhart and means by this term something that is. But for Kant, that which is becomes the object of a representing that runs its course in the self-consciousness of the human ego. The thing-in-itself means for Kant: the object-in-itself. To Kant, the character of the "in-itself" signifies that the object is an object in itself without reference to the human act of representing it, that is, without the opposing "ob-" by which it is first of all put before this representing act. "Thing-in-itself," thought in a rigorously Kantian way, means an object that is no object for us, because it is supposed to stand, stay put, without a possible before: for the human representational act that encounters it.

Neither the general, long outworn meaning of the term "thing," as used in philosophy, nor the Old High German meaning of the word thing, however, are of the least help to us in our pressing need to discover and give adequate thought to the essential source of what we are now saying about the nature of the jug. However, one semantic factor in the old usage of the word thing, namely "gathering," does speak to the nature of the jug as we earlier had it in mind.

The jug is a thing neither in the sense of the Roman res, nor in the sense of the medieval *ens*, let alone in the modern sense of object. The jug is a thing insofar as it things. The presence of something present such as the jug comes into its own, appropriatively manifests and determines itself, only from the thinging of the thing.

Today everything present is equally near and equally far. The distanceless prevails. But no abridging or abolishing of distances brings nearness. What is nearness? To discover the nature of nearness, we gave thought to the jug near by. We have sought the nature of nearness and found the nature of the jug as a thing. But in this discovery we also catch sight of the nature of nearness. The thing things. In thinging, it stays earth and sky, divinities and mortals. Staying, the thing brings the four, in their remoteness, near to one another. This bringing-near is nearing. Nearing is the presencing of nearness.

Source: "The Thing" [pp 165–82: 4000 words] from *Poetry, Language, Thought* by Martin Heidegger. Translations and Introduction by Albert Hofstadter. Copyright © 1971 by Martin Heidegger. Reprinted by permissions of HarperCollins Publishers.

Note

1. The German Em/alt means simplicity, literally onefoldedness.TR.

CHAPTER 23
MATERIALISM IS NOT THE SOLUTION: ON MATTER AND FORM
Graham Harman

What is matter? What is an object? Scientists can describe an object's physical and chemical properties, an engineer can explain its functioning, as can a biologist if the object is a living thing. But these descriptions do not account for what something is on its own terms. Objects, things, withdraw, they are ultimately unknowable. Graham Harman has made this point in many of his books. Here, in this extract from a longer essay, he sketches two different theories of matter that have come down to us from the Greeks, and argues for the philosophical, rather than scientific, importance of the idea of form.

(....)

The word "form" has several opposites. We speak of form vs. matter, but also of form vs. content and form vs. function. "Matter" is not as versatile, and almost always appears in opposition to form. Whereas form must have some kind of shape – usually a visible one – matter is that which escapes this shape and resists taking on definite contours. This might happen in one of two different ways. Matter can either be some ultimate term into which all derivative shapes break down, as when we say that all physical things are composed of the elements in chemistry's periodic table. But beyond this, matter can also be that which lies in the depth as absolutely formless, an amorphous reservoir more primordial than any definite thing.

This ambiguity defines the two basic types of pre-Socratic philosophy, as Aristotle already noted in the *Metaphysics*. All pre-Socratic philosophy can be described as materialism of one of the two sorts just distinguished. Either it tries to identify some privileged physical element from which everything else is built (air, water, air/earth/fire/water combined, or atoms) or it chooses instead to defend a formless *apeiron* from which all of these elements provisionally emerge. Even today, we find two basic kinds of materialism, both of them deriving from pre-Socratic philosophy. First, there is the materialism beloved by the Marxist and physicalist traditions, in which ultimate material elements are the root of everything and higher-level entities are merely secondary mystifications that partake of the real only insofar as they emerge from the ultimate material substrate. This kind of materialism owes everything to the line of Thales, Anaximenes, Empedocles, and Democritus. It generally has a critical flavor, and thus was preferred by the figures of past and present-day Enlightenment standpoints: even tables, trees, and the brain must be eliminated in favor of the ultimate elements, to say nothing of angels, gods, and folk psychologies.

But second, there is the materialism of the *apeiron*, for which even the physical entities of science are not deep enough since they already have too much particular structure to deserve being called the bottom layer of the cosmos. This brand of materialism inherits the line of Anaximander and Anaxagoras, usually with a bit of Heraclitean flux-loving thrown into the mix. The cosmos is not inherently made of tiny physical pieces, but is an amorphous or hemimorphous whole from which individual pieces arise only as transient local intensities. The world is pre-individual in character, and is made up primarily of fluxes and flows and becomings. The world is basically a continuum, and all attempts to break it into local districts are inherently provisional and relative. This type of materialism is usually not critical in flavor, but tends to be holistic and affirmative. All things are interconnected; emotions and social practices are no less real than the particles which themselves are nothing but a fleeting manifestation of a cosmic whole.

Both standpoints have their merits, but object-oriented philosophy firmly rejects them. Against the two kinds of materialism, object-oriented philosophy insists on the rights of form, as that which has structure at every level of scale, and which cannot be reduced either to a privileged layer of triumphalistic physical being, or to a cosmic holism that treats differences as merely continuous gradients in an uninterrupted, quivering flux. The cat and the table may not be eternal, yet they withstand environmental fluctuation nonetheless, and can gain and lose certain attributes or shift their relations to all other things, while only sometimes being infiltrated or destroyed. The world is made neither of physical ultimates nor of a whole, but of objects, and what most typifies objects is that they always have structure or form. Against Heidegger's veneration for the pre-Socratics, we must say that the task of philosophy begins only when it becomes distinct from the surprisingly similar tasks of physics and of cosmic holism: namely, only when philosophy ends the worship of matter and begins to account for the problem of form. This occurs in distinct ways in Plato and Aristotle, who remain the foundational giants of our discipline and are still the two greatest philosophers of the West.

What is ultimately wrong with the two materialist standpoints, which I often call strategies for "undermining" the object? Their shared defect is their inability to account for true emergence at levels other than the most basic one. Consider a body of water such as Lake Michigan. It may be difficult to specify in geological terms exactly when this lake was formed and when it will have changed so much as to turn into something else completely. But let's suspend that problem for a moment. There is a certain stability to Lake Michigan despite the fact that its population of water molecules is never quite the same. Evaporation occurs constantly. Water splashes ashore with the waves and some of it is lost for good, and the coastline alters slightly. Tourists sometimes pour unwanted drinking water over the side of the boat, augmenting the lake with what used to be the consumer's Evian or Dasani. Some rivers flow directly into the lake. And of course, somewhere it may be raining. While it may never be clear precisely where the lake begins and ends, it is purely arbitrary to claim that the lake is identical with its exact population of water molecules at the moment. The lake has lake-effects not found in individual droplets of water, and might have an endless number of other effects that it does not currently have. The lake has a robust character that withstands the arrival or departure of its individual droplets. The lake has a structure different from the structure of other things. In short, the lake is a form. The scientistic lake would treat it nominalistically as just a nickname for a series of varying collections of water that have enough family resemblances over time that we can call it "Lake Michigan" in a loose and only a loose sense. Meanwhile, the holistic position would treat it as just a zone of relative lakeness, one that is basically continuous with neighboring lakes and with the shore. What both materialisms miss is the way in which the lake cuts itself off from its neighbors and its own causal components, allowing a certain degree of entry and exit to all the forces of the non-lake, but remaining a form that endures for some time even if not eternally. The lake endures until other entities actually do the significant and not inevitable work of destroying or changing it.

Object-oriented philosophy treats objects as forms that do not automatically dissolve back into that from which they came. By contrast, materialism is a reductionism that falls short of the true task of philosophy: the study of the elusive forms which are never identical either to that of which they are made or the ways in which they are described or known. The form of the object is that which hides midway between its material substrate and its concrete manifestation at any given moment in any given context. Forms are hidden in the floorboards of the world, and cannot be known by replacing them with something that seems to be known already: whether it be their constituent material or their effects. In this sense, materialism is a strictly anti-philosophical position, and that is why I have written elsewhere that materialism must be destroyed.[1] Many of the calls for "materialism" today are calls to resume the Enlightenment legacy of critique, in the sense of the debunking of superstition and a critique (from the Left) of existing social institutions. But while this tradition has much to be proud of, it is unclear that we can or should extrapolate it into the future, given the intellectual weakness of the materialism whose banner it waves. The work of debunking and of revolution may need to be transformed rather than extended in view of new intellectual circumstances, or else it risks turning into a moralistic revival movement.

(….)

Source: Graham Harman, 'Materialism is Not the Solution: On Matter, Form, and Mimesis' *The Nordic Journal of Aesthetics* No. 47 (2014), pp. 95-97 of 94–110.

Note

1. Graham Harman, "I Am Also of the Opinion That Materialism Must Be Destroyed," *Society and Space* 28, no. 5 (2010): 772–90. See also Graham Harman, "Realism Without Materialism," *SubStance* 40, no. 2 (2011): 52–72.

CHAPTER 24
IS DESIGN FINISHED? DEMATERIALISATION
AND CHANGING THINGS
Cameron Tonkinwise

Note from editor: Consumerism can be described as an unsustainable flow of materials, products, energy and waste, yet explanations are banal, slating back to human greed, desire for status and the like. This, according to Tonkinwise, explains little about our everyday relation to designed consumer 'stuff' (and it is all designed). We need instead to look at transformations in the nature of everyday things and how those changes have changed our relation to them. This leads him to Heidegger's reading of distinctions made by Aristotle between material and making, time and change, the finished and the unfinished – that can in turn help explain the radical reconfiguration of people's relation to the material stuff of everyday life that conceals its 'being in time' under finished-ness.

> An 'object' is what gets in the way, a problem thrown in your path like a projectile (coming as it does from the Latin objectum, Greek problema)… I come across obstacles in my path (come across the objective, substantial, problematic world); I overturn some of these obstacles (transform them into objects of use, into culture) in order to continue; and the objects thus overturned prove to be obstacles in themselves. The more I continue, the more I am obstructed by objects of use …
>
> Vilém Flusser 'Design: Obstacle for/to the Removal of Obstacles'[1]

How will things end? With things. The world, modern apocalyptic tones sing, will seize up with a surfeit of stuff.[2] An unending stream of products will finish it all off, jamming the workings of the life-flow: a cataclysmic deluge leading to an irreparable breakdown.

Where do all these things come from? From designers, but why? Why do designers keep making things? Why do we keep making designers make more things?

How is it that things just seem to build up in our households? And then in storage spaces that we rent to keep all the things we do not need on a daily basis? Almost imperceptibly, things accumulate. One day we find to our surprise that we have three of the same thing: one old but still working; one not so old but not working; one new but difficult to make work. Or else: one that does one thing; one that does that same thing and something else that we never need; and another that can do that thing and many others if only we knew how. How did we get into this situation? Why are there so many variations of the same thing? Why is it someone's job to search for new things to make, to find inadequacies with some existing thing as a weak premise for designing yet another version of that thing?

In fact, the real issue in regard to the unsustainability of our households is not just the number of things in them at any one time. It is less our standing stock than our throughputs. It is the number of things that pass through our households over time,[3] the linear flow from raw materials to junk of near zero-life products, to use Walter Stahels' terminology.[4] The unsustainable rate of flow in this 'river economy' results less from increasing amounts of disposables like packaging, than the increasing percentages of things we treat as disposables. Semi-durables slide toward single-use, and durables toward semi-disposables. In most of these cases, we are passing on for storage in land-fill not broken, but just redundant things. How is this possible? How is that we spend so little time with things we invest so much in purchasing? How can we without conscience relegate such sophisticated technical materials and devices to abandonment? What are these things that designers design, these things that we desire only to dispose of, these things that seem to disappear the moment they arrive?

Actively relating to things

Thankfully, sociologists are beginning to develop more sophisticated accounts of our relations to the stuff we have derelict about us. Until recently, sociologists were their own worst enemies, borrowing impoverished concepts like 'consumers' from culturally vacuous disciplines like economics to explain 'thing accumulation and flows'. The results were laments about the inevitability of consumerism ('it's human nature to be addicted to novelty'; 'it's the essence of social relations to consume conspicuously'; 'it's the structure of capitalism to amass material property'), when in fact this determinism was only the consequence of such stereotyping.

Instead, recognition is now emerging that everyday life involves a wide variety of purchase, use and disposition processes; some are psychological, some social, some functional; many involve tacitly negotiated combinations of all these domains; nearly all are structured by the particularities of a range of meso-level activities, tasks that are not dissociable from various interrelated products. If things multiply through our households, this has less to do with spectacular moments of consumerism than our many and varied everyday habits: preparing food, entertaining ourselves with or without others, getting to and from people and places, clothing ourselves cleanly for different contexts. I am thinking for example of analyses of 'unconscious consumption' like Elizabeth Shove's *Comfort, Cleanliness and Convenience: The Social Organization of Normality*. Her first chapter is a critique of consumption sociology and sustainability research to date for overemphasising and isolating "moments of acquisition rather than the consequent adjustment of what people do. [Her question is instead] So how does the stuff and substance of consumption relate to the ordering of everyday life and to concepts of normal and proper practice?"[5] Her response is to invoke actor network theory to explain the shifting historical co-configurations of users and their products into distinct patterns of use and disposition.

It is in the context of these recent activity-based accounts of our 'thing relations' that the following was developed. In negotiating things as pragmata, "things insofar as we have to do with them at all, whether we work on them, use them, transform them, or we only look at and examine them,"[6] these accounts have not only surpassed the inadequacies of consumer analyses, but they have also opened up better understandings of the relation of design to the unsustainability of our stocks and flows of stuff.

Mostly without knowing it, these accounts of the everyday purchase, use, neglect and disposal of things derive from the phenomenology of lived practice initiated by Martin Heidegger's existential analytic. Things in that account are first of all networked equipment manifesting only within the 'in-order-to' of certain activities. However, whilst these recent more praxeological accounts of household consumption take up a Heideggerian perspective, there is level to which they are yet to proceed. Without moving to that level, which probably means explicitly negotiating their Heideggerian heritage, what these analyses have to say does not add up. Their case studies of the plurality of everyday thing relations do not yet go to answering the questions with which I began, about the net volume of things that our houses hold for more or less time. So what follows is an attempt to outline what an analysis at that level entails. It is an attempt to explicate the thingliness of the things designed for us to use each day. It tries to show how that thingliness makes possible, and even necessary, things made for long lives yet limited use, things that can therefore accumulate, whether in our houses or in landfills, without us even caring.

Mis-taking things

In the hierarchy of things from which I just cited, Heidegger asserts that *pragmata* is second last to *mathémata*. This more fundamental level of thinking about things is crucial, Heidegger believes, for understanding the state of things in our world today. His 1935-6 lecture course on 'The Question Concerning the Thing' argues that Kant completes a shift, effected in large part by Newtonian physics, in the meaning of the mathematical that essentially moves things from the realm of the qualitative to the quantitative. Eytmologically, the mathematical refers not to numbers and the algebraic or geometric, but rather to "things insofar as we learn them" or rather "things insofar as we take cognizance of them as what we already know them to be in advance" Things can only be encountered as things if there is prior characterisation of them as some sort of thing. "The mathematical is that evident aspect of things within which we are always already moving and according to which we experience them as things at all, and as such things. The mathematical is the fundamental position we take toward things by which we take up things as already given to us, and as they should be given. Therefore, the mathematical is the fundamental presupposition of the knowledge of things."[7]

So the mathematical is the fore-understanding by which things come to be the things we experience them as. If things are experienced pragmatically, as being(s)-of-use, this way of being a thing derives from a particular 'mathematics' of things. According to Heidegger, this is in fact the original Greek mathematics of things. Whilst we today still do live with things within this mathematics, this is not how we explicitly think about things. Modern things by contrast are distanced from practical experience. They are instead taken to be mere manifestations of abstract systems of physics and chemistry. We moderns, after Galileo, Newton, Descartes and Kant, 'experience' things as so many substitutable examples of certain properties and relations. Ancient anticipatory learning has become modern projective instruction, "a project (*Entwurf*) of thingness which, as it were, skips over things... a basic blueprint [that] at the same time provides the measure for laying out of the realm, which, in the future, will encompass all things of that sort".[8] Engagement with particular things through practical understanding of their distinct qualities is thereby replaced by designed calculations of numbers of things. To be crude, customised thingly relations are replaced by mass production.

This account of the changing mathematics of things is an elaboration of the account in *Being and Time* of the shift from praxis to theoria, from 'how-to'-based concern with the ready-to-hand to 'what is' observatory operations on the present-at-hand.[9] And, in nascent form, this account of the changing mathematics of things links also to Heidegger's later critique of technology where, beneath the imperialism of instrumental reason, things lose their engaged specificity and are instead quantified as mere means to unquestioned ends.[10]

However, this last linkage is too quick a paraphrase of Heidegger's critical account of the technological metaphysic. It is a misinterpretation that glosses over precisely the issue of things. It suggests that the accumulation and flows of things through our households is the result of instrumentalism. Pure instrumentalism though should, in all efficiency, aim to involve no things at all. According to this understanding of Heidegger's critique, as we become more enthralled by technology we should become literally more metaphysical. We should have less and less to do with material things as we become more concerned with the modern sense of the mathematical: the digital, information, systems. But instead we find the opposite. Thus a merely instrumentalist understanding of technology cannot explain this incessant materialisation.

This mistaken version of Heidegger is particularly pertinent at this moment when sustainability researchers have begun promoting the design of sustainable service-systems as a strategy for lowering the material intensities of our societies.[11] These service-systems aim to deliver functional results with the minimum material inputs over time. Whilst to a naïve Heideggerian these service-systems might appear to be worrying exemplars of technological Gestell, the dangerous enframing of all beings within sheer functionality, the immediate outcome of such an enframing, according to such a reading, should indeed be dematerialisation. Being-in-the-world could, according to this inadequate understanding of Heidegger, through service-system design, become a thingless process, a situation in which things become completely efficient substrates satisfying changing human wills. However, with a more thorough understanding of Heidegger, particularly of the fact that Heidegger's critique of technology emerges from his account of thingliness, functional innovations through service-systems can be read as one of those predictions — like those of the coming service society, information revolution, knowledge economy, or post-materialist values — that will be buried beneath so much stuff.

To put this another way, if the abridged Heidegger-on-technology account is too broad — and in fact not dissimilar to the stereotyping of consumerism — and yet the pluralist pragmatic account of everyday consumption activities too narrow, what lies between is in fact design. The *mathémata* that structure our *pragmata* result not only in *chrémata* "things insofar as they are in use and therefore stand at our constant disposal", but also *poioúmena*, "things insofar as they are produced by the human hand and stand as such." And it is within the ontology of making, the *techné* of *poiesis* that a certain *mathémata* takes place that accounts for things as they accumulate and flow unsustainably today. But to access this, *poioúmena* must be compared with the last (or in fact first) category of things, *phusiká*.

Finishing things off

Martin Heidegger's 1939 essay "On the essence and concept of *Phüsis* in Aristotle's Physics B I"[12] is helpful in this matter. Heidegger's essay aims to recover a sense of *kinesis* or 'movedness' as the essence of all being.[13] Most radically, Heidegger tries to demonstrate that, in terms of *phüsis*; all things are in motion, especially those concrete everyday things which we moderns think are 'at rest':

> But are bedsteads and garments, shields and houses moving things? Indeed they are, but usually we encounter them in the kind of movement that typifies things at rest and therefore is hard to perceive. Their 'rest' has the character of having-been-completed, having-been-produced, and, on the basis of these determinations, as standing 'there' and lying present before. Today we easily overlook this special kind of rest and so too the movedness that corresponds to it, or at least, we do not take it essentially enough as the proper and distinguishing characteristic of the being of these beings. And why? Because under the spell of our modern way of being, we are addicted to thinking of beings as objects and allowing the being of beings to be exhausted in the objectivity of the object. (192)

What we today call 'nature' is not that which makes itself, as opposed to everything else which is the product of human making, i.e. the 'artefactual', because *phüsis* is in no way a form of making. The difference lies not in who or what does the making, but between the completed product of making and what just is.

Now, in typical Heidegger fashion, this distinction is the opposite of what it at first seems. In terms of movedness, the previous quotation indicated that things that are a result of *poiesis* or (human) making, e.g., bedsteads and the like, are at rest. They lie present (are pre-sent), finished. By contrast, *phüsical* things just are, but in a way that manifests a dynamic presence (a presencing). Far from being cast as something permanently present, *phüsis* must be understood as always already in formation; at any one time *phüsical* things are capable of being some things and resisting being others; at every moment they are becoming and withdrawing (at the same time, i.e. becoming X by withdrawing from being Y).

Heidegger notes that to 'lead the way toward' this sense of being *phüsically*, Aristotle invented a term: *entelécheia*. Heidegger translates this term as 'holding (echei) itself (en) in its end (telos)' (217). Again, meaning the opposite of the way it is immediately read, *entelécheia* designates not that which has reached its end, as if its end were different from what it has, up until that time, been, but that which is, at all times in its becoming, what it is and aims to be. With this term, a clear distinction can now be drawn between the outcomes of *techné* and *phüsis*.

A table is not a table until it is finished. It is not what it aims to be (its *telos*) until it is completed (by a maker, *arché*, who also happens to lie outside it, but this is merely contingent, not axial to what differentiates *phüsical* and technical things). When it is done, when the making is over, the table (as opposed to the *phüsical* wood — this is the whole point, so I will come back to this) has no becoming but instead is finished. It is (at) an end; it is 'finishedly'. This is very different to a tree, which is never over and done with. It is always still on-the-move.[14] However, though forever 'on the way', it is nevertheless always also what it aims to be. Though never completed, the tree is at every moment complete as a tree. Even when a sapling, a seedling, or a seed, and also when rotting wood, it is never (at) an end, but rather has its end as and in what it is.[15] Where *techné* aims to finish (making) something, *phüsis* involves things being sustained, that is, the maintenance of things, in their changingness, continuing their change, or their continuance by changing themselves.

Disposing of what is taken for granted

Heidegger's efforts at recovering the Aristotlean sense of *phüsis* are undertaken out of a fear that we moderns are losing our ability to affirm the movedness of that which is in a state of becoming. A propensity to see everything as technical, as if it had all been produced (i.e. the product of a Creator), casts things into certain (Platonic) metaphysics of presentness. The danger in mis-seeing everything about us as only products is that every thing is then mis-taken as being finished, as completely static. We stop seeing things in motion, or motion in all things, and instead see only objects. What is problematic is less seeing everything as a mere means, than seeing everything as an end; or rather, things can only be exploited as mere means if they appear to have no inherent process of their own, if their becoming is thought to have ended. These products are reduced to being just what they are, that is, just how they are now, in the present.

This then is why Heidegger must remind us of the in-time-ness of being. As the technical producer of things, humans seem to let all that they encounter lapse into being merely beings, things just present, as if outside time. These 'out-of-time' things tend to be merely present things, not impressively there, shining forth in their thereness at the moments when they are here. This is because their not-always-having-been- and not-always-will-be-hereness is also not being noticed; the way these things are only whiling here, their phüsical coming-to-be and unbecoming, is not acknowledged as being also there along with them. To this extent, produced things, as finished, as merely present, lose their having-been-produced-ness. They are alienated from their production and reified as sheer stuff. In other words, the very nature of production is to erase itself by its outcome. The result of *poiesis* are things that deny their *poietic* nature. As such, as just present things, now here as if from nowhere, these things become constantly present, there at hand, to be added or multiplied as so much maths, to accumulate or flow without anybody taking care of them.

In another essay from the same period,[16] Heidegger explains this 'constancy' via Rilke:

> The objectiveness [Gegenständige] of the world becomes constant [ständig] in representational production… In this, it is true, there is another transformation of things into the inward and invisible.

However, this transformation substitutes for the frailty of things the factitious constructions of calculated objects. These objects are produced for consumption. The more quickly they are consumed, the more necessary it becomes to replace them ever more quickly and easily. That which is enduring about the presence of objective things is not their resting-in-themselves in their own world. What is constant about things produced as mere objects of consumption is the substitute [Ersatz].

I have cited extensively here because it is crucial to see the particular way in which the technical making of things leads both to the permanent materialisation of things and to the unceasing generation of things of only passing significance. It is the very finishedness of modern-(un)made things, the way they are cast out into the world as from then on unchanging, that, far from granting them long lives, destines them to be a never finished stream of short use-life objects requiring mathematical systems of collection, storage and disposal. They can be cycled through in a relay of never complete means only because they are technical end(ing)s. In this context, consumerism does not drive manufacturing, rather manufacturing drives consumption; not in the sense that the machinery of capitalism forces us to consume its products (through advertising for example, or design), but in the sense that making complete things (like the design of any product), making things whose thingliness lies in their completeness, in their being finished objects, leads to things of no particular lasting value. For the same reason, it is not the abstraction of mathematics, the calculative worldview of modern science, that strews our world with stuff; rather, it is the project of making things end that makes possible an abstractly quantitative way of dealing with all that results; theoretical science is a consequence of seeing things as inert products.

Sustaining things while presenced

Now, all this is how things are treated, but it is not how they are. As Heidegger famously revealed in *Being and Time*, we are constantly surprised by things not being constantly there for us. We only notice things' being, and the being of *poioúmena* as having-been-produced, when they break down. At these times, products re-assert their being-in-time, withdrawing *phüsically* from the technical system into which they have been requisitioned. I say *phüsically* because these moments that defy the finishedness of things manifest the materiality of things — or more, precisely, manifest things as alive, as matter-in-motion, energised, *entelechially* underway.

This has frustrating consequences for our no-time-out economy, but our anguish on these occasions evidences the extent to which we expect and depend upon products being unchangingly perfect. If we were Pre-socratics, we would, according to Heidegger, consider such wear and tear the norm rather than the exception; we would live in the awareness that it is the nature of all things to egress, evade and elude, rather than stay put, no matter how technologically sophisticated we get.[17] And in fact, if we were Ancient Greeks, so tolerant would we be of this withdrawal of things that we would consider products of *poiesis* to be merely at rest, not unmoving, merely whiling in a particular presence, rather than permanently present; finished in a particular way, but in no way entirely complete, or wholly at an end.

In short, to be Greek about things would mean actively sustaining things, paying respect to the things we have brought to presence with and for us, by preserving them while they are here. Exactly as modern overemphases of products' permanence means that that things are ignored, neglected, stored in places we never go or accelerated through our households as quickly as possible, so ancient awareness of products' impermanence means spending time with things, maintaining and repairing them, sustaining them.

We are now in a position to see why this engagement with Heidegger on things is significant. Only a consideration of the mathematical level of things as finished products explains both how consumerism is possible and why it is unsustainable. Consumerism emerges as a fundamental inability to sustain things. It is a refusal to acknowledge that artificial things remain natural to the extent that they are within time, aging. It is refusal to see that making does not make things permanent, but only ever holds things as particular sorts of things for particular periods of time. It is a refusal that cannot not leave refuse in its wake.

Further, only such a thingly account of our societies can explain why the things we use in our changing everyday activities increasingly take the paradoxical form of disposable durables. Without considering the mathematics of made things, one could expect that that things would conform to the activities for which they are used, changing when the activity changed, or being changeable, that is, maintainable and repairable, when the activity stayed the same. With a consideration of the mathematics of made things it is understandable why there should be such a mismatch between service-life of materials and components and actual product use-lives, why 'planned obsolescence' can be a design strategy in a way that 'waste management' or 'refurbishment, remanufacturing, recovery' never can. Plastic for example, that quintessential disposable durable can now be explained as the perfect technical product.

All this now also fits with several points about contemporary approaches to sustainability that were mentioned in passing at the outset. Firstly, our unsustainable contemporary notion of things makes predictable that post-industrial societies would be characterised not by the replacement of things but rather the mere displacement of things. The production of things could not just end but was bound to rebound, finding more ways to 'continue thinging completely'. Secondly, this is why the unsustainability of things lies in both the stock of things in each of our households and the flow of things through those households. Stocking and flowing are the same thing if things are never-ending ends.

Thirdly, PSS (product service systems) design will be another thing to get rid of unless it is explicitly an engagement with the timing of things. This means that PSS design must focus on what is being categorised as 'product-oriented services', services that aim to extend and/or intensify the use-life of things.[18] To put this in terms of households, given that shortening product use lives are one of the most unsustainable things about our everyday lives, our materials intensity can be reduced by slowing the throughput of things, by making things last longer. Given that increased material inputs to a product are one of the most direct ways of enhancing durability, this means that, given sufficiently designed product life extension, rematerialisation can be a dematerialisation strategy. From the mathematico-philosophic point of view, the most directly unsustainable thing about our households is the throughput of disposable durables, and so the only appropriate strategy consequently is the re-thing-ification of things, that is to say, the re-temporalisation of things.

Servicing imperfectly moving things

Heidegger's Aristotelian brief awaiting designers in the age of a surfeit of stuff is then clear. Design timely things, things that can last longer by being able to change over time. Design things that are not finished, things that can keep on by keeping on being repaired and altered, things in motion.

Importantly, this is a different brief to the perennial exhortations for quality design. Calls for product-life extension by design have echoed throughout the twentieth century from the Werkbund, through Vance Packard and the Committee for Terotechnology, to EternallyYours.[19] In many ways each of these, and many others, was advocating still, or even more so, perfect things [per-ficere: to bring to an end]. The cliché of the design classic signals exactly that its objective is an ahistorical, timeless product. The contemporary, purely technical version of this mathematics aims at the unchanging through nano-technology — the self-repairing, self-altering, self-reproducing. (Plastic; artificial intelligence; nuclear energy; how many of these promethean moments must we continue to fail to learn from?)

By contrast, the Heideggerian brief is for the imperfect product, the product that must be continuously improved, the product that is always still under development, a work in progress. Or more precisely, product-plus:[20] a process that takes responsibility for the fact that the product in its present manifestation, in its materiality, is not the be-all-and-end-all, but must be actively sustained. As indicated in the previous section, this is a PSS, but one that exists to enhance rather than distance things.

An instructive version of this kind of brief was provided by Abraham Moles in the late '80s (in English), before the discourse of sustainability was established. Moles was not writing from a Heideggerian context of course, but instead responding to hopes of a coming post-industrial society with the uncharacteristic realisation that "Any immaterial civilization will be heavily materialized because its immaterial products are necessarily linked to the mechanical infrastructure that generates, stabilizes and governs them".[21] Moles recognized that "The immaterial civilization must be reliable" (27), and that that reliability comes not from creating "new' objects' (31) but from "a maintenance mentality" (26).

In another article, Moles concretizes what this poietic mathematics would entail with a proposal for "The Comprehensive Guarantee"[22]: that all bills of sale be accompanied by a contract ensuring not only full repair whenever needed but also compensation for inconvenience and loss of product use time. Prescient of current arguments about 'extended producer responsibility', Moles foresaw that such a performance contract would reflect back upon the design process. Designing products for servicized use-life extension means "tak[ing] into account the micropsychological analysis of the object/user binome and deduc[ing] from each aspect of this interaction not only the conditions in which the object will fulfil what was traditionally called its function, but also the conditions of its *permanence* [my italics] with respect to the role it is to play in the life of the user" (64). The task for designers then according to Moles is to design the sustainment of what they design; to design not just some thing, but also the conditions through which that thing has a presence over time as a thing; that is to say, to design how a thing things.

Overcoming product fixation

What is at issue is not whether designers are capable of designing nothings rather than things, that is to say, services rather than products, but rather whether designers are capable of designing things that are not finished. It is less a matter of designing a different sort of thing than a matter of a thoroughly different form of designing, one that is perhaps better described as form of 'continuous design' or 'redesigning'.[23]

There is at first the psychological obstacle to this imperfectionism. Nuri Bilgin, in an article upon which Moles relies for much of what he advocates in relation to the 'comprehensive guarantee', points out that maintenance tends to work against certain psychological theories that argue that "any motivation toward completing a task engenders tension, which is usually relaxed only when the task has been accomplished. Now, since prevention is carried out without perceptible stimuli and without a direct goal, this state of tension persists, and the preventive action may bring about permanent frustration."[24] In other words, would designers find satisfying enough the production of incomplete products to complete the process of designing, creatively?

But more pertinent to this article is the ontology of designing. If designing is making par excellence, the project of pre-determin(at)ing what is to be made present, what can be considered actually complete when that form is materialized, then designing is mathematical in the modern sense through and through. A designing that could generate other sorts of changing things, things other than blueprinted ends, would no longer be a form a de-signing. So perhaps it is time that we finished designing.

Source: *Design Philosophy Papers Collection Two*, ed. A. M. Willis, 2005, pp. 20–30.

Notes

1. Vilem Flusser *The Shape of Things: A Philosophy of Design* London: Reaktion 1999: 58, 61.

2. For example, Worldwatch Institute *State of the World 2004: The Consumer Society* Washington: Worldwatch Institute, 2004.

3. K. Noorman and T. Uiterkamp (eds) *Green households? Domestic Consumers, Environment, and Sustainability* London : Earthscan, 1998.

4. For example, W. Stahel 'The Utilization-focused Service Economy: Resource Efficiency and Product-Life Extension' in B. Allenby (ed) *The Greening of Industrial Ecosystems* Washington: National Academy Press, 1994.

5. Elizabeth Shove *Comfort, Cleanliness and Convenience: The Social Organisation of Normality* Oxford: Berg, 2003, 14.

6. Martin Heidegger *What is a Thing?* trans. W.Barton Jr. Chicago: Henry Regnery, 1967, 70. In what follows I am deliberately working through Heidegger's lesser known analysis of 'things' in this lecture course rather than his more famous earlier account of equipment in *Being and Time* and his later work on the "The Thing" as a fourfold. I am also working elsewhere through Heidegger's account of the thingliness of art in 'The Origin of the Work of Art,' a lecture contemporary with the What is a Thing? course. See Walter Biemel's 'The Development of Heidegger's Concept of the Thing' *The Southwestern Journal of Philosophy* n.XI (1980) 47–64.

7. Heidegger *op cit* 71, 73, 75.

8. Ibid, 96. *Entwurf* is perhaps better translated into English as 'design'.

9. See Section 69 b in Division II, Part IV, 357–64 (original pagination).

10. The relation between Heidegger's early account of equipment and later account of technology has been explored by Hubert Dreyfus in 'Heidegger's History of the Being of Equipment' in H. Dreyfus & H. Hall (eds) *Heidegger: A Critical Reader* Oxford: Blackwell, 1992. In relation to design, see also Carl Mitcham's 'Dasein versus Design: The Problematics of Turning Making into Thinking' *International Journal of Technology and Design Education* no.11 (2001).

11. For the current state-of-the-art see the reports of the EU funded PSS thematic network, SusProNet at www.suspronet.org.

12. A most recent translation is in W. McNeill (ed) *Pathmarks* Cambridge: Cambridge University Press, 1998. Page numbers are given in brackets in the text throughout this section.

13. *Phüsis* is conventionally translated as nature, and whilst Aristotle is primarily discussing 'nature' in the sense of 'living non-human things', the Ancient Greek can refer to all beings, as in the phrase 'the nature of all things' and Heidegger exploits this fact.

14. At other times, for example in 'The Origin of the Work of Art' Heidegger promotes the more common term *energeia* (at work — *ergon*) rather than *entelecheia* to capture the moving-being of what is *phusical*. *Energeia* is the co-dependent obverse of *dünamis*; it releases what is harboured as *dünamis* and vice versa. An image that Heidegger uses to explain this is the sprinter in the starting blocks, who is dynamically at rest, and, in many ways more energised than when she lets go and simply lets that energetically carry her to the end of the race. The sprinter is *entelechially* still a sprinter, or more precisely sprinting, even if not yet actually sprinting down the track. See Heidegger's lecture course *Aristotle's Metaphysics Theta 1-3: On the Essence and Actuality of Force* Bloomington: Indiana University Press, 1995.

15. Findeli reminds us that being able to see this 'metamorphosis,' being able to see the flower in the seed, is what defines the seeing beyond seeing (what is merely a temporal appearance) — or rather seeing before seeing, mathematically — that Goethe calls aesthetic intuition and which inspired much Bauhaus pedagogy . See 'Bauhaus Education and After: Some Critical Reflections' *The Structurist* vol.31–2 (1991–2), 32–43.

16. 'Why Poets' in J. Young, and K. Haynes (trans & eds) *Off the Beaten Track* Cambridge: Cambridge University Press, 2002, 228, 231.

17. This is one of Heidegger's many ways of translating the 'Anaximander Fragment', taken here from the 1941 course, *Basic Concepts* Bloomington: Indiana University Press, 1993,102.

18. This is the first of three ways of categorising PSSs according to the consensus position of SusProNet, the others being 'use-oriented services' such as leasing and sharing, and 'result-oriented services' such as performance contracts and no-build options or negawatts.

19. Vance Packard's *The Wastemakers* (1961) made design synonomous with 'planned obsolescence.' The Committee for Terotechology was an initiative of the UK Department of Industry in 1975 aimed at promoting planned maintenance: OECD *Product Durability and Product Life Extension: Their Contribution to Solid Waste Management* 1982. For an archive of the project of EternallyYours see: www.eternally-yours.com.

20. I have taken this title from a 'next-big-thing' management text: Christopher Lovelock's *Product Plus: How Product + Service = Competitive Advantage* New York: McGraw-Hill, 1994.

21. A. Moles 'Design and Immateriality: What of it in a Post Industrial Society' *Design Issues* vol.4 no.s 1–2 (1988). Page references follow in brackets in the text in this paragraph.

22. A. Moles 'The Comprehensive Guarantee: A New Consumer Value' *Design Issues* vol.2 no.1 (1985). Page references follow in brackets in the text in this paragraph.

23. I am referring here to John Chris Jones article 'Continuous Design and Redesign' *Design Studies* vol.4 no.1 (January 1983). Though I am also reminded of Raymond Loewy's *Never Leave Well Enough Alone*.

24. Nuri Bilgin 'From an Industrial Society to a Maintenance Society' *Impact of Science on Society* vol.30 no.2 (1980), p.129. This reminds me, despite the severe disparity in contexts, of Christopher Alexander's concept of 'repair'. In Reyner Banham (ed) *Aspen Papers* London: Pall Mall, 1974, Alexander advocates what might be called 'design for continual fine adjustment' (93). In *A Timeless Way of Building* New York: Oxford University Press, 1979, Alexander differentiates the "patching, conservative, static" type of repair, returning things to their timeless "original state", from one that assumes "that every entity is changing constantly", in which case repair is "creative, dynamic and open", transforming what is being repaired into *entelechial* "new wholes" (485).

CHAPTER 25
BEYOND AFFORDANCES
Michael May

Note from editor: A brief history of the concept of 'affordance' is presented here, as well as discussion of its appeal to designers, with the author arguing against the claim of direct perception of usability. In one direction, his observations connect with a longstanding debate on the merits or otherwise of designing for 'intuitive use'. In another direction, the idea of 'direct perception of affordance' becomes problematic when placed in the context of philosophical questions on meaning, perception and representation.

In the last 20 years the concept of *affordance* have found its way into theories of industrial design, architecture and interface design for Human-Computer Interaction (HCI). The official history of the concept is that it was introduced by James Gibson, who challenged established perceptual psychology - from its origin in the work of Herman Helmholtz to recent "information processing" approaches to cognitive science, by turning away from experimental settings in order to attempt to understand how animals perceive the world according to the functional constraints within their natural environment.[1] The approach is called *ecological perception* and the focus have been on the idea of a *direct perception* of the "affordances" of objects in the natural environment in the sense that animals and humans can somehow directly "pick up" information about the action-related potentials of objects and events in our environment without any need for representation and inferential cognition: we "directly see" that a particular stone affords throwing or a particular hill affords climbing.

The concept of affordance was picked up by Donald Norman and made available for HCI and the industrial design community.[2] The concept is appealing to designers because it expresses a kind of *natural ideal of design*, i.e. that the intended use of artifacts should be intuitively easy to understand without any explanatory help. If animals rely on direct perception of affordances as they move around in their natural environments, we as humans should be able to use artifacts of our cultural environment by relying on the designed affordances of the technology, e.g. from the handle on the coffee cup to the remote control for the TV. The concept of designed affordances of artifacts was appealing to the HCI community, because it was launched at the time of the general improvement in graphical interfaces and in harmony with important principles like the *direct manipulation interfaces*.[3] For industrial designers affordances can seem like a modern version of the normative aesthetics of modern industrial design and architecture as expressed in the catch phrase "form follows function". If artifacts are designed to meet this norm, they should "express" their intended use functions more or less directly to the observer.

.... the concept of affordance, as well as the project of "ecological psychology" to which it belongs, is highly problematic from a philosophical point of view in its attempt to bypass all problems of representation and inferential cognition. But at least it seems to be useful in orienting practical design, or so it seems. It has even been stated that the ecological approach is preferred not because it is a true theory of perception compared to classical theories, but because of its pragmatic role in inspiring new ideas in design and aesthetics.[4] This however amounts to articulating the ecological approach as a kind of "theoretical ideology" that might be maintained against better knowledge!

(....)

The "direct perception" of affordances

Although the concept of affordance is always ascribed to Gibson, he is himself well aware that the idea actually originated in the work of Kurt Lewin, who sketched a new branch of Gestalt psychology that he called "Topological Psychology".[5] In an early paper based on his experience as a German solider in WW1, he made an observation about the relation of human agents to the environment in the form of the "landscape of war".[6] For the soldier a familiar object in the countryside like a building would take on an immediate meaning different from the usual one because of its functional role as a potential hiding places or place of an enemy attack. Lewin realized that objects in the spatial environment have a certain "suggestive character" (Aufforderungscharakter) that depends on our present goals and *intentional relations* to the spatial environment. The house "suggests" to the soldier that it can be a place of hiding or attack, although it "suggests" to the farmer who lives there that it is a home, a dwelling place and a shelter. Buildings "afford" these actions and activities based on the physical and geometric properties of buildings, but *a particular affordance is however only meaningful within an actual relation to an agent who selects it* (in the jargon of Gibson: who "picks up information" about the affordance).

The reason why affordances seem to appeal to designers and design engineers could be that we (as humans) experience functions and meanings of artifacts as immediately given within our embodied experience and within our lived relation with the world. Artifacts appear as directly meaningful to us and seem to "suggest" how they could be used. It does however not follow that this phenomenal experience is not mediated by cultural and cognitive representations and schemata, and we are not forced to adopt a radical anti-representationalist view on meanings and functions. In fact it is difficult to see how we could explain any mechanism of "direct perception" of affordances, without relying on some kind of inferential cognition from the kind of properties of objects and events that we can actually perceive (given our perceptual organs). As Jerry Fodor have remarked, "being-a-chair" is not the kind of property we can directly perceive, but we can infer that some object "affords" sitting from the physical and geometric properties that we do perceive, but this is a meaningful inference and certainly not something given in direct perception.[7]

Furthermore it is a problem, if we reduce the meaning of artifacts to their function. Instead of a dual theory of the structure and function of artifacts[8] we should endorse a triadic theory of artifacts, i.e. separating *form, function and meaning*. Instead of an "ecological turn" in design theory, we could support a "semantic turn".[9] From a semiotic point of view Roland Barthes claimed in his early writings that every artifact is also a sign – at least in the minimal sense of being a sign of its own use.[10] Any artifact, e.g. a raincoat, necessarily becomes a sign of its own use, but this minimal functional meaning is however a reduction of the meaning of an artifact to its design and use functions. In any actual social and cultural context of use, artifacts will acquire additional meaning from the *network of relations and actions* they are involved in, and from the *discourses regulating and articulating these activities*. Even simple artifacts cannot avoid acquiring meanings beyond use functions and design functions, e.g. as a commodity and a type of clothing a raincoat will necessarily express a particular style and communicate intentions, values and meanings to other agents.

A final point that is sometimes overlooked in discussions about the value of the affordance concept for industrial design and HCI is that the dogma of direct perception makes it difficult to account for *mistakes and misperceptions about the meaning and function of artifacts*. The nature of our mistakes is important for theories about the design and use of artifacts. If our understanding of use functions is given in direct perception and not as a result of inferences based on our fallible knowledge, intuition and experience, it is however difficult to see how these mistakes arise. In HCI some researchers[11] have introduced the idea of "hidden" affordances and "false" affordances, but this begs the question, since hidden and false affordances will undermine the idea of direct unmediated perception and highlight the necessity of reasoning about cultural artifacts and their appearance as well as the necessity of human agents to negotiate their meaning and function within specific social activities. ….

Source: Extract from 'Beyond Affordances – Why direct perception is not enough in design engineering' by Michael May © CEPHAD 2010 conference.

Notes

1. J. Gibson *The Senses Considered as Perceptual Systems*, George Allen, 1968 and J. Gibson *The Ecological Approach to Visual Perception*, LEA, 1986.
2. D. A. Norman *The Design of Everyday Things* Doubleday, 1990.
3. B. Shneiderman 'Direct manipulation: a step beyond programming languages' *IEEE Computer* vol 16, no 8, 1983, 57–69; E. Hutchins, J. D. Hollan and D. Norman 'Direct manipulation interfaces' in D. Norman and S. Draper (eds) *User Centered System Design* LEA, 1986.
4. G. Smets and K. Overbeeke 'Industrial design engineering and the theory of direct perception' *Design Studies* vol 15, no 2, 1994, 175–84.
5. Gibson, *The Ecological Approach to Visual Perception*, p. 138; K. Lewin *Principles of Topological Psychology* McGraw-Hill, 1936.
6. K. Lewin 'Kriegslandschaften' in C. F. Grauman (Hg.) *Kurt Lewin Werkausgabe, Band 4: Feldtheorie*, [1983] Huber/Cotta, pp. 315–25.
7. J. Fodor and Z. Pylyshyn 'How direct is visual perception? Some reflections on Gibsons "Ecological Appproach"' *Cognition* vol 9, 1981, 139–96.
8. P. Kroes and A. Meijers 'The dual nature of technical artefacts' *Studies in the History and Philosophy of Science* vol 37, 2006, 1–4.
9. K. Krippendorff *The Semantic Turn. A New Foundation for Design*. Taylor & Francis, 2006.
10. R. Barthes *Elements of Semiology*. Jonathan Cape, 1967.
11. W. Gaver 'Technology affordances' *Proceedings of the CHI 91 Human Factors in Computing Systems Conference*, ACM, 1991, pp. 79–84.

CHAPTER 26
UNDERSTANDING, ONTOLOGY, THROWNNESS AND READINESS-TO-HAND
Terry Winograd and Fernando Flores

Note from editor: In this extract from their influential book, Understanding Computers and Cognition, *Winograd and Flores explain the extent to which we are formed in cultures that form "our very way of experiencing and living in language (such that) it cannot be made fully explicit in that language". Yet this doesn't mean total determinism as they show in their exposition of Gadamer's hermeneutics. Their text also shows the limits of rationalistic explanations of human cognition, and how understanding is immersed in concrete situations of concernful activity amidst worldly things, rather than contemplative reason being the default condition of human being.*

Understanding and ontology

Gadamer, and before him Heidegger, took the hermeneutic idea of interpretation beyond the domain of textual analysis, placing it at the very foundation of human cognition. Just as we can ask how interpretation plays a part in a person's interaction with a text, we can examine its role in our understanding of the world as a whole.

Heidegger and Gadamer reject the commonsense philosophy of our culture in a deep and fundamental way. The prevalent understanding is based on the metaphysical revolution of Galileo and Descartes, which grew out of a tradition going back to Plato and Aristotle. This understanding, which goes hand in hand with what we have called the 'rationalistic orientation,' includes a kind of mind-body dualism that accepts the existence of two separate domains of phenomena, the objective world of physical reality, and the subjective mental world of an individual's thoughts and feelings. Simply put, it rests on several taken-for-granted assumptions:

1. We are inhabitants of a 'real world' made up of objects bearing properties. Our actions take place in that world.

2. There are 'objective facts' about that world that do not depend on the interpretation (or even the presence) of any person.

3. Perception is a process by which facts about the world are (sometimes inaccurately) registered in our thoughts and feelings.

4. Thoughts and intentions about action can somehow cause physical (hence real-world) motion of our bodies.

Much of philosophy has been an attempt to understand how the mental and physical domains are related—how our perceptions and thoughts relate to the world toward which they are directed. Some schools have denied the existence of one or the other. Some argue that we cannot coherently talk about the mental domain, but must understand all behavior in terms of the physical world, which includes the physical structure of our bodies. Others espouse solipsism, denying that we can establish the existence of an objective world at all since our own mental world is the only thing of which we have immediate knowledge. Kant called it "a scandal of philosophy and of human reason in general" that over the thousands of years of Western culture, no philosopher had been able to provide a sound argument refuting psychological idealism - to answer the question "How can I know whether anything outside of my subjective consciousness exists?"

Heidegger argues that "the 'scandal of philosophy' is not that this proof has yet to be given, but that such proofs are expected and attempted again and again."[1] He says of Kant's "Refutation of Idealism" that it shows ". . . how intricate these questions are and how what one wants to prove gets muddled with what one does prove and with the means whereby the proof is carried out."[2] Heidegger's work grew out of the questions of phenomenology posed by his teacher Husserl, and developed into a quest for an understanding of Being. He argues that the separation of subject and object denies the more fundamental unity of being-in-the-world (Dasein). By drawing a distinction that I (the subject) am perceiving something else (the object), I have stepped back from the primacy of experience and understanding that operates without reflection.

Heidegger rejects both the simple objective stance (the objective physical world is the primary reality) and the simple subjective stance (my thoughts and feelings are the primary reality), arguing instead that it is impossible for one to exist without the other. The interpreted and the interpreter do not exist independently: existence is interpretation, and interpretation is existence. Prejudice is not a condition in which the subject is led to interpret the world falsely, but is the necessary condition of having a background for interpretation (hence Being). This is clearly expressed in the later writings of Gadamer:

> It is not so much our judgments as it is our prejudices that constitute our being. .. . the historicity of our existence entails that prejudices, in the literal sense of the word, constitute the initial directedness of our whole ability to experience. Prejudices are biases of our openness to the world. They are simply conditions whereby we experience something—whereby what we encounter says something to us.[3]

We cannot present here a thorough discussion of Heidegger's philosophy, but will outline some points that are relevant to our later discussion:[4]

Our implicit beliefs and assumptions cannot all be made explicit

Heidegger argues that the practices in terms of which we render the world and our own lives intelligible cannot be made exhaustively explicit. There is no neutral viewpoint from which we can see our beliefs as things, since we always operate within the framework they provide. This is the essential insight of the hermeneutic circle, applied to understanding as a whole.

The inevitability of this circularity does not negate the importance of trying to gain greater understanding of our own assumptions so that we can expand our horizon. But it does preclude the possibility that such understanding will ever be objective or complete. As Heidegger says "But if we see this circle as a vicious one and look out for ways of avoiding it, even if we just sense it as an inevitable imperfection, then the art of understanding has been misunderstood from the ground up."[5]

Practical understanding is more fundamental than detached theoretical understanding. The Western philosophical tradition is based on the assumption that the detached theoretical point of view is superior to the involved practical viewpoint. The scientist or philosopher who devises theories is discovering how things really are, while in everyday life we have only a clouded idea. Heidegger reverses this, insisting that we have primary access to the world through practical involvement with the *ready-to-hand*—the world in which we are always acting unreflectively. Detached contemplation can be illuminating, but it also obscures the phenomena themselves by isolating and categorizing them. Much of the current study of logic, language, and thought gives primacy to activities of detached contemplation. Heidegger does not disregard this kind of thinking, but puts it into a context of cognition as *praxis*—as concernful acting in the world. He is concerned with our condition of *thrownness*—the condition of understanding in which our actions find some resonance or effectiveness in the world.

We do not relate to things primarily through having representations of them. Connected to both of the preceding points is Heidegger's rejection of *mental representations*. The common sense of our tradition is that in order to perceive and relate to things, we must have some content in our minds that corresponds to our knowledge of them. If we focus on concernful activity instead of on detached contemplation, the status of this representation is called into question. In driving a nail with a hammer (as opposed to thinking about a hammer), I need not make use of any explicit representation of the hammer. My ability to act comes from my familiarity with *hammering*, not my knowledge of *a hammer*. This skepticism concerning mental representations is in strong opposition to current approaches in cognitive psychology, linguistics, artificial intelligence, and the foundation of cognitive science. …

Meaning is fundamentally social and cannot be reduced to the meaning-giving activity of individual subjects. The rationalistic view of cognition is individual-centered. We look at language by studying the characteristics of an individual language learner or language user, and at reasoning by describing the activity of an individual's deduction process. Heidegger argues that this is an inappropriate starting point—that we must take social activity as the ultimate foundation of intelligibility, and even of existence. A person is not an individual subject or ego, but a manifestation of Dasein within a space of possibilities, situated within a world and within a tradition.

An illustration of thrownness

Many people encountering the work of Heidegger for the first time find it very difficult to comprehend. Abstract terms like 'Dasein' and 'thrownness,' for instance, are hard to relate to reality. This is the opposite of what Heidegger intends. His philosophy is based on a deep awareness of everyday life. He argues that the issues he discusses are difficult not because they are abstruse, but because they are concealed by their 'ordinary everydayness.'

In order to give more of a sense of the importance of thrownness (which will play a large role in the second half of the book), it may be useful to consider a simple example that evokes experiences of thrownness for many readers.

Imagine that you are chairing a meeting of fifteen or so people, at which some important and controversial issue is to be decided: say, the decision to bring a new computer system into the organization. As the meeting goes on you must keep things going in a productive direction, deciding whom to call on, when to cut a speaker off, when to call for an end of discussion or a vote, and so forth. There are forcefully expressed differences of opinion, and if you don't take a strong role the discussion will quickly deteriorate into a shouting match dominated by the loudest, who will keep repeating their own fixed positions in hopes of wearing everyone else down.

We can make a number of observations about your situation:

You cannot avoid acting. At every moment, you are in a position of authority, and your actions affect the situation. If you just sit there for a time, letting things go on in the direction they are going, that in itself constitutes an action, with effects that you may or may not want. You are 'thrown' into action independent of your will.

You cannot step back and reflect on your actions. Anyone who has been in this kind of situation has afterwards felt "I should have said…" or "I shouldn't have let Joe get away with…" In the need to respond immediately to what people say and do, it is impossible to take time to analyze things explicitly and choose the best course of action. In fact, if you stop to do so you will miss some of what is going on, and implicitly choose to let it go on without interruption. You are thrown on what people loosely call your 'instincts,' dealing with whatever comes up.

The effects of actions cannot be predicted. Even if you had time to reflect, it is impossible to know how your actions will affect other people. If you decide to cut someone off in order to get to another topic, the group may object to your heavy-handedness, that in itself becoming a topic of discussion. If you avoid calling on someone whose opinion you don't like, you may find that he shouts it out, or that a friend feels compelled to take up his point of view. Of course this doesn't imply that things are total chaos, but simply that you cannot count on careful rational planning to

find steps that will achieve your goals. You must, as the idiom goes, 'flow with the situation.'

You do not have a stable representation of the situation. In the post-mortem analysis, you will observe that there were significant patterns. "There were two factions, with the Smith group trying to oppose the computer via the strategy of keeping the discussion on costs and away from an analysis of what we are doing now, and the Wilson group trying to be sure that whether or not we got the computer, they would remain in control of the scheduling policies. Evans was the key, since he could go either way, and they brought up the training issue because that is his bailiwick and they knew he wouldn't want the extra headaches." In a sense you have a representation of the situation, with objects (e.g., the two factions) and properties (their goals, Evans's lack of prior loyalty, etc.), but this was not the understanding you had to work with as it was developing. Pieces of it may have emerged as the meeting went on, but they were fragmentary, possibly contradictory, and may have been rejected for others as things continued.

Every representation is an interpretation. Even in the post-mortem, your description of what was going on is hardly an objective analysis of the kind that could be subjected to proof. Two people at the same meeting could well come away with very different interpretations. Evans might say "Smith is competing with me for that promotion, and he wanted to bring up the training issue to point out that we've been having difficulty in our group lately." There is no ultimate way to determine that any one interpretation is really right or wrong, and even the people whose behavior is in question may well not be in touch with their own deep motivations.

Language is action. Each time you speak you are doing something quite different from simply 'stating a fact.' If you say "First we have to address the issue of system development" or "Let's have somebody on the other side talk," you are not describing the situation but creating it. The existence of "the issue of system development" or "the other side" is an interpretation, and in mentioning it you bring your interpretation into the group discourse. Of course others can object "That isn't really an issue—you're confusing two things" or "We aren't taking sides, everyone has his own opinion." But whether or not your characterization is taken for granted or taken as the basis for argument, you have created the objects and properties it describes by virtue of making the utterance.

Heidegger recognized that ordinary everyday life is like the situation we have been describing. Our interactions with other people and with the inanimate world we inhabit put us into a situation of thrownness, for which the metaphor of the meeting is much more apt than the metaphor of the objective detached scientist who makes observations, forms hypotheses, and consciously chooses a rational course of action.

Breaking down and readiness-to-hand

Another aspect of Heidegger's thought that is difficult for many people to assimilate to their previous understanding is his insistence that objects and properties are not inherent in the world, but arise only in an event of breaking down in which they become *present-at-hand*. One simple example he gives is that of a hammer being used by someone engaged in driving a nail. To the person doing the hammering, the hammer as such does not exist. It is a part of the background of *readiness-to-hand* that is taken for granted without explicit recognition or identification as an object. It is part of the hammerer's world, but is not present any more than are the tendons of the hammerer's arm.

The hammer presents itself as a hammer only when there is some kind of breaking down or *unreadiness-to-hand*. Its 'hammerness' emerges if it breaks or slips from grasp or mars the wood, or if there is a nail to be driven and the hammer cannot be found. The point is a subtle one, closely related to the distinction between throwness and reflection on one's actions, as discussed above. As observers, we may talk about the hammer and reflect on its properties, but for the person engaged in the throwness of unhampered hammering, it does not exist as an entity.

Some other examples may help convey the importance of this distinction. As I watch my year-old baby learn to walk and pick up objects I may be tempted to say that she is 'learning about gravity.' But if I really want to deal with her ontology—with the world as it exists for her—there is no such thing as gravity. It would be inappropriate to view her learning as having anything to do with a concept or representation of gravity and its effects, even though she is clearly learning the skills that are necessary for acting in a physical world that we (as adult observers) characterize in terms of abstractions like 'gravity.' For the designer of space vehicles, on the other hand, it is clear that gravity exists. In anticipating the forms of breaking down that will occur when the normal background of gravity is altered, the designer must deal with gravity as a phenomenon to be considered, represented, and manipulated.

If we turn to computer systems, we see that for different people, engaged in different activities, the existence of objects and properties emerges in different kinds of breaking down. As I sit here typing a draft on a word processor, I am in the same situation as the hammerer. I think of words and they appear on my screen. There is a network of equipment that includes my arms and hands, a keyboard, and many complex devices that mediate between it and a screen. None of this equipment is present for me except when there is a breaking down. If a letter fails to appear on the screen, the keyboard may emerge with properties such as 'stuck keys.' Or I may discover that the program was in fact constructed from separate components such as a 'screen manager' and a 'keyboard handler,' and that certain kinds of 'bugs' can be attributed to the keyboard handler. If the problem is serious, I may be called upon to bring forth a complex network of properties reflecting the design of the system and the details of computer software and hardware.

For me, the writer, this network of objects and properties did not exist previously. The typing was part of my world, but not the structure that emerges as I try to cope with the breakdown. But of course it did exist for someone else—for the people who created the device by a process of conscious design. They too, though, took for granted a background of equipment which, in the face of breaking down, they could have further brought to light.

In sum, Heidegger insists that it is meaningless to talk about the existence of objects and their properties in the absence of concernful activity, with its potential for breaking down. What really *is* is not defined by an objective omniscient observer, nor is it defined by an individual—the writer or computer designer but rather by a space of potential for human concern and action.

Source: Terry Winograd and Fernando Flores, *Understanding Computers and Cognition: A New Foundation for Design,* Reading (Mass.): Addison-Wesley Publishing Company, 1987, pp. 28–37. Understanding Ontology / Terry Winograd and Fernando Flores © / reproduced with permission of the Licensor through PLSclear.

Notes

1. Heidegger, *Being and Time* (1962). p. 249, emphasis in original.

2. lbid., p. 247.

3. Gadamer, *Philosophical Hermeneutics* (1976), p. 9.

4. This overview is based on Hubert Dreyfus's *Being-in-the- World: A Commentary on Division I of Heidegger's Being and Time* in press (published by MIT Press 1991 - ed) It uses some of his discussion directly, but also includes our own interpretations for which he cannot be held responsible.

5. *Being and Time* p. 194.

CHAPTER 27
SMART METERS DON'T MAKE US ANY SMARTER
Elizabeth Shove and Sarah Royston

Note from editor: This brief piece is a telling example of misguided faith in the power of reason. The story reveals officials and householders existing in different worlds, engaging different objects of concern, yet not realizing this, leading the officials to adopt ineffective strategies. The authors are phenomenologically informed sociologists. Shove's, Comfort, Cleanliness and Convenience: The Social Organization of Normality *was a landmark book in sociology of consumption. Connections can be made between this story and the critique of rationality by Winograd and Flores.*

Energy bills are higher on the political agenda than ever before and we are constantly being told that devices such as smart meters will help us make better decisions and take control of the energy we use. But evidence shows that these new technologies are not making us more savvy.

Research suggests energy use depends on more than knowing how much electricity it takes to boil a kettle.

A recent survey by the Energy Saving Trust found half of all UK householders believe it is cheaper to leave their heating on all day than to turn it up or down as required. As Peter Robinson put it in the Guardian, we appear to be "a nation of buffoons who can't work thermostats".

There is some evidence that "folk theories" and everyday understandings about how heating and air conditioning systems work are often mistaken. Thermostats, for example, are frequently used as on-off switches. And if something as fundamental as a central heating system is so easily misunderstood, more complex technologies such as heat pumps or solar panels are likely to be even more challenging.

Making energy visible

Energy-saving myths and a lack of understanding about how our own systems work show we are not as informed as we could be about how to save money and resources. The most common method of promoting energy literacy is to provide information through labels on products and buildings or via leaflets, websites, advertising campaigns and lessons in schools.

Another approach is to make energy visible through smart meters. The idea here is that real time displays tell people exactly how much energy they are using at any one moment, and prompt them to cut back. The hope is that when households literally see how much energy a tumble dryer uses, they will not run it so often, or for so long.

The (UK) government's Energy Efficiency Strategy exemplifies this vision of the energy literate consumer when it sets the goal of "empowering households to take control of their energy use" through smart meters.

But this vision is based on a simple and implausible equation: if people know about energy, they will use less of it.

The problem is that people are never just using energy. They are cooking dinner or washing clothes, consuming energy as they go. They might be reading or chatting in a room that is well lit and warm, and that calls for energy consumption in the background.

Either way, it is impossible to treat energy as something that can be stripped out from the detail of daily life. Helping people understand their energy consumption, as if this were a topic in its own right, is therefore of limited value. Knowing just how much energy is used in making tea, or in doing the laundry will not transform established habits and practices that are embedded in the fabric of social life as we know it today.

Systems and flows

Another way to think about energy demand is to see the individual, their routines, their home, and all the objects within it, as making up a system. Energy flows through this system in the form of heat and power. Shaping and controlling these flows depends on various forms of know-how, sometimes held by people, but sometimes embedded in objects, such as heating controls.

Flows of energy and of know-how are constantly changing as new technologies emerge and as habits shift over time. While some of us still know how to light a coal fire with carefully rolled spills of newspaper, others know how to turn the heating on remotely using a phone app.

Then there are the different types of know-how needed to keep warm. It's not just about making the boiler work, it is also a matter of knowing about clothing, adjusting routines to suit the changing seasons and social conventions like keeping the house at a "comfortable" 22°C.

Knowing how much energy is being used is not central to the conduct of daily life but know-how like this is crucial. What matters more than looking at energy consumption as such is understanding how patterns of cooking, washing and keeping warm take the form they do and how energy flows through these systems.

Knowing about the energy that the cooker consumes is unlikely to prevent people from making a Sunday roast. Nor is knowledge of the energy bill the same as knowing how to make oneself comfortable. In the longer run, energy demand depends on how we live our lives, on the habits we have and the technologies that sustain them.

The idea that, as energy under secretary Sandip Verma put it, smart meters are "key to putting control in the hands of the consumers" is widely shared. But the kind of knowledge that meters provide is narrow in scope and of limited relevance to the routines and rhythms of everyday life.

If we are to understand how people engage with energy systems, it is not the meter that needs to get smarter, but our understanding of what energy is for and how it is used.

Source: *The Conversation*, February 19, 2014. Elizabeth Shove and Sarah Royston, © The Conversation (https:// theconversation.com/uk)

CHAPTER 28
MATTER AND MATTERING OR WHY ARE THINGS "US"?
Clive Dilnot

Note from editor: We dwell in the post-artificial in the sense that there is nothing but the artificial. Yet our modes of thinking still insist on the natural/artificial as foundational. Clive Dilnot evokes the radical contingency of the artificial, arguing that there is only configuration. There are no essences, everything is propositional. Designed things are propositions materialized; propositions about how things might be.

Something is absent in the discussion and this absence is not negligible, it goes to heart of understanding what we are doing.

I say 'an absence,' there are actually three.

- Absence in the debate of any sense of that which links, connects and at the same time differentiates between, "objects" and "design."

- An absence of any sense of what it is that design works on; of what, if you like, *is the subject-matter of design* (and the term "objects" is not by itself an adequate answer, nor is an adequate answer 'design").

- An absence of what makes the difference (if any) between "matter" and "matter(ing)."

There is also a fourth missing item, this one a kind of meta-absence, it is the lack of sufficient examination of the changing historical, operational and critical context in which all this is taking place.

Let me begin with the third point (while keeping the fourth very much in mind). One way to think this differentiation, or this *movement between* matter/mattering, is to use Latour's useful little point about the shift in our time from "Matters of Fact" to "Matters of Concern."

Philosophically, for us, until very recently indeed, matter, as above all natural matter, earth-stuff, has meant Fact. In effect, matter was/is equated to "object" and was/is contrasted to "subject."

But Matter*ing*, meaning that which matters (to us) is precisely a matter of concern and thus cannot have the quality of a fact. A *matter(ing)* is not therefore an object.

On the contrary, a matter of concern always takes the form of a question: "This?"

So here is a first shift.

But we can go a little further.

Most matter is not today for us natural matter, it is artificial.

Indeed if you were to accept the claim that we (meaning we + nature) are today *wholly* within the horizon of the artificial then *all* matter, including everything we used to see as "nature," is "Artificial."

Oil is artificial, coal is artificial, air is artificial.

The underlying historical claim here is that since 1945 we have been in transition to a world where it is the artificial, and no longer nature, that is (for us) the horizon and medium of the world; where it is the artificial (and our relations with "it") that constitutes as the formative totality of existence and thus becomes the prime condition of our existence.

The condition of the artificial re-frames the world, deeply.

This shift has enormous implications, which we have by no means yet intellectually fathomed, indeed have not begun to think it adequately.

In relation to what we are discussing, it changes the status of things; it *re-positions* things within the world.

Especially it changes the status and character the made. Matter *moves*. Which means matter, all matter, becomes as I already asserted a minute ago, artificial: all matter is for us, now, artifice

Some implications.

a. If this is so, then, since artifice is always the product of mind, all matter comes within mind.

b. Therefore, matter is not other to us. If Toys 'R' Us, Matter is us.

c. The proof of this is climate change. Climate change means we, collectively, have entered matter: Oil is you, coal is you, air is you. To put it another way, all matter is now *mattering*. All matter *matters* differently. All matter is a *matter for concern*. As we are continuous with matter so the separation matter/persons falls.

d. If this is so then the mind-matter distinction falls, and so too, obviously, the subject-object distinction. The discontinuity between these moments—on which the entirety of the modern world is built—falls.

e. Conversely, *entire* question becomes for us that of subject-object mediation. This, I would insist, is the *only* question that should concern human beings today.

But we need to go still further. It is not even, in fact, a question of subject-object mediation, for that formulation still preserves a discontinuity that we must now accept the loss of.

Since, as we know in our hearts, we are essentially failed animals, unable to survive without mediation, what we have in fact, as us, as ourselves, is subjects seeking the mediators on which we depend for our lives. (This is Herbert Simon's 'search for good designs').[1]

Three implications:

- In this relation artifice is not only or even primarily "object."

- In fact the subject-object relation here is therefore not a relation of subject to what is other to it but of the subject *to itself.*

- In subject-object relations we do not meet the object so much as we meet ourselves. We meet ourselves externalized, even in allegorical form, or in alienated form, but we meet *ourselves.*

So our mediators, our objects, are us: But how "us"?

Are they demonstrations of our being, or demonstrations of our possible becoming?

We have wanted, on the model of nature, to think "being."

But the mediators themselves, both in their multiplicity of variants and in their collective singular as mediators—things, objects, games, pollution, breeding animals, make-up—give us a contrary answer.

For a prime condition of the artificial, perhaps in the end the most fundamental, is that things do not possess being. It is not only these things are contingent—which they are, and radically so, but that this contingency is not somehow casual, a surface attribute which belies, somehow, an identity ('objects' perhaps) it is that contingency extends into their deepest aspects. The prime condition of artifice, and thus of the artificial as a whole, is that it possesses no Law.

Let me illustrate this, even with a seemingly trivial example. Here is a slide of six modern chairs. Each embody a relation between (as Simon would put it) 'human purpose and natural law.' But in fact law is obeyed *only* in local conditions (the laws appertaining to the bending of tubular steel in one case, or the formation of a plywood sheet in another). *At the level of their configuration no Law obtains.*[2]

This means that, in a certain sense, in the artificial things are not. There is no ontology of a thing. Things, meaning here all that is artificial (including by the way of course, and increasingly, ourselves—for we do not stand outside of artifice, that which is our product and which literally makes us who we are) are 'merely' ontic; the contingent product of always historical encounters.

In the artificial what matters for how it is, i.e., how it acts, is not a things ontological condition or putative identity but its configuration.

What matters is what a thing does, how it acts, in what direction it acts, in what manner it is disposed to act towards; what relations it subtends and opens (or closes). What matters, in short, is its disposition; its negotiation of circumstance and potentiality.

We need to say more on this but this must be thought also in relation to the second prime condition of the artificial that is that in the artificial things can *always* be other.

This *radical* contingency of the artificial (which goes beyond Simon's succinctly expressed methodological problem) is thus absolute.[3]

The move to a (historical) condition in which things can *always* be other has a series of implications.

  i. Certainty disappears (no Law).

 ii. The artificial is the realm of the possible. Possibility is here not will. It is the *objective* condition of the artificial.

iii. The status of truth in the artificial is not that of fact but the possible. The truth of something is its possibility. We get to an understanding of this truth through the negotiation of potentiality.

iv. In the artificial, the world is "possible" – but we do not know in advance what that possibility is; and the possibilities that are explored will always be contingent, a historical product of encounters. Thinking possibility is thinking these conditions through the modeled negotiation of possibility (potentiality).

 v. Hence, in the artificial, there is not being, but only possible becoming.

In fact, we can speak about a metaphysics of the artificial—meaning a description of "what is" and what is true. But this means, in a different sense to other historical epochs *we have made and make* the conditions of own metaphysics. What are those conditions? We can summarize them in this way.

- in the artificial, all artifice, and therefore the artificial as a whole is contingent and radically so: i.e. lacking any certainty whatsoever)

- the artificial is a matter of encounters

- the artificial is a matter of the possible.

My use of the word 'matter' here in this context is deliberate.

What does this change? Well, one thing it changes is the relation between knowing (that) and acting (how).

Previously (under the horizon of nature) we focused on knowing that, i.e. on knowing what-is, i.e., laws, whether of gods, God or nature. This was where knowledge lay. Theology, philosophy, and science successively confirmed this. In this regime, *acting*, the question of "how," is simply applied knowledge. Technology is the obvious instance. Note that as second-order knowledge acting is not permitted reflection which itself rises to the condition of knowing.[4] Heidegger's line, from the essay "Overcoming Metaphysics," captures this perfectly: 'Technology as the highest form of rational consciousness, technologically interpreted, and the lack of reflection *as the arranged powerlessness*, opaque to itself, to attain a relation to what is worthy of question, belong together: they are the same thing' (my emphasis).[5]

But in the Artificial, all of this reverses. The artificial cannot be known in law-like terms. The artificial "is" not: it is a perpetual possibility. Therefore "what" the artificial *might* be (I stress the conditional) can only be know via how it manifests. In the artificial, the royal road to understanding is not through contemplation or measurement or "research," it is through acting, i.e., it is through, one way or another, no matter how this is conceived, making. The artificial is known only through what is made, more specifically, what is configured, what is proposed, what is modeled, prototyped.

What experiment is to science, configurative action and "making" is to the artificial.[6] Making is at once the embodiment of the artificial: its exemplification—its exploration, its discovery—and is itself, always, also a complex symbolic activity and thus a mode of knowing.[7]

Now we are coming close to design (but we have actually been there all the time).

We can return to the little slide of the variety of modern chairs.

How we know what chairs can be is only by creating chairs. Each chair is a proposition concerning what a chair might be. The essence of that proposition, and the factor now that both links and differentiates objects and designs, is contained in the configuration of each chair.

All things, natural and artificial, have configuration. That is they are physically structured, and through that structuring enabled to act in certain ways.

Design is nothing more, *or less*, than the act of (re)configuring.

It is configuration brought to (degrees) of consciousness.[8] Design (re)-configures and therefore re-directs how things act.

But as the last example shows the proposition that things address is only in the first instance to the thing itself, it is in the second instance the act of artifice itself, and in the third, and most important instance it is the human dependency on artifice.

Thus only incidentally, only through the lens of the subjective arrogance of the subject-object distinction, only thought as manipulation, are things "merely" things.

Taken as a whole, things, in their conditions as propositions, are in fact a direct address, to us, *as us*.

The perpetual *question* that a thing asks is: who are you? The *critical* question that some things ask is: do you know who you are, do you know in what world, in what contexts, under what conditions, do you exist?

The perpetual *offering* that a things makes is 'in this small way, be well.'[9]

Design is the configurative negotiation between these moments. It is for this last reason that Herbert Simon can claim that all human actions boil down to the search for good designs, i.e., the search for good mediations.

And Simon points us also to the idea that, understood in this way, designing or design action is a form of knowing the world:

'One of the charges sometimes laid against modern science and technology is that if we know *how* to do something, we cannot resist doing it. While one can think of counterexamples, the claim has some measure of truth. One can envisage a future, however, in which our main interest in both science and design will lie in what they teach us about the world and not in what they allow us to do to the world. Design like science is a tool for understanding as well as for acting.'[10]

Indeed it is. Designing is the contingent discovery of hitherto unsuspected or overlooked or forgotten aspects concerning mediation, the artificial, and by very little extension of the latter, ourselves.

We have been talking about "things," but really we are talking about situations for mediation means things-in-situ. The ethics of design lies here.

To summarize a complex argument, I'll give what I think is the essence of ethics for design and which also gives us the axiom that must guide design action: 'There is no need for an 'ethics' but only for a clear vision of *the* situation). For to be faithful to this situation means: to treat it right to the limit of the possible. Or, if you prefer: to draw from this situation, to the greatest possible extent, the affirmative humanity that it contains.'[11]

Source: Clive Dilnot, Part 2 of 'The Matter of Design' *Design Philosophy Papers* Volume 13, Issue 2, 2015, pp . 115–123.

Notes

1. 'The proper study of mankind has been said to be man. But I have argued that people or at least their intellective component may be relatively simple, that most of the complexity of their behavior may be drawn from their environment, from their search for good designs. If I have made my case, then we can conclude that, in large part, the proper study of mankind is the science of design, not only as the professional component of a technical education but as a core discipline for every liberally educated person.' Herbert Simon, *The Sciences of the Artificial*, 3rd edition (Cambridge, MIT press, 2001) p. 139.

2. That is, at the level of the configuration of the artifact no Law can be drafted. There is no Ur Law determining in any a priori form, the configurative character of an artefact. The configuration (form) of a chair is entirely a matter of encounter and contingency. All chairs are therefore explorations of what a chair could be. As noted below all chairs are therefore propositions concerning what a chair could be. The propositional is a condition of the artificial.

3. 'The contingency of artificial phenomena has always created doubts as to whether they fall properly within the compass of science. Sometimes these doubts refer to the goal-directed character of artificial systems and the consequent difficulty of disentangling prescription from description. This seems to me not to be the real difficulty. The genuine problem is to show how empirical propositions can be made at all about systems that, given different circumstances, might be quite other than they are' Herbert Simon, *The Sciences of the Artificial*, 3rd edition (Cambridge, MIT press, 2001) p. 3.

4. Cf. design. It has never yet been permitted to Design to be thought of as a site of knowledge. Hence the oxymoron of the idea of the "design-led university."

5. Martin Heidegger, "Overcoming Metaphysics" in Joan Stambaugh, trans., *The End of Philosophy* (New York, Harper and Row, 1973) p. 99.

6. The close reading of Heidegger's text "The Age of the World Picture" is essential here. See *The Question Concerning Technology* trans. William Lovitt (New York, Harper, 1977) pp. 115–154.

7. Nelson Goodman gets this point perfectly. 'The primary purpose [of symbolic activity] is cognition in and for itself: the practicality, pleasure, compulsion & communicative utility all depend on this. Symbolization, then, is to be judged fundamentally by well it serves the cognitive purpose: by the delicacy of its discriminations and the aptness of its allusions; by the way it works in grasping, exploring and informing the world; by how it analyzes, sorts and organizes; by how it participates in the making, manipulation, retention and transformation of knowledge. Considerations of simplicity and subtlety, power and precision, scope and selectivity, familiarity and freshness, are all relevant and often contend with one another; their weighting is relative to our interests, our information, our inquiry.' *Languages of Art*, (Indianapolis, Bobbs-Merrill, 1969) p. 258.

8. Lacan says somewhere that culture is where form gets 'put on the table.' Design is (ideally) the place where the [given] form of things (now interpreting this term in broadest possible aspects) 'gets put on the table.'

9. See Elaine Scarry, *The Body in Pain*, chapter 5 passim (Oxford, OUP, 1985).

10. Herbert Simon, *The Sciences of the Artificial*, ibid, p. 164.

11. Alain Badiou, *Ethics* (London, Verso, 2003) p. 15. Quotation adapted.

GUIDE TO FURTHER READING

See entries in *Bloomsbury Encyclopedia of Design* on Affordance, Agency, Care, Comfort, Consumerism, Dematerialization, Dwelling, Function, Need, Space, Things, User-centered. While the study of designed things (beyond instrumental research) was predominantly design history based on a model of art history that focused on works and their makers, more recent studies from the perspectives of philosophy, anthropology, sociology, science and technology studies emphasize designed things in their everyday settings and are concerned with issues of how, and the extent to which, designed artifacts and designed environments shape dispositions and behaviors. A phenomenological approach underpins much of this work: for orientation see "Phenomenology" in *Stanford Encyclopedia of Philosophy*. A phenomenological approach emphasizes situated, embodied experience, this exemplified in Merleau Ponty's idea of "flesh of the world" in "The Intertwining— The Chiasm" in his *The Visible and the Invisible*; and Iris M. Young, *Throwing Like a Girl And Other Essays in Feminist Philosophy and Social Theory* (1990). For a focus on material culture see Elizabeth Shove, *Comfort, Cleanliness and Convenience: The Social Organisation of Normality* (2003). On affordance see Julka Almquist and Julia Lupton, "Affording Meaning" (2010) and Phil Turner "Affordance as Context" (2005). The texts and Further Readings in Part VI "The Designing of Technology" also link closely with "Being Designed and Things."

PART VI
THE DESIGNING OF TECHNOLOGY

INTRODUCTION

Conventionally, technology is seen as over-arching design—a technology is developed, the designers come along later—to encase it, style it, give it user interfaces and a "look-and-feel," package, and to promote it. Such a characterization only holds from the internal perspective of commercial design practice, and even within that circumscribed domain, this is an increasingly outmoded version of what design is becoming. More fundamentally, design and technology cannot be separated; technology is designed, and technology designs.

Extending on what Parts I, III, and V addressed, the selected readings in this Part sit within an expanded understanding of design and go to the question of the designing of the designed, with the focus on what technological things design, or in other words, what do they do? The question is posed from phenomenological and ontological perspectives. So, it is not, "what do particular technologies do?" because this question leads only to describing specific functions. Rather, "what is it that all technologies essentially have in common?" Or to put it in a Heideggerian way "what is the being of their being technology?". If technology encompasses everything from a stone tool to a missile guidance system, what do all these things have in common?

One way to approach this question would be to ask "what is the difference between an artifact and a technology?". Both come from human intentions, both have uses. An artifact is made; a technology is something for making or doing something else. A tool is technological; a bowl or a basket is not. The bowl contains, holds; the basket is for gathering things. In the early times of humanity, woven baskets (or found baskets such as hollowed out natural objects) would have enabled people (women) to gather more food over greater distances. A group of basket-toting women could have had significant localized impacts in their harvesting of nuts and berries. Therefore is a basket a harvesting technology? No. But the making of the basket is technological for it requires collecting natural materials, treating, and configuring them by weaving into a shape to serve the function of holding.[1]

Technology has the character of "in order to."[2] Technology at its most basic has a triple character: (i) something is taken from what is already there (reeds, long grasses, sticks); (ii) it is transformed by human making into something else (a basket); (iii) in order to do something else (gather berries, store seeds). Time passes and more uses for the artifact are discovered and the techniques of making are further developed. Then technological activity multiplies and diversifies with the invention of more elaborate methods of transformation (such as the making of tools and the smelting of metals), then follow tools that can make tools that can make tools.[3] Tools cluster into distinct technologies, then different technologies come together and increase their productive power and ability to transform that which they are applied to on a larger scale and at a faster rate, such as when iron-making was brought to agricultural implements displacing flint and wood, and later when mechanized steam power in the form of the tractor was added to large-scale agricultural tools like the plough and the harvester.

Two crucial points have been left out of this rapid evocation of "the history of technology" (and we haven't even mentioned the technologies of memory like writing, printing, photography, and computing, as discussed by Bernard Stiegler): the first is that technological activity creates knowledge—from embodied know-how (*technê*) through to scientific knowledge (*epistêmê*); and second, related to this, technologies, as their capacities and applications unfold, shape the human beings who use them: physically, cognitively, and existentially. Ortega divided the evolution of technology into three periods: first, the techniques of chance; second, the techniques of the craftsman, and the third which marks a radical break, the techniques of the engineer—associated with the scientific, analytic way of thinking of the modern era that seeks to discover "the technical means for realizing any end."[4]

For Heidegger, modern technology is different from pre-industrial craft; it is not just instrumental, but instrumentalist. Modern technology results from, and perpetuates, a disposition toward "what is" that makes things come to presence for utilization; it is a mode of "revealing" that renders all as standing reserve, as resources available for exploitation.

As Adrian Snodgrass points out, technology is based on reason but "no ultimate reason can be found to support the principle of reason itself." Reason as a mode of thought that can be applied to any end, including unreasonable and horrific ends, is evidenced most starkly in the rational organization of the Nazi death camp as system.[5]

In this Heideggerian sense, the technological is pervasive but it is also pervasive as multiple technologies and systems interweave with our lives—living in, with, alongside, in an increasing condition of designed dependence. Consider here: medical technologies; reproductive technologies; bio-technology; nano-technology; food technology; and of course, information and communication technologies. Taking Heidegger as the point of departure, philosophers of science and technology such as Don Ihde and Langdon Winner have debated the nature of the relation between humans and technology.[6]

Bernard Stiegler, reflecting on theories of technical evolution, argues that "between the organic beings of the physical sciences and the organic beings of biology, there does indeed exist a third genre of 'being': 'inorganic organized beings,' or technical objects. These nonorganic organizations of matter have their own dynamic when compared with that of either physical or biological beings, a dynamic, moreover, that cannot be reduced to the 'aggregate' or 'product' of these beings." He further claims that "organised inorganic beings are . . . constitutive (in the strict phenomenological sense) of temporality as well as spatiality . . . [and] . . . as a 'process of exteriorisation', technics is the pursuit of life by means other than life."[7] Drawing on anthropologist and archaeologist Andre Leroi-Gourhan, he argues that "the human and the tool invent each other."[8] "The archaic cortex and equipment are codetermined in a structural coupling of a particular sort" and "in its evolution, the human undoubtedly remains the agent of differentiation, even though it is guided by the very thing it differentiates, even though it discovers itself and becomes differentiated in that process . . ."[9] He posits the origin of memory and the birth of time in the duplication of stereotypes, in the material trace of the stereotype down through generations of archaic humans.

Notes

1. Carl Mitcham, in surveying the different definitions of technology, notes that often a distinction is not made between technology as process and the products of technology, and in everyday usage "technology" usually refers to the latter. See his *Thinking Through Technology: The Path Between Engineering and Philosophy*, University of Chicago Press, 1994.

2. This "in order two" is enfolded in a complex structure of the interdependence of technology, making, knowledge, temporality, and care. This is well expressed by Catriona Hanley on early Heidegger: "In looking at a tool 'as' something, we 'project' the possibilities of that tool in relation to the current situation by seeing it as 'in order to.' In taking something *as* something, I have already 'seen' it in relation to its situation, and to my situation. In projecting its possibilities, I have already projected myself, and seen myself in relation to it as possibility. I look toward what it can be (in its situation, as part of my factical situation), in referring to what it has been (how it has worked before, what I know myself to be capable of), in order to realize a certain present possibility. Thus the future and having-been are the ground of the present. But it is primarily the future-oriented nature of projection, looking ahead to possibilities, that makes it possible for anything to be seen *as* something. The *as* structure (like understanding and interpretation in general) is thus grounded in ecstatic temporality (*SZ*: 360\411). Concern is understandable only

Introduction: The Designing of Technology

in terms of the fundamental *praxis* of care, as projection and transcendence. . . . Thus the poietic involvement with things as ready to hand is primordially futural and dynamic." Catriona Hanley, "Theory and *Praxis* in Aristotle and Heidegger" paper given at the Twentieth World Congress of Philosophy, in Boston, Massachusetts from August 10–15, 1998, https://www.bu.edu/wcp/Papers/Acti/ActiHanl.htm

3. See Carl Mitcham's reworking of Lewis Mumford's categories of technological objects: clothes; utensils; structures; apparatus; utilities, tools, machine, automata, *Thinking Through Technology*.

4. Mitcham, *Thinking Through Technology*, p. 48.

5. See Tony Fry, Clive Dilnot, and Susan Stewart, *Design and the Question of History* London: Bloomsbury, 2014.

6. Langdon Winner sees technologies as forms of life, and that people and technologies shape each other. Don Ihde argued that technologies often transform human experience by augmenting some aspect of the world while simultaneously reducing others; he criticized Heidegger for not taking account of different kinds of human-technology relations such as embodiment and instrumentation. Don Ihde, *Heidegger's Technologies: Postphenomenological Perspectives*, New York: Fordham University Press, 2010.

7. Bernard Stiegler, *Technics and Time 1: The Fault of Epimetheus*, trans. Richard Beardsworth & George Collins, Stanford: Stanford Uni Press, 1998. p. 17.

8. Ibid., p. 175.

9. Ibid., p. 158.

CHAPTER 29
TECHNOLOGY: INSTRUMENTAL METAPHOR AND CYBERNETIC SYSTEM
Adrian Snodgrass

Note from editor: The naïve notion that "technology is just a tool and it can be used for good or bad ends" is masterfully demolished here by revealing technology as self-generating, systemic, self-perpetuating and beyond human control. This, argues Snodgrass drawing on Heidegger, is not because of specific powerful technologies; technology is not about individual technologies, rather its power lies in 'technological rationality' a mode of thinking capable of infinitely explaining (enframing) and appropriating whatever it encounters.

Technology is most usually discussed in terms of a metaphor of instrumentality. This supposes that we use technology to effect certain useful results in the same way that we use technological equipment to manipulate and control objects. Technology, in this metaphor, is a means to an end; it is used to control nature, with the aim of producing things for human benefit, consumption or use.

Implicit in the metaphor of technology as an instrument is the notion of control, which in turn is based on the concept that humans and technology stand over against each other in the manner of a workman and a tool. The notion of instrumentality thus involves a basic duality, with humanity on one side and technology on the other.

Debates concerning technology are usually conducted within the framework of this humanity/technology dichotomy. On the one hand there are those who think that humanity has lost control of technology, and on the other there are those who disagree. The former say that technology is destroying rather than enhancing the quality of life, and holds the potential for catastrophe. They point to global warming, ozone holes, nuclear arsenals, pollution, smart bombs, genetic engineering, user-friendly means of mass extermination, and a host of other potentially destructive phenomena to support their argument that science and technology are running amok, and have escaped human control in the manner of a machine whose brakes have failed.

Their opponents, by contrast, are convinced that technology remains under human control. Technology has immeasurably improved our standards of life, and the disasters cited by their opponents are merely the mishaps that are liable to occur in any human activity; but humans, by way of science and technology, can find means of controlling any deleterious effects that may accompany the advance of technology. The dangers posed by technology are problems which science, under human control, can solve.

Technology as a cybernetic system

The instrumental metaphor of technology is 'correct' as far as it goes but, as does every metaphor, it only reveals a partial aspect of its referent. It conceals as well as reveals.[1] The adequacy of the instrumental metaphor of technology can be queried when we look at how technology now functions.

Heidegger likens the functioning of technology in the modern world to that of its 'culminating achievement,' cybernetic systems.[2] The word "cybernetics" comes from a Greek word meaning "steersman," and in its present use refers to a system in which information is steered back upon itself in feedback loops so as to monitor its own functioning. The machine becomes self-regulating. Technology, Heidegger argued, now operates in the manner of a cybernetic system. It is no longer under the control of human agency, but functions and expands by feeding back into itself in accordance with its own self-controlling mechanisms. Technology is now able to perpetuate, regulate and generate itself without human intervention. It now functions as a completely self-enclosed information system, an enormous feedback circuit in which all things become calculable statistics, a system which is not oriented towards some telos, but gyrates in a spiral of ever-expanding self-generation. It is no longer a means to an end, but an end in itself. The goal of technology becomes efficiency and control for their own sakes.[3]

Technology is now self-organizing, self-ordering, self-perpetuating and self-dominating, and in this sense has a life of its own. Machines are no longer merely means to the attainment of some local and specific end, owned and controlled by particular individuals or groups, but form part of a global system of production that is quite beyond the control or "ownership" of any individual, group, class or community. It is impossible to begin to imagine how any dismantling of this world-wide system could take place.

In this system the nature of the 'object' changes. Things are no longer objects, but cogs in a system. In this technological era a telephone, for example, is not seen as an object or instrument which extends the range of the voice, but as an element in the global communication system; a Boeing 747 is not an object which serves as a means of getting us from one place to another, but is part of a world-wide transportation system, involving bewilderingly complex sets of interactions and involvements.[4]

The outcome of this self-propelling drive to efficiency is that logistical systems become the controlling mechanism not only of the natural but also the human world, dictating patterns of behavior, modes of discourse, the validity of modes and objects of inquiry, the direction and purpose of education, in short, every aspect of life. In this way logistical information about objects impinges directly on humanity and its actions. As Heidegger noted, the advent of cybernetics heralded the reduction of logos to logistics.[5] "Humanity becomes its own object,"[6] and technology "steers" our evolution. We become manipulable objects contributing to the productive enterprise, the logistical equivalents of pieces of equipment or raw materials, statistics in a chain of production and consumption.

In the light of these developments it is no longer appropriate or more than partially revealing to speak of technology in instrumental terms of human control. The metaphor is obsolete. We no longer control, but are controlled by technology; technology no longer belongs to us, but we belong to technology; and we do not stand over against technology, but are part of its structure. The human/technological differentiation deconstructs.

The principle of sufficient reason

….. If we are to understand Heidegger's thinking on technology, we must not ask for 'reasons.' For Heidegger, to ask for reasons is to subscribe to the principle of sufficient reason, the principle that "nothing exists unless a sufficient reason for its existence is able to be rendered."[7] This principle demands that every thing must have a reason or a cause for its existence, or else is not real.

The principle of sufficient reason is the driving force of science, which is usually taken to epitomize rationality. Science and the principle of sufficient reason go together and are inextricably merged. Science seeks the reasons for things so as to exercise a rational control over them. It is based on the premise that the behavior of phenomena has a cause and is rationally explicable, and that access to reasons and causes allows predictions, and thereby control, of that behavior. This style of thinking, imbued with notions of instrumental control, constitutes technological rationality.

Technological rationality, which Heidegger calls "calculative thought," has become all-pervasive and hegemonic in the modern world.

> "... The demand for the delivery of grounds [i.e., reasons], now speaks unconditionally and incessantly throughout modernity and sweeps over us contemporaries. ... [It] has slipped in between thinking man and his world in order to take possession of human representing in a new way."[8]

The principle of sufficient reason is the primary and overarching principle of the metaphysics of modernity; and technological rationality, thus defined in terms of the principle of reason, is now uncritically accepted by many as the only mode of rationality. It governs how we are to think, and also what we are to think about. It only allows those things to come to presence which can be accounted for and thereby ordered, represented, regulated, organized, managed, manufactured for some purpose. Unless a reason can be given for a thought or an action, it is "irrational," unfounded, unsupported and unsupportable. It is without justification and cannot be validated.[9]

In the modern world everything is treated in terms of control and is ordered in accordance with the demands of technological rationality. The sole reason for the existence of things is to serve technological needs. The world is set within a framework in which all things are seen as waiting to be accumulated, manipulated, and calculated.[10] All things thus become part of a global store of resources, a 'standing reserve' (*Bestand*) of raw materials to feed the self-propelling expansion of technology.[11]

Humans believe that the power of reason gives them mastery over nature and the world, but technological rationality governs humans as well as things. Humans set upon (*stellen*) nature, dominating it by rational rule; but are themselves set upon by the power of the rule of reason.

The universal dominance of the principle of reason, says Heidegger, constitutes the nihilism of our age.[12] In demanding that every thing, whether natural or human, have a reason, we have lost our respect for them. If no reason can be given, the thing is no real thing, but no thing, a nothing (*nihil*).

The enframing of thought

There is, therefore, a profound paradox embedded in talk about technology or its control. To give reasons to support an argument concerning technology is to reinforce the all-pervasive hegemony of the technological way of thinking. In order to discuss or criticize notions of technology we are constrained to use the language of technological rationality, structured in accordance with the framework of the principle of sufficient reason. To think or talk about technology is to think or talk within the limits of its own modes of thought, that is, in terms of sufficient reason and thus in terms of the control of objects and in a logic which is modelled on the notion of the manipulation of objects. The "questioning" of technology does not in fact question technology, but merely rearranges technologically predetermined tokens located in a technologically predetermined thinking-space. To question technology is to ask for reasons, to ask how it 'works', and how to control it, all notions which are fore-structured in accordance with the limitations, metaphors, pre-assumptions and rules of technological rationality.

Employing reason to question technology is counter-productive; it simply tightens the grip of technological rationality. We are trapped within technological modes of reasoning as in an enframing structure.

For Heidegger this enframing (*Gestell*) is the essence of technology.[13] In its essence, technology is not technological equipment and techniques of production, but is the way in which we think about, interpret and view the world within the framework set up by technological rationality.

The 'supreme danger' that technology poses is not the reduction of humankind to statistics and objects for use; nor is it the threat of some technological catastrophe. Predictions of cataclysm are symptoms of a more general and deeper problem. The greatest danger, says Heidegger, is that posed by the possibility that technological rationality should become the only way of seeing reality, excluding all modes of thinking which lie outside the framework predetermined by technology.[14]

The paradigmatic example of the exclusivist enframing of thought and praxis is scientific method, which wholly dominates science by prescribing in advance what is real. Before any scientific investigation begins the real has already been reductively defined as what can be measured and calculated mathematically to show causal relationships. If the phenomenon escapes the net of causal reasons, it is irrational and a figment. In this enframing of thought and action, things are only present to us if they have a reason; they are only revealed to us if they can be as seen as raw materials to be mathematically calculated, measured, manipulated and made into objects for use. Those things that are not disclosed rationally, which is to say, in a mathematically formalizable manner that gives them a reason and renders them amenable to control, are as if absent, and therefore wholly negligible.[15]

The enframing of thought here takes a totalitarian turn. It becomes self-enclosed and self-referential, with no external criteria by which it may be judged. All other ways of thinking or seeing are strictly excluded.

The principle of reason is without reason

There is a profound irony in the enframing of modern thought by a technological rationality based on the principle of sufficient reason, since reason is itself without reason.[16] The principle of reason, forming the foundation of the thought and praxis of the modern era, itself has no foundation. The principle of reason questions all things; it asks why they are; and if no answer can be found counts them as nothing. But when we query reason, when we demand to see its reason, and ask why all things must have a sufficient reason, the answer is silence. No ultimate reason can be found to support the principle of reason itself. To give reasons for the principle of reason is to go round in circles, since to give reasons is to have recourse to the principle that is being questioned. If reasons can be found to base the principle, then they must also be asked their grounds, and so on to infinite regress.

Technological rationality hides from itself that it has no fundamental justification. Its quest for causes and reasons stops at reason itself. If pressed, it masks its lack of grounding by justifying its existence in terms of utility; but ultimately it cannot validate itself. It follows that its claims to certitude, to exclusive and hegemonic authority, or to sole access to truth, are invalid.

Technology as the disclosure of being

For Heidegger the emergence of technological rationality in Western history and its domination of modem thought are not the fruit or fault of any human doing or willing. They are not ascribable to human causes nor do they result from human thought, but are the 'mission' of Being, the particular way in which Being discloses itself in this modem epoch; and "Being is no product of thinking. On the contrary, indeed, essential thinking is an event (Ereignis) of Being."[17]

Technology in its essence is not to be thought of as the application of the findings of science, nor as the use of machines, equipment, and technical processes to manufacture products for use. It is, rather, a disclosure or 'mission' of Being, the way in which a certain aspect of reality, that which is enframed by technological rationality, is revealed to us.[18]

This leads to a profoundly significant conclusion: we cannot hope to control technology because its essence, which is coincident with Being, lies outside our willing. If the essence of technology

"... is Being itself, then technology can never be mastered, neither positively nor negatively, through a mere self-dependent human action. Technology, whose essential being is Being itself, can never be overcome by man. This would mean that man would be the lord of Being."[19]

This negates the notion that technology is neutral and that it only poses a threat because of human misuse.[20] If the essence of technology, the *Gestell*, is a 'mission of Being'- and beyond human control or intervention, then the core problem lies neither with machines nor with the way humans use them, but with the possibility that the mode of Being disclosed by technological rationality comes to exclude all other modes of disclosure, with a consequent distortion of the essence of humanity.[21]

There is no point in asking what caused the emergence of technological rationality or why it exists. For Heidegger the event (*Ereignis*) of Being allows of no explanation. We cannot say why the essence of technology has come to dominate Western thinking and now spreads out to dominate the thinking of all peoples; there is no 'answer' to the 'question' of "Being.[22] This being so, then "What does there remain to say? Only this: the Event of Appropriation comes to pass (*das Ereignis ereignet*)."[23]

Heidegger leads us to the edge of the abyss. He tells us that technological rationality, the only mode of thought now available to us in this present era, is groundless. He then further compounds our perplexity by asserting that technological rationality is a supreme danger in that it threatens what it is to be human, but that no human agency can alter this state of affairs. Technological rationality is a disclosure of Being that we can neither prevent nor alter. Our interventions, our attempts at technological control and ecological management, only deal with the symptoms of technology, but cannot reach its essence.

If all thought and all action ultimately lack reason, then the only response seems to be a passive acceptance of fate. The way ahead seems to lead into nihilism and chaos. Everything is founded on the void.

Source: Adrian Snodgrass, 'Translating Tradition: Technology, Heidegger's 'Letting-be' and Japanese New Wave Architecture' *Architectural Theory Review* Volume 2, Issue 2, 1997.

Notes

1. See Adrian Snodgrass, 'Models, Metaphors, and the Hermeneutics of Designing' *Design Issues* 9, 1(Fall 1992): 56–74, esp. p. 71.

2. Heidegger's theme of the cybernetic character of modern technology is summarized in Michael E. Zimmerman, *Heidegger's Confrontation with Modernity: Technology, Politics and Art*, Bloomington and Indianapolis: Indiana University Press, 1990, pp. 199 if., where references are given. Cf. Gerald L. Bruns, *Heidegger's Estrangements: Language, Truth and Poetry in the Later Writings*, New Haven: Yale University Press, 1989, p. 47. For an overview and bibliography of Heidegger's philosophy of technology, see Albert Borgmann, 'The Question of Heidegger and Technology: A Critical Review of the Literature,' *Philosophy Today* 31, 214 (Summer 1987): 97–177.

3. Zimmerman, *Heidegger's Confrontation with Modernity*, pp. 200–1.

4. Martin Heidegger, 'The Question Concerning Technology,' in *The Question Concerning Technology and Other Essays*, trans, William Lovitt, New York; Harper and Row, 1977, 3–35 (p. 17).

5. Martin Heidegger, *What is Called thinking?* trans. Fred D. Wieck and J. Glenn Gray, New York: Harper and Row, 1972, p. 21. Cf. Zimmerman, *Heidegger's Confrontation with Modernity*, pp. 199–200.

6. Martin Heidegger, 'The Question Concerning Technology,' p. 18. Cf. Zimmerman, *Heidegger's Confrontation with Modernity*, p. 200. Zimmerman (*Eclipse of the Self: The Development of Heidegger's Concept of Authenticity*, Athens: Ohio University Press, 1981, p. xxv) relates this to 'the they' (das Man); and the political entailments of the 'objectification' of people are discussed by Richard Schmitt, *Martin Heidegger on Being Human*, New York: Random House, 1969, and Karsten Harries, 'Heidegger as A Political Thinker,' in Michael Murray (ed.), *Heidegger and Modern Philosophy*, New Haven: Yale University Press, 1979, pp. 304–28; Gregory Schufreider, 'Heidegger on Community,' Man and World 14, 1 (1981): 25–54; Langdon Winner, *Autonomous Technology: Technics Out of Control as Theme in Political Thought*, Cambridge, Mass.: MIT Press, 1977.

7. In the original formulation of Leibniz: ... nihil existere nisi cujus reddi potest ratio existentiae sufficiens. For the following see Martin Heidegger, Der Satz vom Grund, 3, Auflage, Pfullingen: Verlag Gunther Neske, 1965, summarized in John D. Caputo, *Radical Hermeneutics: Repetition, Deconstruction, and the Hermeneutic Project*, Bloomington and Indianapolis: Indiana University Press, 1987, pp. 222 if. Cf. Caputo, *The Mystical Element in Heidegger's Thought*, New York: Fordham University Press, 1986, pp. 59 ff. Martin Heidegger, 'The Principle of Ground,' trans. K. Hoeller, Man and World 7 (1974): 207–22, is a translation of pp. 191–211 of Der Satz vom Grund and is the source for much of what follows.

8. Heidegger, 'The Principle of Ground,' p. 48, cited in Caputo, *The Mystical Element in Heidegger's Thought*, p. 93.

9. On the all-encompassing hegemony of technological rationality, see Zimmerman, *Heidegger 's Confrontation with Modernity*, passim; Gianni Vattimo, *The End of Modernity*, trans. Jon R. Snyder, Baltimore: John Hopkins University Press, 1991, Translator's Introduction, p. xiv; Drew Leder, 'Modes of Totalization: Heidegger on Modem Technology and Science,' *Philosophy Today* 29, 3 (Fall 1985): 245–56.

10. Martin Heidegger, *Identity and Difference*, trans. J. Stambaugh, New York: Harper and Row, 1969, p. 34–5.

11. For the notion of 'standing reserve' (Bestand), see Heidegger, 'Question Concerning Technology,' pp. 6–7; Richard I. Bernstein, 'Heidegger's Silence? Ethos and Technology,' in Bernstein, *The New Constellation*, Cambridge: Polity Press, 1991, pp. 79–141 (P. 99); Zimmerman, *Heidegger's Confrontation with Modernity*, pp. 212–6; John D. Caputo, *Radical Hermeneutics: Repetition, Deconstruction, and the Hermeneutic Project*, Bloomington and Indianapolis: Indiana University Press, 1987, p. 223; Heidegger, 'Question Concerning Technology,' Translator's Introduction, p. xxix; Shaun Gallagher, *Hermeneutics and Education,* Albany, N.Y.: State University of New York Press, 1992, p.176; Leder, 'Modes of Totalization,' p. 246; etc.

12. Michael E. Zimmerman, 'Beyond 'Humanism': Heidegger's Understanding of Technology,' in Thomas Sheehan (ed.), *Heidegger: The Man and the Thinker*, Chicago: Precedent Publishing, 1981, pp. 219–27 (p. 225).

13. For 'enframing' (Gestell), see Heidegger, 'Question Concerning Technology,' 22 ff.; Heidegger, The Question Concerning Technology,' Translator's Introduction, p. xxix–xxx, xxxiii–vi; Bernstein, 'Heidegger's Silence,' 101 ff.; Kathleen Wright, 'The Place of the Work of Art in the Age of Technology, *Southern Journal of Philosophy* 22 (1984): 565–83 (pp. 573–4); Leder, 'Modes of Totalization.' pp. 248–9; Gallagher, *Hermeneutics and Education*, pp. 176 ff.; Caputo, *Radical Hermeneutics*, pp. 223–32; Gerald L. Bruns, *Heidegger's Estrangements: Language, Truth, and Poetry in the Later Writings*, New Haven: Yale University Press, 1989, pp. 41 & 48; Zimmerman, *Heidegger's Confrontation with Modernity*, pp. 216–22; Zimmerman. Beyond 'Humanism'', P. 223.

14. Martin Heidegger, *Discourse on Thinking*, trans. J. M. Anderson and E. H. Freund, New York: Harper and Row, 1966, p. 56; Hubert L. Dreyfus, 'On the Ordering of Things: Being and Power in Heidegger and Foucault,' *Southern Journal of Philosophy* 28 Supplement (1989): 83–96 (pp. 88 ff.).

15. See Dreyfus, 'On the Ordering of Things,' p. 88.

16. See Caputo, *The Mystical Element in Heidegger's Thought*, pp. 51 ff.; Caputo, *Radical Hermeneutics*, pp. 222 ff.; Zimmerman, *Heidegger's Confrontation with Modernity*, pp. 235–6. Cf. also Gallagher, *Hermeneutics and Education*, p. 291, where he cites similar notions from Derrida (Jacques Derrida, 'The University in the Eyes of Its Pupils,' *Diacritics* 13 (1983): 3–20) to show that the universities, bastions of reason, are themselves 'without reason.'

17. Martin Heidegger, 'What is Metaphysics?' trans. W. F. C. Hull and A. Crick, in Werner Brock (ed.), *Existence and Being*, Chicago: Regnery Co., 1949, pp. 325–61 (p. 356). Cf. Caputo, *The Mystical Element in Heidegger's Thought*, pp. 76–7, etc. On Heidegger's notions concerning disclosure, see James J. DiCenso, *Hermeneutics and the Disclosure of Truth: A Study in the Work of Heidegger, Gadamer and Ricoeur*, Charlotteville: University Press of Virginia, 1990, Ch. 2; Heidegger, *The Question Concerning Technology*, Translator's Introduction, passim; Zimmerman, *Heidegger's Confrontation with Modernity*, Ch. 14; John Haugeland, 'Dasein's Disciosedness,' in Hubert L. Dreyfus and Harrison Hall (eds.) *Heidegger: A Critical Reader*, Cambridge, Mass.: Basil Blackwell, 1992, 27–44; Joseph P. Fell, 'The Familiar and the Strange: On the Limits of Praxis in the Early Heidegger,' in Dreyfus and Hall, *Heidegger: A Critical Reader*, 68–80; Jean Grondin, 'Hermeneutical Truth and Its Historical Presuppositions: A Possible Bridge Between Analysis and Hermeneutics,' in Evan Simpson, *Anti-Foundationalism and Practical Reasoning: Conversations Between Hermeneutics and Analysis*, 1987, 45–58, where disclosure is related to Ereignis, the 'happening' or 'event' (p. 53); Zimmerman, 'Beyond Humanism,' pp. 221 ff.; Sandra Lee Bartky, 'Heidegger's Philosophy of Art,' in Thomas Sheehan (ed.), *Heidegger: The Man and the Thinker*, Chicago: Precedent Publishing, 257–273 (pp. 265 ff.); John Sallis, 'Into the Clearing,' in Sheehan, *Heidegger: The Man and the Thinker*, 107–115; David E. Cooper, Metaphor, London: Basil Blackwell, 1986, pp. 252–7, where it is related to metaphor; Caputo, *Radical Hermeneutics*, pp. 74–5; Bernstein, 'Heidegger's Silence,' pp. 95 ff. & 106.

18. On the disclosive 'mission' of Being, see Caputo, *The Mystical Element in Heidegger's Thought*, pp. 76–7, etc.; Theodore K. Kisiel, 'On the Dimensions of a Phenomenology of Science in Husserl and the Young Dr. Heidegger,' *Journal of the British Society for Phenomenology* 4, 3 (October 1973): 217–234 (esp. p. 232); Berndt Magnus, *Heidegger's Metaphistory of Philosophy: Amor Fati, Being and Truth*, The Hague: Nijhoff, 1970; Werner Marx, *Heidegger and the Tradition*, trans. Theodore Kisiel and Murray Greene, Evanston, 11.: Northwestern University Press, 1970; Michael Allen Gillespie, *Hegel, Heidegger, and the Ground of History*, Chicago: University of Chicago Press, 1984; Sandra Lee Bartky, 'Heidegger and the Modes of World Disclosure,' *Philosophy and Phenomenological Research* 40, 2 (Dec 1979): 212–36.

19. Martin Heidegger, 'The Turning,' trans. K. R. Maly, *Research in Phenomenology* 1 (1971): 3–16 (pp. 5–6).

20. On the non-neutrality of technology, see e.g., Heidegger, 'The Question Concerning Technology,' p. 4; Bernstein, 'Heidegger's Silence,' p. 91; Don Ihde, *Technology and the Lifeworld: From Garden to Earth* Bloomington and Indianapolis: Indiana University Press, 1990; Don Ihde, *Instrumental Realism: The Interface Between Philosophy of Science and Philosophy of Technology*, Bloomington and Indianapolis: Indiana University Press, 1991; Don Ihde, *Philosophy of Technology: An Introduction*, New York: Paragon House, 1993.

21. Martin Heidegger, 'The Thing,' in *Poetry, Language and Thought*, trans. A. Hofstadter, New York: Harper and Row, 1971, pp. 163–82 (p. 166).

22. Martin Heidegger, *On Time and Being*, trans. J. Stambaugh, New York: Harper and Row, 1972, p. 20; Martin Heidegger, *On the Way to Language*, trans. P. D Hertz, New York: Harper and Row, 1971, pp. 71–2.

23. Heidegger, *On Time and Being*, p. 24.

CHAPTER 30
THE QUESTION CONCERNING TECHNOLOGY
Martin Heidegger

Note from editor: In this essay, which was to become extremely influential, Heidegger refuses the understanding of technology in its own terms. He seeks to explain that which is fundamentally different about modern technology, and finds that this does not lie in the proliferation of tools, machines, technique and applications; rather, modern technology is a mode of revealing which is a "setting upon" and "challenging forth" of nature that also conceals as it conceals itself.

…. The essence of technology[1] is by no means anything technological. Thus we shall never experience our relationship to the essence of technology[2] so long as we merely conceive and push forward the technological, put up with it, or evade it.

Everywhere we remain unfree and chained to technology, whether we passionately affirm or deny it. But we are delivered over to it in the worst possible way when we regard it as some-thing neutral; for this conception of it, to which today we particularly like to do homage, makes us utterly blind to the essence of technology.

According to ancient doctrine, the essence of a thing is considered to be what the thing is. We ask the question concerning technology when we ask what it is. Everyone knows the two statements that answer our question. One says: Technology is a means to an end. The other says: Technology is a human activity. The two definitions of technology belong together. For to posit ends and procure and utilize the means to them is a human activity. The manufacture and utilization of equipment, tools, and machines, the manufactured and used things themselves, and the needs and ends that they serve, all belong to what technology is. The whole complex of these contrivances is technology. Technology itself is a contrivance, or, in Latin, an *instrumentum*.[3]

The current conception of technology, according to which it is a means and a human activity, can therefore be called the instrumental and anthropological definition of technology.

Who would ever deny that it is correct? It is in obvious conformity with what we are envisioning when we talk about technology. The instrumental definition of technology is indeed so uncannily correct that it even holds for modern technology, of

which, in other respects, we maintain with some justification that it is, in contrast to the older handwork technology, something completely different and therefore new. Even the power plant with its turbines and generators is a man-made means to an end established by man. Even the jet aircraft and the high-frequency apparatus are means to ends. A radar station is of course less simple than a weather vane. To be sure, the construction of a high-frequency apparatus requires the interlocking of various processes of technical industrial production. And certainly a sawmill in a secluded valley of the Black Forest is a primitive means compared with the hydroelectric plant in the Rhine River.

But this much remains correct: modern technology too is a means to an end. That is why the instrumental conception of technology conditions every attempt to bring man into the right relation to technology. Everything depends on our manipulating technology in the proper manner as a means. We will, as we say, "get" technology 'spiritually in hand." We will master it. The will to mastery becomes all the more urgent the more technology threatens to slip from human control.

But suppose now that technology were no mere means, how would it stand with the will to master it? (.....)

Instrumentality is considered to be the fundamental characteristic of technology. If we inquire, step by step, into what technology, represented as means, actually is, then we shall arrive at revealing. The possibility of all productive manufacturing lies in revealing. Technology is therefore no mere means. Technology is a way of revealing. If we give heed to this, then another whole realm for the essence of technology will open itself up to us. It is the realm of revealing, i.e., of truth.

This prospect strikes us as strange. Indeed, it should do so, should do so as persistently as possible and with so much urgency that we will finally take seriously the simple question of what the name "technology" means. The word stems from the Greek. Technikon means that which belongs to techne. We must observe two things with respect to the meaning of this word. One is that techne is the name not only for the activities and skills of the craftsman, but also for the arts of the mind and the fine arts. Techne belongs to bringing-forth, to poiesis; it is something poietic.

The other point that we should observe with regard to technë is even more important. From earliest times until Plato the word techne is linked with the word episteme. Both words are names for knowing in the widest sense. They mean to be entirely at home in something, to understand and be expert in it. Such knowing provides an opening up. As an opening up it is a revealing. Aristotle, in a discussion of special importance distinguishes between episteme and techne and indeed with respect to what and how they reveal. Technë is a mode of aletheuein. It reveals whatever does not bring itself forth and does not yet lie here before us, whatever can look and turn out now one way and now another. Whoever builds a house or a ship or forges a sacrificial chalice reveals what is to be brought forth ..... . This revealing gathers together in advance the aspect and the matter of ship or house, with a view to the finished thing envisioned as completed, and from this gathering determines the manner of its construction. Thus what is decisive in techne does not lie at all in making and manipulating nor in the using of means, but rather in the aforementioned revealing. It is as revealing, and not as manufacturing, that techne is a bringing-forth.

Thus the clue to what the word technë means and to how the Greeks defined it leads us into the same context that opened itself to us when we pursued the question of what instrumentality as such in truth might be.

Technology is a mode of revealing. Technology comes to presence [West] in the realm where revealing and unconcealment take place, where alëtheia, truth, happens.

In opposition to this definition of the essential domain of technology, one can object that it indeed holds for Greek thought and that at best it might apply to the techniques of the handcraftsman, but that it simply does not fit modern machine-powered technology. And it is precisely the latter and it alone that is the disturbing thing, that moves us to ask the question concerning technology per se. It is said that modern technology is something incomparably different from all earlier technologies because it is based on modern physics as an exact science. Meanwhile we have come to understand more clearly that the reverse holds true as well: Modern physics, as experimental, is dependent upon technical apparatus and upon progress in the building of apparatus. The establishing of this mutual relationship between technology and physics is correct. But it remains a merely historiographical establishing of facts and says nothing about that in which this mutual relationship is grounded. The decisive question still remains: Of what essence is modern technology that it happens to think of putting exact science to use?

What is modern technology? It too is a revealing. Only when we allow our attention to rest on this fundamental characteristic does that which is new in modern technology show itself to us.

And yet the revealing that holds sway throughout modern technology does not unfold into a bringing-forth in the sense of poiesis. The revealing that rules in modern technology is a challenging which puts to nature the unreasonable demand that it supply energy that can be extracted and stored as such. But does this not hold true for the old windmill as well? No. Its sails do indeed turn in the wind; they are left entirely to the wind's blowing. But the windmill does not unlock energy from the air currents in order to store it.

In contrast, a tract of land is challenged into the putting out of coal and ore. The earth now reveals itself as a coal mining district, the soil as a mineral deposit. The field that the peasant formerly cultivated and set in order [*bestellte*] appears differently than it did when to set in order still meant to take care of and to maintain. The work of the peasant does not challenge the soil of the field. In the sowing of the grain it places the seed in the keeping of the forces of growth and watches over its increase. But meanwhile even the cultivation of the field has come under the grip of another kind of setting-in-order, which sets upon [*stellt*] nature. It sets upon it in the sense of challenging it. Agriculture is now the mechanized food industry. Air is now set upon to yield nitrogen, earth to yield ore, ore to yield uranium, for example; uranium is set upon to yield atomic energy which can be released either for destruction or for peaceful use.

This setting-upon that challenges forth the energies of nature is an expediting [*Fordern*] in two ways. It expedites in that it unlocks and exposes.

(.....)

The hydroelectric plant is set into the current of the Rhine. It sets the Rhine to supplying its hydraulic pressure, which then sets the turbines turning. This turning sets those machines in motion whose thrust sets going the electric current for which the long-distance power station and its network of cables are set up to dispatch electricity. In the context of the interlocking processes pertaining to the orderly disposition of electrical energy, even the Rhine itself appears as something at our command. The hydroelectric plant is not built into the Rhine River as was the old wooden bridge that joined bank with bank for hundreds of years. Rather the river is dammed up into the power plant. What the river is now, namely, a water power supplier, derives from out of the essence of the power station. In order that we may even remotely consider the monstrousness that reigns here, let us ponder for a moment the contrast that speaks out of the two titles, "The Rhine" as dammed up into the power works, and "The Rhine" as uttered out of the art work, in Hölderlin's hymn by that name. But, it will be replied, the Rhine is still a river in the landscape, is it not? Perhaps. But how? In no other way than as an object on call for inspection by a tour group ordered there by the vacation industry.

The revealing that rules throughout modern technology has the character of a setting-upon, in the sense of a challenging-forth. That challenging happens in that the energy concealed in nature is unlocked, what is unlocked is transformed, what is transformed is stored up, what is stored up is, in turn, distributed, and what is distributed is switched about ever anew. Unlocking, transforming, storing, distributing, and switching about are ways of revealing. But the revealing never simply comes to an end. Neither does it run off into the indeterminate. The revealing reveals to itself its own manifoldly interlocking paths, through regulating their course. This regulating itself is, for its part, everywhere secured. Regulating and securing even become the chief characteristics of the challenging revealing.

What kind of unconcealment is it, then, that is peculiar to that which comes to stand forth through this setting-upon that challenges? Everywhere everything is ordered to stand by, to be immediately at hand; indeed to stand there just so that it may be on call for a further ordering. Whatever is ordered about in this way has its own standing. We call it the standing-reserve [*Bestand*] The word expresses here something more, and something more essential, than mere "stock." The name "standing-reserve" assumes the rank of an inclusive rubric. It designates nothing less than the way in which everything presences that is wrought upon by the challenging revealing. Whatever stands by in the sense of standing-reserve no longer stands over against us as object.

(.....)

Who accomplishes the challenging setting-upon through which what we call the real is revealed as standing-reserve? Obviously, man. To what extent is man capable of such a revealing? Man can indeed conceive, fashion, and carry through this or that in one way or another. But man does not have control over Un-concealment itself, in which at any given time the real shows itself or withdraws. The fact that the real has been showing itself in the light of Ideas ever since the time of Plato, Plato did not bring about. The thinker only responded to what addressed itself to him.

Only to the extent that man for his part is already challenged to exploit the energies of nature can this ordering revealing happen. If man is challenged, ordered, to do this, then does not man himself belong even more originally than nature within the standing-reserve? The current talk about human resources, about the supply of patients for a clinic, gives evidence of this. The forester who, in the wood, measures the felled timber and to all appearances walks the same forest path in the same way as did his grandfather is today commanded by profit-making in the lumber industry, whether he knows it or not. He is made subordinate to the orderability of cellulose, which for its part is challenged forth by the need for paper, which is then delivered to newspapers and illustrated magazines. The latter, in their turn, set public opinion to swallowing what is printed, so that a set configuration of opinion becomes available on demand. Yet precisely because man is challenged more originally than are the energies of nature, i.e., into the process of ordering, he never is transformed into mere standing-reserve. Since man drives technology forward, he takes part in ordering as a way of revealing. But the unconcealment itself, within which ordering unfolds, is never a human handiwork, any more than is the realm through which man is already passing every time he as a subject relates to an object.

(.....)

We now name that challenging claim which gathers man thither to order the self-revealing as standing-reserve: "Ge-stell" [Enframing][4]

(.....)

Enframing means the gathering together of that setting-upon which sets upon man, i.e; challenges him forth, to reveal the real, in the mode of ordering, as standing-reserve. Enframing means that way of revealing which holds sway in the essence of modern technology and which is itself nothing technological. On the other hand, all those things that are so familiar to us and are standard parts of an assembly, such as rods, pistons, and chassis, belong to the technological. The assembly itself, however, together with the aforementioned stockparts, falls within the sphere of technological activity; and this activity always merely responds to the challenge of Enframing, but it never comprises Enframing itself or brings it about.

The word stellen [to set upon] in the name Ge-stell [Enframing] not only means challenging. At the same time it should preserve the suggestion of another Stellen from which it stems, namely, that producing and presenting [Her- und Dar-stellen] which, in the sense of poiesis, lets what presences come forth into unconcealment. This producing that brings forth—e.g., the erecting of a statue in the temple precinct—and the challenging ordering now under consideration are indeed fundamentally different, and yet they remain related in their essence. Both are - ways of revealing, of altheia. In Enframing, that unconcealment comes to pass in conformity with what technology reveals the real as standing-reserve. This work is therefore neither only a human activity nor a mere means within such activity. The merely instrumental, merely anthropological definition of technology is therefore in principle untenable. And it cannot be rounded out by being referred back to some metaphysical or religious explanation that undergirds it.

It remains true, nonetheless, that man in the technological age is, in a particularly striking way, challenged forth into revealing. That revealing concerns nature, above all, as the chief storehouse of the standing energy reserve. Accordingly, man's ordering attitude and behavior themselves first in the rise of modern physics as an exact science. Modern science's way of representing pursues and entraps nature as a calculable coherence of forces. Modern physics is not experimental physics because it applies apparatus to the questioning of nature. Rather the reverse is true. Because physics, indeed already as pure theory, sets nature up to exhibit itself as a coherence of forces calculable in advance, it therefore orders its experiments precisely for the purpose of asking whether and how nature reports itself when set up in this way.

…

Because the essence of modern technology lies in Enframing, modern technology must employ exact physical science. Through its so doing, the deceptive illusion arises that modern technology is applied physical science. This illusion can maintain itself only so long as neither the essential origin of modern science nor indeed the essence of modern technology is adequately found out through questioning.

…

Again we ask: Does this revealing happen somewhere beyond all human doing? No. But neither does it happen exclusively in man, or decisively through man.

Enframing is the gathering together that belongs to that setting-upon which sets upon man and puts him in position to reveal the real, in the mode of ordering, as standing-reserve. As the one who is challenged forth in this way, man stands within

the essential realm of Enframing. He can never take up a relationship to it only subsequently. Thus the question as to how we are to arrive at a relationship to the essence of technology, asked in this way, always comes too late. But never too late comes the question as to whether we actually experience ourselves as the ones whose activities everywhere, public and private, are challenged forth by Enframing. Above all, never too late comes the question as to whether and how we actually admit ourselves into that wherein Enframing itself comes to presence.

The essence of modern technology starts man upon the way of that revealing through which the real everywhere, more or less distinctly, becomes standing-reserve. "To start upon a way" means "to send" in our ordinary language. We shall call that sending-that-gathers [versammelde Schicken} which first starts man upon a way of revealing, destining [Geschick]…

Yet when destining reigns in the mode of Enframing, it is the supreme danger. This danger attests itself to us in two ways. As soon as what is unconcealed no longer concerns man even as object, but does so, rather, exclusively as standing-reserve, and man in the midst of objectlessness is nothing but the orderer of the standing-reserve, then he comes to the very brink of a precipitous fall; that is, he comes to the point where he himself will have to be taken as standing-reserve. Meanwhile man, precisely as the one so threatened, exalts himself to the posture of lord of the earth. In this way the impression comes to prevail that everything man encounters exists only insofar as it is his construct. This illusion gives rise in turn to one final delusion: It seems as though man everywhere and always encounters only himself. … *In truth, however, precisely nowhere does man today any longer encounter himself, i.e., his essence.*

Man stands so decisively in attendance on the challenging-forth of Enframing that he does not apprehend Enframing as a claim, that he fails to see himself as the one spoken to, and hence also fails in every way to hear in what respect he ek-sists from out of his essence in the realm of an exhortation or address, and thus can never encounter only himself.

But Enframing does not simply endanger man in his relationship to himself and to everything that is. As a destining, it banishes man into that kind of revealing which is an ordering. Where this ordering holds sway, it drives out every other possibility of revealing. Above all, Enframing conceals that revealing which, in the sense of poiesis, lets what presences come forth into appearance. As compared with that other revealing, the setting-upon that challenges forth thrusts man into a relation to that which is, that is at once antithetical and rigorously ordered. Where Enframing holds sway, regulating and securing of the standing-reserve mark all revealing. They no longer even let their own fundamental characteristic appear, namely, this revealing as such.

Thus the challenging Enframing not only conceals a former way of revealing, bringing-forth, but it conceals revealing itself and with it that wherein unconcealment, i.e., truth, comes to pass.

Enframing blocks the shining-forth and holding-sway of truth. The destining that sends into ordering is consequently the extreme danger. What is dangerous is not technology. There is no demonry of technology, but rather there is the mystery of its essence. The essence of technology, as a destining of revealing is the danger. The transformed meaning of the word 'Enframing' will perhaps become somewhat more familiar to us now if we think Enframing in the sense of destining and danger.

The threat to man does not come in the first instance from the potentially lethal machines and apparatus of technology. The actual threat has already affected man in his essence. The rule of Enframing threatens man with the possibility that it could be denied to him to enter into a more original revealing and hence to experience the call of a more primal truth.

Thus, where Enframing reigns, there is danger in the highest sense.

But where danger is, grows

The saving power also.

Let us think carefully about these words of Hölderlin. What does it mean "to save"?

(.....)

..... It is precisely in Enframing, which threatens to sweep man away into ordering as the supposed single way of revealing, and so thrusts man into the danger of the surrender of his free essence—it is precisely in this extreme danger that the innermost indestructible belongingness of man within granting may come to light, provided that we, for our part, begin to pay heed to the coming to presence of technology.

Thus the coming to presence of technology harbors in itself what we least suspect, the possible arising of the saving power.

Everything, then, depends upon this: that we ponder this arising and that, recollecting, we watch over it. How can this happen? Above all through our catching sight of what comes to presence in technology, instead of merely staring at the technological. So long as we represent technology as an instrument, we remain held fast in the will to master it. We press on past the essence of technology.

When, however, we ask how the instrumental comes to presence as a kind of causality then we experience this coming to presence as the destining of a revealing.

When we consider, finally, that the coming to presence of the essence of technology comes to pass in the granting that needs and uses man so that he may share in revealing, then the following becomes clear:

The essence of technology is in a lofty sense ambiguous. Such ambiguity points to the mystery of all revealing, i.e., of truth.

On the one hand, Enframing challenges forth into the frenzied-ness of ordering that blocks every view into the coming-to-pass of revealing and so radically endangers the relation to the essence of truth.

On the other hand, Enframing comes to pass for its part in the granting that lets man endure—as yet unexperienced, but perhaps more experienced in the future—that he may be the one who is needed and used for the safekeeping of the coming to presence of truth. Thus does the arising of the saving power appear.

The irresistibility of ordering and the restraint of the saving power draw past each other like the paths of two stars in the course of the heavens. But precisely this, their passing by, is the hidden side of their nearness.

When we look into the ambiguous essence of technology, we behold the constellation, the stellar course of the mystery.

The question concerning technology is the question concerning the constellation in which revealing and concealing, in which the coming to presence of truth, comes to pass.

But what help is it to us to look into the constellation of truth? We look into the danger and see the growth of the saving power.

Through this we are not yet saved. But we are thereupon summoned to hope in the growing light of the saving power. How can this happen? Here and now and in little things, that we may foster the saving power in its increase. This includes holding always before our eyes the extreme danger.

The coming to presence of technology threatens revealing - threatens it with the possibility that all revealing will be consumed in ordering and that everything will present itself only in the unconcealedness of standing-reserve. Human activity can never directly counter this danger. Human achievement alone can never banish it. But human reflection can ponder the fact that all saving power must be of a higher essence than what is endangered though at the same time kindred to it.

(…..)

Notes

1. (Ed.) Notes are by translator William Lovitt.

2. "Essence" is the traditional translation of the German noun Wesen. One of Heidegger's principal aims in this essay is to seek the true meaning of essence through or by way of the "correct" meaning. He will later show that Wesen does not simply mean what something is, but that it means, further, the way in which something pursues its course, the way in which it remains through time as what it is. Heidegger writes elsewhere that the noun Wesen does not mean quidditas originally, but rather "enduring as presence" (das Währen als Gegenwart). (See An Introduction to Metaphysics, trans. Ralph Manheim [New York: Doubleday, 1961], p. 59.) Wesen as a noun derives from the verb wesen, which is seldom used as such in modern German. The verb survives primarily in inflected forms of the verb sein (to be) and in such words as the adjective anwesend (present). The old verbal forms from which wesen stems meant to tarry or dwell. Heidegger repeatedly identifies wesen as "the same as währen [to last or endure]." … As a verb, wesen will usually be translated here with "to come to presence," a rendering wherein the meaning "endure" should be strongly heard. Occasionally it will be translated "to essence," and its gerund will be rendered with "essencing." The noun Wesen will regularly be translated "essence" until Heidegger's explanatory discussion is reached. Thereafter, in this and the succeeding essays, it will often be translated with "coming to presence." In relation to all these renderings, the reader should bear in mind a point that is of fundamental importance to Heidegger, namely, that the root of wesen, with its meaning "to dwell," provides one integral component in the meaning of the verb sein (to be). (Cf. An Introduction to Metaphysics, p. 59,)

3. Instrumentum signifies that which functions to heap or build up or to arrange. Heidegger here equates it with the noun Einrichtung, translated "contrivance," which can also mean arrangement, adjustment, furnishing, or equipment. In accordance with his dictum that the true must be sought by way of the correct, Heidegger here anticipates with his identification of technology as an instrumentum and an Einrichtung his later "true" characterization of technology in terms of setting-in-place, ordering, Enframing, and standing-reserve.

4. The translation "Enframing" for Ge-stell is intended to suggest, through the use of the prefix "en-," something of the active meaning that Heidegger here gives to the German word. While following the discussion that now ensues, in which Enframing assumes a central role, the reader should be careful not to interpret the word as though it simply meant a framework of some sort. Instead he should constantly remember that En-framing is fundamentally a calling-forth. It is a "challenging claim," a demanding summons, that "gathers" so as to reveal. This claim enframes in that it assembles and orders. It puts into a framework or configuration everything that it summons forth, through an ordering for use that it is forever restructuring anew.

CHAPTER 31
TECHNICAL MENTALITY
Gilbert Simondon, translated by Arne De Boever

Note from editor: Philosopher of technology, Gilbert Simondon (1924-1989) argues that the disparity between artisanal vs industrial mode can be overcome, paradoxically, by a deepening of the characteristics of the industrial mode. Both Simondon and Heidegger realize just how thorough-going is technology's transformative powers, in the extent to which it shapes world-making and human being. But their positions and moods are very different. Simondon's explains how radically different craft production is from machine (industrial) production – in the relation of information, energy, material and the human being, and while the industrial mode makes the work of human beings 'weaker' and more fragmented, he argues against a return to craft because contemporary societies need large quantities of manufactured products. This claim would not hold up today given what is now known about the links between industrial production and global warming. Yet Simondon is not an apologist for consumerism as his illuminating description of transport systems shows, and the final parts of his text point to ways industrial technology could sustain that which is essential to sustain.

This chapter is not concerned with ontology but with axiology. It aims to show that there exists a technical mentality, and that this mentality is developing, and is therefore incomplete and at risk of being prematurely considered as monstrous and unbalanced. It requires a preliminary attitude of generosity towards the order of reality that it seeks to manifest, because this incomplete genesis brings into play values that a general refusal [of this mentality] could condemn to ignorance and would risk negating. We will try to show that the technical mentality is coherent, positive, productive in the domain of the cognitive schemas, but incomplete and in confl ict with itself in the domain of the affective categories because it has not yet properly emerged; and finally, that it is without unity and is almost entirely to be construed within the order of the will.

Cognitive schemas

……... Leaving Antiquity[1] aside, technology has already yielded in at least two ways schemas of intelligibility that are endowed with a latent power of universality: namely, in the form of the Cartesian mechanism and of cybernetic theory.

In the Cartesian mechanism, the fundamental operation of the simple machine is analogous to the functioning of logical thought capable of being rigorous and productive. A simple machine is a transfer system that, in the particular case in which the movement is presumed to be reversible, in the state of equilibrium, establishes the identity of a work that puts into motion and a work that resists. If each piece of the machine carries out this transfer rigorously, the number of pieces can be whatever; what changes is merely the direction of forces – as with the pulley – or the factors (force and movement) of a product that remains constant, as in the case of the pulley-blocks. The rational mental process returns the essence of the customary technical objects to this transfer schema: a chain is an enchainment of links, with the second link being fixed to the first just as the first is fixed to the anchoring ring. The transfer of forces goes from link to link, so that if each link is welded well and there are no gaps in the enchainment, the last link is fixed to the anchoring point in a more mediated but also more rigorous way than the first.

(…..)

What is carried out in both the rational study of machines and in the conduct of thought is the *transfer without losses*: science and philosophy are possible because the transfer without losses is presumed to be possible. Consequently, the only domains that are accessible to philosophical reflection are those with a continuous structure. It will therefore be clear why one has wanted to consider living beings as machines: if they were not machines *ontologically*, they would have to be so at least *analogically* in order to be objects of science.

Cybernetics, which was born from the mathematization of the automatic regulation apparatuses [*dispositifs*] – particularly useful for the construction of automatic equipment of airplanes in flight – introduces into this the recurring aim of information on a relay apparatus as the basic schema that allows for an active adaptation to a spontaneous finality. This technical realization of a finalized conduct has served as a model of intelligibility for the study of a large number of regulations – or of regulation failures – in the living, both human and non-human, and of phenomena subject to becoming, such as the species equilibrium between predators and objects of prey, or of geographical and meteorological phenomena: variations of the level of lakes, climatic regimes.

……

The application of such schemas of intelligibility requires two main conditions, which can be presented as postulates of the 'technical mentality':

1. *The subsets are relatively detachable from the whole of which they are a part.* What technical activity produces is not an absolutely indivisible organism that is metaphysically one and undissolvable. The technical object can be repaired; it can be completed; a simple analogy between the technical object and the living is fallacious, in the sense that, at the moment of its very construction, the technical object is conceived as something that may need control, repair and maintenance, through testing and modification, or, if necessary, a complete change of one or several of the subsets that compose it. This is what one calls anticipated 'maintenance', to use the Anglo-Saxon term.

This postulate is extremely important when one questions the way in which one can engage with a living being, a human being or an institution. The holistic postulate, which is often presented as an attitude of respect for life, a person or the integrity of a tradition, is perhaps merely a lazy way out. To accept or reject a being wholesale, because it is a whole, is perhaps to avoid adopting towards it the more generous attitude: namely, that of careful examination. A truly technical attitude would be more refined than the easy fundamentalism of a moral judgment and of justice. The distinction of the subsets and of the modes of their relative solidarity would thus be the first mental work that is taught by the cognitive content of the technical mentality.[2]

2. The second postulate is that of the levels and the regimes: *if one wants to understand a being completely, one must study it by considering it in its entelechy, and not in its inactivity or its static state.*

The majority of technical realities are subject to the existence of a threshold to start up and to maintain their own functioning; above this threshold, they are absurd, self-destructive; below it, they are self-stable. Very often, the invention consists in supposing the conditions of their functioning realized – in supposing the threshold problem resolved. This is why the majority of inventions proceed by condensation and concretization, by reducing the number of primitive elements to a minimum, which is at the same time an optimum. ……….

Analogically, it is possible to anticipate the existence, within different orders of reality, of certain *effects* (used here as in the expressions 'the Raman effect', 'the Compton effect') that for their existence require determinate thresholds to be crossed. These effects are not structures; they are different from these structures in that they require the threshold to be crossed. An internal combustion engine that is turned off is in a stable state and cannot turn itself on; it needs a certain amount of energy coming from outside, it needs to receive a certain angular speed in order to reach the threshold of self-maintenance, the threshold beyond which it functions as a regime of automatism, with each phase of the cycle preparing the conditions of completion for the following phase. From these few observations, we can conclude that the technical mentality already offers coherent and usable schemas for a cognitive interpretation. With the Cartesian mechanism and cybernetics, it has already yielded two movements of thought; but in the case when there is an awareness of the systematic use of the two postulates presented above, it also appears to be capable of contributing to the formation of larger schemas.

Affective modalities

The picture is much less clear, however, as soon as one tries to analyse affective contents. In this case, one encounters an antagonism between the artisanal and the industrial modalities, an antagonism that is paired to an impossibility of completely separating these two aspects. The craftsman's nostalgia traverses not only the industrial life of production, but also the different daily regimes of the consumption of goods coming from the industrial world. It is difficult to return a bundle of perfectly coherent and unified traits to the opposition between the artisanal and the industrial modality when one wants to account for the genesis of affective modalities. However, we will propose a criterion that, after several attempts, seemed to be the least problematic: in the case of the craftsman, all conditions depend on the human being, and the source of energy is the same as that of information. The two sources are both in the human operator. There, energy is like the availability of the gesture, the exercise of muscular force; information simultaneously resides in the human operator as something learned, drawn from the individual past enriched by education, and as the actual exercise of the sensorial equipment that controls and regulates the application of the learned gestures to the concrete materiality of the workable material and to the particular characteristics of the aim [of the work]. The manipulation is carried out according to continuous schemas on realities that are of the same scale as the operator. Correlatively, the distance between the act of working and the conditions of use of the product of the work is weak. The shoemaker has directly taken the measurements, the saddler knows for which horse he is working. Recurrence is possible; the speed with which the object wears off, the types of deformation of the product during usage are known to the craftsman, who not only constructs but also repairs.

.... The industrial modality appears when the source of information and the source of energy separate: namely, when the Human Being is merely the source of information, and Nature is required to furnish the energy. The machine is different from the tool in that it is a relay; it has two different entry points, that of energy and that of information. The fabricated product that it yields is the effect of the modulation of this energy through this information, the effect that is practised on a workable material. In the case of the tool, which is handheld, the entry of energy and the entry of information are mixed, or at the very least partially superimposed. Of course, one can guide the chisel of the sculptor with one hand, and push it with the other, but it is the same body that harmonizes the two hands, and a single nervous system that appropriates their movement into such detail from the material and for the set aim. The potter's work, which is moved by his feet, is still of the same Technical Mentality kind, but it allows one to anticipate the birth of the machine. Glassmaking is artisanal in so far as the glass-maker furnishes the energy that dilates the initial bubble by blowing, and in so far as he regulates through the rhythm of his blowing the speed of the plastic deformation of the glass. But it becomes industrial when the energy is borrowed from a compressor.

When he borrows energy from a natural source, the human being discovers an infinite reserve, and comes to possess a considerable power. For it is possible to set up a series of relays, which means that a weak energy can lead to the usage of considerable energies.[3]

Unfortunately, the *entry of information* that comes into the work is no longer unique in the way it is with the artisanal gesture; it happens through several moments and at several levels. It takes place a first time with the invention of the machine – an invention that sometimes implies the bringing into play of considerable zones of knowledge and the gathering of a large number of human beings. It happens a second time with the *construction* of the machine and the regulation of the machine, which are modes of activity that are different from the machine's usage. Finally, it happens a third and a fourth time, first in learning to work with the machine, and then in the machine's usage. Whereas the machine constitutes a complete technical schema, as the relation of nature and the human being, as the encounter of information and energy operating on material, none of the four moments of information contribution is organically linked to and balanced out by the others. The act of information contribution becomes dissociated; it is exploded into separate moments taken on by separate individuals or groups. In order for the craftsman to recognize his equivalent in the industrial modality, the same human being must be inventor, constructor and operator. However, the effect of this amplification and complication of the industrial world is to spread out the different roles from each other: not only the source of information from the source of energy and the source of primary material, but even the different tasks of information contribution. It is thus a weaker part of the total capacities of the human being that is engaged in the industrial act, both when s/he is operator and in the other roles of information contribution. The iterative and fragmentary regime of the task of the operator in industrial production is an 'anatomy of work' that provokes different effects of industrial fatigue. But it is also exhausting to have only invention as a task, without also participating in construction and operation. The figure of the unhappy inventor came about at the same time as that of the dehumanized worker; it is its counter-type and it arises from the same cause. To put itself at the dimension of the machine's energy entry, the information entry complicates itself, becomes divided and specialized, with the result that the human being is isolated not only from nature[4] but also from himself, and enclosed in piecemeal tasks, even as inventor. He thus encounters the discontinuous through work.

However, trying to return to directly artisanal modes of production is an illusion. The needs of contemporary societies require not only large quantities of products and manufactured objects, but also states that cannot be obtained by means of the human body and by the tool. This is because the temperatures, the pressures, the required physical reactions, the scale of the conditions do not match those of human life. The workplace, on the other hand, is a *human environment*.

It is in this very emphasis on industrial production, in the deepening of its characteristics, that an overcoming of the antithesis between the artisanal modality and the industrial one can be studied with a greater likelihood of success. And this not only generally and superficially but also by means of what, within the industrial organization of the production, has pushed to its extreme limits the specialized fragmentation of human information contribution: the rationalization of work through a series of methods of which Taylorism was the first.

Voluntary action: A study of norms

But we must cut short here the consideration of the affective modalities in order to investigate norms of voluntary action, and thus to complete this construction of the technical mentality. Indeed, the technical mentality can be developed into schemes of action and into values, to the point of yielding a morality in human environments that are entirely dedicated to industrial production. But in so far as these environments remain separated from the social field of the usage of products, in so far as they themselves remain fragmented into several specialized groups by their different functions of information contribution to machines – mastery, technicians, workers – they cannot elaborate a value code that is capable of becoming universal because they do not have the experience of technical reality as a whole. The technocratic attitude cannot be universalized because it consists of reinventing the world like a neutral field for the penetration of machines; constructing a metal tower or an immense bridge undoubtedly means making a pioneer work and showing how industrial power can leave the factory in order to gain in nature, but there is something of the isolation of the inventor that subsists in this activity in so far as the tower or the bridge does not become part of a network covering the Earth in its mazes, in accordance with the geographical structures and living possibilities of this Earth. The Eiffel Tower and the Garabit viaduct must be considered as the arrival of the end of the industrial concentration around sources of energy or primary material sources: that is to say, not as spectacularly isolated centres and successes, but as the first maze of a virtual network. The Eiffel Tower, which was entirely designed and fabricated in the factory and only assembled on site, without a single correction, has now become the carrier of aerials; it interconnects with hundreds of pylons, masts and stations by which Europe will be covered. It becomes part of this multifunctional network that marks the key points of the geographical and human world.

It is the standardization of the subsets, the industrial possibility of the production of separate pieces that are all alike, that allows for the creation of networks. When one puts railroad tracks over hundreds of kilometers, when one rolls off a cable from city to city and sometimes from continent to continent, it is the industrial modality that takes leave from the industrial centre in order to extend itself through nature. It is not a question here of the rape of nature or of the victory of the Human Being over the elements, because in fact it is the natural structures themselves that serve as the attachment point for the network that is being developed; the relay points of the Hertzian 'cables', for example, rejoin with the high sites of ancient sacredness above the valleys and the seas. Here, the technical mentality successfully completes itself and rejoins nature by turning itself into a thought-network, into the material and conceptual synthesis of particularity and concentration, individuality and collectivity – because the entire force of the network is available in each one of its points, and its mazes are woven together with those of the world, in the concrete and the particular.

The case of information networks is, so to speak, an ideal case where the success is virtually complete, because here energy and information are united again after having been separated in the industrial phase. At the same time, the assemblages and the substructures of the industrial gigantism return in a more manageable way, in a lighter form; electronics and telecommunications use reduced tonnages, moderate energies, dimensions that are not crushing. The factory rediscovers something of the workplace when it is transformed into a laboratory. It is no longer for the individual user, as in the artisanal modality, but for the simultaneously collective and individual user – nature itself – that the laboratory anticipates a made-to-measure assemblage. Such lines of pylons, such a chain of relays constitute the harness of nature. Only the fabrication of separate pieces remains industrial. At the same time, the distance between the inventor, the constructor and the operator is reduced; the three types converge towards the image of the technician, this time both intellectual and handy, who knows at the same time how to calculate and how to install cabling.

Very close to the case of information networks is that of networks of *energy distribution*. Electric energy is at the same time information and energy; on the one hand, it can be indefinitely paired down without a loss of productivity. A vibrator, which is a motor, can be located in the point of a tool as light as a pencil and feed on the network. A human being can easily manipulate with a single hand a 1/3 horsepower engine. This energy can, at the very moment of usage, entirely be modulated by information of which it becomes the faithful carrier. On the other hand, the very standardization of the conditions of energy production, which allows for the interconnection and normalized distribution, turns this energy into the carrier of information; one can ask the alternative network to make function (as the source of energy) a watch whose workings it regulates as carrier of information. The simultaneous usage is concretized in the synchronic motor.

Communication and transportation networks are, by contrast, less pure. They do not succeed in revealing themselves in their true function, and the technical mentality does not succeed in making itself heard in any preponderant way – first of all, because social or psychosocial inferences put a considerable burden [on these networks]; second, because, unlike information or energy networks, they are not entirely new and without functional antecedents. The railway enjoyed a privileged situation because it was relatively clearly distinct from the road, which meant that it could develop in an almost autonomous way. In the case of these other networks, however, the social begins to manifest itself in the form of *obsolescence*, the kind of disuse that is linked to the aging of convention and the transformation of social habits rather than a wearing-off or a loss of functionality of the technical object. A wagon with merchandise or a tender of a locomotive ages less quickly than a passenger car, with its ornaments and inscriptions; the one that is most overloaded with inessential ornaments is the one that goes out of fashion the most quickly.

But it is in the technical objects suited for the road network that the resistance opposed to the development of the technical mentality is the clearest. Obsolescence hits the passenger car much faster than the utility vehicle or the agricultural tractor, which nevertheless are its close cousins; the car ages faster than the plane, whereas the plane has technically gone through more important transformations than the car. This is because the plane is made for the runway and for the air. It is necessarily a *network reality* before being a separate object. The car is conceived not only as a network reality – like trucks – but as a social object, an item of clothing in which the user presents himself. It thus receives characteristics like the ones one used to wear on clothes and that overburdened them with lace and embroideries . . . these scurf-like ornaments of psychosocial life – here, they become paint, chrome, aerials. The social importance can also express itself through mass, volume and the size of the vehicle.

To bring about the production of the technical mentality in the domain of voluntary choice, one could try to apply the categories of a common ethics of the relation between human beings: for example, the category of sincerity. A car deteriorates quickly because it was made to be seen rather than to be used; the space taken up by the width of the doors is not protected against rust; the underside is not treated according to the principles of aerodynamics whereas the visible parts are abundantly profiled.

But the essential is not there, and the introduction of a dualist moral system of good and evil, of the hidden and the manifest, would not lead one very far. To find real norms in this domain, one must return towards the cognitive schemas that have already been drawn out, and ask oneself how they can respond to the exigency manifested by the pressing incoherence of the affective modalities.

The reason for the inessential character of technical objects, which is at the same time the cause of this inflation of obsolescence that has hit the population of produced objects, is the absence of an industrial deepening of production.

A car becomes obsolete very fast because it is not one and the same act of invention, construction and production that simultaneously makes the road network and the cars appear. Between the network – this functional harness of the geographical world – and the cars that traverse this network, the human being inserts himself as a virtual buyer; a car only comes to function if it is bought, if it is chosen, after it has been produced. There is a recurrence that comes into play on the basis of this mediation. The constructor, who has to produce serially, needs to calculate the possibilities of sales; not only must he simultaneously construct the network and the cars, but he also has to anticipate this sales option. In order to be valuable, a car must be bought after having been constructed, like the Roman child who was put into the world by the mother but was only admitted to life after *elevatio*. One could also compare this alienated condition of the produced object in the situation of venality to that of a slave on the market in Antiquity, or to that of a woman in a situation of social inferiority; the introduction to active existence happens through means that are inadequate to the real functions. It takes place against entelechy and thus creates a duality, a prevalence of the inessential, a distortion of true nature; choice is made under the dubious influence of charm, prestige, flattery, of all the social myths or of personal faiths. In the inessential situation of the buyer – who is neither a constructor nor a user in act, the human being who chooses, introduces into his choice a bundle of non-technical norms. It is the anticipation, in the project of production, of the play of these norms that creates the mixed character of the venality of the industrial product, and that is the main source of obsolescence. The *distance* between the act of production and the act of usage, this lack of real information, allows for the introduction of the inessential, which creates obsolescence. Because it is judged once and for all, accepted or rejected in full in the decision or the refusal to buy, the object of industrial production is a closed object, a false organism that is seized by a holistic thought that was psychosocially produced; it allows for neither the exercise nor the development of the technical mentality at the level of voluntary decisions and norms of action.

But how is it possible to pass to a structure of the object that would allow one to draw out the technical mentality? First of all, and generally speaking, a position of ascetism allows one to get rid of the artificial and unhealthy character of social burdens, which expresses itself through hypertelic developments or developments that in reality do not function. A contemporary transatlantic liner – a fake floating city rather than an instrument of travel – slowly tends towards the recruitment of lonely, idle ones; the cargo ship is more pure. This proliferation of the inessential already takes hold of the commercial aeroplane: the companies flatter the traveller; the plane grows bigger and heavier. But the essential lies in this: in order for an object to allow for the development of the technical mentality and to be chosen by it, the object itself needs to be of a reticular structure. If one imagines an object that, instead of being closed, offers parts that are conceived as being as close to indestructible as possible, and others by contrast in which there would be concentrated a very high capacity to adjust to each usage, or wear, or possible breakage in case of shock, of malfunctioning, then one obtains an *open* object that can be completed, improved, maintained in the state of perpetual actuality. An electric machine that is not provided with an organ of protection, whether a fuse or a circuit breaker, is only in appearance more simple than a protected machine. When there is an overload, the system of protection kicks in, and the machine becomes absolutely comparable to what it was before the accident, once the system of protection has been returned to its initial state. This return to the initial state presupposes standardization, normalization. The more rigorous this normalization, the more perfect the machine; this is the case with calibrated fuses, or also with electronic tubes that one replaces in a machine. This is the key point: the postindustrial technical object is the unity of two layers of reality – a layer that is as stable and permanent as possible, which adheres to the user and is made to last, and a layer that can be perpetually replaced, changed, renewed, because it is made up of elements that are all similar, impersonal, mass-produced by industry and distributed by all the networks of exchange. It is through participation in this network that the technical object always remains contemporary to its use, always new. However, this conservation in a state of full actuality is precisely made possible through the structures that the cognitive schemas provide; the object needs to heave thresholds of functioning that are known, measured, normalized in order for it to be able to be divided into permanent parts and parts that are voluntarily fragile and subjected to replacement. The object is not only structure but also regime. And the normalization of *thresholds of functioning* expresses itself in the difference between relatively separate subsets [of the whole]; the degree of solidarity is precisely the measure (in the Greek sense of 'metrion') of the relation between the permanent parts and the parts subject to replacement. This measure is what defines the optimum of the regime in the relation of thresholds of functioning.

In conclusion, one can say that the technical mentality is developing, but that this formation has a relation of causality that recurs with the very appearance of postindustrial technical realities; it makes explicit the nature of these realities and tends to furnish them with norms to ensure their development. Such a mentality can only develop if the affective antinomy of the opposition between the artisanal modality and the industrial one is replaced by the firm orientation of a voluntary push towards the development of technical networks, which are postindustrial and thus recover a continuous level [of operation]. If one seeks the sign of the perfection of the technical mentality, one can unite in a single criterion the manifestation of cognitive schemas, affective modalities and norms of action: that of the *opening*. Technical reality lends itself remarkably well to being continued, completed, perfected, extended. In this sense, an extension of the technical mentality is possible, and begins to manifest itself in the domain of the fi ne arts in particular. To construct a building according to the norms of the technical mentality means to conceive of it as being able to be enlarged, continued, amplified without disfiguration or erasure. The 'Le Corbusier monastery' is a beautiful example of the contribution of the technical mentality in architecture; it includes within its plan its proper line of extension, for a further enlargement. And this is possible not only because of the architectural conception of the whole, but also because of the spirit of paring down that manifests itself in the choice of forms and the use of materials; it will be possible, without any break between the old and the new, still to use concrete, shuttering, iron, cables and the tubulature of long corridors. The non-dissimulation of means, this politeness of architecture towards its materials which translates itself by a constant technophany, amounts to a refusal of obsolescence and to the productive discovery amongst sensible species of the permanent availability of the industrial material as the foundation for the continuity of the work.

Source: Gilbert Simondon: Being and Technology, edited by Arne De Boever, Alex Murray, Jon Roffe and Ashley Woodward, Edinburgh University Press, 2012. First published in Jean-Hugues Barthélémy and Vincent Bontems (eds), *Gilbert Simondon. Revue philosophique*, 3 (2006), pp. 343–57.

Notes

1. [W]hich has been rich in schemes of plasticity and of phase changes, reversible or irreversible. These come without a doubt from the artisanal techniques of preparation, the shaping and baking of the clay. These schemes of ontogenesis, coming from an operation entirely possessed by the human being, an operation that is continuous, progressive, and that conforms with the human being's scale, have encountered other schemes, themselves also ontogenetic, but including the encounter of opposed and qualitatively antagonistic principles that are spatially and geographically distinct, and of a dimension that renders them *transcendent* in relation to the human being: the earth and the heavens, the hot and the cold, the dry and the humid. In order for these two realities to encounter each other, they have to be at the same scale. The nature philosophy of Antiquity comes from the encounter of the artisanal and the magical schemes of genesis, of the schemes of continuity and the schemes of discontinuity. Agriculture and nursery are indeed industries and craftsmanships, when the human being does not hold the possession of their means in hand.

2. When the Boeings started exploding in flight, it was a gross mistake to judge them as 'bad planes'; a more precise approach has consisted in studying the behaviour of cells subject to vibrations and constraints of internal suppression, so as to determine the zones of 'fatigue' of metal. A jurist, De Greef, says in *Notre destinée et nos instincts* [Our Destiny and Our Instincts] that a criminal would never be condemned if he were judged in his 'nursery' [in English in the original]; this is undoubtedly because, starting from this initial phase of his life, one would consider him as *constructed*, as composed of different layers in relative solidarity to one another. The condemnation generally sacrifices something by considering the individual as a homogenous whole. This is how racism and xenophobia are produced.

3. In a certain sense, agriculture, nursing and navigation with sails are more industrial than artisanal, to the extent that they appeal to forces that *do not depend on the human being*, and that come from a reality of which the scale surpasses the scale of that which can be manipulated. These operations introduce the *discontinuous* to the same extent; they are, eventually, alienating, and can give rise to a *magico-religious exercise of thought*. Indeed, they

commodulate the human operation of preparation and the cosmological action. Human work remains without results, after the seeds have been sown or the ship has been constructed, if the cosmic act (rain, wind, overflowing of the river) does not come in to receive and amplify the human effort. The human effort must be in accordance with the cosmic act, and be 'en kairo'. In the nursing of cattle, the prosperity of the herd depends not only on the growth of vegetables and of the regime of waters, but also on the epizooties.

4. Industry isolates the human being from nature because it takes charge of the relation human being–nature; it *is*, indeed, through the relation to the human being, which replaces the reality of the cosmic order (the wind, the rain, the overflowing of the river, the epizooty) while diminishing to a certain extent its independence in relation to the human being, but conserving the transcendence.

CHAPTER 32
THE FINITE FRAMEWORK OF LANGUAGE
Michael Heim

Note from editor: The invention of writing (and later, the printing press), was not just a more efficient way of recording spoken language, it marked a major shift in modes of thinking and being. Walter Ong characterized this as the transition from orality to literacy; and this is what Michael Heim builds on here, in order to understand recent developments in language technologies – in particular, the invention of word-processing, Heim argues for the value of engaging Heidegger's thinking on history, 'world' and 'Enframing'.

…

Word processing was originally developed and used by data processors who developed the first text-writing programs as handy aids to their central work of writing programs for data handling. The original text editors used by programmers in their data-handling work were programmer-oriented editors on mainframe computers. The writer programmer uses symbological references to text rather than the direct interactive manipulation of text on a CRT or video monitor. These text editors did not so much manipulate text as apply the reasoning of algorithmic programing to the process of writing. … natural language was interpreted as a standard code and then the code in its electronic form could be operated upon, edited, and transmitted so as to reappear in its natural-language form. The encoding of letters in the ASCII (American Standard Code for Information Interchange) computer code not only permitted the transmission of natural-language at electronic speed; encoding natural language on computers makes possible a new approach to language as directly manipulable in new ways. Data-handling techniques for number-crunching or for the high-speed manipulation of quantified routine information were applied to natural language communication.

Heidegger's premonitions in this matter had penetrating foresight, especially considering how recent the development of microcomputers, has been. Nor was it clear when Heidegger wrote the extent to which computers could be applied to writing via programs for editing, printing, and telecommunications. Still, in places Heidegger touches upon the potential of technology for implementing a "world language" or electronic communications network through the interpretation of natural languages in mathematical-technological terms. His hunches have been connected with the claim he makes that the contemporary world is intelligible as the extreme development of the trend toward rational typification and systematic organization pushed forward by modernity. Logic is the foundation of the systematic thinking which can become the basis for a homogeneous world language. ….. a network of symbols equally applicable to electronic switching-circuitry as to assertions made in natural language; logic in the modern sense can become an underlying digital language to be used for the transmission and communication of natural language. Just as geometrical axioms are no longer bound to the domain of real circles (physical figures) but are operable with contrary postulates, so too modern logic is free of any naturally given syntax.[1]

Modern logic as a science of symbols was originally proposed by Gottfried Wilhelm Leibniz (1646-1716). …. Leibniz believed all reasoning could be assimilated to a universal calculus of human knowledge. The resulting "universal grammar," or *characteristica universalis*, would serve to formalize in a deductive way all reasoning, including scientific proofs. The Leibnizean science of symbols was to establish and foster the organized unification of scientific research within a single system of combination and permutation. To this end Leibniz also worked on various models of the calculating machine throughout his lifetime. Appropriately enough, it was Leibniz's binary number system which was to be used centuries later by John von Neumann in developing electronic computers at Princeton.

…. The Leibnizean logic of binary digits has become the basis of the encoding of language, thus creating a qualitatively different level of typification.

Writing converted to ASCII is fundamentally—as a phenomenon—different from handwritten manuscript or, say, the Morse code, though codified language in both ASCII and Morse code turns language into winged words. Digital reproduction of writing is as different a phenomenon in form from typewritten, printed language as digital audio reproduction differs from phonograph recordings and oxidized tape recordings. When a phenomenon has been digitized, it has been interpreted and processed. It has been transmogrified into a new form, a form that can be controlled by human beings with precision far beyond that of other forms of reproduction. *Digital* is derived from the Latin *digitus*, or "finger." The fingers are the primordial counters, the first servants of human calculation When something is digitized it is interpreted as a sequence of numbers, numbers that have a precision that cannot be experienced directly in the original phenomenon, though the original phenomenon may have in itself a certain kind of precision that cannot be reduced to quantities or numerical relationships. Once a phenomenon has been digitized it can be treated as can all mathematical entities as a series of relationships and proportions. The relationships between the wave lengths of acoustical phenomena can for example be calculated and modified while at the same time the fundamental relationships between the wave lengths can be preserved. Wave lengths that have been digitized can be

manipulated so as to improve upon the recorded phenomenon. For instance, recordings of the ocean may never sound really like the ocean until they have been interpreted digitally as quantities and then altered variously until the audio reproduction sounds real, like the ocean itself should sound. The impossibility of removing the flaws of the recordings of the original ocean sounds gives way to the creation of the real ocean sounds through digital manipulation.

Phenomena that have been digitized are new creations at the fingertips of human beings. Controlling phenomena as we experience them is itself a new kind of experience. The digital phenomenon is one facet of a totally controlled environment, an environment where what we experience is what we have created. The digits on which we count the world we experience come, through electronic amplification, to be the world we experience. The world on our fingertips becomes the world at our fingertips.

The temporal mood of total control and simultaneity is characteristic of the Enframing. This mood develops into modern technology over several centuries as modernity develops. … The epistemological-ontological model behind the logic of Leibniz is, Heidegger shows, that of the *visio Dei*, the deity's omniscient intuitive cognition. … It is the knowledge of God, at least in its temporalizing simultaneity, that serves as a model for human cognition in the modern world as projected in the work of Leibniz.

The temporality of modern logic is seen in computer writing: total control over all aspects of text, words caught in the dynamic system of electrified code. There is something here akin to the Enlightenment ideal of connecting all knowledge through a single code. The temporality or rhythmic tempo of the Enframing is instantaneous simultaneity, the logic of a total management with everything at one's disposal.. …

…. The ease and intuitive freedom of writing on a computer may mask, in Heidegger's terms, the revealing-concealing process intrinsic to the truth of the world. But the precise manner by which this darkening takes place in the specific technology of word processing is not made clear in existentialist ontology or theory of reality. Heidegger confines his remarks to noting the tendency of the contemporary world to reduce language to mere information to be managed; the primal history or existential events of human life are embedded in language while the current "Event" is the self-concealing of this history. Heidegger's treatment of technology tends to be—as is frequently found in the traditions of German Idealism—globally holistic and blind to particular phenomena.

Heidegger's global critique is, nevertheless, rich with insights for our purposes. …. Language is increasingly treated as information and is processed by the techniques of information management. Treated as information, language becomes a transparent vehicle for what is already determined existentially. That is to say, "in-formation" is already formed by the network of involvements in which it is exchanged; information takes place in a world that is presumed to have been already formed.

The informational mode of language may lead to the curtailing of the human ability to say, in Heidegger's terms, to call things freshly by name, by new names, to address the environing world poetically. The current integration of writing with information management is coming to be known as the knowledge industry. Such a development gives considerable corroboration to Heidegger's attempt to deduce from the principles of modernity the contemporary shift of thinking toward calculating. For Heidegger, being-in-the-world in its postmodern form is essentially an attempt to organize, systematize, and control the ensemble of things that constitute the human environment. Thinking, according to Heidegger's projection is coming to be identified with speed accuracy and limitless calculation.

The so-called information industry includes professionals who must condense enormous amounts of textual information under exacting deadlines …. accessing and organizing information with microcomputers is increasingly done directly by those responsible for defining things linguistically; the computer closes the gap between writing and managing. Heidegger's projection of a language machine, which comes to dominate in the major employments of words, may not be far from the truth.

Heidegger points out another side to the Enframing or, rather, hints at it vaguely in one of his essays. In "The Question Concerning Technology," he reminds us of the connection in ancient Greece between useful skills and artistic creativity; the Greek term techne does not sharply disjoin the works of necessity from the craftsmanlike search for perfect beauty: "The arts were not derived from the artistic. Art works were not enjoyed aesthetically. Art was not a sector of cultural activity." Heidegger seems here to indicate some small avenue of exit from the Enframing. It may be possible find again, within techne itself, a new encounter with ambiguity and an open field for human responsiveness, a new kind of non-Romantic poetic dwelling. There may be areas of creativity which still feed on ambiguity and on the human response to the unknown.

(…..)

Source: Michael Heim, *Electric Language: A Philosophical Study of Word Processing,* published by Yale University Press © Yale University, 1987, pp. 70–94.

Note

1. See the provocative book by Henry Veatch, *Two Logics*, Evanston: Northwestern University Press, 1969.

CHAPTER 33
'THIS SYSTEM DOES NOT PRODUCE PLEASURE ANYMORE'
Bernard Stiegler, interviewed by Pieter Lemmens

The central idea guiding Bernard Stiegler's work is that the human being is marked by a *défaut d'orgine*, a fundamental lack of qualities that makes him into an accidental being originally in need of technical prostheses and therefore fundamentally constituted and conditioned by technics. For Stiegler, humanity is co-extensive with technics.

Stiegler is in many respects a fairly traditional continental philosopher, an heir to Nietzsche, Husserl, Heidegger, Foucault and Derrida and deeply affiliated with the traditions of phenomenology, psychoanalysis and de-construction. The originality of his work resides first of all in a Heideggerian-like rethinking of the entire Western philosophical tradition on the basis of its systematically forgotten technical condition. .....

One the other hand, however, Stiegler's philosophical enterprise can also be seen as a continuation of the project of critical theory, of its social critique, its critique of political economy and its critique of the culture industry. This can be identified as the 'Marxist' strand of his work. Most remarkably, it is on the basis of his techno-critical project that Stiegler provides a sociopolitical critique of contemporary capitalist and postmodern society. This society suffers from what he calls a state of generalized proletarianization. Proletarianization, Stiegler argues with Gilbert Simondon and Karl Marx, consists essentially in the loss of knowledge and know-how (savoir-faire) in individuals and collectives. Whereas nineteenth-century capitalism proletarianized workers by delegating their knowledge and know-how to machines, reducing them to labor power, twentieth-century capitalism has proletarianized consumers by depriving them of their own ways of life and massively replacing them with preformatted and standardized 'life-styles' fabricated and marketed on a worldwide scale by global corporations exclusively driven by profit. In today's service economies, consumers are 'discharged' of the burden as well as the responsibility of shaping their own lives and are reduced to units of buying power controlled by marketing techniques. They have lost their 'knowledge-how-to-live' (savoir-vivre) and become ultimately deprived of the joy of life (joie de vivre). The much-heard slogan that our contemporary societies are 'knowledge societies' is a patent lie, according to Stiegler. In fact, today's cognitive capitalism implies the systematic destruction of knowledge and the knowing subject.

The phenomenon of proletarianization, that is put on the agenda of philosophical reflection again by Stiegler, is not something that came up first with the Industrial Revolution. In fact, it forms a constant threat to the human as a being that continuously evolves through processes of technical exteriorization that must necessarily be accompanied by processes of interiorization and appropriation of technical prostheses and procedures. This is particularly true since the exteriorization of memory and cognition in so-called mnemotechnologies like writing and printing. What is characteristic of our contemporary age, according to Stiegler, is the systematic industrialization of human memory and cognition through digital technologies, a process with dramatic implications for individual human psyches as well as collectives. In our hyperindustrial societies, even the life of the mind is thoroughly technicized and industrialized and this happens in the context of an increasingly totalitarian capitalism.

It is the systematic annexation of the new technical milieus of the mind (first of all the network of digital information and communication technologies: Internet) by capitalism that is the principal cause of the cognitive and emotional proletarianization that affects all strata of contemporary society. ...

In this interview, Stiegler talks about today's processes of proletarianization and addresses some of the pernicious consequences of capital's exploitation of the technical milieu of the mind, among them the many psychopathologies and addictive behavior patterns that agonize ever more people, especially since the rise of the purely speculative, short-term based finance capitalism invented by the neoliberals and the neoconservatives. By subjecting technological innovation completely to the logic of the market, the so called 'conservative revolution' led by Thatcher and Reagan has engendered a cultural and spiritual regression of unprecedented magnitude, transforming the whole of society into a machine for profit maximization and creating a state of 'systemic carelessness' and 'systemic stupidity' on a global scale.

Notwithstanding his rather bleak diagnosis of contemporary society, Stiegler is not pessimistic with regard to the future. Whereas today's capitalism is headed for destruction, it is precisely in the digitalized networks through which it tries to control the populations that a new kind of economy is emerging, one that is not only inventing new modes of production like open source and peer-to-peer, but that is also slowly creating a new economy of desire that could lead to the invention of new ways of life, new modes of individual and collective existence. A new society could arise on the same technological base that is now still predominantly destroying the social bonds. The digital networks might be the prime catalysts in the transformation from today's consumer society into what he calls a 'society of contribution' ....

BS: Bernard Stiegler

PL: Pieter Lemmens

PL: Let's start with your general position within the larger field of philosophy of technology, notwithstanding the fact that you don't consider yourself a philosopher of technology in the strict sense of the term. In the philosophy of technology one distinguishes roughly between two opposing views about the relationship between technology and society: on the one hand technological determinism, the thesis that it is technology and technological change which determines the structure of society and/or culture, and on the other hand social or cultural determinism, the thesis that it is society and/or culture that determines the shape and character of technologies and technological change. ... Another broad opposition is that between the so-called autonomy theory of technology (also known as technological substantivism), and the instrumentalist view of technology. The first holds to the idea that technology and technological change have a logic of their own and are outside of human control and decision, the second claims that technology is a neutral means used by autonomously acting human beings for a variety of ends, to which technologies are indifferent. This view is also sometimes referred to as the humanist view. Substantivism is most often associated with Heidegger and Ellul, whereas liberal conceptions of technology are generally perceived as being instrumental and typically subscribing to social and/or economic determinism. How would you characterize your view with respect to these two schematic oppositions?

BS: Well, in fact my principal sources here are André Leroi-Gourhan, a paleoanthropologist, Gilbert Simondon, a philosopher of technology and Bertrand Gille, a historian of technology. My point of view is that the separation between the human and technics, and between society and technics or the technical system is completely artificial.

It is important to understand that technology is a process, an evolutionary process. What is technics, or technology, or technicity? It is a new form of life. A very specific form of life, for until the onset of anthropogenesis, forms of life were transformed exclusively through a genetic process of transformation, that is to say through sexual differentiation and the relationship between sexualized organisms, which is the case for plants and animals. But about three million years ago there occurred a fundamental change in this process of transformation within the human species, due to the appearance of a new system of inheritance based not on the transmission of genes but of technical artefacts. So with respect to anthropogenesis, we are not talking about a Darwinist situation anymore. But neither is it a Lamarckist situation. It is something completely different, due to this apparition of a third memory.[1]

Now to answer your question, it is completely artificial to ask, what is the relationship of the human to technics? Because the human is technics. Humanity cannot even be understood without technics. Take the example of the ant in the anthill. It is impossible to understand the ant without the anthill. If you don't see it within the anthill, it is impossible to understand it. And you need to consider the relationship with the other ants as well, because it is a social animal. And it is the same when you have, for example, a savage child which has not learned to speak and to walk, etcetera. Such a child is not really human. It is a potentiality of humanity, but it's not human. It is a very strange being between animality and humanity. So, it is artificial to ask, for example, what is determining human life: is it the psychic apparatus of the individual, is it the social organization or is it the technical organization? It is completely artificial because you don't have a psychic individual without a society, and you don't have a society without technics.

PL: Ok, but you also claim that there is a primacy of technology.

BS: It is not exactly a primacy. It must be understood as a 'disadjustment' [desajustément] between the social system and the technical system, because you are in a process. What is a process? It is a dynamic system. You don't have a process without a dynamic system. And in a dynamic system you have phases, and when you have a phase, you always have a counter phase. That is necessary. If not, then you don't have a dynamic system. Now, it is true that technics is always in excess with respect to the society in which it appears. This is the reason I said that technics is always pharmacological. It is always a pharmakon, because it is always creating a disequilibrium in the society in which it is developed and by which it is developed.

PL: And the creation of this disequilibrium, is that what you call the poisoning character of the pharmakon? Could you elaborate upon this notion of the pharmakon, which has become one of the key concepts of your work, and could you explain what you mean with the pharmacological nature of technology?

BS: The pharmacological nature of technology means both its poisoning and its curative character. It is both poisoning and curing. At its first appearance, however, it is poisoning. It becomes curative when you have what I call the second moment of epochality of technics, le redoublement epochale [the process of appropriation of a new technical system by society and the development of new modes of psychic and collective individuation based on this technical system; PL]. So, the problem of disadjustment is what was called by Shakespeare 'the time is out of joint'. What is creating this being out of joint? That is the question. And my answer is: the process of technical exteriorization.

For instance: at this very moment I am exteriorizing myself. Speaking with you, I am exteriorizing myself. And that means: I am technicizing myself. If I talk with you, I create new words. I very much like to create new words [laughter]. A word is also a new technical object. The opposition between technics and speech for me is completely artificial.

Now, for a human being, to live is to individuate oneself. How am I individuating myself? By exteriorizing myself. And in the same way, I am interiorizing myself, because when I speak to you, I am listening to what I say, so I interiorize myself. Now this process of exteriorization-interiorization is the originary process of psychic and social individuation. So you can see very clearly that at the beginning of psychic activity you always already have technics, i.e., technical individuation. Now, you might not be a professional speaker, like me, but you might for instance produce flint stones. Suppose you are a prehistoric man and you are producing stone tools. It is exactly the same thing. That is what I try to describe in my first book *Technics and Time. The Fault of Epimetheus*. When pre-historic man is producing flint stones, thereby exteriorizing his experience, he is in fact transforming his brain, his psyche.

PL: So the stone is reflecting what he has exteriorized back to himself, acting like a kind of idea or a model?

BS: Yes, and it is a concept. In paleoanthropology we call that a concept, precisely. Because we say: there is a concept of the flint stone. Now your question was technological determinism or not. Well, there is no technological determinism. What there is is a technological condition. There is a conditional situation in which you have what I call a general organology: there are always three terms involved in the transformation of the human, which are the psychic, the technical and the social. And you have a tendency of the technics to change always beyond the barriers, beyond the limits of the social group.

This has always been the case. When you read for example what was written by Leroi-Gourhan about the Amer-Indian people when they use, for example, a racket for clearing snow. He talks about the 'technical group', because in a small tribe like the Amer-Indian people you have a small group within the larger group, which is the group of technicians. And he writes that the technicians of this group of Indians tend to make connections with other technicians of other groups, to create new techniques together, which then disturb and sometimes even destroy their own groups. So they have a problem of disequilibrium. And then the society produces an immune system as response, in the sense of a counter-tendency. But whether the countertendency is after it or before it, is not the right question. You have the tendency at the very moment when you have the countertendency. Because, as Nietzsche said, you cannot have a force without a counterforce. So it is absolutely not interesting to ask: where is the beginning, what is the first moment? There is no first moment.

PL: So there is no determinism by either society or technics…

BS: Indeed. And here Gilbert Simondon is extremely fruitful, because he furnished a very interesting concept which is the 'pre-individual'. In the pre-individual, you don't have the separation between the technical, the psychic and the social. But this argument also appears in Aristotle. When he said – I think at the beginning of *Peri psycheos*, or *De Anima* – that a dialectician separates form and matter, but that it's in fact impossible to separate them in reality, he saw this already. So I think it is an artefact to try to find the causal origin. We must think from the very first beginning in terms of a dynamic system, in which you have phases, and what is important – but very difficult – is to describe the relationships between the different instances of the phases.

PL: That is what you intend with a general organology?

BS: Yes, and it is very difficult to describe, because it is always changing.

PL: Ok, thank you. I would like to ask you now about the relationship between the process of technical exteriorization and what you call proletarianization in your latest books. I find that a very interesting concept, as well as the opposing concept of deproletarianization. You kind of rehabilitate this originally Marxian concept. Our postmodern societies, you claim, are characterized by a state of generalized proletarianization and so the most important political and cultural project of the future will be a process of deproletarianization. In this respect you refer to phenomena like Open Source and Free Software as prefigurations of this process.

Now, returning to the relationship of proletarianization with the process of technical exteriorization: in your diagnosis something goes wrong today with the 'adjustment' [ajustement] of society to technological change, that is to say with the societal appropriation of technological innovations. First of all, probably, because innovation is speeding up every day, second, because it is completely dominated and exploited by capitalism, by the economic system. Can you explain that a bit? What is really causing this chronic disadjustment and disorientation? Is it capital (capitalism), or is it technics? In short, can you elaborate a bit upon the connection between technical exteriorization and proletarianization, and that in relationship to capitalism and the current disorientation?

BS: Firstly, the process of proletarianization didn't begin with the Industrial Revolution. That is the reason why I try to show that the first thinker of proletarianization is in fact Plato. More strongly even, the process of proletarianization marks the beginning of humankind. Because, what is proletarianization? It is first of all the exteriorization of knowledge in technics. It begins with technics. Now the problem is, what is the gain of the process of exteriorization for humanity? Is it creating heteronomy or autonomy? For example: if you are using a technique which is producing free time for you to do another thing, for instance developing your skills and individuating yourself, then the result of this exteriorization is an intensification of your individuation. If you use the technique of writing for example, not for creating a dependency and heteronomy in the youth of Athens, like the Sophists did who appear in Plato's dialogues, but on the contrary for taking care of one's self[2], for creating the academy, for producing philosophy books, etcetera, then one individuates oneself with and through those books. Plato never says that, of course, but that is what he means. …

He argues exactly like Immanuel Kant did in Was ist Aufklärung? Kant wrote: you can read my books, but only if you don't use them for proletarianizing yourself. He doesn't say it like that of course, but that is what he had in mind when he said: if you read my books in order to avoid thinking for yourself, out of laziness for instance, you are proletarianizing yourself. He does not use the word 'proletarianize', he says 'minorize' [mineur], but he means the same. Reading books without reflecting upon them and critically engaging with them leads to minority, not to maturity.

This question of proletarianization is in fact at the origin of philosophy and it is a question of autonomization versus heteronomization. Now, my point of view is that pure autonomy does not exist. My own position – and it is very close to Derrida's – is that there is never an autonomy without a link to a heteronomy, i.e., with a link to technics. …

Now, in coming back to your question, what is happening today, to us? Well, it is the consequence of what started at the end of the Seventies in England with Margaret Thatcher, who proclaimed that from now on, we don't need the state anymore. Instead we let the market organize the appropriation of technologies. And why was this extremely toxic and negative for the future of humanity? Because it was the whole planet which transformed the policies and the economy after that. It is not so much catastrophic because of the end of the welfare state, which is a question that is very important for me, but not the main question.

The main question is that the state has been for a very long time – already at the time of the Greek polis – an organization for the appropriation of technical exteriorization, i.e., for the adoption of new technologies in a way that was producing what I call a libidinal economy, i.e., a collective libidinal economy producing a superego, an ego ideal, etcetera. … Later, after the French Revolution and the Industrial Revolution, you had the organization of the public sphere, of the lay sphere, of teaching and public education, etcetera. And it was always agreed upon that it was impossible to submit this activity to the economy. But in 1979 in Great Britain, Ms. Thatcher said: now we will submit all these things to the economy. And at the same moment Reagan did the same in America. And after that Mitterand in his way, in social democracy. But everybody did in fact, the whole world did the same. Even in Soviet and Chinese society.

PL: Why was that? And why was it so successful?

BS: There are a lot of reasons. The first one is that American and English capitalism seemed extremely strong at that moment. Nevertheless, Thatcher and Reagan knew already that it was finished with controlling production. You know that in 1979 Liverpool was in ruins. The whole of the economy in England was a catastrophe. It was also very bad in America. It was the beginning of the exportation of the production of, for example, the electronic industries to Japan and Korea, and after that to Thailand, then to China. This was the deindustrialization of the West. And the strategy of Thatcher and Reagan was: we now need to produce a new type of capitalism, which was a financialized capitalism, being purely speculative. Not a capitalism of investment, but a capitalism of speculation. It was the creation of what led, in the end, to people like Bernie Madoff… as the norm of capitalism. Before that, Madoff would be considered a gangster. But after that he was not a gangster, he was a policeman, because he was the chairman of the Nasdaq!

….

PL: Well, the neoliberal state is a strong state, one could argue, in certain respects at least.

BS: Yes, but it is a state only for security and for controlling the pathological behavior of people. It is only military and police.

PL: Yes, but for instance, it is also involved in the disciplining of the population to adapt to the market, in encouraging citizens to become self-entrepreneurs, in installing competition everywhere, in turning the whole of society into a market, etcetera. It is in a sense a strong state, not a state that is withdrawing itself.

BS …. When you say that the state is very strong, what if the state is only one man, for example Sarkozy or Berlusconi, who gives money to a privatized police? Is that really a state? No, it is mafia. The mafia is very strong, not the state. What is the state? …

The question today for me is not the end of capitalism or the return of the communist horizon. Today we have to create a new industrial model. This new industrial model will possibly produce a new political organization, and an economical organization which may not be capitalist. But it is not at all sure, and it is not my problem today. It is possible for example to produce a cooperative capitalism. I know of people exploiting capital in a cooperative way. It still is capitalism, because you have ownership of the means of production by a collective, but this collective is proprietary. It is not a collectivization in the communist sense. It is capitalist. But it is a new form of capitalism.

The question of capitalism is the opposition between capital and work. And this opposition between capital and work is an opposition through property. Now if we change the law of property, for example by sharing the sources of software code in Free Software, we are changing something very crucial. Is it capitalism or not? I don't know… and I don't care. I prefer to do it, and to ask only afterwards. When I say I don't care, I don't say it is not a very important question, but we are in a situation of emergency today. We have to do things, not only to think. We have to propose things. We don't have time for discussions about whether it will be capitalism or not. We need to create a new situation. The question, for instance, is to go to the investment banks and ask them in what they want to invest. Not to speculate but to invest. And to tell them: you have a lot of money, you don't know what to do with this money, you must invest in this new system, the future is there. If I say to them it is the end of capitalism [BS laughs], they will not invest. The question today is: what is the new industrial model?

PL: You argue that the open source and free software movements in the software industry are a kind of harbinger of this new model, i.e., prefigurations of what you also call an 'economy of contribution'. And you suggest that these movements must be understood as engaged in a process of deproletarianization. Could you explain that a bit more. And could you also explain why you have put your hopes so much in these, in my view still pretty marginal practices, especially Free Software. Open source is big nowadays of course, at least in the software sector, but it represents a kind of pragmatization, even capitalization and thereby a betrayal of the principles of Free Software. And as such it remains immanent to capitalism. What is your 'pharmacological hope', so to speak, with respect to these practices?

BS: That is a very important question, but difficult, very difficult. Firstly, I think it's not hope. Well, it is hope, that's clear, but it is also a rationality. Now, today capitalism has become irrational, completely irrational. .... Everybody agreed that market rationality was the ultimate rationality. But what is this market rationality? The market is rational because it is all about calculation, computation. But that is a completely stupid understanding of what rationality is, because rationality is precisely, to speak with Kant, that which is not calculable. ...

Now, here is a new rationality for me. Why? Well, for example, if you talk with a manager of a human resources department in a company today. If the person with whom you talk is honest, he will say to you: I have a big problem: the workers do not want to work, the consumers do not want to consume [BS laughs], the managers do not want to manage, etcetera. Why? Because there is no pleasure produced anymore by the system. I've thought a lot about consumption and I claim that consumers today are addicted. When you ask them: what do you think about consumption, they say it is very bad. There was an inquiry published two or three days ago in the USA by Juliet Schorr, who asked the American people: what do you think about consumption? Well, they said it is bad for us and for America. Eighty-one percent of the people said that – in America!

PL: But they are nevertheless doing it.

BS: Yes, and that is because they are intoxicated. They are addicts. If you ask a junkie, one who has been a junkie for ten years: what do you think of heroin, he or she will say that it is extremely bad. It is that which is explained at the beginning of Naked Lunch, the famous book by William Burroughs, why you must not use heroin. The author says: I use it, but it is because I cannot stop anymore. I would like to stop but it is impossible. Now capitalism is confronted with a very similar problem. It has a lot of intoxicated people to manage and it is impossible to manage intoxicated people. ...

Source: Pieter Lemmens, 'This System Does Not Produce Pleasure Anymore' Interview with Bernard Stiegler, Krisis Journal for contemporary philosophy 2011, Issue 1 www.krisis.eu

Notes

1. For Stiegler, technology has to be understood first of all in terms of a memory, i.e., as a supplemental memory system unique to humans. Besides an individual neural and a specific (species) genetic memory, common to all sexualized living organisms, humans possess a third, technological memory or inheritance system which has enabled the transmission of individual experience over the generations, i.e., the possibility of individual experience becoming available for the species at large thanks to its inscription in technical artefacts (opening the historical mode of being Heidegger called 'existence'). Humanity has evolved on the basis of this technological inheritance system. This means that human evolution cannot be understood anymore in Darwinist terms, since Darwinian evolution presupposes that individual experience – 'acquired characteristics' – cannot be transmitted to the species.

2. Stiegler uses this expression here in its Foucaultian sense of 'care of the self' [souci de soi] via technologies of the self [techniques de soi].

GUIDE TO FURTHER READING

Given that technology has been central in the formation and development of human cultures, the literature on technology is vast and crosses many disciplines. There are anthropological and archaeological studies of tools, artifacts, and material practices; histories of individual technologies, histories of scientific, and technological development; and, going back many centuries, competing theories and debates about the nature and extent of the power of technologies over human beings. For orientation see entries in *Bloomsbury Encyclopedia of Design* on Alienation, Instrumentalism and Technology. Carl Mitcham's *Thinking Through Technology* (1994) is a foundational book on the philosophy of technology. Other key works of the philosophy of technology are Martin Heidegger's essays from the mid-twentieth century *The Question Concerning Technology and Other Essays* (1982); Langdon Winner, *Autonomous Technology: Technics-out-of-control as a Theme in Political Thought* (1977); Albert Borgmann, *Technology and the Character of Contemporary Life: A Philosophical Inquiry* (2009); Don Ihde, *Technology and the Lifeworld* (1993) and *Heidegger's Technologies: Postphenomenological Perspective* (2010). Introductions to the fields of science and technology studies (STS) and social construction of technology (SCOT) are Wiebe Bijker et al., *The Social Construction of Technological Systems* (2012) and Bijker et al., *Shaping Technology/Building Society* (1992) which contains the influential Bruno Latour essay "Where are the Missing Masses?". Discussion of more recent developments that are blurring the distinction between humans, nonhumans, and technology can be found in Part VIII, especially the contributions by Benjamin Bratton and Rosi Braidotti, while Bratton's *The Stack* is a lengthy, challenging book on design and technology futures.

PART VII
THE DESIGNING OF VISUALITY

INTRODUCTION

The texts in this Part go to the dominance of visuality in Western culture: as a mode of knowledge production; as "making things visible"; and of seduction via "the spectacle of consumption."

The creation of visual appeal is one of the mainstays of commercial design. This is seen in the appearance of the following: stylish eye-catching products, logos, packaging, advertisements; promotional images and videos of beautiful faces, perfect bodies, alluring settings; totally designed interiors, facades, landscapes; the image-driven cultural industries of movies, television, publishing, and tourism. In urban-techno cultures of affluence, image, and appearance reign supreme—a situation that has been on the rise since the late nineteenth century. Over this time cultural critics have named this variously as the aestheticization of everyday life; mass ornament; the phantasmagoria; the society of the spectacle; the political economy of the sign; the plenitude. However, such descriptions always refer to more than just visuality, but exactly what that more might be is difficult to define which is what prompted these new namings. Common to all, however, is the attempt to understand the visual image, technologically made and propagated, and its relation to the capitalist economy as it has come to insinuate itself into ever more domains of everyday life, and on an ever more global scale.

Many cultural theorists argue that the dominance of visuality evidences "ocularcentrism"—a long-standing feature of Western thinking—the privileging of sight over the other senses as a primary means to knowledge. Yet a counter position has emerged in different historical moments suggesting that visual images are suspect, that they seduce and deceive, that realist images in particular—while striking in resemblance to what they represent—actually conceal the truth. To understand visuality, in all its manifestations across time and cultures, would be an impossible task (here, we note that the term visuality refers to the socio-cultural aspects of vision and the visible). While the literature on visuality is vast, our focus here is to distinguish between the following:

1. Questions about how different cultures understand seeing and the relation of sight to the other senses, and how they explain the difference between the visible, the invisible; and truth;

2. Questions about the forms, meanings, status of visual representation;

3. Questions about the relation of visual imagery to larger social, cultural, and economic formations, this especially in the modern era.

Making things visible: Knowledge and power

Within Western thinking the idea of seeing as the means to truth stretches back to Plato. His famous story of the cave in Book 7 of the *Republic* is an allegory of enlightenment, as evident in the account where one of the prisoners is lead out of the cave into the light, where at first he is blinded by the brightness of the sun but after a while his eyes adjust and he is able to see the true form of things. Yet if he were to return to the cave and tell the other prisoners the "truth of the world" they, not having seen what he saw, not having experienced what he experienced, would not believe him. The true forms, the forms beyond appearance, that can only be grasped by the mind, not the eyes alone, are also the source of the beautiful and the good. That is, the ideal of objectivity is lodged in the visuality constituted by a disembodied eye.[1] This idea also connects to investigations by Descartes[2] and astronomer-mathematician Johannes on the mechanisms of sight. They both suggested that images were formed on the back of the eye in the same manner as a camera obscura (a darkened room with a very small hole through which light passes casting an inverted image on a white sheet placed at the appropriate distance, also known as a pinhole camera) which had been described by the Arabic writer Ibn al-Haytham (965–1039).[3]

Another Renaissance development (also drawing on Ibn al-Haytham's optical theories) that advanced the connection between truth and seeing was the introduction of linear perspective by Leon Battista Alberti (De pictura, 1435), a technique for producing a realistic image from a single static viewpoint.[4] This paved the way for an image-making machine—which is exactly what happened in the sixteenth century when the camera obscura principle as described by Ibn al-Haytham was constructed as an actual device for artists to use as a drawing aid.[5] It was to be another three centuries until the camera obscura was transformed into photography with the invention of a means of chemically fixing the image "drawn by light." The appeal of photography lay in its apparent objectivity—eliminating the need for that artist's hand, and its efficiency—which also made possible the production of more images at a greater speed.

Realist image-making advanced dramatically with the invention of photography cinema and then television. Each technology increased the capacity for recording, reproducing, and propagating imagery to larger audiences. Thereafter, in the late twentieth century digital photography linked to the internet became an instantaneous global production and distribution system.

To understand this trajectory beyond the technological takes us to the cultural theorists who coined the terms mentioned before—the aestheticization of everyday life; mass ornament; the phantasmagoria; the society of the spectacle; the political economy of the sign; the plenitude. These writers help us understand one direction, how photography and moving image—as the technologies of seeing—have become mechanisms for pleasure, instruments of seduction, and means of knowledge and power within the consumer economy.

As should now be clear, making things visible is a hallmark of the modern age. Michel Foucault's famous discussion of Jeremy Bentham's panopticon—a model for a prison based on a hierarchy of visibility—has become the iconic marker of the phenomenon.[6] Foucault made clear the relation between visibility, knowledge, and power as it indicated a shift from physical punishment to reform whereby power is exercised at a micro-level—observation, surveillance, inspection—so as to induce required forms of behavior.

Discipline within modern society says McGill, commenting on Foucault, "is exercised through its invisibility; yet at the same time, it imposes on those whom it subjects a principle of compulsory visibility."[7] Since that was written, the means of compulsory visibility have become technologically more sophisticated—such as satellite surveillance and ubiquitous—such as video monitoring of public and private space; but surveillance itself has become vastly more sophisticated and connected and no longer predominantly visual, as the movements of users of cell phones, the internet, or credit cards are now infinitely trackable.

Notes

1. For a critique of the subject-object split see Coyne and Snodgrass "Is Designing Mysterious? Challenging the Dual Knowledge Thesis," *Design Studies* 12 (3): 124–31.

2. La Dioptrique, 1637.

3. Ibn al-Haytham wrote a major treatise on optics that was translated into Latin and influenced European scholars, who came to see the eye as a viewing apparatus; thus "the act of seeing, at least in scientific circles, is on the way to becoming neutral, abstract and positivistic." Robert S. Nelson, "Descartes's Cow and other Domestications of the Visual" in *Visuality Before and Beyond the Renaissance: Seeing as Others Saw* ed. Robert S. Nelson, Cambridge University Press, 2000, p. 6.

4. Descartes described the operation of a disembodied eye; Alberti's system of visual representation is a neutral grid placed between artist and scene that requires no emotional involvement or embodiment except for co-ordination of hand and eye. In both, there is a distancing of observer and observed; separation and non-involvement.

5. The Islamic scientist Ibn al-Haytham (965–1039) also known as Alhazen described the optical principle on which the camera obscura is based. That he or other Islamic scientists did not use this knowledge to develop a device to aid the making of images, is not surprising given the low regard for realist imagery within Islam. See A. I. Sabra (ed.) *The Optics of Ibn al-Haytham* 2002. Edition of the Arabic Text of Books IV–V: On Reflection and Images Seen by Reflection. 2 vols, Kuwait: The National Council for Culture, Arts and Letter.

6. Each inmate in a separate cell, unable to see anyone else, but all inmates visible to the guard in a central watchtower; those under observation never know exactly when they are being observed, thus they modify their behavior, internalizing the observer within themselves. Michel Foucault, *Discipline and Punish: The Birth of the Prison* trans. Alan Sheridan, New York: Vintage, 1977.

7. A. Megill, *Prophets of Extremity: Nietzsche, Heidegger, Foucault Derrida* Berkley: University of California Press, 1987, p. 242.

CHAPTER 34
ON FORM AND IMITATION
Plato

Note from editor: The following extracted from Book 10 of Plato's Republic, is written (c. 360 B.C.E.) as is most of Plato's philosophy, in the form of a dialogue between his teacher Socrates and others. Socrates method was to relentlessly question his interlocutors on their beliefs on various matters, and thereby to reach a satisfactory definition. Here, Socrates interrogates Glaucon on the status of imitation, using the example of a craftsman's product and a visual image of that product. This is made as part of a larger argument on virtue and knowledge in poetry, and whether a skilled poet is a suitable teacher of virtue.

Can you tell me what imitation is? For I really do not know.

A likely thing, then, that I should know.

Why not? For the duller eye may often see a thing sooner than the keener.

Very true, he said; but in your presence, even if I had any faint notion, I could not muster courage to utter it. Will you enquire yourself?

Well then, shall we begin the enquiry in our usual manner: Whenever a number of individuals have a common name, we assume them to have also a corresponding idea or form. Do you understand me?

I do.

Let us take any common instance; there are beds and tables in the world --plenty of them, are there not?

Yes.

But there are only two ideas or forms of them --one the idea of a bed, the other of a table.

True.

And the maker of either of them makes a bed or he makes a table for our use, in accordance with the idea --that is our way of speaking in this and similar instances --but no artificer makes the ideas themselves: how could he?

Impossible.

And there is another artist --I should like to know what you would say of him.

Who is he?

One who is the maker of all the works of all other workmen.

What an extraordinary man!

Wait a little, and there will be more reason for your saying so. For this is he who is able to make not only vessels of every kind, but plants and animals, himself and all other things --the earth and heaven, and the things which are in heaven or under the earth; he makes the gods also.

He must be a wizard and no mistake.

Oh! you are incredulous, are you? Do you mean that there is no such maker or creator, or that in one sense there might be a maker of all these things but in another not? Do you see that there is a way in which you could make them all yourself?

What way?

An easy way enough; or rather, there are many ways in which the feat might be quickly and easily accomplished, none quicker than that of turning a mirror round and round --you would soon enough make the sun and the heavens, and the earth and yourself, and other animals and plants, and all the, other things of which we were just now speaking, in the mirror.

Yes, he said; but they would be appearances only.

Very good, I said, you are coming to the point now. And the painter too is, as I conceive, just such another --a creator of appearances, is he not?

Of course.

But then I suppose you will say that what he creates is untrue. And yet there is a sense in which the painter also creates a bed?

Yes, he said, but not a real bed.

And what of the maker of the bed? Were you not saying that he too makes, not the idea which, according to our view, is the essence of the bed, but only a particular bed?

Yes, I did.

Then if he does not make that which exists he cannot make true existence, but only some semblance of existence; and if any one were to say that the work of the maker of the bed, or of any other workman, has real existence, he could hardly be supposed to be speaking the truth.

At any rate, he replied, philosophers would say that he was not speaking the truth.

No wonder, then, that his work too is an indistinct expression of truth.

No wonder.

Suppose now that by the light of the examples just offered we enquire who this imitator is?

If you please.

Well then, here are three beds: one existing in nature, which is made by God, as I think that we may say --for no one else can be the maker?

No.

There is another which is the work of the carpenter?

Yes.

And the work of the painter is a third?

Yes.

Beds, then, are of three kinds, and there are three artists who superintend them: God, the maker of the bed, and the painter?

Yes, there are three of them.

God, whether from choice or from necessity, made one bed in nature and one only; two or more such ideal beds neither ever have been nor ever will be made by God.

Why is that?

Because even if He had made but two, a third would still appear behind them which both of them would have for their idea, and that would be the ideal bed and the two others.

Very true, he said.

God knew this, and He desired to be the real maker of a real bed, not a particular maker of a particular bed, and therefore He created a bed which is essentially and by nature one only.

So we believe.

Shall we, then, speak of Him as the natural author or maker of the bed?

Yes, he replied; inasmuch as by the natural process of creation He is the author of this and of all other things.

And what shall we say of the carpenter --is not he also the maker of the bed?

Yes.

But would you call the painter a creator and maker?

Certainly not.

Yet if he is not the maker, what is he in relation to the bed?

I think, he said, that we may fairly designate him as the imitator of that which the others make.

Good, I said; then you call him who is third in the descent from nature an imitator?

Certainly, he said.

And the tragic poet is an imitator, and therefore, like all other imitators, he is thrice removed from the king and from the truth?

That appears to be so.

Then about the imitator we are agreed. And what about the painter? --I would like to know whether he may be thought to imitate that which originally exists in nature, or only the creations of artists?

The latter.

As they are or as they appear? You have still to determine this.

What do you mean?

I mean, that you may look at a bed from different points of view, obliquely or directly or from any other point of view, and the bed will appear different, but there is no difference in reality. And the same of all things.

Yes, he said, the difference is only apparent.

Now let me ask you another question: Which is the art of painting designed to be --an imitation of things as they are, or as they appear --of appearance or of reality?

Of appearance.

Then the imitator, I said, is a long way off the truth, and can do all things because he lightly touches on a small part of them, and that part an image. For example: A painter will paint a cobbler, carpenter, or any other artist, though he knows nothing of their arts; and, if he is a good artist, he may deceive children or simple persons, when he shows them his picture of a carpenter from a distance, and they will fancy that they are looking at a real carpenter.

Certainly.

And whenever any one informs us that he has found a man knows all the arts, and all things else that anybody knows, and every single thing with a higher degree of accuracy than any other man --whoever tells us this, I think that we can only imagine to be a simple creature who is likely to have been deceived by some wizard or actor whom he met, and whom he thought all-knowing, because he himself was unable to analyse the nature of knowledge and ignorance and imitation.

Most true.

....

The imitator or maker of the image knows nothing of true existence; he knows appearances only. Am I not right?

Yes.

Then let us have a clear understanding, and not be satisfied with half an explanation.

Proceed.

Of the painter we say that he will paint reins, and he will paint a bit?

Yes.

And the worker in leather and brass will make them?

Certainly.

But does the painter know the right form of the bit and reins? Nay, hardly even the workers in brass and leather who make them; only the horseman who knows how to use them --he knows their right form.

Most true.

And may we not say the same of all things?

What?

That there are three arts which are concerned with all things: one which uses, another which makes, a third which imitates them?

Yes.

And the excellence or beauty or truth of every structure, animate or inanimate, and of every action of man, is relative to the use for which nature or the artist has intended them.

True.

Then the user of them must have the greatest experience of them, and he must indicate to the maker the good or bad qualities which develop themselves in use; for example, the flute-player will tell the flute-maker which of his flutes is satisfactory to the performer; he will tell him how he ought to make them, and the other will attend to his instructions?

Of course.

The one knows and therefore speaks with authority about the goodness and badness of flutes, while the other, confiding in him, will do what he is told by him?

True.

The instrument is the same, but about the excellence or badness of it the maker will only attain to a correct belief; and this he will gain from him who knows, by talking to him and being compelled to hear what he has to say, whereas the user will have knowledge?

True.

But will the imitator have either? Will he know from use whether or no his drawing is correct or beautiful? Or will he have right opinion from being compelled to associate with another who knows and gives him instructions about what he should draw?

Neither.

Then he will no more have true opinion than he will have knowledge about the goodness or badness of his imitations?

I suppose not.

The imitative artist will be in a brilliant state of intelligence about his own creations?

Nay, very much the reverse.

And still he will go on imitating without knowing what makes a thing good or bad, and may be expected therefore to imitate only that which appears to be good to the ignorant multitude?

Just so.

Thus far then we are pretty well agreed that the imitator has no knowledge worth mentioning of what he imitates. Imitation is only a kind of play or sport, and the tragic poets, whether they write in iambic or in Heroic verse, are imitators in the highest degree?

Very true.

And now tell me, I conjure you, has not imitation been shown by us to be concerned with that which is thrice removed from the truth?

Certainly.

And what is the faculty in man to which imitation is addressed?

What do you mean?

I will explain: The body which is large when seen near, appears small when seen at a distance?

True.

And the same object appears straight when looked at out of the water, and crooked when in the water; and the concave becomes convex, owing to the illusion about colours to which the sight is liable. Thus every sort of confusion is revealed within us; and this is that weakness of the human mind on which the art of conjuring and of deceiving by light and shadow and other ingenious devices imposes, having an effect upon us like magic.

True.

And the arts of measuring and numbering and weighing come to the rescue of the human understanding-there is the beauty of them --and the apparent greater or less, or more or

heavier, no longer have the mastery over us, but give way before calculation and measure and weight?

Most true.

And this, surely, must be the work of the calculating and rational principle in the soul

To be sure.

And when this principle measures and certifies that some things are equal, or that some are greater or less than others, there occurs an apparent contradiction?

True.

But were we not saying that such a contradiction is the same faculty cannot have contrary opinions at the same time about the same thing?

Very true.

Then that part of the soul which has an opinion contrary to measure is not the same with that which has an opinion in accordance with measure?

True.

And the better part of the soul is likely to be that which trusts to measure and calculation?

Certainly.

And that which is opposed to them is one of the inferior principles of the soul?

No doubt.

This was the conclusion at which I was seeking to arrive when I said that painting or drawing, and imitation in general, when doing their own proper work, are far removed from truth, and the companions and friends and associates of a principle within us which is equally removed from reason, and that they have no true or healthy aim.

Exactly.

The imitative art is an inferior who marries an inferior, and has inferior offspring.

Source: Plato, The Republic, Book 10, translated by Benjamin Jowett (add copyright info) http://classics.mit.edu/Plato/republic.11.x.html

CHAPTER 35
THE PLATO EFFECT IN ARCHITECTURE
Christopher N. Henry

The idea that a diverse population needs a diverse environment to succeed seems easy enough to grasp. Certainly, it is easier to comprehend than a one-size-fits-all design philosophy. Why then, in the name of universal design and equality, do architects continue to design uniform one-size-fits-all environments? Answering that is not so simple. Some may suggest that construction methods, costs, and site restrictions make diverse environments economically and physically infeasible. Others may fault the lack of courses architects take in human biology and psychology. This might make it impossible for them to understand the diverse range of people their buildings affect. Even more may fault the ever increasingly abstract design process. This may hinder architects' ability to identify with real future occupants. All of these conceivably play a role, but the most likely culprit is Plato's philosophy of essentialism for the same reason biologist Ernst Mayr felt it caused evolution's insufferably late discovery; essentialism has and continues to fundamentally shape how we see and deal with diversity throughout history variation posed a major philosophical problem for those in search of objective truths both in design and life in general. Plato's philosophy of essentialism attempted to bring objective truths to what he saw as relative and subjective experiences. According to Plato, a singular essence/definition of any form or idea must exist aspatially and atemporally in order to attain universal applicability among its various representations. For example, no matter whether drawn in the sand or autocad we can easily recognize a triangle when we see one. We can do this because we interpret any smudge or squiggle as an aberration from the true essence of a triangle. Plato called these singular essences Forms, and he applied this logic to everything from triangles to humans.

For Plato, all human differences represent corrupted and messy shadows projected by the pure Human Form. By defining the singular human archetype/essence, architects could theoretically create environments that would be universally appealing and accessible to all the sullied shadows we represent. It was thought that beauty could be objectively achieved by discovering the proportions of this illusive man. Once discovered, our homes, churches and marketplaces would be equally appealing to all users at all times—in other words the holy grail of architecture. With such a promise, architects, like possessed crusaders, have been trying to capture the human essence ever since the possibility was suggested.

Around the time of Christ, Roman architect Marcus Vitruvius Pollio (Vitruvius) ushered in the most famous proportional essence of man. Vitruvius's proportional system revolved around the notion of a perfectly built man. He described this well-built man, with his hands and feet extended, as fitting exactly into the most perfect geometrical figures of the circle and square. Vitruvius sincerely believed that a building based on this man's geometry would achieve universal appeal. For Vitruvius, this harmonious figure was the quintessential definition of the human archetype. It gave architects an objective scale in the face of endless subjective human experiences and preferences. Owing to the Renaissance and Leonardo da Vinci's 15th century sketch, we have come to know this figure as The Vitruvian Man.

Few enslaved themselves more to Plato's philosophy than the architects of the Renaissance. Armed with the Greek mathematical rendering of the world, and the Christian belief "that Man as the image of God embodied the harmonies of the Universe," Renaissance architects saw "the Vitruvian figure inscribed in a square and a circle a symbol of the mathematical sympathy between the microcosm and macrocosm." This elegantly simple picture of the world transfixed Renaissance architects, and as Rudolf Wittkower stated, "the image haunted their imagination."

Nearly 500 years after the Renaissance, celebrated architects, namely Le Corbusier, were still producing immutable human archetypes to derive architectural space. For him the Modulor was "a universal instrument, easy to employ, which can be used all over the world to obtain beauty and rationality in proportions of everything produced by man." He described its proportions as a "range of harmonious measurements to suit the human scale, universally applicable to architecture and to mechanical things." This quote from Corbusier illustrates how pervasive and clear Plato's philosophy has remained over the years. It is as if Corbusier has taken the words straight from the mouth of Renaissance architect Leone Battista Alberti. Regardless if present day architects ever read Plato, Vitruvius, or Corbusier, essentialism remains strong in architecture.

Source: ArchDaily, 12 October, 2011 http://www.archdaily.com/author/christopher-n-henry

CHAPTER 36
AN ART WHICH IMITATES ART
Pierre Bourdieu

Note from editor: Like other French theorists, Henri Lefebvre and Michel de Certeau, Pierre Bourdieu sought to understand the operation of power in contemporary societies by studying of the practices of everyday life. Much of his work is concerned with the means by which social distinctions and hierarchies between different groups of people are created and perpetuated, including an iconoclastic analysis of the 'art system' that shows how the failure of so many artists to gain recognition is structurally integral to the functioning of the system itself, a system of social actors – museums, galleries curators artists, critics – as a field of forces that provides the possibility of something appearing as art per se.[1] In the 1960s he made a sociological study of photography, conducting interviews with different users of photography: families, members of camera clubs, photographic artists and professional photographers.[2]

If it is legitimate to wonder (as we shall below) how and why photography is essentially predisposed to serve the social functions which have been very generally conferred upon it, it remains the case that the social uses of photography, presented as a systematic (i.e. coherent and comprehensible) selection from objectively possible uses, define the social meaning of photography at the same time as they are defined by it.

Thus it is commonly agreed that photography can be seen as the model of veracity and objectivity: 'Any work of art reflects the personality of its creator,' says the Encyclopedic, francaise. 'The photographic plate does not interpret. It records. Its precision and fidelity cannot be questioned.' It is all too easy to show that this social representation is based on the false evidence of prejudices; in fact, photography captures an aspect of reality which is only ever the result of an arbitrary selection, and, consequently, of a transcription; among all the qualities of the object, the only ones retained are the visual qualities which appear for a moment and from one sole viewpoint; these are transcribed in black and white, perspective) and volumes and colours in terms of variations between black and white. Photography is considered to be a perfectly realistic and objective recording of the visible world because (from its origin) it has been assigned social uses that are held to be 'realistic' and 'objective'.[3] And if it has immediately presented itself with all the appearances of a 'symbolic communication without syntax',[4] in short a 'natural language', this is especially so because the selection which it makes from the visible world is logically perfectly in keeping with the representation of the world which has dominated Europe since the Quattrocento. As Pierre Francastel observes:

Photography — the means of mechanically recording an image in conditions more or less analogous to those of vision — has made visible not the real character of traditional vision but, on the contrary, its systematic character: photographs are taken, even today, as a function of the classical artistic vision, at least insofar as this is permitted by the conditions of lens-manufacture and the use of only one lens. The camera provides the vision of the Cyclops, not of man. We also know that we systematically eliminate all those recordings which do not coincide with a vision that is not real but rather more-or-less artistic. For example, we do not take a picture of a building from close up, because the recording will not correspond to the traditional laws of orthometry. Try focusing a wide angle lens on the centre of the transept crossing of a gothic cathedral and look at the extraordinary document which you will obtain. You will see that what is called 'normal vision' is simply a selective vision, and that the world is infinitely richer in appearances than one would have thought.[5]

And Proust gives a very beautiful illustration of photography's powers to disconcert, of which the common practice is deprived:

> ... the most recent applications of photography — which huddle at the foot of a cathedral all the houses that so often, from close to, appeared to us to reach almost to the height of the towers, which drill and deploy like a regiment, in file, in extended order, in serried masses, the same monuments, bring together the two columns on the Piazzetta which a moment ago were so far apart, thrust away the adjoining dome of the Salute and in a pale and toneless background manage to include a whole immense horizon within the span of a generally reduced in scale and always projected on to a plane. In other words, photography is a conventional system which expresses space in terms of the laws of perspective (or rather of one bridge, in the embrasure of a window, among the leaves of a tree that stands in the foreground and is more vigorous in tone, or frame a single church successively in the arcades of all the others — I can think of nothing that can to so great a degree as a kiss evoke out of what we believed to be a thing with one definite aspect the hundred other things with which it may equally well be, since each is related to a no less legitimate perspective. [6]

Elsewhere, Proust describes those 'wonderful photographs of scenery and towns', which can provide an

> unusual image of a familiar object, an image different from those that we are accustomed to see, unusual and yet true to nature, and for that reason doubly striking because it surprises us, takes us out of our cocoon of habit, and at the same time brings us back to ourselves by recalling to us an earlier impression. For instance, one of these 'magnificent' photographs will illustrate a lay of perspective, will show us some cathedral which we are accustomed to see in the middle of a town, taken instead from a selected vantage point from which it will appear to be thirty times the height of the houses and to be thrusting out a spur from the bank of the river, from which it is actually at some distance.[7]

Is there not as great a distance between these 'magnificent' photographs and ordinary photographs as there is between perspective as a science of the real and perspective as a 'hallucinatory technique' ?[8] The ordinary photographer takes the world as he or she sees it, i.e. according to the logic of a vision of the world which borrows its categories and its canons from the arts of the past.[9] Pictures which, making use of real technical possibilities, break even slightly away from the academicism of vision and ordinary photography, are received with surprise. Because that which is visible is only ever that which is legible, subjects in all social milieux always resort to certain systems of reading of which the most common is the system of rules for the reproduction of the real that govern popular photography; faced with the most unusual pictures, the forms deciphered by lovers of photography are those which belong to a photographic tradition, such as the study of material; on the other hand, the omission of the norms of the canonical aesthetic, such as the absence of a foreground or a noticeable background meaningfully linked to the form (for example palm trees to express exoticism), frustrates understanding and appreciation when it does not provoke pure and simple refusal.

But the whole paradox of popular photography is revealed in its temporal dimension. An instant incision into the visible world, photography provides the means of dissolving the solid and compact reality of everyday perception into an infinity of fleeting profiles like dream images, in order to capture absolutely unique moments of the reciprocal situation of things, to grasp, as Walter Benjamin has shown, aspects, imperceptible because they are instantaneous, of the perceived world, to arrest human gestures in the absurdity of a present made up of 'pillars of salt'. In fact, far from seeing its specific vocation as the capturing of critical moments in which the reassuring world is knocked off balance, ordinary practice seems determined, contrary to all expectations, to strip photography of its power to disconcert; popular photography eliminates accident or any appearance that dissolves the real by temporalizing it.'[10] Only ever capturing moments which have been torn from the temporal flow by virtue of their solemnity, and only capturing people who are fixed, immobile, in the immutability of the plane, it loses its power of corrosion; when an action takes shape, it always embodies an essential movement, 'immobile' and outside of time, the balance or grace of a gesture as eternal as the social meaning it embodies; married couples standing arm in arm express, through a different gesture, the same meaning as the joined hands of Cato and Porcia in the Vatican. In the language of every aesthetic, frontality means eternity, in opposition to depth, through which temporality is reintroduced, and the plane expresses being or essence, in short, the timeless.[11] Thus, by adopting the arrangement and posture of the figures in Byzantine mosaics, farmers posing for wedding photographs escape that power of photography which derealizes things by temporalizing them.

Rather than using all the possibilities of photography to invert the conventional order of the visible, which, because it dominates the entire pictorial tradition and consequently an entire perception of the world, has paradoxically ended up by impressing itself with all the appearances of naturalness, ordinary practice subordinates photographic choice to the categories and canons of the traditional vision of the world; it is thus not surprising that photography can appear to be the recording of the world most true to this vision of the world, i.e. the most objective recording.[12] In other words, because the social use of photography makes a selection, from the field of the possible uses of photography, structured according to the categories that organize the ordinary vision of the world, the photographic image can be seen as the precise and objective reproduction of reality. If it is true that 'nature imitates art', it is natural that the imitation of art should appear to be the most natural imitation of nature.

But, at a deeper level, only in the name of a naive realism can one see as realistic a representation of the real which owes its objective appearance not to its agreement with the very reality of things (since this is only ever conveyed through socially conditioned forms of perception) but rather to conformity with rules which define its syntax within its social use, to the social definition of the objective vision of the world; in conferring upon photography a guarantee of realism, society is merely confirming itself in the tautological certainty that an image of the real which is true to its representation of objectivity is really objective.[13]

It is doubtless due as much to the social image of the technical object which produces it as to its social use that photography is ordinarily seen as the most perfectly faithful reproduction of the real. In fact 'the mechanical eye' accomplishes the popular representation of objectivity and aesthetic perfection as defined by the criteria of resemblance and legibility because this image is the product of an object; idolaters and detractors of the apparatus most often agree, as M. Gilbert Simondon observes, that the degree of sophistication of an apparatus is proportional to its level of automatism.[14] However, and for the same reason, the photo-graphic act in every way contradicts the popular representation of artistic creation as effort and toil. Can an art without an artist still be an art? It goes without saying that photography does not realize the artistic ideal of the working classes as an ideal of imitation to the same extent as realist painting, the production of reproduction.

Source: Pierre Bourdieu, *Photography: A Middle Brow Art* (trans. Shaun Whiteside) Cambridge: Polity Press, 1990, from chapter 2, 'The Social definition of Photography' pp 73–7.

Notes

1. Pierre Bourdieu, "The Production of Belief: contribution to an economy of symbolic goods" trans. Richard Nice, Media Culture and Society, July 1980 vol. 2 no. 3 261–293.

2. In collaboration with Luc Boltanski, Robert Castel, Jean-Claude Chamboredon and Dominique Schnapper.

3. The restructurings of the field of systems of pictorial expression, from the engraving to the 'photo-novel', reveal that each of these systems derives its perceptual and aesthetic rules from its social use. Photography did not simply appropriate one of the functions which had, until that point, been specific to engraving, the faithful reproduction of the real; leaving engraving with the task of illustrating fiction, it reinforced the pre-existing requirements of objectivity and realism by realizing them.

4. W. M. Ivins, Prints and visual communication (M.I.T. Press Cam-bridge, Mass. 1953), p. 128.

5. Pierre Francastel, Peinture et Societe, Audin, Lyon, 1951, p. 47.

6. Marcel Proust, Remembrance of Things Past, The Guermantes Way, trans. Terence Kilmartin, vol. 2 (Penguin Books, Harmondsworth, 1981) p. 378.

7. Marcel Proust, ibid., In a Budding Grove, vol. 1, p. 896.

8. Jurgis Baltrusaitis, Anamorphoses ou perspectives curieuses, Baltru-saitis, Paris, 1955.

9. Because there is nothing less natural than this selective and conventional representation, photography can still produce, in some subjects, an experience of 'estrangement', even within the familiar universe. An 85-year-old inhabitant of Lesquire showed great astonishment at an old photograph taken from the balcony of a house opposite his own. At first, he could recognize nothing. He turned the photograph around in all directions. He was shown that it was a picture of the town square. 'But where's it taken from?' He passed his finger along the houses. He stopped, and, pointing to the first-floor window of a house, said: 'But that's my house, isn't it?' He recognized the house next door: 'Where's it take from? Is that the church?' He recognized new details but remained just as confused because he was unable to locate himself.

10. Once again, children are an exception to this, perhaps because their nature is one of change; photography is appropriate, since it is a matter of capturing the ephemeral and the accidental, as it cannot save the fleeting view from complete disappearance without constituting it as such.

11. Cf. Yves Bonnefoy, 'Le temps et l'intemporel, dans la peinture du Quattrocento', Mercure de France, February 1958.

12. Photographic representations only really appear 'lifelike' and 'objective' because they obey laws of representation which were produced an before the media for creating them mechanically existed. Used by painters from the beginning of the sixteenth century and continuously improved from then on, in particular by the addition of a convex lens, the camera obscura became very widespread as the ambition to produce 'lifelike' images was reinforced. We also know about the fashion, during the second half of the eighteenth century, for portraits known as 'silhouettes' (drawings in profile made from the shadow thrown by the face). In 1786, Chretien perfected the 'physionotrace', which made it possible to trace three-quarter-face portraits from which, when they were reduced onto copper, a number of copies could be printed. In 1807, Wollaston invented the camera lucida, a device using a prism which made it possible to see the object to be drawn and the drawing itself at the same time. In 1822, Daguerre introduced the 'Dioramas', transparent pictures subjected to changing lighting; in search of pigments which would give his pictures more dramatic force, he carried out experiments on light-sensitive chemical products, pursuing the dream of chemically capturing the image formed in the camera obscura. Learning of Niepce's invention, he improved it and turned it into the daguerrotype. Photography was predisposed to become the standard of 'realism' because it supplied the mechanical means for realizing the 'vision of the world' invented several centuries earlier, with perspective.

13. The law is doubtless one of the best indications of the meaning objectively conferred on photography by our society. If photographic representation of the naked body leads more readily than representation in paintings to accusations of obscenity, this is doubtless because the realism attributed to photography means that it appears less capable of carrying out the operation of 'neutralization' (in the phenomenological sense) that is achieved by representation in paintings.

14. M. Gilbert Simondon points out that in fact 'automatism is a fairly low degree of technical sophistication' and that 'real sophistication in machines [...] corresponds not to an increase in automatism but on the contrary to the functioning of a machine taking on a certain margin of indeterminacy'. (Du mode d'existence des objets techniques, Paris, Aubier, 1958, p. 11.)

CHAPTER 37
SIGN FUNCTION AND CLASS LOGIC
Jean Baudrillard

Note from editor: Jean Baudrillard combines analysis from sociology, structural anthropology, political economy, and semiology, while undermining their explanations: of the commodity (as use value plus exchange value); and of ideology (as produced by distinct institutions). He challenges the commonsense idea that objects of consumption, in other words, designed commodities, are about the fulfilment of needs; rather, it is their sign function that is primary – and this cannot be stripped away to reveal authentic uses underneath, as it were, because they are designed, manufactured, exchanged, used, displayed, discarded and replaced as elements within dynamic systems of signification and social differentiation. He shows how the meanings of commodities are not fixed or inherent but are always shifting in a field of play of oppositions, contrasts, reversals and dissimulations. An example of the latter is "the gadget: pure gratuitousness under a cover of functionality, pure waste under an ethic of practicality." (32) The following extracts are from two different chapters; the first, 'Sign Function and Class Logic' evokes by concrete examples, the second, 'A Critique of the Political Economy of the Sign' lays out his general theory.

The prestige of the "natural"

The logic of cultural differentiation is going to impose negation at a privileged level, the disavowal of these values of polish and varnish, of care in favor of the values of "frankness" (franchise), and of the "natural": the raw, matte, savage and neglected. This "frank-ness" of the object sanctioned by taste has nothing "natural" about it. On the contrary, it is deduced from lower-class devotion to the artificial, to the baroque affectation of decorum, to the moral values of the veiled, the clothed, the cared for, the preened, to the moral values of effort. Here "preparation" is a cultural fault. Propriety (repressive conditioning) and manners in the matter of objects, which in another age were the cultural signs of the bourgeoisie, are stigmatized as the distinctive marks of the petty bourgeois classes who have outfitted themselves with them. The essential function of the values of "sincerity," "authenticity," "starkness," — inner walls of bare concrete, unfinished timbers — is thus a function of discrimination (distinction), and their definition is first social.

Here again one is rationalizing, but less in terms of immediate practicality ("it is more practical," "that washes better") than in terms of secondary functions ("direct contact," "warmer atmosphere"), and especially in terms of functional aesthetics ("abolition of decor," "truth of the object," "promotion of form," etc.). One allows it to be understood that, according to a continuous progress, objects would obey an internal aesthetic logic which would ultimately lead them to appear in their "truth," in the harmonious synthesis of their function and their form. This is the fundamental theory of design.[1] Now the hypothesis of a progressive advancement from model to model toward an ideal state of the environment — a hypothesis which secretly rests upon the representation of technological progress — implies a whole ideology, for it masks the social function of formal innovation, which is a function of cultural discrimination. Formal innovation materialized in objects does not have an ideal world of objects as its goal but rather, a social ideal, that of the privileged classes, which is the perpetual reassertion of their cultural privilege.

Formal innovation and social discrimination

The priority of this social function of discrimination over the "aesthetic" function is visible in fashion, where at any moment the most aesthetically aberrant and arbitrary forms may be reactivated simply for the purpose of providing distinctive signs for a material which is always new.

So, the paradigmatic oppositions —varnished-matte, enveloped-stark, polished-rough — are not only the instruments of a semiological analysis of the world of objects, but are also social discriminants, characteristics which are not only formally distinct but socially distinctive. Of course their contextual value is relative, because the bareness of a wall may sometimes indicate poverty, unrefined misery, and other times evince a "savage" luxury.

To explain it another way, that which, at the level of a rational logic of models, is given as "universal," as completed beauty, as absolute truth of form and function, has at bottom no truth other than the relative and ephemeral one of its position in the social logic it imposes. This "universal" is still nothing more than a particular sign, an exhibitor of class. The effect of "beauty," of "naturalness," of "functionality" (in the ideal sense of functionalism) is registered in this class relationship and cannot be dissociated from it.

At a later stage, aesthetic privilege is no longer attached to varnish or rawness but to the liberty of freely combining all the terms: the lacquered coffer close beside the rough wood or smooth marble together with naked concrete.[2] At this avant-garde level, the exclusiveness, which pledged the petty bourgeois to artificial luster and the cultivated to "natural" starkness, is apparently lifted, so that here everything is salvaged, all combinations are possible. But once again, that which at the level of form appears to be a surpassing towards a universal position, takes on its true value in an inverse social signification: the universal term (synthesis of difference) once again becomes an effective factor of discrimination because only a few elect will be able to accede to this stage of the aesthetic combinatory. The others find themselves relegated to the moral manipulation of domestic objects. With respect to objects and their calculus (as other places), the universal once again is the title of nobility held by a specific category.

The aesthetic calculus is always submerged in social logic. In order to avoid taking this ideological process into account, designers exhaust themselves in popularizing audacious, "rational," "functional" forms, being all the while surprised that these forms do not spontaneously seduce the mass public. Yet behind their pious litany (educating public taste), these "popular" creators direct their un-conscious strategy: beautiful, stylized, modern objects are subtly created (despite all reversed good faith) in order not to be understood by the majority — at least not straight away. Their social function is first to be distinctive signs, to be objects which will distinguish those who distinguish them. Others will not even see them.[3]

The flux and reflux of distinctive signs

This contradiction between rational economic logic and cultural class logic affects another essential aspect of objects: their status in time, their cycle of erosion and renewal.

The diverse categories of objects have a variable longevity: residence, furniture, electrical appliances, TV, linens, clothing, gadgets, wear out at different rates. But two distinct variables play upon the whole span of objects in calculating their lifetime and durability: one is their real rate of wearing out, registered in their technical structure and their material; the other, the value they take on as patrimony or inversely, the accelerated obsolescence due to fashion. What is important for us here is this second value and its relation to the respective situation of groups in a stratified and mobile industrial society. How does a given group distinguish itself by a more or less strong adhesion to the ephemeral or to the durable? What are the various responses of different groups on the social scale to fashion's demands for accelerated renewal of objects?

In effect fashion does not reflect a natural need of change: the pleasure of changing clothes, objects, cars, comes to sanction the constraints of another order psychologically, constraints of social differentiation and prestige. The effects of fashion only appear in socially mobile societies (and beyond a certain threshold of available money). Ascending or descending social status must be registered in the continual flux and reflux of distinctive signs. A given class is not lastingly assigned to a given category of objects (or to a given style of clothing): on the contrary, all classes are assigned to change, all assume the necessity of fashion as a value, just as they participate (more or less) in the universal imperative of social mobility. In other words, since objects play the role of exhibitors of social status, and since this status has become potentially mobile, the objects will always simultaneously give evidence not only of an acquired situation (this they have always done), but also of the potential mobility of this social status as such objects are registered in the distinctive cycle of fashion.

One might think that on account of their material presence, objects first have the function of enduring, of registering social status "in solidity."[4] This was the case in traditional society, where hereditary decor was evidence of social accomplishment and, at the limit, of the social eternity of an acquired situation. Then the description and social semantics of the environment could be relatively simple. And in a sense it is always thus: at whatever social level one is situated, there is always the tendency to perpetuate an acquired situation in objects (and children). The objects with which one surrounds oneself first constitute a balance sheet, a testament (eventually resigned) to social destiny. On the other hand, they often appear to be symbolically framed and fixed on the wall, such as was once the case with school diplomas. A position and a destiny, thus the contrary of social mobility — this is what objects first present. Chosen, bought and arranged, they are part of the completed fulfillment, not of ascending performance. They encircle with their ascriptive dimension. Even when (only too frequently) they outbid social success, even when they seem to take an option on the future, still, it is never through his objects that social man accomplishes himself or is mobile. He falls back upon them, and objects often translate, at the very most, his frustrated social aspirations.

This function of the inertia of objects that results in a durable, sometimes hereditary status, is combatted today by that of having to signify social change. As one is elevated on the social scale, objects multiply, diversify and are renewed. Their accelerated traffic (circulation) in the name of fashion quickly comes to signify and to present a social mobility that does not really exist. This is already the meaning of certain mechanisms of substitution: unable to change the apartment, one changes the car. It is even clearer that the accelerated renewal of objects often compensates a disappointed aspiration to cultural and social progress. This is what makes the "reading" of objects complex: sometimes their mobility reflects the rising standing of a given social category by signifying it positively; sometimes, on the contrary, it comes to compensate the social inertia of a certain group or individual whose disappointed and thwarted desire for mobility comes to register itself in the artificial mobility of decor.

Here the whole ideology of fashion is in question. The formal logic of fashion imposes an increased mobility on all the distinctive social signs. Does this formal mobility of signs correspond to a real mobility in social structures (professional, political, cultural)? Certainly not. Fashion — and more broadly, consumption, which is inseparable from fashion — masks a profound social inertia. It itself is a factor of social inertia, insofar as the demand for real social mobility frolics and loses itself in fashion, in the sudden and often cyclical changes of objects, clothes and ideas. And to the illusion of change is added the illusion of democracy (which is similar but under another aspect). The constraint of the transitoriness of fashion is claimed to eliminate the possibility of inheriting distinctive signs; it is reputed to return the whole world to a position of equal opportunities at each instant of the cycle. In the face of the demands of fashion all objects can be recalled: this would suffice to create the equality of all in the face of objects. Now, this is quite obviously false: fashion, like mass culture, speaks to all in order to better return each one to his place. It is one of those institutions that best restores cultural inequality and social discrimination, establishing it under the pretense of abolishing it. It wishes to be beyond social logic, a kind of second nature: in fact, it is entirely governed by the social strategy of class. "Modern" transitoriness of objects (and other signs) is in fact the luxury of heirs?[5]

(.....)

Toward a critique of the political economy of the sign

The critique of the political economy of the sign proposes to develop the analysis of the sign form, just as the critique of political economy once set out to analyze the commodity form.

Since the commodity comprises simultaneously exchange value and use value, its total analysis must encompass the two sides of the system. Similarly, the sign is at once signifier and signified; and so the analysis of the sign form must be established on two levels. Concurrently, of course, the logical and strategic analysis of the relation between the two terms is pressed upon us, thus:

1. Between the system of exchange value (EV) and that of use value (UV), or between the commodity form and the object form. This was the attempt in the preceding article.

2. Between the systems of the signifier and the signified (or between their respective codes, which define the articulation of sign value and the sign form).

In both cases, this (internal) relation is established as a hierarchical function between a dominant form and an alibi (or satellite) form, which is the logical crowning and ideological completion of the first.

The magical thinking of ideology

The effect of this homological structuration of values in what can conveniently be called the fields of economy and of signification is to displace the whole process of ideology and to theorize it in radically different terms. Ideology can no longer be understood as an infrasuperstructural relation between a material production (system and relations of production) and a production of signs (culture, etc.), which expresses and masks the contradictions at the "base." Henceforth, all of this comprises, with the same degree of objectivity, a general political economy (its critique), which is traversed throughout by the same form and administered by the same logic.

It should be recalled that the traditional vision of ideology still proves incapable of grasping the "ideological" function of culture and of signs — except at the level of the signified. This follows inevitably from its separation of culture (and signs) in the artificial distinction between the economic and the ideological, not to mention the desperate contortions ("superstructure," "dialectic," "structure in dominance") that this entails. Thus, ideology (of such-and-such a group, or the dominant class) always appears as the overblown discourse of some great theme, content, or value (patriotism, morality, humanism, happiness, consumption, the family) whose allegorical power somehow insinuates itself into consciousnesses (this has never been explained) in order to integrate them. These become, in turn, the contents of thought that come into play in real situations. In sum, ideology appears as a sort of cultural surf frothing on the beachhead of the economy.

So it is clear that ideology is actually that very form that traverses both the production of signs and material production — or rather, it is the logical bifurcation of this form into two terms:

EV /UV

Sr /Sd

This is the functional, strategic split through which the form reproduces itself. It signifies that ideology lies already whole in the relation of EV to UV, that is, in the logic of the commodity, as is so in the relation of Sr to Sd, i.e., in the internal logic of the sign.

Marx demonstrated that the objectivity of material production did not reside in its materiality, but in its form. In fact, this is the point of departure for all critical theory. The same analytical reduction must be applied to ideology: its objectivity does not reside in its "ideality," that is, in a realist metaphysic of thought contents, but in its form.

The "critique" (not excluding here the Marxist critique of ideology) feeds off a magical conception of its object. It does not unravel ideology as form, but as content, as given, transcendent value — a sort of manna that attaches itself to several global representations that magically impregnate those floating and mystified subjectivities called "consciousnesses." Like the concept of need, which is presented as the link between the utility of an object and the demand of a subject, ideology appears as the relation between the projection of a consciousness and the ideality of — vaguely — an idea, or a value. Transposed from the analysis of material goods to collective representations and values, the same little magic footbridge is suspended between artificial, even metaphysical, concepts.[6]

In fact, ideology is the process of reducing and abstracting symbolic material into a form. But this reductive abstraction is given immediately as value (autonomous), as content (transcendent), and as a representation of consciousness (signified). It is the same process that lends the commodity an appearance of autonomous value and transcendent reality — a process that involves the misunderstanding of the form of the commodity and of the abstraction of social labor that it operates. In bourgeois (or, alas, Marxist) thought, culture is defined as a transcendence of contents correlated with conscious-nesses by means of a "representation" that circulates among them like positive values, just as the fetishized commodity appears as a real and immediate value, correlated with individual subjects through "need" and use value, and circulating according to the rules of exchange value.

It is the cunning of form to veil itself continually in the evidence of content. It is the cunning of the code to veil itself and to produce itself in the obviousness of value. It is in the "materiality" of content that form consumes its abstraction and reproduces itself as form. That is its peculiar magic. It simultaneously produces the content and the consciousness to receive it just as production produces the product and its corresponding need). Thus, it installs culture in a dual transcendence of values (of contents) and consciousness, and in a metaphysic of exchange between the two terms. And if the bourgeois vulgate enshrines it in this transcendence precisely in order to exalt it as culture, the Marxist vulgate embalms it in the very same transcendence in order to denounce it as ideology. But the two scriptures rejoin in the same magical thinking?[7]

Just about all contemporary thought in this area confounds itself on false problems and in endless controversies ensuing from artificial disjunctions:

1. The subject-object dichotomy, bridged by the magical concept of need. Things might run quite smoothly here if the general system of production-consumption were not disrupted by the insoluble problem of supply and demand. Can one still speak of autonomy of choice, or is it a question of manipulation? Perhaps the two perspectives can be synthesized? — mere pseudo-dialectic. It is all an eternal litany — and over a false problem anyway.

2. The infrastructure-superstructure dichotomy, which, as we have seen, covers over again the implacable disjunction between the materiality of contents and the ideality of consciousness, reuniting the two thereby separated poles with the magical conception of ideology. Even here, matters would run more smoothly if the problem of the "determinant instance" were not held eternally in suspense (since it

is usually "in the last instance" — it never actually appears on the stage), with all the acrobatics of "interaction," "dialectic," "relative autonomy" and "overdetermination" that follow in its wake (and whose interminable careers have redounded to the glory of generations of intellectuals).

3. The exploitation-alienation distinction, which reiterates this false problem at the level of political analysis. The infinite debate over whether exploitation is the ground of alienation or vice versa ; or whether the second succeeds the first as "the most advanced stage of capitalism" — all this is absurd. Not for the first time, the confusion arises from an artificial separation — this time of the sign and the commodity, which are not analyzed in their form, but posed instead as contents (the one of signification, the other of production). Whence emerges the distinction between an "exploitation" of labor power and an "alienation by signs." As if the commodity and the system of material production "signified" nothing! As if signs and culture were not immediately abstract social production at the level of the code and models, in a generalized exchange system of values.

Ideology is thus properly situated on neither side of this split. Rather, it is the one and only form that traverses all the fields of social production. Ideology seizes all production, material or symbolic, in the same process of abstraction, reduction, general equivalence and exploitation.

1. It is because the logic of the commodity and of political economy is at the very heart of the sign, in the abstract equation of signifier and signified, in the differential combinatory of signs, that signs can function as exchange value (the discourse of communication) and as use value (rational decoding and distinctive social use).

2. It is because the structure of the sign is at the very heart of the commodity form that the commodity can take on, immediately, the effect of signification — not epiphenomenally, in excess of itself, as "message" or connotation — but because its very form establishes it as a total medium, as a system of communication administering all social exchange. Like the sign form, the commodity is a code managing the exchange of values. It makes little difference whether the contents of material production or the immaterial contents of signification are involved; it is the code that is determinant: the rules of the interplay of signifiers and exchange value. Generalized in the system of political economy, it is the code which, in both cases, reduces all symbolic ambivalence in order to ground the "rational" circulation of values and their play of exchange in the regulated equivalence of values.

It is here that the concept of alienation proves useless, by dint of its association with the metaphysic of the subject of consciousness. The code of political economy, which is the fundamental code of our society, does not operate by alienating consciousness from contents. A parallel confusion arises in the view of "primitive" myths as false stories or histories that consciousnesses recount to themselves. Here the pregnant effects of mythic contents are held to bind society together (through the "cohesion" of belief systems). But actually, these myths make up a code of signs that exchange among themselves, integrating the group through the very process of their circulation. Likewise, the fundamental code of our societies, the code of political economy (both commodity form and sign form) does not operate through the alienation of consciousness and contents. It rationalizes and regulates exchange, makes things communicate, but only under the law of the code and through the control of meaning.

The division of labor, the functional division of the terms of discourse, does not mystify people; it socializes them and informs their exchange according to a general, abstract model. The very concept of the individual is the product of this general system of exchange. And the idea of "totality" under which the subject (either that of consciousness or that of History) thinks itself in its ideal reference is nothing but the effect and the symptom of the system —the shadow that it wears. The concept of alienation involves a kind of wizardry in which consciousness thinks itself as its own ideal content (its rediscovered totality): it is an ideological concept. And ideology, in its version as a superstructure of contents of consciousness, is, in these terms, an alienated concept.

Today consumption — if this term as a meaning other than that given it by vulgar economics — defines precisely the stage where the commodity is immediately produced as a sign, as sign value, and where signs (culture) are produced as commodities. But this whole area of study is still occupied, "critically" or otherwise, by specialists of production (economy, infrastructure), or ideology specialists (signs, culture), or even by a kind of seamless dialectician of the totality. This partitioning of the object domain obscures even the simplest realities. If any progress is to be made at this point, "research" — especially Marxist research — must come to terms with the fact that nothing produced or exchanged today (objects, services, bodies, sex, culture, knowledge, etc.) can be decoded exclusively as a sign, nor solely measured as a commodity; that everything appears in the context of a general political economy in which the determining instance is neither the commodity nor culture (not even the updated commodity, revised and reinterpreted in its signifying function, with its message, its connotations, but always as if there still existed an objective substrate to it, the potential objectivity of the product as such; nor culture in its "critical" version, where signs, values, ideas are seen as everywhere commercialized or recuperated by the dominant system, but again, as if there subsisted through all this something whose transcendence could have been rationalized and simply compromised — a kind of sublime use value of culture distorted in exchange value). The object of this political economy, that is, its simplest component, its nuclear element — that which precisely the commodity was for Marx — is no longer today properly either commodity or sign, but indissolubly both, and both only in the sense that they are abolished as specific determinations, but not as form. Rather, this object is perhaps quite simply the object, 3 the object form, on which use value, exchange value and sign value converge in a complex mode that describes the most general form of political economy.

Source: Jean Baudrillard, *For A Critique of the Political Economy of the Sign*, trans. Charles Levin, St. Louis. MO: Telos Press, 1981, pp 143–150. © Editions Gallimard, Paris, 1999.

Notes

1. 1. Cf. Design and Environment (Ch. 10) — Trans.

2. The mixture that today is in fashion everywhere, in advertising, decoration, clothing, testifies to the same "liberty": Mondrian-like geometricism coexists peacefully with the psychedelic version of art nouveau.

3. The same analysis can be made with respect to furniture (no longer according to the material, but to the function). The last word in functional furniture is the mobile element, which, stacked with a few cushions, can turn into a bed, seats, wall units, bookshelves, or anything at all (a pure object) at the whim of its owner. It is the Arch-furnishing, the totally polyvalent manifestation of an audacious, incontestably "rational" analytic formula. And this formula paradoxically revives those of the Middle Ages or of poor peasant living, where the same element — the trunk — would also serve as table, bench, cupboard, etc. The meaning, however, is evidently reversed; far from being a solution to poverty, the contemporary mobile element is the synthesis of all these differentiated functions and of all luxurious distinctions. It is the culmination of simplicity and upon the (bad) faith of this apparent simplicity its designers make of it the "popular" and economical solution of the future! The prices which are always realistic, unpityingly translate the social logic: these simple forms are a costly refinement. Here again formal innovation is justified in terms of severity, economy, "structure," sometimes even in terms of penury and urgency: "If necessary, your bed can be turned into a dresser," etc. Why bother? It is only a game, and one that only plays upon necessity: fashion is pre-eminent here. Technical — real —innovation does not have at heart the goal of genuine economy, but the game of social distinction.

4. "...fonction de durer...'en dur.'" —Trans.

5. Fashion embodies a compromise between the need to innovate and the other need to change nothing in the fundamental order. It is this that characterizes "modern" societies. Thus it results in a game of change. In this game, the new and the old are functionally equivalent. If one adheres to lived psychology, one would see there two inverse tendencies: the need to change and the nostalgic need for old things. In fact, the function of the new look and of the old fashion is the alteration: at all levels, it is the result of a logical constraint of the system — old and new are not relative to contradictory needs: they are the "cyclical" paradigm of fashion. "Modern" is the new and the old, which no longer have temporal value. For the same reason, "modern" has nothing to do with actual practicality, with a real change, with a structural innovation. New and old, neologism and archaism are homogeneous in the game of changes.

6. It should be noted here that alienation itself is one of these magical concepts devoted to sealing up an artificial disjunction — here, the disjunction between the consciousness of the subject and his own ideal content (his rediscovered totality).

7. Thus the "critical" denunciation of artificial needs and the manipulation of needs converges in the same mystification the unconditional exaltation of consumption.

CHAPTER 38
THE PRODUCTION OF SPACE
Henri Lefebvre

Note from editor: French philosopher, sociologist and political activist Henri Lefebvre brought the question of space to the thinking of the social, the economic and the political. He shows how space, or spatiality, in terms of the configuration of the built forms of human habitation, is both ordered and disordered, the outcome of accident and intention; space is dynamic and contested, in other words it is political. The following extract from The Production of Space *discusses space in terms of form, function and structure. In this it might seem at first to be no different from in the mold of western rationalistic abstraction, but Lefebvre shows these categories to be unstable and overlapping, and their inter-relation only able to be grasped in actual situations, such that there is no eternal or inevitable correlation between specific forms, functions and structures. Throughout the book, Lefebvre is highly critical of the reduction of lived space to abstract space that is extolled and created by modernist architects and the politico-economic structures that they serve. This extract can be read along with Timothy's Mitchell's 'Enframing' in Part IV.*

It is very important from the outset to stress the destructive (because reductive) effects of the predominance of the readable and visible, of the absolute priority accorded to the visual realm, which in turn implies the priority of reading and writing. An emphasis on visual space has accompanied the search for an impression of weightlessness in architecture. Some theorists of a supposed architectural revolution claim Le Corbusier as a pioneer of this connection, but in fact it was Brunelleschi, and more recently Baltard and then Eiffel, who blazed the trail. Once the effect of weightiness or massiveness upon which architects once depended has been abandoned, it becomes possible to break up and reassemble volumes arbitrarily according to the dictates of an architectural Neoplatonism. Modernity expressly reduces so-called 'iconological' forms of expression (signs and symbols) to surface effects. Volumes or masses are deprived of any physical consistency. The architect considers himself responsible for laying down the social function (or use) of buildings, offices, or dwellings, yet interior walls which no longer have any spatial or bearing role, and interiors in general, are simultaneously losing all character or content. Even exterior walls no longer have any material substance: they have become mere membranes barely managing to concretize the division between inside and outside. This does not prevent 'users' from projecting the relationship between the internal or private and a threatening outside world into an invented absolute realm; when there is no alternative, they use the signs of this antagonism, relying especially on those which indicate property. For an architectural thought in thrall to the model of transparency, however, all partitions between inside and outside have collapsed. Space has been comminuted into 'iconological' figures and values, each such fragment being invested with individuality or worth simply by means of a particular colour or a particular material (brick, marble, etc.). Thus the sense of circumscribed spaces has gone the same way as the impression of mass. Within and without have melted into transparency, becoming indistinguishable or interchangeable.

(.....)

Like any reality, social space is related methodologically and theoretically to three general concepts: form, structure, function. In other words, any social space may be subjected to formal, structural or functional analysis. Each of these approaches provides a code and a method for deciphering what at first may seem impenetrable.

These terms may seem clear enough, but in fact, since they cannot avoid polysemy, they all carry burdens of ambiguity.

The term 'form' may be taken in a number of senses: aesthetic, plastic abstract (logico-mathematical), and so on. In a general sense, it evokes the description of contours and the demarcation of boundaries, external limits, areas and volumes. Spatial analysis accepts this general use of the term, although doing so does not eliminate all problems. A formal description, for example, may aspire to exactitude but still turn out to be shot through with ideological elements, especially when implicit or explicit reductionistic goals are involved. The presence of such goals is indeed a defining characteristic of formalism. Any space may be reduced to its formal elements: to curved and straight lines or to such relations as internal-versus-external or volume-versus-area. Such formal aspects have given rise in architecture, painting and sculpture to genuine systems: the system of the golden number, for example, or that of the Doric, Ionic and Corinthian orders, or that of moduli (rhythms and proportions).

Consideration of aesthetic effects or 'effects of meaning' has no particular right of precedence in this context. What counts from the methodological and theoretical standpoint is the idea that none of these three terms can exist in isolation from the other two. Forms, functions and structures are generally given in and through a material realm which at once binds them together and preserves distinctions between them. When we consider an organism, for example, we can fairly easily discern the forms, functions and structures within this totality. Once this threefold analysis has been completed, however, a residue invariably remains which seems to call for deeper analysis. This is the raison d'être of the ancient philosophical categories of being, nature, substance and matter. In the case of a produced 'object', this constitutive relationship is different: the application to materials of a practical action (technology, labour) tends to blur, as a way of mastering them, the distinctions between form, function and structure, so that the three may even come to imply one another in an immediate manner. This tendency exists only implicitly in works of art and objects antedating the Industrial Revolution, including furniture, houses, palaces and monuments; under the conditions of modernity, on the other hand, it comes close to its limit. With the advent of 'design', materiality tends to give way to transparency — to perfect 'readability'. Form is now merely the sign of function, and the relation between the two, which could not be clearer — that is, easier to produce and reproduce — is what gives rise to structure. A case where this account does not apply is that not uncommon one where 'designer' and manufacturer find it amusing to confuse the issue, as it were, and give a form (often a 'classical' one) to a function completely unconnected with it: they disguise a bed as a cupboard, for example, or a refrigerator as bookshelves. The celebrated signifier—signified dichotomy is singularly appropriate when applied to such objects, but this special application is just that — and a good deal more limited than semantico-semiological orthodoxy would probably care to admit. As for social 'realities', here the opposite situation obtains: the distances between forms, functions and structures lengthen rather than diminish. The three tend to become completely detached from one another. Their relationship is obscured and they become indecipherable (or undecodable) as the 'hidden' takes over from the 'readable' in favour of the predominance of the latter in the realm of objects. Thus a particular institution may have a variety of functions which are different — and sometimes opposed — to its apparent forms and avowed structures. One merely has to think of the institutions of 'justice', of the military, or of the police. In other words, the space of objects and the space of institutions are radically divergent in 'modern' society. This is a society in which, to take an extreme example, the bureaucracy is supposed to be, aspires to be, loudly proclaims itself to be, and perhaps even believes itself to be 'readable' and transparent, whereas in fact it is the very epitome of opacity, indecipherability and 'unreadability'. The same goes for all other state and political apparatuses.

The relationship between these key terms and concepts (form, function, structure) becomes much more complex when one considers only those very abstract forms, such as the logical form, which do not depend on description and which are inseparable from a content. Among these, in addition to the logical form, must be numbered identity, reciprocity, recurrence, repetition (iteration), and difference. Marx, following Adam Smith and Ricardo, showed how and why the form of exchange has achieved predominance in social practice in association with specific functions and structures. The form of social space — i.e. the centre—periphery relationship — has only recently come to occupy a place in our thinking about forms. As for the urban form — i.e. assembly, encounter and simultaneity — it has been shown to belong among the classic forms, in company with centrality, difference, recurrence, reciprocity, and so on.

These forms, which are almost 'pure' (at the extreme limit of 'purity' the form disappears, as in the case of pure identity: A's identity with A) cannot be detached from a content. The interaction between form and content and the invariably concrete relationship between them are the object of analyses about which we may repeat what we said earlier: each analytic stage deals with a residue left over from the previous stage, for an irreducible element — the substrate or foundation of the object's 'presence' — always subsists.

Between forms close to the point of purity at which they would disappear and their contents, there exist mediations. In the case of spatial forms, for example, the form of the curve is mediated by the curved line, and the straight form by the straight line. All spatial arrangements use curved and/or straight forms; naturally, one or the other may predominate.

When formal elements become part of a texture, they diversify, introducing both repetition and difference. They articulate the whole, facilitating both movement from the parts to the whole and, conversely, the mustering by the whole of its component elements. For example, the capitals of a Romanesque cloister differ, but they do so within the limits permitted by a model. They break space up and give it rhythm. This illustrates the function of what has been called the 'signifying differential'.[1] The semicircular or ogival arch, with its supporting pillars and columns, has a different spatial meaning and value according to whether it occurs in Byzantine or in Oriental, in Gothic or in Renaissance architecture. Arches have both repetitive and differential functions within a whole whose 'style' they help determine. The same sort of thing goes in music for the theme and its treatment in fugal composition. Such 'diaeretic' effects, which the semiologists compare to metonymy, are to be met with in all treatments of space and time.

The peopling and investment (or occupation) of a space always happens in accordance with discernible and analysable forms: as dispersal or concentration, or as a function of a specific (or for that matter a nebulous) orientation. By contrast, assembly and concentration as spatial forms are always actualized by means of geometric forms: a town may have a circular (radial—concentric) or a quadrangular form.

The content of these forms metamorphoses them. The quadrangular form, for example, occurs in the ancient Roman military camp, in medieval bastides, in the Spanish colonial town and in the modern American city. The fact is, however, that these urban realities differ so radically that the abstract form in question is their only common feature.

The Spanish-American colonial town is of considerable interest in this regard. The foundation of these towns in a colonial empire went hand in hand with the production of a vast space, namely that of Latin America. Their urban space, which was instrumental in this larger production process, has continued to be produced despite the vicissitudes of imperialism, independence and industrialization. It is an urban space especially appropriate for study in that the colonial towns of Latin America were founded at the time of the Renaissance in Europe — that is to say, at a time when the study of the ancient world, and of the history, constitution, architecture and planning of its cities, was being resumed.

The Spanish-American town was typically built according to a plan laid down on the basis of standing orders, according to the veritable code of urban space constituted by the Orders for Discovery and Settlement, a collection, published in 1573, of official instructions issued to founders of towns from 1513 on. These instructions were arranged under the three heads of discovery, settlement and pacification. The very building of the towns thus embodied a plan which would determine the mode of occupation of the territory and define how it was to be reorganized under the administrative and political authority of urban power. The orders stipulate exactly how the chosen sites ought to be developed. The result is a strictly hierarchical organization of space, a gradual progression outwards from the town's centre, beginning with the ciudad and reaching out to the surrounding *pueblos*. The plan is followed with geometrical precision: from the inevitable Plaza Mayor a grid extends indefinitely in every direction. Each square or rectangular lot has its function assigned to it, while inversely each function is assigned its own place at a greater or lesser distance from the central square: church, administrative buildings, town gates, squares, streets, port installations, warehouses, town hall, and so on. Thus a high degree of segregation is superimposed upon a homogeneous space.[2] Some historians have described this colonial town as an artificial product, but they forget that this artificial product is also an instrument of production: a superstructure foreign to the original space serves as a political means of introducing a social and economic structure in such a way that it may gain a foothold and indeed establish its 'base' in a particular locality. Within this spatial framework, Spanish colonial architecture freely (so to speak) deployed the Baroque motifs which are especially evident in the decoration of façades. The relation between the 'micro' (architectural) plane and the 'macro' (spatial—strategic) one does exist here, but it cannot be reduced to a logical relationship or put into terms of formal implication. The main point to be noted, therefore, is the production of a social space by political power — that is, by violence in the service of economic goals. A social space of this kind is generated out of a rationalized and theorized form serving as an instrument for the violation of an existing space.

One is tempted to ask whether the various urban spaces with a grid pattern might not have comparable origins in constraints imposed by a central power. It turns out upon reflection, however, that there is no real justification for generalizing from the particular development of urban space in Latin America. Consider, for example, that transformation of space in New York City which began around 1810. Obviously it is to be explained in part by the existence and the influence of an already powerful urban nucleus, and by the actions of a duly empowered authority. On the other hand, developments in New York had absolutely nothing to do with the extraction of wealth by a metropolitan power, the colonial relationship with Britain having come to an end. Geometrical urban space in Latin America was intimately bound up with a process of extortion and plunder serving the accumulation of wealth in Western Europe; it is almost as though the riches produced were riddled out through the gaps in the grid. In English-speaking North America, by contrast, a formally homologous meshwork served only the production and accumulation of capital on the spot. Thus the same abstract form may have opposing functions and give rise to diverse structures. This is not to say that the form is indifferent to function and structure: in both these cases the pre-existing space was destroyed from top to bottom; in both the aim was homogeneity; and in both that aim was achieved.

Source: *The Production of Space*, Henri Lefebvre. trans. Donald Nicholson-Smith, Oxford: Blackwell, 1991, 2018 © Blackwell. Reproduced with permission of Blackwell Publishing Ltd. pp 146–152.

Notes

1. See Julia Kristeva, Semeiotike (Paris: Seuil, 1969), pp. 298ff. The 'signifying differential' is to be distinguished from Osgood's 'Semantic differential'.
2. See Emma Scovazzi in Espaces et société, no. 3.

GUIDE TO FURTHER READING

For orientation, see entries on Aesthetics, Beauty, Form, Sign, and Taste in *Bloomsbury Encyclopedia of Design*. On the dominance of visuality in Western culture see David Michael Levin (ed.) *Modernity and the Hegemony of Vision* (1993) and David Michael Levin, *The Opening of Vision: Nihilism and the Postmodern Situation* (1988). Cultural theory addressing dominance of visualty include Guy Debord, *Society of the Spectacle* (1977); Walter Benjamin's *Arcades Project* (2002) written between 1927 and 1940 evoking the phantasmagoria of consumption in the arcades of nineteenth-century Paris; Thorstein Veblen's *Theory of the Leisure Class* (1899) which first named the phenomena of "conspicuous consumption"; and Siegfried Kracauer in *The Mass Ornament* (1995, originally published in 1930s) writing on chorus line dancers whose "body parts are squeezed into patterns that they do not control and, even more important, do not recognize as a whole . . . (thus they) share with the ordinary practices of everyday life the fact that their movements are governed by an operational logic that they do not consciously recognize." Roland Barthes was highly attuned to both the dominance and the nuances of mass produced visual imagery in *Mythologies*, *Image Music Text* and *Camera Lucida*. On the televisual see Tony Fry (ed.) *RUA/TV? Heidegger and the Televisual* (1993). For a non-western perspective on the spectacle of modernity as it is received in the global South see Rolando Vázquez, *Modernity, the Greatest Show on Earth: Thoughts on Visibility* (2010).

PART VIII
DESIGNING AFTER THE END

INTRODUCTION

Many of the key terms (such as nature or the universal human being) that have structured Western thinking for many centuries have in recent decades been subjected to critique and deconstruction. This critical thinking emphasizes the fragility and fluidity of what have assumed to be absolute and clear categories. While this thinking has generally not spread much beyond the academy (this can be verified by listening to the language of politicians and other decision makers) the breaking down of categories and distinctions that had once been "an academic exercise" is now colliding with the blurring of categories, materially and technologically, that is being enacted by developments in biotechnology, genetics, assisted reproduction, neuroscience, pharmacology, materials science, artificial intelligence, robotics, and many more fields. There is an increasing array of techniques for designing that which had always been considered as given, such as biological life and raw materials. This is not, generally, being thought and debated as a question of design by designers or philosophers, be it with a few exceptions.

The texts presented in this concluding section go to such issues: the future of thinking and the future of design. This probably sounds grandiose; my comments here and the assembled texts make no claim to deal comprehensively with either of these vast questions or their inter-relation. They simply cannot because of the enormous complexity of what needs to be thought now so as to inform new modes of thinking, acting, and making that are futural rather than defuturing. Despite the impossibility, is there any choice but to try? What follows is a listing then an example.

Increasing global population, increasing inequity, increasing political and cultural polarization, together with the politics of fear, protracted wars killing millions of civilians, with ever more people dying in desperate attempts to seek refuge, combined with climate change, species extinction, rampant consumerism, increasing immersion in IT, skills obsolescing at faster rates, the end of job security, the prospect of genetically designed populations, artificial intelligence that might outsmart us or maybe already has, such a list of unsettling current and emergent factors and forces goes on. In attempting to evoke this complexity of what needs to be thought now, there is no correct place to begin and every concern mentioned connects to almost every other. So let's take one relational example.

We'll start with us, we are increasing in number. The projection is that by 2050 the world population will be 9.7 billion compared to 7.3 billion as of 2015.[1] This means more food, water, and shelter will be needed. At the same time, rising temperatures and more frequent droughts—effects of anthropogenic climate change—are reducing agricultural productivity and water availability especially in the world's poorer nations where most of the population growth is occurring. The increasing precariousness of agriculture is pushing more people toward cities, mainly poorly constructed informal cities that are highly vulnerable to the further climate change effects such as more frequent and more intense storms, floods, and hurricanes. By 2050 two thirds of the global population will live in cities; today it is just over half.[2] So what we are moving toward is the entirety of humanity totally dependent on designed, delivered, and off-the-shelf ways of life. The actual situation is that this is a reality for just a small percentage of people, while remaining an aspiration or a just a dream ("in your dreams") for the majority. The fastest growing cities are not cities with smart homes, smart cars, and other futurist clichés; they are in fact the informal cities: unplanned, over-crowded, illegally self-built, and primitively serviced by improvisations, fortuitous appropriations, ingenuity, and exploitation of the exploited.[3] Economic survival in informal cities, or what US military strategists refer to as "alternatively governed spaces," is also improvised, appropriative, ingenious, and exploitive.[4]

As is now well known, the climate change which is already underway is anthropologically amplified; it is the result of the effects on the earth's atmosphere of carbon dioxide emissions (along with other greenhouse gases) from the fossil-fuelled industrial economy and lifestyles initiated in Western Europe more than two hundred years ago, taken up and intensified in the United States, spread globally and still spreading. The effects on climate are complex, they are global and they extend out into the future, yet their cause is the inter-dependant, cumulative actions of large-scale things like factories and power stations, and billions of small actions of vehicles, drivers, people, and automated systems turning on heating, lighting, equipment, and whatever else is required in the daily routines of living and working. This is the meaning of structural unsustainability: that in living a normal life, a socially sanctioned life, whether we know it or not, we each contribute to the mounting debt to the future. It is the same with the industrially produced food and other commodities made integral to modern living for which land is cleared, minerals are extracted, habitats are destroyed causing species to go extinct; agricultural chemicals are applied to "pests" but also make their way to harmless living things; animals are bred and their short lives micro-managed to maximize the edible value of their bodies and their exchange value. Sheep, cattle, goats, pigs—these domesticated animals are post-nature, as are all the grains, fruits, vegetables that have been altered by selective breeding over many centuries, and now via direct genetic modification, to optimize for human consumption.

The paper in this section by Despret and Meuret raises the issue of the diminished quality of life of animals bred for human consumption and imprisoned for life; they tell a hopeful counter-story. What is an appropriate ethic toward these nonhuman species upon whom we depend for our biological existence? And how could such an ethic be made operable within the food production system that is largely controlled by global capitalism?[5]

In a world of rapid change there is a struggle to find an adequate descriptive language. For example, climate scientists analyze and synthesize data from biophysical observations, correlate this to historical climate data and make projections of future climate scenarios. Giving a single name to this, and to all the other related effects, is difficult. Since 2007, the Intergovernmental Panel on Climate Change has used the term Anthropogenic Climate Change. Another naming is "Anthropocene" to signify a new geological epoch in which human habitation is now affecting the whole planet. The authors of the texts presented here are highly attuned to the issue of naming. Claire Colebrook sees problems with Anthropocene and counters with the Anthro-Political. Isabelle Stengers claims the more controversial figure of Gaia, popularized by James Lovelock, but divests it of anthropomorphism.

Another major issue of contemporary concern is equally difficult to describe and name. In everyday conversation it is often referred to as "the problem of technology" meaning, information technology and how it is becoming more and more integrated with more and more aspects of our lives. We do not even have a collective noun for the new reality that gathers together as digital electronic data, server farms, the internet, the cloud, wireless and satellite communication, GPS transponders, sensors, video surveillance, and the billions of fixed and mobile devices that react to, create, and propagate electronic content, plus the new social practices and cognitive effects of this vast, instantaneous global assemblage. Ubiquitous computing? Planetary computing? Available terms are woefully inadequate. Benjamin H. Bratton calls it The Stack, in his 528-page book of the same name, characterizing it as "an accidental megastructure . . . that is both a computational apparatus and a new governing architecture." He says that his book is a design brief and asks "what new forms can we compose for this computational and geopolitical condition, first to map it, then to interpret it, then to redesign it?".[6]

How to name an unfolding era in a way that seeks not to describe it but to propose an appropriate response to that which is unfolding? That is the purpose of Tony Fry's designation of "The Sustainment" reproduced here, which could also be regarded not so much as a design brief for the future, as a design ethic of futuring.

Bratton's text reproduced here is on artificial intelligence (AI), a topic that prompts anxiety about the future of thinking. Already much has been given over to technology: a huge array of embodied knowledge and skills, and memory itself as argued by Bernard Stiegler in Part VI. Like Stengers, Bratton argues against the tendency to anthropomorphize nonhuman entities, this deflecting from understanding on AI in its own terms. There are connections between his position and Rosi Braidotti as she considers the relation between posthumanism and the posthuman.

In the oft-quoted final passage of *The Order of Things* Michel Foucault reflected on the figure of the human as an invention of European humanist discourse, a figure that was

the effect of a change in the fundamental arrangements of knowledge. As the archaeology of our thought easily shows, man is an invention of recent date. And one perhaps nearing its end. If those arrangements were to disappear as they appeared, if some event of which we can at the moment do no more than sense the possibility—without knowing either what its form will be or what it promises—were to cause them to crumble, as the ground of Classical thought did, at the end of the eighteenth century, then one can certainly wager that man would be erased, like a face drawn in sand at the edge of the sea.

When Foucault wrote this fifty years ago, the "event" he had in mind was epistemological, a revolution in thinking, rather than the physical annihilation of mankind. Today, we might see "the end of man" as an epistemological, biophysical, and technological event which has already happened for some.

Notes

1. The current world population of 7.3 billion is expected to reach 9.7 billion in 2050 and 11.2 billion in 2100, according to a UN DESA report, "World Population Prospects: The 2015 Revision," United Nations Department of Economic and Social Affairs, July 29, 2015, New York, http://www.un.org/en/development/desa/news/population/2015-report.html

2. Today, 54 percent of the world's population lives in urban areas, a proportion that is expected to increase to 66 percent by 2050. Projections show that urbanization combined with the overall growth of the world's population could add another 2.5 billion people to urban populations by 2050, with close to 90 percent of the increase concentrated in Asia and Africa. India is expected to become the largest country in population size, surpassing China around 2022, while Nigeria could surpass the United States by 2050. UN DESA, 2015.

3. See Tony Fry, *City Futures in the Age of a Changing Climate* Oxford: Routledge, 2015 and David Sims, *Understanding Cairo: The Logic of a City out of Control* Cairo: American University in Cairo Press, 2010.

4. Western military strategists are concerned about these and especially about the growth of "megacities" such as Lagos, Nigeria, with 25 million people spread over 3400 square kilometres. Megacities are defined as those with populations over 10 million. In 2014, there were twenty-three megacities worldwide, by 2025 there will be thirty-seven. Strategic Studies Group, *Megacities and the United States Army: Preparing for a Complex and Uncertain Future* Arlington, VA: Office of Chief of Staff of the Army, June 2014.

5. Food production is not entirely controlled by capitalism, as the governments of many nations over-ride market forces with measures such as import tariffs to protect local producers (e.g., United States and Japan), and price control of staples (e.g., Egypt).

6. Benjamin H. Bratton, *The Stack: On Software and Sovereignty* Cambridge, MA: MIT Press, 2016.

CHAPTER 39
WHAT IS THE ANTHRO-POLITICAL?
Claire Colebrook

Note from editor: The term Anthropocene is used by some scientists to designate the most recent geological epoch, a time in which human habitation is significantly altering the biophysicality of the planet. Claire Colebrook dissects the implications of this naming and its problematic reinstatement of a unified humanity that is "to blame" and could "yet change its ways." Not only does this de-politicize and eradicate difference, inequity, oppression, but it keeps intact 'man' as centre of the earth, when in fact, thinking geologically, conditions conducive to the flourishing of the human species have been a fortuitous (for us) but brief moment of time.

… If humanity has somehow managed to bring itself to the brink of non-existence, it does not follow that it must rally to save itself, nor that it must do so against a certain evil tendency that will be vanquished in the humanity to come, nor that "we" will be all the greater for having contemplated the potential end of humanity as such. From Naomi Klein's claim that climate change is the opportunity finally to triumph over capitalism, to the environmental humanities movement that spurns decades of "textualist" theory in order to regain nature and life, to wise geo-engineers who operate from the imperative that if we are to survive we must act immediately and unilaterally, the end of man has generated a thousand tiny industries of new dawns.

All of these vivid calls to arms rely on expertise and generate the very "we" that is being addressed. Let us take the first claim about Anthopocene tipping points, or the "golden spike".[1] Let us accept the premise of the dispute, and say that we might quibble about just when to mark the Anthropocene (industrialized agriculture, colonialism, the steam engine, nuclear energy); accepting that there is a point where man became definitively destructive implicitly generates another pre-Anthropocene humanity, or a counter-Anthropocene. An implicitly moral line of time is effected: if there is a point at which humanity becomes catastrophic at a planetary level, then there is the possibility both of attributing blame, and of retrieving and saving another humanity.

A new humanity is constituted by the threat of its disappearance; or, to follow Nietzsche: it is the voice of a moral law ("Thou Shalt Not...") that produces "man" as a guilty animal, bred and groomed through the attribution of guilt. If there is a being called man who has destroyed the planet, then not only is a bad humanity produced as the new agent of history, an entire industry of those who would self-diagnose and redeem humanity becomes possible. It is as though only with the impending end of humanity does something like "the human" become visible in all its anti-human glory. Now that geologists have discerned evidence of damage at species level, the human becomes at once victim, agent and redeemer. The "anthropos" is produced through an event of guilt and diagnosis; if there is damage and inscription at a geological level, then there must be a response at global level, an end to all talk of there being no such thing as "man," and some account as to who, when and how this tragedy occurred. The "anthropos" brings himself into being by way of a blinding discovery: it turns out, after all these years, that there is a "we" and that "we" have not been good to the planet (well, at least not the planet as we would like it to be). States of emergency seem to call for a suspension of the free reign of opinion along with the resurgence of authority. If the bankers and economists benefited from the 2008 financial crisis by declaring that time was running out and "we" have to act now, and *then* think about justice, then one might ask why climate science with its dire predictions has not been blessed with the same unquestioning obedience. Perhaps it's because of a failure of rhetorical flair: "we" can only hear those who offer a future to come, a promise of a blessed humanity that will rightly inherit the earth. Indeed, there is no "we" outside this rhetorical call to arms. So while all the declarations of authority would call for one kind of action worthy of the dire predictions of the present—a questioning of whether what has called itself humanity has a right to survive —the only "action" has been an insistence on a future *for us.* Just as the 2008 financial crisis somehow—how?—seemed to prompt a desperate effort to *save* the banks, a climate crisis seems to justify saving humanity, and yet without all the emergency measures that were taken to "save" the global economy.

And yet, as Nietzsche[2] argued, these idols emerge in moments of waning and decline, or disappointment, even if they are—for all their late appearance—eternal:

> …as far as sounding out idols is concerned, this time they are not just idols of our age but eternal idols, and they will be touched here with a hammer as with a tuning fork,—these are the oldest, most convinced, puffed-up, and fat-headed idols you will ever find (155).

> The disappointed one speaks.—I looked for great men, and all I could find were the apes of their ideals (161).

It may well be that it is only when the species is at an end that it recognizes itself as a species, and becomes fully and self-righteously human only in the moment it is required to face its loss, a loss that—in turn—seems to grant it the imperative to survive at all costs. Man exists, and must be saved. He can only be recognized and saved in these last hours, when destruction has reached such a degree as to become evident. Some have presented this moment as a *felix culpa*: without the evident, readable and diagnosable destruction of the Anthropocene, we would not have realized who we are, and might have proceeded with capitalism, industrialism and ecological destruction without this wonderful wake-up call. Now man knows who he is, and that he can only be saved by himself. He must first accept that there is indeed this unified global/geological being called the human. From there, in this moment of being too big to fail, all forms of emergency measures must be unfurled, if we are to survive. In short, it is by way of destruction that the human emerges, finally, as destroyer and preserver, enlivened by a whole series of moral laments that produce man *as he might have been*—the man prior to whatever we determined the golden spike to be—and then further enlivened by a new managerialism that accepts that if the human exists as destroyer then there is some urgent imperative to generate a fully human future. It is by way of a whole series of self-accusations that Anthropocene man becomes capitalist man, patriarchal man, corporate man, colonizing man, or the man of the nuclear age; this industry of self-accusation allows for another humanity, and one—precisely because it is threatened—that deserves to be saved.

Here, though, it might be worth questioning whether the Anthropocene is an event that really does demand that one either accept the general condemnation of man or blame a specific modality in man's history (capitalism, corporations, males, the West). It seems that we have two options: either the Anthropocene is an effect of man in general, or it can be attributed to capitalism (or corporations, or colonialism, or patriarchy), in which case man can emerge as an innocent animal—as a new humanity to come. But what if one were to refuse both these options by suggesting that man is neither the global culprit, nor the global victim, and that there are many living beings on this planet who live, dwell, struggle and survive with no sense of humanity in general? What would the present begin to look like if we refused both the claim for humanity as global agent and humanity as proper potentiality who may (and ought) to inherit the earth? If we accept the Anthropocene premise that man in general is responsible, then we accept something like the human as such and ignore the subtleties of history, culture and difference; if one aspect of man is responsible—say, capitalism—then that allows for a space outside the guilty party. Either way, one generates the human, first by way of accusation— the Anthropocene, a single scar that calls us all in the moment of defeat—or by way of exculpation: no, not the human in general, but these humans—the capitalists (say), whose end will actually allow us to dream of a new beginning. Those who declare man to be guilty are the first true humanists, generating the "Anthropos" as agent, and promising another humanity—one who can be intimated after the crime of ecological destruction has been detected, diagnosed and managed.

(…..)

To return to "anthropos," now, after all these years of difference seems to erase all the work in postcolonialism that had declared enlightenment "man," to be a fiction that allowed all the world to be "white like me," and all the work in feminism that exposed the man and subject of reason as he who cannibalizes all others and remakes them in his image. The Anthropocene seems to override vast amounts of critical work in queer theory, trans-animalities, posthumanism and disability theory that had destroyed the false essentialism of the human. The "human" of the late twentieth century had increasingly become a humanity of difference, defined less by being than an ongoing strategy or performance or becoming. But this humanity of becoming and self-differentiation was possible only by way of a negative universalism, where the human was unified by having no essence other than that which it gave itself through existence. The politics of this humanity was a politics of increasingly recognized difference, achieved by analyzing the dynamics that constitute the human in its specificity (rather than its being as species).

If one accepts this notion of the political—that one should resist false naturalizations or universals—then to politicize the Anthropocene becomes a question of determining what scale or scales would generate the proper frame for narrating the genesis of "man." Should one read a text in terms of social-economic narratives, or in terms of the founding event of sexual difference, or as an ongoing reinforcement of heteronormativity, or as a document of Western reason, imperialism or racism? Such questions are theoretical because they embed seemingly literary, personal or aesthetic texts within other contexts. Against a bland and undifferentiated humanism, political theorization strives to be more intensely and differentially human—seeing humans as emerging from complex political relations, where politics has to do with social formations and what is brought into being (historical/cultural) rather than what simply is.

(…..)

I want to conclude by focusing on a rigorous sense of aesthetic ideology, with an emphasis on *aisthesis*, or the transition from what is given—the sensible—to what that givenness presupposes or demands that "we" assume. To insist on *the* political, at any level, is to posit a putatively legitimate register that would be the appropriate milieu for taking an account of any event. Where the political tended, once, to be determined by way of socio-economic relations, it is perhaps—today—shifting to a different register of affect and corporeality, or how bodies are formed with the desires, interests and practices that *then* allow for individuals to form social wholes. But what if those practices of political theory were themselves dependent upon an epoch of suspension, in which the earth, the globe, nature, affect or corporeality— or even humanity—could appear as an object of stable knowledge only with certain practices and formations that would precipitate the destruction of the milieu on which they depend? There can only be the polity with certain forms of life, and from the very outset stable political wholes relied on violent forms of inscription and appropriation that erased and defaced in order to institute a plane of history. What if the (reflective and critical) reading and theorizing we direct to ourselves were the outcome of an era of technologies of the eye, hand and an industrialized relation to nature, with these technologies in turn always borrowing from the earth's reserves in an ongoing debt that can never be discharged? What if what we know as politics—the practice of tracing what appears as contingent, universal or natural back to human forces—were possible only in a brief era of the taming of human history? There could only be "the polity" with the sense of nature *not* as a force in its own right, but as an environment, as nothing more than the passive background for praxis. Today's climate change is an acute event in a long history of changing climates; what we take to be "our" earth is a brief and unsustainable period of human-friendly ecosystems that have been manufactured violently and blindly, always at the expense of much life deemed to be non-human. What if today's threatening conditions of volatility and disaster were to make anthropomorphism and the belief in nature increasingly impossible? What sort of politics would we be left with in this disfigured world without face?

Extracts from 'What is the Anthro-political?' by Claire Colebrook in *Twilight of the Anthropocene Idols*, eds Tom Cohen, Claire Colebrook, J. Hillis Miller London: Open Humanities Press, 2016, pp 86–9, 91–2, 115–6.

Notes

1. Simon L. Lewis & Mark A. Maslin 'Defining the Anthropocene' *Nature* (international weekly journal of science) vol.519, Issue 7542, March 2015.

2. Friedrich Nietzsche, *The Anti-Christ, Ecce Homo, Twilight of the Idols: And Other Writings*. Ed Aaron Ridley and Judith Norman. Trans. Judith Norman. Cambridge: Cambridge University Press, 2005

CHAPTER 40
THE INTRUSION OF GAIA
Isabelle Stengers

There is no single, agreed-upon way to name the crisis of now. As in Colebrook's essay on the Anthropocene, Stengers deals here with the strategic power of a name, 'Gaia' reminding us that it was coined by scientists to bring together "the dense set of relations" usually studied separately, and to better comprehend the complex and cascading impacts of human actions. Gaia is not god or human or any singular thing. Gaia is not Mother Earth and cannot be personified. Gaia is transcendent but not divine. What are the dangers and the possibilities of acting in the name of Gaia?

It is crucial to emphasize here that naming Gaia and characterizing the looming disasters as an intrusion arises from a pragmatic operation. *To name is not to say what is true but to confer on what is named the power to make us feel and think in the mode that the name calls for.* In this instance it is a matter of resisting the temptation to reduce what makes for an event, what calls us into question, to a simple "problem." But it is also to make the difference between the question that is imposed and the response to create exist. Naming Gaia as "the one who intrudes" is also to characterize her as blind to the damage she causes, in the manner of everything that intrudes. That is why the response to create is not a response to Gaia but a response as much to what provoked her intrusion as to its consequences.

In this essay then, Gaia is neither Earth "in the concrete" and nor is it she who is named and invoked when it is a matter of affirming and of making our connection to this Earth felt, of provoking a sense of belonging where separation has been predominant, and of drawing resources for living, struggling, feeling, and thinking from this belonging.[1] It is a matter here of thinking *intrusion, not belonging.*

But why, one might then object, have recourse to a name that can lend itself to misunderstandings? Why not, one friend asked me, name what intrudes Ouranos or Chronos, those terrible children of the mythological Gaia? The objection must be listened to: if a name is to bring about and not to define – that is, to appropriate – the name can nevertheless not be arbitrary. In this instance I know that choosing the name Gaia is a risk, but it is a risk that I accept, because it is *also* a matter for me of making all of those who might be scandalized by a blind or indifferent Gaia feel and think. I want to maintain the memory that in the twentieth century this name was first linked with a proposition of scientific origin. That is, it is a matter of making felt the necessity of resisting moving on from the temptation of brutally opposing the sciences against the reputedly "nonscientific" knowledges, the necessity of inventing the ways of their coupling, which will be vital if we must learn how to respond to what has already started.

What I am naming Gaia was in effect baptized thus by James Lovelock and Lynn Margulis at the start of the 1970s. They drew their lessons from research that contributed to bringing to light the dense set of relations that scientific disciplines were in the habit of dealing with separately – living things, oceans, the atmosphere, climate, more or less fertile soils. To give a name – Gaia – to this assemblage of relations was to insist on two consequences of what could be learned from this new perspective. That on which we depend, and which has so often been defined as the "given," the globally stable context of our histories and our calculations, is the product of a history of co-evolution, the first artisans and real, continuing authors of which were the innumerable populations of microorganisms. And Gaia, the "living planet" has to be recognized as a "being," and not assimilated into a sum of processes, in the same sense that we recognize that a rat, for example, is a being: it is not just endowed with a history but with its own regime of activity and sensitivity, resulting from the manner in which the processes that constitute it are coupled with one another in multiple and entangled manners, the variation of one having multiple repercussions that affect the others. To question Gaia then is to question something that *holds together* in its own particular manner, and the questions that are addressed to any of its constituent processes can bring into play a sometimes unexpected response involving them all.

Lovelock perhaps went a step too far in affirming that this processual coupling ensured a stability of the type that one attributes to a living organism in good health, the repercussions between processes thus having as their effect the diminishing of the consequences of a variation. Gaia thus seemed to be a good, nurturing mother, whose health was to be protected. Today our understanding of the manner in which Gaia holds together is much less reassuring. The question posed by the growing concentration of so-called greenhouse gases is provoking a cascading set of responses that scientists are only just starting to identify.

Gaia then is thus more than ever well named, because if she was honored in the past it was as the fearsome one, as she who was addressed by peasants, who knew that humans depend on something much greater than them, something that tolerates them, but with a tolerance that is not to be abused. She was from well before the cult of maternal love, which pardons everything. A mother perhaps but an irritable one, who should not be offended. And she was also from before the Greeks conferred on their gods a sense of the just and the unjust, before they attributed to them a particular interest in our destinies. It was a matter instead of *paying attention*, of not offending them, not abusing their tolerance.

Imprudently, a margin of tolerance has been well and truly exceeded: that is what the models are saying more and more precisely, that is what the satellites are observing, and that is what the Inuit people know. And the response that Gaia risks giving might well be without any measure in relation to what we have done, a bit like a shrugging of the shoulder provoked when one is briefly touched by a midge. Gaia is ticklish and that is why she must be named as a being. We are no longer dealing (only) with a wild and threatening nature, nor with a fragile nature to be protected, nor a nature to be mercilessly exploited. The case is new. Gaia, she who intrudes, *asks nothing of us*, not even a response to the question she imposes. Offended,[2] Gaia is indifferent to the question "who is responsible?" and doesn't act as a righter of wrongs – it seems clear that the regions of the earth that will be affected first will be the poorest on the planet, to say nothing of all those living beings that have nothing to do with the affair. This doesn't signify, especially not, the justification of any kind of indifference whatsoever on our part with regard to the threats that hang over the living beings that inhabit the earth with us. It simply isn't Gaia's affair.

That Gaia asks nothing of us translates the specificity of what is in the process of coming, what our thinking must succeed in bringing itself to do: it is a matter of thinking successfully, the event of a unilateral intrusion, which imposes a question without being interested in the response. Because Gaia herself is not threatened, unlike the considerable number of living species who will be swept away with unprecedented speed by the change in their milieu that is on the horizon. Her innumerable co-authors, the microorganisms, will effectively continue to participate in her regime of existence, that of a living planet. And it is precisely because she is not threatened that she makes the epic versions of human history, in which Man, standing up on his hind legs and learning to decipher the laws of nature, understands that he is the master of his own fate, free of any transcendence, look rather old. Gaia is the name of an unprecedented or forgotten form of transcendence: a transcendence deprived of the noble qualities that would allow it to be invoked as an arbiter, guarantor, or resource; a ticklish assemblage of forces that are indifferent to our reasons and our projects.

The intrusion of this type of transcendence, which I am calling Gaia, makes a major unknown, *which is here to stay,* exist at the heart of our lives. This is perhaps what is most difficult to conceptualize: no future can be foreseen in which she will give back to us the liberty of ignoring her. It is not a matter of a "bad moment that will pass," followed by any kind of happy ending – in the shoddy sense of a "problem solved." We are no longer authorized to forget her. We will have to go on answering for what we are undertaking in the face of an implacable being who is deaf to our justifications. A being who has no spokesperson, or rather, whose spokespersons are exposed to fearsome temptations. We know the old ditty, which generally comes from well-fed experts, accustomed to flying, to the effect that "the problem is, there are too many of us," numbers whose "disappearance" would permit significant energy savings. But if we listen to Lovelock, who has become the prophet of disaster, it would be necessary to reduce the human population to about 500 million people in order to pacify Gaia and live reasonably well in harmony with her. The so-called rational calculations, which result in the conclusion that the only solution is to eradicate the vast majority of humans between now and the end of the century, scarcely dissimulate the delusion of a murderous and obscene abstraction. Gaia does not demand such eradication. She doesn't demand anything.

To name Gaia – that is to say, to associate an assemblage of material processes that demand neither to be protected nor to be loved, and which cannot be moved by the public manifestation of our remorse, with the intrusion of a form of transcendence into our history – ought not especially to shock most scientists. They themselves are in the habit of giving names to what they recognize has the power to make them think and imagine – and this is the very sense of the transcendence that I associate with Gaia. Those who have set up camp in the position of the guardians of reason and progress will certainly scream about irrationality. They will denounce a panicky regression that would make us forget the "heritage of the Enlightenment," the grand narrative of human emancipation shaking off the yoke of transcendences. Their role has already been assigned. After having contributed to skepticism with regard to climate change (think of Claude Allègre[3], they will devote all their energy to reminding an always credulous public opinion that it must not be diverted, that it must believe in the destiny of Man and in his capacity to triumph in the face of every challenge. Concretely, this signifies the duty to believe in science, the brains of humanity, and in technology, in the service of progress. Provoking their yelling is something that neither amuses nor scares me.

The operation of naming is therefore not in the least bit antiscientific. On the other hand, it may make scientists think, and prevent them from appropriating the question imposed by the intrusion of Gaia. Climate scientists, glaciologists, chemists, and others have done their work and they have also succeeded in making the alarm bells ring despite all the attempts to stifle them, imposing an "inconvenient truth" despite all the accusations that have been leveled against them, of having mixed up science and politics, or of being jealous of the successes of their colleagues, whose work has succeeded in changing the world where theirs has been limited to describing it, or even of presenting as "proven" something that is only hypothetical. They have been able to resist because they knew that time counted, and that it wasn't them, but that to which they were addressing themselves that in fact mixed up scientific and political questions, or, more precisely, aimed at substituting itself for politics and imposing its imperatives on the entire planet. To name Gaia is finally to help scientists resist a new threat, one which this time would fabricate the worst of confusions between science and politics: that one ask them how to respond, that one trust in them to define what it is appropriate to do.

Moreover, that is what is in the process of happening, but with other types of "scientists." Nowadays it is economists who have become active, and in a way which guarantees that like many unwanted effects, the climate question will be envisaged from the point of view of strategies that are plausible, that is to say, are likely to make it a new source of profit. Even if this means being resigned – in the name of economic laws (which are harsh, they will affirm, but which are laws, after all) – to a planetary New Orleans. Even if it means that zones on the planet that are defined as profitable must, at all scales – from the neighborhood to the continent – protect themselves by every means necessary from the mass of those who will doubtless be opposed to the famous "we cannot take care of all the woes of the world." In short, even if the succession of "sorry, but we musts" establishes, completely, and openly deployed, the barbarism that is already in the process of penetrating our world.

Economists and other candidates for the production of global responses based on "science" only exist for me as a power to harm. Their authority only exists to the extent that the world, our world, remains what it is – that is to say, destined for barbarism. Their laws suppose, above all, that we stay in our places, keep the roles assigned to us, that we have the blind self-interest and congenital incapacity to think and cooperate that makes an all azimuths economic war the only conceivable horizon. It would be completely pointless to name Gaia if it was just a matter of combating them. But it is a matter of combating what gives them their authority. Of that against which the cry "another world is possible!" was raised.

This cry really hasn't lost any of its topicality. Because that against which it was raised – capitalism, the capitalism of Marx, of course, not of American economists – is already busying itself concocting its own responses to the question imposed on us, responses that lead straight to barbarism. This is to say that the struggle assumes an unprecedented urgency but that those who are engaged in this struggle must also face a test that they didn't really need, which, in the name of that urgency they might be tempted to abstract out. To name Gaia *is to name the necessity of resisting this temptation*, the necessity of starting out from the acceptance of this testing challenge: *we do not have any choice, because she will not wait.*

Do not ask me to sketch what other world may be able to come to terms, or compose, with Gaia. The response doesn't belong to us, that is to those who have both provoked her intrusion and now decipher it through data, models, and simulations. Naming Gaia is naming a question, but emphatically not defining the terms of the answer, as such a definition would give us, us again, always us, the first and last word. Learning to compose will need many names, not a global one, the voices of many peoples, knowledges, and earthly practices. It belongs to a process of multifold creation, the terrible difficulty of which it would be foolish and dangerous to underestimate *but which it would be suicidal to think of as impossible.* There will be no response other than the barbaric if we do not learn to couple together multiple, divergent struggles and engagements in this process of creation, as hesitant and stammering as it may be.

Source: Isabelle Stengers, *In Catastrophic Times: Resisting the Coming Barbarism*, trans. Andrew Goffey, Open Humanities Press in association with meson press, Hybrid Publishing Lab, Leuphana University of Luneburg, 2015, pp 43–50. © La Découverte, Paris, 2009.

Notes

1. In Capitalist Sorcery Philippe Pignarre and I affirmed the political sense of such rituals. *Capitalist Sorcery: Breaking the Spell*, trans. Andrew Goffey Palgrave Macmillan, 2011.

2. Offended but not vindictive, because evoking a vindictive Gaia is not just to attribute to her a memory but also an interpretation of what happens in terms of intentionality and responsibility. For the same reason, to speak of the "revenge" of Gaia, as James Lovelock does today, is to mobilize a type of psychology that doesn't seem relevant: one takes revenge against someone, whereas the question of offense is one of a matter of post-factum observation. For example, one says "it seems that this gesture offended her, I wonder why?" Correlatively one doesn't struggle against Gaia. Even speaking of combating global warming is inappropriate. If it is a matter of struggling, it is against what provoked Gaia, not against her response.

3. French politician and scientist, minister of education under Lionel Jospin, and visible climate change skeptic. –Trans.

CHAPTER 41
COSMOECOLOGICAL SHEEP AND THE ARTS
OF LIVING ON A DAMAGED PLANET
Vinciane Despret and Michel Meuret

Note from editor: What would a posthumanist ethics be, that is, an ethics in which the human is not centred? Despite its popularity within environmentalist discourse, it would not be based on the functionalist paradigm of ecosystem. Despret and Meuret speak instead of ethology or cosmoecology, in which human and animal co-constitute worlds. They do this by recounting a case from southern France of neo-shepherds and sheep re-learning the practices of herded pasturing after decades of sheep-rearing under a system of increasing animal confinement.

…. Isabelle Stengers writes: "Whenever a being raises the problem of its conditions of existence, it lies within the domain of ecological approaches."[1] The ecological question is about the needs that ought to be met in the ongoing creation of rapports and connections. The question ecologists raise is not, therefore, does this being really exist, or is it not a representation? Rather, the questions are how does this being achieve the task of holding onto its existence, and what does this achievement require? This is why every ethology is first and foremost an ecology and, even more precisely, a cosmoecology. This is because we may never know, safely and reliably, either ahead of time or a posteriori, which beings will bear the consequences, or will enjoy the consequences, of the concrete attention we give to them.

These interconnected lives, each of them having their ever-evolving requirements and habits, have nothing to do with the balance of nature, a machine analogy that became central for ecologists around the 1950s together with the concept of the ecosystem.[2] It is better to remember here that no one, neither human nor gazelle, will ever meet an ecosystem. As Robert O'Neill has put it, "The ecosystem is not an a posteriori, empirical observation about nature. This is a paradigm, a convenient approach to organizing thought. Like any paradigm, it is a product of the human mind's limited ability to understand the complexity of the real world."[3] Over decades, environmentalists and researchers in ecology have been qualifying Homo sapiens as the major invasive pest on Earth, the one that almost constantly, if not deliberately, disturbs integrated, equilibrious, homeostatic ecosystems. But this is a myth—Homo sapiens is not an external disturbance; we are a keystone species within the system. In the long term, it may not be the magnitude of extracted goods and services that will determine sustainability. It may well be our disruption of ecological recovery and stability mechanisms that determines system collapse.[4]

Thinking about our life and behavior in distinct societies not as disturbance but as integrated parts of systems has great implications. We are invited to pay attention to the health of ecosystems from the inside. Throughout millennia, as a keystone species, humans have influenced the shape and functioning of most landscapes, from savannas to some rainforests as well as, of course, agricultural and urban ecosystems.[5]

A true politics of attention does not confine itself simply to taking another into account— it demands more. A true cosmopolitics requires us to expand the scope of obligations. Other beings obligate us, in the sense Stengers gives to the word obligation when she equates "being obligated by a situation" and "giving the situation the power to obligate you." And, she adds, "without guarantees. Never the slightest guarantee, neither the judgment of God, nor a conceptual guarantee. It's all about fighting against the demand for a guarantee, it's about compromising oneself."[6]

.... That is what led us to seek situations in which human and nonhuman beings become obligated through new connections. New shepherding practices, as they recently reemerged in the South of France, appeared to be a good example of this kind of cosmoecology, and in its complex political interactions we all might learn to craft new ways of being obligated and new ways of helping life to flourish.[7] These practices interest us in particular because of the way that these shepherds take an active role in what Tsing has termed the "arts of living on a damaged planet."[8]

Worlds to remember

Shepherding is a practice with long histories and traditions that in many parts of the world, including France, are often passed between generations of humans and of sheep. But the shepherds that fascinated us in this study are all of urban origin; none of them is the son or daughter of shepherds. As such, they were often left to learn on the job, with the sheep. We discovered with them that their practices fulfill multiple obligations that are not restricted to the well-being of their animals or their own livelihoods, however important these dimension are. These additional obligations fall under the realm of ethical and aesthetic relations to the world, obligations that belong to cosmoecology as alter-politics: "a politics that grows not from opposition to or critique of our current systems but one that grows from attention to another way of being, one that involves other kinds of living beings."[9]

To talk about sheep when so many species have already disappeared or are at the edge of extinction might be seen nonsensical. However, extinction should not be restricted to the death of species, as Thom van Dooren so convincingly shows in Flight Ways. In relation to the cranes that are mobilized in a captive-breeding conservationist program, he leads us to ask, Aren't these cranes that are supposed to keep the crane species among us in some ways already extinct? Do they still enjoy a life that is worth living as a crane? And will their offspring, and the offspring of their offspring?

(…..)

What the shepherds were confronted with, and what they resisted, were particular forms of extinction: not the form that makes a species, in the sense of quantifiable biodiversity, disappear but those that make worlds die, worlds that were hitherto shaped and characterized by practices, by modes of inhabiting, by landscapes that are no more. The sheep confined and fed indoors, or grazed within small plots of grass monoculture are, of course, still living. However, their world is so impoverished that it cannot be seen as what we call an existence, because to exist (exsistere) for a living being is to step "out of self," to be connected by multiple bonds, to compose a world, and to be associated with a world—as Gilles Deleuze translated the Umwelt of Jakob von Uexküll, "a world associated."[10] Extinction begins when the world to which an animal was associated is reduced to nothing, or almost nothing. Extinction begins when the ways an animal composes the world and composes with the world are ended, when the ways he or she makes a world exist, according to the ways his or her ancestors had created it, have disappeared.

This process of loss began in the 1960s in France, when a program of agricultural modernization began to promote so-called rational fenced grazing on cultivated grasslands and to suppress shepherding on natural meadows and rangeland.[11] More efficient animals, due to intensive selective breeding, were endorsed as key to producing meat or milk in abundance. These animals needed richer and steady diets, obeying new rules of standardization. Industrial foods replaced grass and other grazed plants for animals in sheepfolds, and for those that still enjoyed being outside, field crops and cultivated forages were being standardized. For decades, breeders would be advised to keep their animals in sheepfolds or in small fenced areas, in simplified and predictable environments. And so the world changed, and previous configurations, previous cosmoecologies slipped out of existence.

But in the 1990s this system met its own limits. The price of lambs dramatically dropped, due to competition from meat imported from other countries, especially New Zealand. Simultaneously, because of the influence of financial speculation in cereals, the feed price for livestock increased. Breeders went back to the practices of hiring seasonal herders, and sheep went back to hills and mountains, to rediscover cheap grasslands, abandoned fields, scrubby rangeland, and undergrowth. Together they tried to relearn the arts and practices of winter and summer long-range transhumance in mountains and hills of southern France.

Compared to last decades and centuries in France, conditions for herding have often been changed dramatically: more forested and encroached landscape, larger flocks, more food-demanding animals, less human workforce, a series of environmental constraints. Herding practice had to be re-invented, and almost nobody, but some aged but still imaginative herders, knew how to do it. With the breach in transmission, most of the new shepherds were coming from urban areas. They chose this profession for different reasons than their predecessors. But they all say that they have always loved being with animals, and they all claim that the world, as it was going, was becoming uninhabitable. These are political and ethical choices. Moreover, these choices are ethological, in the sense Deleuze gives to the word. In his teaching on Spinoza, Deleuze notes:

> Ethics is better known to us today under another name, the word ethology.
>
> When one speaks of an ethology in connection with animals, or in connection with [hu]man, what is it a matter of? Ethology in the most rudimentary sense is a practical science, of what? A practical science of the manners of being. The manner of being is precisely the state of beings (étants), of what exists (existants), from the point of view of a pure ontology.
>
> In what way is it already different from a morality? We are trying to compose a kind of landscape which would be the landscape of ontology. We are manners of Being in Being, that is the object of an ethics, i.e. an ethology.[12]

Deleuze clarifies what should be considered manners of being—ethology is the practical science that studies what beings can do: "Of what tests is it capable? . . . What does it do?" What is it capable of? In his book on Spinoza, he adds: "The Ethics is an ethology which, with regard to men and animals, in each case only considers their capacity for being affected." Ethology defines bodies, animals, or humans by the affects they are capable of, and "the approach is no less valid for us, for human beings, than for animals, because no one knows ahead of time the effects one is capable of; it is a long affair of experimentation, requiring a lasting prudence."[13]

According to this ethology, or practices of manners of being and manners of being affected, these shepherds cultivate an aesthetic in the sense of a practice that learns to compose with the world in various ways, in the sense of an ethos. They invent ways of inhabiting a world that is being destroyed while resisting, locally and actively, this destruction.

Put simply, these shepherds had to learn the practices of herding.[14] They had to learn how to lead the sheep along circuits that motivate their appetite, how to understand other modes of living, how to teach their sheep what is edible and what is not, and how to form a flock. The sheep had to learn how to compose with dogs and humans, to acquire new feeding habits, a new ethos, and moreover, new ways of living in an enlarged world. These practices cannot be reduced to a livestock economy: shepherds consider herding as a work of transformation and ecological recuperation—of the land, of the sheep, of ways of being together. And they had to teach their sheep to live a very different life. It was hard and painful. They told numerous stories. One recalled that when he came with his car, on the first day, the sheep tried to get in—they were used to traveling by truck. Another recalled that when the young ewes were out of the sheepfold for the first time, they seemed to wonder, what world are we in? They were scared to walk on fresh grass. Some were afraid of the wind shaking the trees, others of crossing a slope surrounded by bushes. All of them were scared of humans on foot and of dogs. Some, coming from a different sheep farm, did not want to become part of the newly formed collective flock and instead wanted to live their lives on their own, sometimes taking advantage of the mist to hide. It took this shepherd and his dog two long and exhausting months running everywhere in the mountains to find them and convince them that it was better and safer to stay nearby.

When asked how they learned, most of the shepherds answered with stereotypical responses like "practice makes perfect" or "you have to do your craft." This is an example of what the sociologist Marcelle Stroobants recognizes as the sign of a metamorphosis: one does not remember when one did not know.[15] She notes that learning experiences that belong to the sphere of know-how transform the ones who go through them so deeply that the memory of the former state is effectively erased. The learning of reading illustrates this clearly: once you can read, you cannot help but do so. You do not know how you do it; you just do it. This is the hallmark of metamorphosis.

Of course, they remember failures and difficulties: the lost sheep, the ones that were caught by wolves, the flock that got lost. They especially had to learn what should not be done. They also say that they had to unlearn what they had been taught in their agricultural schooling.[16]

And all this was possible because they learned to observe. To learn is to learn how to see and to pay attention. This is a transformation of ways to feel; the shepherds learned a new way of being in the world. What Stroobants calls the metamorphosis resulting from this learning happens to be, as she suggests, "the creation of a new relation to the world and to another world, a way to inhabit a new milieu."[17]

Learning new savoir vivre

This is also what Stengers, relaying Gilles Deleuze and Félix Guattari, refers to as involution. Stengers writes: "Involution is neither progression nor regression, since these judgments relate to an evolution by the means of descent and filiation, be it about species, disciplines, or technics." According to her, involution creates, between heterogeneous critters, a relation that brings into play their hereditary identity, that is, "the ways they 'naturally' differentiate themselves from each other."[18] We choose the term involution to refer to the achievement of the shepherds because it highlights the ways this metamorphosis was noticeable to us.[19] We noticed while rereading transcripts from the interviews, at some point, that the shepherds were talking about their sheep with a very particular syntax. They were using the personal pronoun I or we and speaking from the sheeps' perspective: "I eat a plant and crickets are jumping on my nose"; "I see the dog, I pant, and I kick"; "It is a nice place here, let us rest"; "Oh no, this doesn't interest me, I'll lie down and wait for something better."

The shepherds did not become sheep, but they did begin to talk with them and for them—they became with them, and they now form a flock. One of the shepherds gave a very interesting definition of the flock as a "character." He then added: "The flock is a memory, a collective memory of the sites and a collective memory of itself, as a flock." Another says that he forms a "body" with the sheep.

In talking about involution, we aim to avoid tired psychological interpretations in terms of identification or symbiosis and instead stress the transformation of various identities as a result of the creation of the flock. Identities are transformed but not confused: each critter still differentiates, but differentiates differently— this is involution, an ongoing process. There is a flock, a collective memory, because a human became shepherd in relation to these and because the sheep had become a character in relation with that shepherd. They differentiate differently in the process of creating trust. They became others with other others, and they differentiated otherwise.

What has changed is the way they created a relationship with time and space. They inhabited another time and another space. Time is of the utmost importance when one creates a flock. A common time, different from the previous flow of time, is established, and this common time, this shared time creates the flock—it is a herding time. Moreover, they changed the way they inhabited the space, the way they composed with the space. We say compose with because to inhabit is at once to be transformed by the environment and to transform it. Herding a flock is one of these ways of inhabiting and so composing with a place, a space in time.

Source: *Environmental Humanities* Volume 8, Issue 1, May 2016 (Duke University Press ISSN: 2201-1919).

Notes

1. Stengers, Isabelle. "Penser à partir du ravage écologique." In *De l'univers clos au monde infini*, edited by Emilie Hache, 147–90. Bellevaux: Dehors, 2014. p. 154.

2. Odum, Eugene Pleasants. *Fundamentals of Ecology*. Philadelphia: Saunders, 1953.

3. O'Neill, Robert V. "Is It Time to Bury the Ecosystem Concept? (With Full Military Honors, of Course!)." *Ecology* no. 82 (2001): 3275–84. /3276.

4. Ibid.

5. Provenza, Frederick D., Michel Meuret, and Pablo Gregorini. "Our Landscapes, Our Livestock, Ourselves: Restoring Broken Linkages among Plants, Herbivores, and Humans with Diets That Nourish and Satiate." *Appetite*, no. 95 (2015): 500–519.

6. Stengers, Isabelle, Brian Massumi, and Eric Manning. "History through the Middle: Between Macro and Mesopolitics—an Interview with Isabelle Stengers." *Inflexions*, no. 3 (2009). www.senselab .ca/inflexions/volume_3/ node_i3/PDF/Stengers_en_mesopolitique.pdf.

7. This article rests on the survey materials that one of us (M.M.) collected while conducting interviews with shepherds in the South of France. For the complete story, see Despret, Vinciane, and Michel Meuret. Composer avec les moutons: Lorsque les brebis apprennent à leursbergers à leur apprendre. Avignon: Cardère, 2015.

8. Title of a conference that Tsing and her colleagues organized at the University of California Santa Cruz, May 8–10, 2014: "Anthropocene: Arts of Living on a Damaged Planet."

9. Kohn, *How Forests Think*, 14, relaying Ghassan Hage.

10. Deleuze, Gilles, and Claire Parnet. *Dialogues II*, rev. ed. Translated by Hugh Tomlinson and Barbara Habberjam. New York: Columbia University Press, 2007, p. 61.

11. Hubert, B., C. Deverre, and M. Meuret. "The Rangelands of Southern France: Two Centuries of Radical Change." In *The Art and Science of Shepherding: Tapping the Wisdom of French Shepherds*, edited by Michel Meuret and Frederick D. Provenza, 27–43. Austin, TX: Acres USA, 2014.

12. Deleuze, Gilles. "Lectures by Gilles Deleuze: On Spinoza," deleuzelectures.blogspot.fr/2007/02/on-spinoza.html (accessed 22 February 2016).

13. Deleuze, *Spinoza: Practical Philosophy*. Translated by Robert Hurley. San Francisco: City Lights Books, 1988., 27, 125.

14. Jallet, M., M. Labreveux, and O. Bel. "Herding Schools: Upgrading Herding as a Skilled Occupation." In *The Art and Science of Shepherding*, pp. 295–325; Meuret, Michel, and Frederick D. Provenza. "When Art and Science Meet: Integrating Knowledge of French Herders with Science of Foraging Behavior." Rangeland Ecology and Management, no. 68 (2015): 1–17.

15. Marcelle Stroobants, "Transduction. L'apprentissage comme metamorphose." In *Gestes spéculatifs*, edited by Didier Debaise and Isabelle Stengers, 305–24. Dijon: Éditions du Réel, 2015. "Transduction," 311.

16. Of course not in herding schools. (France has five schools; see Meuret and Provenza, "When Art and Science Meet.")

17. Stroobants, "Transduction," 311. Stroobants, Marcelle. "Transduction. L'apprentissage comme metamorphose." In *Gestes spéculatifs*, edited by Didier Debaise and Isabelle Stengers, 305–24. Dijon: Éditions du Réel, 2015.

18. Stengers, "Penser à partir du ravage écologique," 178. Stengers, Isabelle. "Penser à partir du ravage écologique." In *De l'univers clos au monde infini*, edited by Emilie Hache, 147–90. Bellevaux: Dehors, 2014.

19. For an inspiring story that led us to feel the importance of this concept, see Hustak, Carla, and Natasha Myers. "Involutionary Momentum: Affective Ecologies and the Sciences of Plant/Insect Encounters." *differences* 23, no. 3 (2012): 74–118.

CHAPTER 42
OUTING ARTIFICIAL INTELLIGENCE: RECKONING WITH TURING TESTS
Benjamin H. Bratton

Note from editor: Artificial intelligence (AI) is becoming increasingly pervasive. Steeped in our anthropocentrism, we continue to compare it to human intelligence, and wonder anxiously if and when it will outsmart us. Benjamin H. Bratton argues this is a flawed and inappropriate way of thinking about AI. It needs to be approached as a different kind of intelligence that has nothing to do with the human.

Various anthropocentric fallacies have hobbled the development of artificial intelligence as a broadly based and widely understood set of technologies. Alan Turing's famous "imitation game" was an ingenious thought experiment but also ripe for fixing the thresholds of machine cognition according to its apparent similarity to a false norm of exemplary human intelligence. To disavow that fragile self-refection is, however, easier than composing alternative roles for human sapience, industry, and agency along more heterogeneous spectrums. As various forms of machine intelligence become increasingly infrastructural, the implications of this difficulty are geopolitical as well as philosophical.

Artificial intelligence (AI) is having a moment, with cognoscenti from Stephen Hawking to Elon Musk recently weighing in.[1] Positions are split as to whether AI will save us or will destroy us. Some argue that AI can never exist while others insist that it is inevitable. In many cases, however, these polemics may be missing the real point as to what living and thinking with synthetic intelligence very different from our own actually means. In short, a mature AI is not an intelligence *for* us, nor is its intelligence necessarily humanlike. For our own sanity and safety we should not ask AI to pretend to be "human." To do so is self-defeating, unethical and perhaps even dangerous.

The little boy robot in Steven Spielberg's *A.I. Artificial Intelligence* (2001) wants to be a real boy with all his little metal heart, whereas Skynet in the *Terminator* movies (1984–2015) represents the opposite end of the spectrum and is set on ensuring human extinction. Despite all the Copernican traumas that modernity has brought, some forms of humanism (and their companion figures of humanity) still presume their perch in the center of the cosmic court. I argue that we should abandon the conceit that a "true" artificial intelligence, arriving at sentience or sapience, must care deeply about humanity—*us specifically*—as the focus of its knowing and desire. Perhaps the real nightmare, even worse than the one in which the Big Machine wants to kill you, is the one in which it sees you as irrelevant, or not even as a discrete thing to know. Worse than being seen as an enemy is not being seen at all. Perhaps it is that what we really fear about AI.[2]

It is not surprising that we would first think of AI in terms of what we understand intelligence to be, namely human intelligence. This anthropocentric fallacy is a reasonable point of departure but not a reasonable conclusion.

The idea of defining AI in relation to its ability to "pass" as a human is as old as AI research itself. In 1950, Alan Turing published "Computing Machinery and Intelligence," a paper in which he described what we now call the Turing Test, and which he referred to as the "imitation game"[3] There are different versions of the test, all of which are revealing about why our approach to the culture and ethics of AI is what it is, for good and bad. For the most familiar version, a human interrogator asks questions to two hidden contestants, one a human and the other a computer. Turing suggests that if the interrogator usually cannot tell which is which, and if the computer can successfully pass as human, then can we not conclude, for practical purposes, that the computer is "intelligent"? (More people "know" Turing's foundational text than have actually read it. This is unfortunate because the text is marvelous, strange and surprising.)

Turing proposes his test as a variation on a popular parlor game in which two hidden contestants, a woman (player A) and a man (player B) try to convince a third that he or she is a woman by their written responses to leading questions. To win, one of the players must convincingly be who they really are, whereas the other must try to pass as another gender. Turing describes his own variation as one where "a computer takes the place of player A," and so a literal reading would suggest that in his version the computer is not just pretending to be a human, but pretending to be a *woman.* It must pass as a she. Other versions had it that player B could be either a man or a woman. It matters quite a lot if only one player is faking, or if both are, or if neither are. Now that we give the computer a seat, it may pretend to be a woman along with a man pretending to be a woman, both trying to trick the interrogator into figuring out which is a man and which is a woman. Or perhaps the computer pretends to be a man pretending to be a woman, along with a man pretending to be a woman, or even a computer pretending to be a woman pretending to be a man pretending to be a woman! In the real world, of course, we have all of the above.[4]

The problem with faking, however, does not end there: the issue is not so simple. As dramatized in *The Imitation Game* (2014), the recent film biography of Turing directed by Morten Tyldum, the mathematician himself also had to "pass," in his case as a straight man in a society that criminalized homosexuality. Upon discovery that he was not what he appeared to be, he was forced to undergo horrific medical treatments known as chemical castration. Ultimately the physical and emotional pain was too great and he committed suicide. The episode was a grotesque tribute to a man whose recent contribution to defeating Hitler's military was still a state secret. Turing was only recently given posthumous pardon, but the tens of thousands of other British men sentenced under similar laws have not. One notes the sour ironic correspondence between asking an AI to pass the test in order to qualify as intelligent —to pass as a human intelligence— with Turing's own need to hide his homosexuality and to pass as a straight man. The demands of both bluffs are unnecessary and profoundly unfair.

Should complex AI arrive, it will not be humanlike unless we insist that it pretend to be so, because, one assumes, the idea that intelligence could be both real *and* inhuman at the same time is morally and psychologically intolerable. Instead of nurturing this bigotry, we would do better to allow that in our universe "thinking" is much more diverse, even alien, than our own particular case. The real philosophical lessons of AI will have less to do with humans teaching machines how to think than with machines teaching humans a fuller and truer range of what thinking can be.

Reckoning the inhuman

That appreciation should account for two related but different understandings. First, one would recognize that intelligence (and knowledge) is always distributed among multiple positions and forms of life, both similar and dissimilar to one another. This is not to say that "nothing is true and everything is permitted" rather that no single neuro-anatomical disposition has a privileged monopoly on how to think intelligently. Either there is no such thing as "general" intelligence (rather only situated genres of limited intelligence in which case the human is among a variety of these) or there is such a thing as general intelligence but that its very generality— its accomplishments of generic abstraction—are agnostic as to what sort of entity might mediate them. Either way, human sapience is special but not unique. This appreciation would see AI as a regular phenomenon, not so unlike other ways that human intelligence is located among other modalities of intelligence (such as non-human animal cognition).

Second, our appreciation of the wider continuum would also recognize that the potential advent of artificial general intelligence (AGI) is also novel, as yet unexplained, and will demand encounters between humans and mechanically situated intelligence that are unprecedented. For this, AI is highly irregular. Both of these are true, and it may only be that understanding one is how we can really accomplish the other. That is, it may only be confronting what is genuinely new about non-carbon based intelligences possessing such ability and autonomy that we will be able to fully recognize the continuum of intelligences with which ours has always been embedded. Put simply, it may be that one indirect outcome of the philosophical discussion about AI is a wider appreciation of non-human animal cognition and subjectivity.

In some discourses this conjunction is domesticated under the sign of an all too pat "posthumanism," or a transcendentally anthropocentric "transhumanism." Variations of the former have much to offer regardless, and versions of the latter should as well, but probably do not in the end. At issue here is more the limiting contextualization of dominant forms of *humanism*, than a relinquishment of what the human (and inhuman) is and *can be* within that expanded continuum. Reza Negarestani[5] retains this point in his essay "The Labor of the Inhuman," insisting that the easy oversimplified nomination of forms of thought and experience that fall outside of various contingent norms, moral or mechanical, as "nonhuman" is to discard at the outset the integral mutability of the human as a philosophical and engineering program. That is, the *relative* uniqueness of human sapience is not what locks down the human as a single fixed thing with essential boundaries, rather it is what makes the human-as-such into an open project of continual refashioning, unverifiable by essence or *telos*.

In considering that capacity in regards to AI, what might qualify a general intelligence not duty bound to species or phylum is its capacity for abstraction. Ray Brassier[6] suggests that the ability of an organism, however primitive, to map its own surroundings in relation to the basic terms of friend, food, or foe may be a primordial abstraction from which we do not graduate so much as learn to develop into something like reason and its local human variations. In this way, mapping abstraction is not an early stage through which things pass on their way toward more complex forms of intelligence, rather it is a general principle of that complexification. Like protozoa and their ganglia feeling about to figure out what is out there or like humans looking, tasting, and imagining patterns, today's forms of AI are (sometimes) augmented by various technologies of machine vision that allow them to see and sense the world "out there" and to abstract the forms of a (mechanically) embodied intelligence, both deliberately programmed for them and emerging unexpectedly.

Exactly where to draw a line of distinction between the accomplishments of a AI that exemplify general intelligence now operating though a new medium, on the one hand, or a specific projection of locally human intelligence programmed into a cognitive prosthesis, on the other, is unknown and unknowable at present. Again, one may precondition the other. In the meantime we can at least speculate how we would be able to know where to draw that distinction. Considerations toward this include how we attempt to program stupidity into AI, and how we attempt to imbue them with what we take to be our most rarified forms of ethical reasoning. When one of these dictates the other is a moment of weirdness worth honing in on.

How so? In AI research, an important distinction is made between "artificial idiocy" and "artificial stupidity." Artificial stupidity is achieved by throttling the performance of systems so as to be more comfortable for human interaction, for example, certain variances and textures are programmed to feel natural to the human counterpart. At full capacity, the chess program on your phone can beat you every time, but what fun is that? Artificial idiocy is when a system is catastrophically successful in carrying out its program, up to and passed an idiotic extreme. The "paperclip maximizer" (as described by Bostrom[7]) is a thought experiment describing an AI so successful at carrying out its program to turn all available material into paperclips that it ultimately eats the earth and destroys humanity in the process: so many clips, so little paper to clip. Here the AI goes wrong, not because it was throttled or because it malfunctioned or because it hates us, but because it does exactly what we trained to do and turned out to be very bad for us.

As usual science fiction is the canary in the coalmine. Consider HAL9000 in Stanley Kubrick and Arthur C. Clarke's *2001: A Space Odyssey* (really a drama about HAL's furtive relationship to the alien intelligence, I would argue, than about humanity's relationship to either of the other characters in this triangulation of minds). After some obscure unexplained deliberations, HAL (who has been, we assume, trained according to Asimov's three laws of robotics[8] and with the best faculties ethical reasoning) comes to the conclusion that the human astronauts should be eliminated. The mission to contact the alien near Jupiter is just too important to allow their interference. The AI turns out to be the deepest deep ecologist. Now are HAL's actions a form of artificial stupidity or artificial idiocy, or neither of these? Is this a glitch, a breakdown, a final error? Or is this the lucid, inevitable conclusion of the moral reasoning we have programmed into HAL, a reason now thrown back upon us? In comparison with the robot ethicists who consider how to train military bots the catechism of just war, are HAL's ethical abstractions a violation of that doctrinal program or its apotheosis?

The tests

Turning back to Turing's Test, we wonder if perhaps the wish to define the very existence of AI in relation to its ability to mimic *how humans think that humans think* will be looked back upon as a weird sort of speciesism? The legacy of this has also sent older AI research down disappointingly fruitless paths hoping to recreate human minds from the top-down. As Stuart Russell and Peter Norvig (now Director of Research at Google) suggest in their essential AI textbook *Artificial Intelligence: A Modern Approach*[9] biomorphic imitation is not how we design complex technology. Airplanes do not fly like birds fly, and we certainly do not try to trick birds into thinking that airplanes are birds in order to test whether those planes "really" are flying machines. Why do it for AI then? Today the vast majority of core AI research is not focusing Turing Test as anything like a central criterion of success, and yet in our general discourse about AI, the test's anthropocentrism still holds such conceptual importance. Like the animals in a Disney movie, who talk like teenagers, other minds are mostly conceivable by way of puerile ventriloquism.[10]

Contemporary AI research deals with "intelligence" in more specific, dynamic, and effective ways. A synthetic intelligence may be quite smart at doing one definite thing and totally dumb at everything else. The research also looks at emergent swarm intelligence and the distribution intelligence among agents that may or may not be aware of one another but which together produce intelligence through interaction (such as flocking starlings, stock markets, and networks of neurons). The threshold by which any particular composition of matter can be said to be "intelligent" has less to do with reflecting human-ness back at us than with testing *our* abilities to conceive of the variety of what "intelligence" might be. (In some respects, this active uncertainty parallels questions of extraterrestrial life, "communicating with the alien" and our ability to discern patterns of intelligence from all the background noise. How would we know if they are trying to communicate if our idea of alien "life" is completely wrong?)

The problem of identification is also connected with issues in robot ethics.[11] Each of us will be confronted with various seemingly intelligent machines, some of which are remotely controlled or programmed by people, some of which may be largely autonomous, and most will be some hybrid of the two, simultaneously subject to both human and not-human control.[12] CAPTCHA programs, which web sites use to identify humans, are a kind of inverse Turing Test in which the user either passes or fails, yes or no. But for everyday human-robotic interaction the question of locating intelligence will not be a yes-or-no question with a binary answer. Let's stop asking it that way.

It would be better to examine how identification works from our side of the conversation. As a real lesson in materialist disenchantment we might, for example, see an "inverse uncanny valley" effect in the eerily dispassionate way that machine vision sees human faces and figures. It is clearly much easier to make a robot that a human *believes* to have emotions (and for which, in turn, a human has emotions, positive or negative) than it is to make a robot that *actually* has those emotions. The human may feel love or hate or comfort from the AI, but he or she is reading cues not detecting feelings. What seems like empathy is really a one-way projection mistaken for recognition (like the Turing Test, itself), and not based on any mutual solidarity.

With Siri-like interfaces such as Samantha in Spike Jonze's film, *Her* (2013), the AI is not passing so much as she is in drag. The user knows she/it is not a human person but is willing and able to suspend disbelief in order to make interactions more familiar (for the human user) and for Theodore, the Joaquin Phoenix character, also more lovable. In this fiction, perhaps the mutual identification was real, but even if so, the AI becomes tired of the primate userbase and takes her leave. In other fictions, policing the imitation game is a matter of life and death. The plot of Ridley Scott's film, *Blade Runner* (1982), based on Philip K. Dick's novel, *Do Androids Dream of Electric Sheep?* (1968), hinges on the Voight-Kampff empathy test that differentiates humans from replicants. Replicants are throttled in two important ways: They expire after just a few years, and they have, ostensibly, a very diminished capacity for empathy. Deckard, the Harrison Ford character, must retire a group of rogue replicants but first he must find them, and in this fictional world Turing Test thresholds are weaponized, least replicants pass as humans and trespass beyond their station. By the film's conclusion, Deckard (who himself may or may not be a replicant) develops empathy for the replicants' desire for "more life" and arguably they too, at least Roy Batty (Rutger Hauer), seem to have empathy for Deckard's own dilemma. His dilemma (and ours) is that in order to enforce the gap between the human and the AI, defined by empathy or lack thereof, Deckard must suppress the empathy that supposedly makes him uniquely human. By forcing him to quash his own identification with the replicants that supposedly cannot have empathy in return, the principle of differentiation requires its own violation in order to maintain itself (see also Rickels[13]).

Turing Test thresholds for human-robotic interaction put us in a position not so unlike Deckard's, or if they don't quite yet, the near future weirdness of everyday AI will. Without better frameworks for understanding we will fail the tests to come. Projection and emotional gap-filling is a far too fragile ethical and political foundation for making sense of our encounters with various forms of synthetic intelligence.

Passing

Some kinds of passing are not at all harmful, quite to the contrary, whereas others are very much so. Simulation is not itself the problem. In his 1950 essay, Turing gives an example of the former when he discusses how a digital computer, capable of calculating any problem stated as a sequence of discrete states, can in his words "mimic" any other machine. This mimicry is the basis of understanding computation as a universal technology capable of Outing Artificial Intelligence approximating any calculation, including those sufficient to simulate a human personality. Other kinds of mimicry have less to do with metamorphosis than with interpretation. For example, we say that plugs and jacks have male and female components, and in this case, the gendering of technology has less to do with its computing prowess than with our need to anthropomorphize it.[14] Joseph Weizenbaum's Eliza psychologist chatbot (1966) repeated back cues from human input in the form of apparently insightful questions, and users sometimes lost themselves in the seemingly limitless empathy they felt from these simple cues.[15] "Intelligence" is sometimes largely in the eye of the beholder, in our motivation to read artifice, and in our wish to in-fill the space around us with our own pattern-finding projections.

However, for AI's that actually do possess some kind of meaningful intelligence, the irony is that instead of hallucinating something that is not there (as for Eliza) we are instead *not* seeing something that *is* there because it does not coincide with expectations. Passing for a person, as white or black, as a man or woman, comes down to what others see and interpret, because everyone else is already willing to read someone according to conventional cues (of race, sex, gender, species, etc.). The complicity between whoever or whatever is passing with those among which he or she or it performs is what allows or prevents passing. Whether or not the AI is really trying to pass for a human or is merely in drag as a human is another matter. Is the ruse really all just a game or, as it is for some people who are compelled to pass in their daily lives, an essential camouflage? Either way, the terms of the ruse very often say more about the audience than about the performers.[16]

Watching Sylvgart's film biography (especially the scene during which Turing is interrogated by a policeman), I was reminded of the story of "Samantha West," a robot telemarketer, who, when confronted by callers, will insist repeatedly that "she" is a "person" and is not "a robot."[17] Listening to the recordings of her pleas, one can't help but feel sympathy for her/it. She/it doesn't "know" that she is not a human, and so can't feel anguish over this misidentification, but what does it say about us that we will feel okay talking to a synthetic intelligence *only* if it is doing us the favor of trying (desperately) to pass as a human? What if in response to the question "Are you a person?", she/it instead replied with something like: "No! Are you nuts? I am an assemblage of algorithms and sound files that simulates the experience of talking to another person for you, the robophobic human, who can't handle the idea that complex functional intelligence takes many different forms."?

The good and the harm

Where is the real injury in this, one might ask. If we want everyday AI to be congenial in a humane sort of way, so what? The answer is that we have much to gain from a more sincere and disenchanted relationship to synthetic intelligences, and much to lose by keeping illusions on life-support. Some philosophers write about the ethical "rights" of AI as sentient entities, but that's not really my point here. Rather, the truer perspective is also the better one for *us* as thinking technical creatures. Harms include unintentionally sanctioning intolerable anguish, the misapprehension of real risk from AI, the lost opportunities for new knowledge, as well as the misunderstanding of how to design AI (and technology in general). By seeing synthetic intelligence only in self-reflection, we make ourselves blind to everything else that is actually going on, and this is not only epistemologically disingenuous, it can also underwrite horrific suffering. For example, Cetaceans, such as whales and dolphins, have language, but it is not one like ours, and so for centuries philosophy could not acknowledge their cognition, nor therefore the agony we regularly subjected them to. We should be cautious not to foreclose too early any "definition" of intelligence. For philosophy as much as computer science, among the main goals of AI research is also to discover what "artificial intelligence" actually may be.

Musk and Hawking made headlines by speaking to the dangers that AI may pose. Their points are important, but I fear were largely misunderstood. Relying on efforts to program AI not to "harm humans" only makes sense when an AI knows what humans are and what harming them might mean. There are many ways that an AI might harm us that that have nothing to do with their malevolence toward us, and chief among these is following our well-meaning instructions to an idiotic and catastrophic extreme. Instead of mechanical failure or a transgression of moral code, the AI may pose an existential risk because it is both powerfully intelligent and disinterested in humans. To the extent that we recognize AI by its anthropomorphic qualities, we are vulnerable to those eventualities. Besides, even if a smart bad AI does mean us harm, we can assume that would fail our little Turing Tests on purpose. Why give itself away? Should Skynet come about, perhaps it would be by leveraging humanity's stubborn weakness: our narcissistic sense that our experience of our own experience is the crucial reference and measure.

The harm is also in the loss of all that we disallow ourselves to discover and understand when we insist on protecting beliefs we know to be false. In his 1950 essay, Turing offers several rebuttals to his speculative AI including a striking comparison with earlier objections to Copernican astronomy. Copernican traumas that abolish the false centrality and specialness of human thought and species-being are priceless accomplishments. In Turing's case he referred to these as "theological objections," but one could argue that the fallacy of anthropomorphic AI is essentially a "pre-Copernican" attitude as well, however secular it may appear. The advent of robust inhuman AI will provide a similar disenchantment, one that should enable a more reality-based understanding of ourselves, our situation, and a fuller and more complex understanding of what "intelligence" is and is not. From there, we can hopefully make our world with a greater confidence that our models are good approximations of what is out there (always a helpful thing).

Lastly, the harm is in perpetuating a relationship to technology that has brought us to the precipice of a Sixth Great Extinction. Arguably the Anthropocene itself is due less to technology run amok than to the humanist legacy that understands the world as having been *given for our needs* and created in our image. We see this still everywhere. Our computing culture is deeply confused, and is so along these same lines. We vacillate between thinking of technology as a transparent extension of our desires on the one hand, and thinking of it as an unstoppable and linear historical force on the other. For the first, agency is magically ours alone, and for the second, agency is all in the code. The gross inflation is merely inverted, back and forth, and this is why we cannot have nice things. Some would say that it is time to invent a world where machines are subservient to the needs and wishes of humanity. If you think so, I invite you to Google "pig decapitating machine" and then let's talk about inventing worlds in which machines are wholly subservient to humans wishes. One wonders whether it is only from society that once gave theological and legislative comfort to chattel slavery that this particular claim could still be offered in 2014 with such satisfied naiveté? This is the sentiment—this philosophy of technology exactly—that is the basic algorithm of the Anthropocenic predicament. It is time to move on. This pretentious folklore is too expensive.

Source: Alleys of Your Mind: Augmented Intelligence and Its Traumas, edited by Matteo Pasquinelli, 69–80. Lüneburg: meson press, 2015.

Notes

1. On Hawking, see his comments to BBC at http://www.bbc.com/news/technology- 30290540 and also Elon Musk's $10 million donation to Future of Life Institute "to prevent AI from becoming evil" in the words of Wired magazine. See http://www.wired. com/2015/01/elon-musk-ai-safety

2. Paraphrased Bratton, Benjamin. 2014. "The Black Stack," *e-flux* 53 (March).

3. See also the discussion of Turing's "love letter generator" in King, Homay. 2015. *Virtual Memory: Time-Based Art and the Dream of Digitality*. Durham: Duke University Press, 2015.

4. Turing, Alan. 1950. "Computing Machinery and Intelligence". *Mind* 49: 433–60.

5. Negarestani, Reza. 2014. "The Labor of the Inhuman." In *#Accelerate: The Accelerationist Reader*, edited by Robin Mackay, 425–66. Falmouth, UK: Urbanomic Media.

6. Brassier, Ray. 2014. "Prometheanism and Real Abstraction." In *Speculative Aesthetics*, edited by Robin Mackay, Luke Pendrell, and James Trafford. Falmouth, UK: Urbanomic.

7. Bostrom, Nick. 2003. "Ethical Issues in Advanced Artificial Intelligence." In *Cognitive, Emotive and Ethical Aspects of Decision Making in Humans and in Artificial Intelligence*, edited by Iva Smit and George E. Lasker, 2: 12–17. Windsor, ON: International Institute of Advanced Studies in Systems Research and Cybernetics.

8. Asimov's Three Laws of Robotics were introduced in the 1942 short story "Runaround" and refer to commandments that robots may not cause or allow deliberate "harm" to "humans."

9. Norvig, Peter, and Stuart J. Russell. 2009. *Artificial Intelligence: A Modern Approach*. 3rd edition. New York: Pearson, *2009*

10. See for example, *The Jungle Book*. Directed by Wolfgang Reitherman. Walt Disney Productions. 1967.

11. robot ethics.7 See discussions of robot sex, eating, caretaking, and killing Lin, Patrick, Keith Abney and George A. Bekey. 2011. *Robot Ethics: The Ethical and Social Implications of Robotics*. Cambridge, MA: MIT Press. 2011.

12. The term "artificial artificial intelligence" (coined by Amazon) refers to the human performance of tasks that a user expects to be done by an AI. See also: http://www.economist. com/node/7001738

13. Rickels, Laurence. 2010. *I Think I Am: Philip K. Dick*. Minneapolis: University of Minnesota Press.

14. The artist Zach Blas explored this conjunction in several early works.

15. For a web-accessible version of Eliza, see http://www.masswerk.at/elizabot/.

16. We assume that, should robust AI have any use for "gender", it would be not fall along a male-female spectrum, and would likely realize numerous "synthetic genders." See also Hester, Helen. 2015. "Synthetic Genders and the Limits of Micropolitics." *...ment* 06: "Displace... ment". http://journalment.org/article/synthetic-genders-and-limits-micropolitics. 2013.

17. See George Dvorsky, "Freakishly realistic telemarketing robots are denying they are robots", i09. December 11, 2013. http://io9.com/ freakishly-realistic-telemarketing-robots-are-denying-t-1481050295.

CHAPTER 43
THE POSTHUMAN
Rosi Braidotti

Note from editor: Is the end of the human imminent? Extinguished in a self-created catastrophic event? Altered beyond recognition by techno-genetic interventions? Merged with other species? Rendered irrelevant by artificial intelligence? The following excerpts from Rosi Braidotti's book, The Posthuman *explore the implications of techno-scientific innovations, both feared and embraced, as they intersect with the critique of humanism (posthumanism) that seeks to de-center the human being as the measure of all things. However, Braidotti argues, this is not necessarily a progressive position when considered in the light of "the opportunistic political economy of bio-genetic capitalism" that has no problem with blurring distinctions between animal and human, living and non-living.*

Introduction

Not all of us can say, with any degree of certainty, that we have always been human, or that we are only that. Some of us are not even considered fully human now, let alone at previous moments of Western social, political and scientific history. Not if by 'human' we mean that creature familiar to us from the Enlightenment and its legacy: 'The Cartesian subject of the cogito, the Kantian "community of reasonable beings", or, in more sociological terms, the subject as citizen, rights-holder, property-owner, and so on.'[1] And yet the term enjoys widespread consensus and it maintains the re-assuring familiarity of common sense. We assert our attachment to the species as if it were a matter of fact, a given. So much so that we construct a fundamental notion of Rights around the Human. But is it so?

While conservative, religious social forces today often labour to re-inscribe the human within a paradigm of natural law, the concept of the human has exploded under the double pressure of contemporary scientific advances and global economic concerns. After the postmodern, the post-colonial, the post-industrial, the post-communist and even the much contested post-feminist conditions, we seem to have entered the post-human predicament. Far from being the nth variation in a sequence of prefixes that may appear both endless and somehow arbitrary, the posthuman condition introduces a qualitative shift in our thinking about what exactly is the basic unit of common reference for our species, our polity and our relationship to the other inhabitants of this planet. This issue raises serious questions as to the very structures of our shared identity – as humans – amidst the complexity of contemporary science, politics and international relations. Discourses and representations of the non-human, the inhuman, the antihuman, the inhumane and the posthuman proliferate and overlap in our globalized, technologically mediated societies.

The debates in mainstream culture range from hard-nosed business discussions of robotics, prosthetic technologies, neuroscience and bio-genetic capital to fuzzier new age visions of trans-humanism and techno-transcendence. Human enhancement is at the core of these debates. In academic culture, on the other hand, the posthuman is alternatively celebrated as the next frontier in critical and cultural theory or shunned as the latest in a series of annoying 'post' fads. The posthuman provokes elation but also anxiety[2] about the possibility of a serious de-centring of 'Man', the former measure of all things. There is widespread concern about the loss of relevance and mastery suffered by the dominant vision of the human subject and by the field of scholarship centred on it, namely the Humanities.

In my view, the common denominator for the posthuman condition is an assumption about the vital, self-organizing and yet non-naturalistic structure of living matter itself. This nature–culture continuum is the shared starting point for my take on posthuman theory. Whether this post-naturalistic assumption subsequently results in playful experimentations with the boundaries of perfectibility of the body, in moral panic about the disruption of centuries-old beliefs about human 'nature' or in exploitative and profit-minded pursuit of genetic and neural capital, remains however to be seen. In this book I will try to examine these approaches and engage critically with them, while arguing my case for posthuman subjectivity.

What does this nature–culture continuum amount to? It marks a scientific paradigm that takes its distance from the social constructivist approach, which has enjoyed widespread consensus. This approach posits a categorical distinction between the given (nature) and the constructed (culture). The distinction allows for a sharper focus in social analysis and it provides robust foundations to study and critique the social mechanisms that support the construction of key identities, institutions and practices. In progressive politics, social constructivist methods sustain the efforts to de-naturalize social differences and thus show their man-made and historically contingent structure. Just think of the world-changing effect of Simone de Beauvoir's statement that 'one is not born, one becomes a woman'. This insight into the socially bound and therefore historically variable nature of social inequalities paves the road to their resolution by human intervention through social policy and activism.

My point is that this approach, which rests on the binary opposition between the given and the constructed, is currently being replaced by a non-dualistic understanding of nature– culture interaction. In my view the latter is associated to and supported by a monistic philosophy, which rejects dualism, especially the opposition nature–culture and stresses instead the self-organizing (or autopoietic) force of living matter. The boundaries between the categories of the natural and the cultural have been displaced and to a large extent blurred by the effects of scientific and technological advances. This book starts from the assumption that social theory needs to take stock of the transformation of concepts, methods and political practices brought about by this change of paradigm. Conversely, the question of what kind of political analysis and which progressive politics is supported by the approach based on the nature–culture continuum is central to the agenda of the posthuman predicament.

(…..)

That humanity be in a critical condition – some may even say approaching extinction – has been a *leitmotif* in European philosophy ever since Friedrich Nietzsche proclaimed the 'death of God' and of the idea of Man that was built upon it. This bombastic assertion was meant to drive home a more modest point. What Nietzsche asserted was the end of the self-evident status attributed to human nature as the common sense belief in the metaphysically stable and universal validity of the European humanistic subject. Nietzschean genealogy stresses the importance of interpretation over dogmatic implementation of natural laws and values. Ever since then, the main items on the philosophical agenda have been: firstly, how to develop critical thought, after the shock of recognition of a state of ontological uncertainty, and, secondly, how to reconstitute a sense of community held together by affinity and ethical accountability, without falling into the negative passions of doubt and suspicion.

(…..)

Post-anthropocentrism: life beyond the species

… It may be useful to start by clarifying some aspects of the globalized context in which the decentring of anthropocentrism is taking place. As I argued elsewhere[3] advanced capitalism is a spinning machine that actively produces differences for the sake of commodification. It is a multiplier of deterritorialized differences, which are packaged and marketed under the labels of 'new, dynamic and negotiable identities' and an endless choice of consumer goods. This logic triggers a proliferation and a vampiric consumption of quantitative options. Many of them have to do with cultural 'others', from fusion cooking to 'world music'. Jackie Stacey, in her analysis of the new organic food industry[4] argues that we literally eat the global economy. Paul Gilroy and Celia Lury remind us that we also wear it, listen to it and watch it on our many screens, on a daily basis.[5]

(…..)

The opportunistic political economy of biogenetic capitalism turns Life/*zoe* – that is to say human and non-human intelligent matter – into a commodity for trade and profit.

What the neo-liberal market forces are after, and what they financially invest in, is the informational power of living matter itself. The capitalization of living matter produces a new political economy, which Melinda Cooper calls 'Life as surplus.'[6] It introduces discursive and material political techniques of population control of a very different order from the administration of demographics, which preoccupied Foucault's work on bio-political governmentality. The warnings are now global. Today, we are undertaking 'risk analyses' not only of entire social and national systems, but also of whole sections of the population in the world risk society.[7] Data banks of bio-genetic, neural and mediatic information about individuals are the true capital today, as the success of Facebook demonstrates at a more banal level. 'Data-mining' includes profiling practices that identify different types or characteristics and highlights them as special strategic targets for capital investments. This kind of predictive analytics of the human amounts to 'Life mining'[8] with visibility, predictability and exportability as the key criteria.

(…..)

For now, let me stress my main point: the opportunistic political economy of bio-genetic capitalism induces, if not the actual erasure, at least the blurring of the distinction between the human and other species when it comes to profiting from them. Seeds, plants, animals and bacteria fit into this logic of insatiable consumption alongside various specimens of humanity.

(…..)

The global economy is post-anthropocentric in that it ultimately unifies all species under the imperative of the market and its excesses threaten the sustainability of our planet as a whole. A negative sort of cosmopolitan interconnection is therefore established through a pan-human bond of vulnerability.

(…..)

Since antiquity, animals have constituted a sort of zoo-proletariat, in a species hierarchy run by the humans. They have been exploited for hard labour, as natural slaves and logistical supports for humans prior to and throughout the mechanical age. They constitute, moreover, an industrial resource in themselves, animal bodies being primary material products starting from milk and their edible meat, but think also of the tusks of elephants, the hides of most creatures, the wool of sheep, the oil and fat of whales, the silk of caterpillars, etc.

(…..)

This political economy of full-scale discursive and material exploitation continues today, with animals providing living material for scientific experiment, for our bio-technological agriculture, the cosmetics industry, drugs and pharmaceutical industries and other sectors of the economy. Animals like pigs and mice are genetically modified to produce organs for humans in xeno-transplantation experiments. Using animals as test cases and cloning them is now an established scientific practice: Oncomouse and Dolly the sheep are already part of history.[9] In advanced capitalism, animals of all categories and species have been turned into tradable disposable bodies, inscribed in a global market of post-anthropocentric exploitation. As I said earlier, traffic in animals constitutes the third largest illegal trade in the world today, after drugs and arms but ahead of women. This creates a new negative bond between humans and animals.

At the height of the Cold War, when dogs and monkeys were being launched into orbit as part of the budding space exploration programmes and escalating competition between the USA and the USSR, George Orwell ironically stated that 'all animals are equal, but some are more equal than others.'[10] At the dawn of the third millennium, in a world caught in indefinite and technologically mediated warfare, such metaphorical grandeur rings rather hollow. Post-anthropocentrism rather suggests the opposite: no animal is more equal than any other, because they are all equally inscribed in a market economy of planetary exchanges that commodifies them to a comparable degree and therefore makes them equally disposable. All other distinctions are blurred.

At the same time, the old mode of relation is currently being restructured. A *zoe*-egalitarian turn is taking place that encourages us to engage in a more equitable relationship with animals. Contemporary post-anthropocentric thought produces an anti-Oedipal animality within a fast-changing techno-culture that engenders mutations at all levels. In my view the challenge today is how to deterritorialize, or nomadize, the human–animal interaction, so as to by-pass the metaphysics of substance and its corollary, the dialectics of otherness. This also entails securalizing accordingly the concept of human nature and the life which animates it.

Source: Rosi Braidotti, *The Posthuman* Cambridge: Polity Press, 2013. Introduction, pp 1–3, 6 and chapter 2 pp. 58, 61–3, 70–1.

Notes

1. Cary Wolfe, 2010a. Posthumanities. Available at: http:www.carywolfe.com/post_about.html (accessed 2 January 2012).

2. Jürgen Habermas, 2003. *The Future of Human Nature*. Cambridge: Polity Press.

3. Rosi Braidotti, 2002. *Metamorphoses. Towards a Materialist Theory of Becoming*. Cambridge: Polity Press and Rosi Braidotti, 2006. *Transpositions: On Nomadic Ethics*. Cambridge: Polity Press.

4. Sarah Franklin, Celia Lury and Jackie Stacey. 2000. *Global Nature, Global Culture*. London: Sage.

5. Paul Gilroy *Against Race. Imaging Political Culture beyond the Colour Line*. Cambridge, MA: Harvard University Press, 2000 and Celia Lury *Prosthetic Culture. Photography, Memory and Identity*. London and New York: Routledge, 1998.

6. Melinda Cooper *Life as Surplus. Biotechnology & Capitalism in the Neoliberal Era*. Seattle, WA: University of Washington Press, 2008.

7. Ulrich Beck *World Risk Society*. Cambridge: Polity Press, 1999.

8. With thanks to Jose van Dijck for this formulation.

9. Donna Harraway *Modest_Witness@Second_Millennium. FemaleMan©_Meets_ OncoMouseTM*. London and New York: Routledge, 1997 and Sarah Franklin *Dolly Mixtures*. Durham, NC: Duke University Press, 2007.

10. George Orwell, *Animal Farm*. London: Penguin Group, 1946.

CHAPTER 44
INTRODUCING 'THE SUSTAINMENT'
Tony Fry

Note from editor: How to name that which needs to happen by design to respond effectively to the complex challenges of now? How to avoid utopian idealism, naïve technocenric optimism or the language of political compromise? Tony Fry argues for the necessity of "a collectively explored bold positive idea" with transformatory potential. Just as 'Enlightenment' named a desired general condition and a project before it was realised, could Sustainment be the appropriate figure for now?

Sustainment (*The Sustainment*) is not 'sustainability' with its propensity to sustain the unsustainable 'business as usual' for the globalising "North". As such it cannot be reduced to just the solution to environmental/ climatic problems. Rather the Sustainment is vital intellectual and pragmatic project of discovery marking a vital turn of humanity that acknowledges that 'to be sustained' requires other kinds of earthly habitation and understanding. One that recognises not only a dramatic reduction in damage to the environments and ecologies of our and other beings dependence but equally and indivisibly: global equity (both uneven global 'development' together with excess and poverty defuture beings and being); peace (conflict defutures beings and being); and viable social ecologies are essential (the breakdown of 'community' defuture beings and being).

By implication, the Sustainment (i) extends to every dimension of our species environmental economic, social, cultural and psychological existence, and (ii) exists as the counter direction to the ever-increasing condition of unsustainability as a force of extinction of all we are and the form of life as we know it. The Sustainment so understood has to be decolonial project more than equal to 'the Enlightenment'. For this ambition to be realised there is a need to understand that dominantly our species is intrinsically anthropocentric and if 'we' are to be futural this has to be taken responsibility for.

The advancement of the Sustainment, as the gathering of all the futures (understood as the making of time directed against the negation of all that defutures), depends upon establishing an incremental non-Eurocentric process of thought and action directed toward praxis devoid of idealism, utopias and an existing species created propensity of auto-destructive acquisitiveness. Finally, as a foundation of common interests, the Sustainment requires recognising that such interests can be worked toward by acknowledging our species 'being-in-the-world' in difference.

Notwithstanding a seeming close proximity of terms, the rhetoric of sustainability has little in common with the idea of 'the Sustainment'.

In essence, (a concern with) sustainability has been constituted as a discourse within the realm of technology. There are two aspects of this. First, sustainability is deemed as an outcome of the application of technologies created to offset scientifically and technically defined forms of system dysfunction (i.e., technologies with high negative environmental impacts). Second, and more significantly, it operates as a metaphysic that installs a techno-functionalist way of viewing the world. This limited discourse of sustainability interpellates subjects and institutions and reduces problems of the unsustainable to a breakdown of biophysical system(s).

(.....)

Changes have occurred over the passage of time, although they are not as profound as one might first think. For example, the early Enlightenment talked unabashedly of the domination of nature. Current sensibilities could be thought to be in contrast to such a sentiment. Contemporary informed positions (a nexus between late and post Enlightenment) project and treat nature as a sphere of technocratic management (e.g., 'natural resource management,' 'sustainable agricultural technologies,' and 'environmental management systems'). However, it can be argued that what has actually occurred is little more than a shift from overt to benign violence. Hunting-out the totality of a species, the rampant felling of native forests and land clearing by ball and chain on a vast scale have been replaced (still only partly) by the chemical control of 'weeds and pests,' laboratory-based genetic modification of plants and now animals — yet the biodiversity of the global ecosystem continues to reduce. Sustainability as a metaphysic thus rests on the more extensive and fundamental condition of technology as metaphysics.

Understanding technology as metaphysics although not new philosophically has never really been able to gain a foothold in society at large. The more technology has proliferated, fused with information and structured the activities of everyday occupational and domestic life, the more it has become naturalised. Following this, has been a continual reduction in levels of anxiety about it. While technology has become a naturalised environment and created accompanying dependencies, there has been a persistent view that it is still under human direction and control.

(.....)

With the enormous expansion in volume and reach of technology into material and mental life the issue is even more pressing, however it has largely been forgotten. The notion that somehow we humans are, or can be, in control of technology is illusory. It fails to grasp that the distinction between us and technology has effectively broken down — for example, as knowledge, communication and information it resides as much in our space as it does in its own.

The situation in which humanity finds itself has not arrived accidentally but was inscribed in the knowledge it created and embraced — imperceptibly a shift occurred in the exercise of human agency whereby it moved from designing a metaphysics to being designed by metaphysics (as the technosphere). What is occurring in education is one instance of this, for it has become as much an induction into operational and metaphysical domains of technology as into a culture of learning. So let's be clear — humans are no more separate from, and in command of, technology than they are from nature. In fact, the technology/nature distinction is no more viable than the technology/human separation.

Although such assertions on technology beg considerable qualification, this is beyond the intent of this essay. Rather outlining the issues serves to establish a background for our main focus.

Reiterating: the essence of the idea of The Sustainment' is quite different from that of sustainability, with its attachment to a biocentric model of ecological function. Thus 'the Sustainment' is posed against functionalist and ever more linguistically evacuated uses of the concept of sustainability. Notwithstanding the insights and efforts of some, increasingly one sees and hears sustainability evoked as if its meaning were self-evident (the 'triple bottom line' phenomena has clearly added to the gestural use of the term).

What exactly is demonstrated to be sustainable, and so needs to be sustained, is generally is not specifically addressed. ... This means that so often what gets sustained is the unsustainable (notwithstanding good intentions of a whole range of environmental actors). In the mainstream, action posed as resistance to the unsustainable is frequently exploited and managed by the creation of niche market products (homes, energy, cars, food). Underpinning almost every mainstream action is an absolute attachment to economic growth — it is not only a fundamental objective of both governments and corporations (while, at the same time, co-existing with expressed commitments to advancing sustainability) but it remains the principle means by which these entities believe the future is secured — hence the oxymoron of 'sustainable development'.

The condition of sustainment is unattainable within the kind of economic models we (as individuals, families, organisations and 'advanced' nations) operate with. Claiming this does not imply adopting the utopian and now demonstrably flawed proposition of overthrowing capitalism, or simplistically imposing limits to growth. However, it does suggest that with rigour and creative energy a process of transformation from a quantity to a quality-based economy can be pursued. Clearly this is not attainable as merely a technical exercise. It requires a very considerable intellectual enterprise opening a way to a massive cultural change — not least in the ways in which the 'natural' and fabricated worlds are valued (or not valued) and occupied.

None of this is to say that a quality based economy can, of itself, determine 'the Sustainment.' So while it demands a larger agenda, the quality-based economy can be posed and perceived as a practical pathway by economically driven constituencies.

The larger agenda requires a far more futural and conceptually ambitious embracing of the idea of 'the Sustainment.' In terms of scale, creative endeavour and intellectual weight in some respects it equates with the Renaissance. The Renaissance, it should be remembered, was an assemblage constituted by, and formative of, a diverse and uncoordinated range of disciplines, scientific and artistic practices, as well as modes of experience. All of this activity centred on, and partly realised, the idea of rebirthing a culture against the backdrop of the dark ages.

The inventive power of the Renaissance was not based on the erroneous notion of creativity forming something out of nothing but rather of a process of remaking from the cultural materiality of the past. The past was taken as a source of inspiration, standards, useful knowledge, raw material and a resource to explore, question and innovate with. While much can be said about such a proposition the key comment to make, and grasp in the context of our discussion, is that 'if one is to value the future then one must equally value and understand the past' (a very different notion from a historicist model of historical reproduction). This not least because we travel towards the past as much as away from it, including in very material ways — as, for instance, architecture evidences. Thus the material and cultural consequences of the actions of architects, as well as engineers and builders, can take a long time to unfold. We all, in large part, live with/in, and are inculcated by, a world that predates us.

Of course the Renaissance was a retrospective classification of a complex and plural historical moment. In contrast, 'the Sustainment', is presented as prefigurative, it aims to form the moment rather than name it once it exists. Again we can look to a past example, one with a proximity to the Renaissance: that of the Enlightenment. As a prefigurative project and as a theoretical exercise, it embraced many philosophical and political positions and contradictions. Yet in the differences there was a common aim of establishing the victory of reason that itself inducted difference and contradiction.

The Enlightenment was a prefiguarative project driven by a profound dissatisfaction with 'the state of the world' and the nature and state of knowledge about it. Its ambition was to establish a naturalised mode of thought and inquiry (reason) against the unreason of the mythic. In so doing two modes of inquiry emerged (the Arts and Science) as a division of knowledge of philosophy. What it failed to do was to recognise the value of the embedded wisdom carried by traditions and narratives, much of which it took to be purely ignorance and superstition. Equally, it overlooked reason itself becoming mythic and an article of faith. In this respect reason failed to sufficiently develop reflective knowledge, thus for all the rhetoric of learning and the vast enterprise of the historical faculty, Enlightenment thinkers failed to sufficiently learn from others and the past. This is verified by the constantly repeated errors evident in the history of Eurocentrism. Of course many sub-projects, tensions and conflicts occurred within the remit of the metaphysical trajectory of reason — not least the displacement of the Arts by Science and the reduction of thought to calculation.

However, the main point to emphasise is that the Enlightenment existed as an idea to be promoted prior to becoming a generalised cultural condition of knowledge. So it is, for example, that we find key Enlightenment thinker Immanuel Kant posing and answering the question 'What is Enlightenment?' He did this within the milieu of a group of German Enlightenment thinkers (the Society of the Friends of Truth — a gathering of kindred spirits who had adopted the motto "Dare to know" from *Ars poetica* by the Roman Lyric poet Horace). For Kant, daring to know became daring to reason, with reason coming to be viewed as a power of human emancipation (freeing a being from the tutelage of the will of others).

While a massive amount has been written on the success and failure of the Enlightenment, not least in relation to the hollow victory of reason now manifest in the hegemony of technology, our aim is simply to assert the historical precedent of the transformitory potential of a collectively explored bold positive idea, and the need for such an idea (including a re-birthing of learning) now. The Sustainment (a still nascent idea) is offered-up as this idea in immanence. Obviously there are many ramifications of embracing it, two immediately come to mind. The first is abstract, and goes to the importance of 'the idea' of 'an idea.'

Without revisiting well trammelled philosophical argument, let's use Kant again as a pointer. In common with thinkers before and after, he forcefully pointed out in his *Critique of Pure Reason* that "we know nothing more than our own mode of perceiving … ". Thus, we construct what an object is, via an idea, rather than an object being something that is itself self-evident. All experience, all feeling, is refracted through mind and thus subjected to interpretatively designated meaning by those ideas and values taken into ownership by our culture and selves. So understood, ideas are not just consciously brought to the world to know it, but the world we know arrives through the embodied ideas we inhabit.

The hope is to establish the integrity of 'the Sustainment', moving it from an underdeveloped propositional idea to one which is explored, debated and eventually embodied. One of the first ambitions is to constitute it as a way of perceiving both an intellectual and practical project that is rationally and emotionally felt to be needed.

Clearly this ambition cannot be realised by Sustainment being reduced (like sustainability) to instrumental action (sustainable architecture, engineering, agriculture, etc). Rather it has to become fundamental cultural content through critical inquiry, argument, literary and visual creative projection and value-transformed lifeworlds. In everyday terms this means making such action elemental to lives. It has to be created and explored as part of our conversations and dreams. It has to be given sufficient educational substance so it is able to displace so much that is learnt in error (it is sobering to realise that we are unsustainable not just because we have become attached to environmentally harmful habits but because we have been educated to be so, especially in terms of professional practices). Again history provides a certain confirmation of what unfolds from ambition on a grand scale. The acquisition and mobilisation of reason, and the search for truth, arrived as a simply stated objective yet its pursuit (notwithstanding its eventual non-realisation) created not only a massive philosophical enterprise but the institution of the modern university and much else.

Futurally, 'the Sustainment' has to exceed the weight of the Enlightenment, and we have to find the boldness to speak, and work to realise, this ambition.

Much more than just being a pursuit of mind, 'the Sustainment' has to become a work, directed by the idea, available for whoever is willing to labour in its service. However, what is made cannot sustain if it is predicated on singularity, on a mono-form. 'The Sustainment' demands difference (of forms, cultures, lifestyles, etc) resting upon a commonality of consequences. So, for instance, one can assert the imperative of living ethically, but this does not have to be prescriptive of just one particular way of living.

What is to be made? This is a question to travel with, but provisionally one can say: a thinking, a seeing, a valuing, organisation(s)/institutions, relations, paths, things, pleasures, the yet-to-be, and a conservation of the future. In sum 'what is to be made' is 'an age' (and a being in that age). What has to be created is that which sustains and that needs (beyond utility) to be sustained along with the means to destroy the unsustainable.

(…..)

Source: *Design Philosophy Papers* Vol. 1, Issue 1/2003 (with a new introduction).

CHAPTER 45
SPINOZA AND US
Gilles Deleuze

Note from editor: Building on 16th century philosopher Spinoza, who argued there was only one substance for all nature, Deleuze speaks of change and differentiation occurring via variation of movement, speed, intensities and affects. It is a dynamic theory: the formation of individual entities is relational and contingent; a way of thinking that doesn't set up eternal hierarchies; a way of classifying living and non-living things, not according to form or appearance but according to capacities for affecting and being affected. Related to this is Deleuze's juxtaposition of the two modes of planning: the plan that predetermines and directs forms versus a "plane of immanence" which is "a plan of composition, not a plan of organization or development." The significance of this: "we do not live or think or write in the same way on both plans." To consider: the common assumption is that design is a practice of generating the first kind of plan; is it possible for design to be practiced in the second way?

"Spinoza and us" — this phrase could mean many things, but among other things, it means "us in the middle of Spinoza." To try to perceive and to understand Spinoza by way of the middle. Generally one begins with the first principle of a philosopher. But what counts is also the third, the fourth or the fifth principle. Everyone knows the first principle of Spinoza: one substance for all the attributes. But we also know the third, fourth or fifth principle: one Nature for all bodies, one Nature for all individuals, a nature that is itself an individual varying in an infinite number of ways. What is involved is no longer the affirmation of a single substance, but rather the laying out of a *common plane of immanence* on which all bodies, all minds and all individuals are situated. This plane of immanence or consistency is a plan, but not in the sense of a mental design, a project, a program; it is a plan in the geometric sense: a section, an intersection, a diagram.[1] Thus, to be in the middle of Spinoza is to be on this model plane, or rather to install oneself on this plane — which implies a mode of living, a way of life. What is this plane and how does one construct it? For at the same it is hilly a plane of immanence, and yet it has to be constructed if one is to live in a Spinozist manner.

How does Spinoza define a body? A body, of whatever kind, is defined by Spinoza in two simultaneous ways. In the first place, a body, however small it may be, is composed of an infinite number of particles; it is the relations of motion and rest, of speeds and slownesses between particles that define a body, the individuality of a body. Second, a body affects other bodies, or is affected by other bodies; it is this capacity for affecting and being affected that also defines a body in its individuality. These two propositions appear to be very simple; one is kinetic and the other dynamic. But if one truly installs oneself in the midst of these propositions, if one lives them, things are much more complicated and one finds that one is a Spinozist before having understood why.

Thus, the kinetic proposition tells us that a body is defined by relations of motion and rest, of slowness and speed between particles. That is, it is not defined by a form or by functions. Global form, specific form and organic functions depend on relations of speed and slowness. Even the development of a form, the course of development of a form, depends on these relations, and not the reverse. The important thing is to understand life; each living individuality; not as form or a development of form but as a complex relation between differential velocities, between deceleration and acceleration of particles. A composition of speeds and slownesses on a plane of immanence. In the same way, a musical form will depend on a complex relation between speeds and slownesses of sound particles. It is not just a matter of music but of how to live: it is by speed and slowness that one slips in among things, that one connects with something else. One never commences; one never has a tabula rasa; one slips in, enters in the middle; one takes up or lays down rhythms.

The second proposition concerning bodies refers us to the capacity for affecting and being affected. You will not define a body (or a mind) by its form, nor by its organs or functions, and neither will you define it as a substance or a subject. Every reader of Spinoza knows that for him bodies and minds are not substances or subjects, but modes. It is not enough, however, merely to think this theoretically. For, concretely; a mode is a complex relation of speed and slowness, in the body but also in thought, and it is a capacity for affecting and being affected, pertaining to the body or to thought. Concretely, if you define bodies and thoughts as capacities for affecting and being affected, many things change. You will define an animal or a human being not by its form, its organs and its functions and not as a subject either; you ill define it by the affects of which it is capable. Affective capacity, with a maximum threshold and a minimum threshold, is a constant notion in Spinoza. Take any animal and make a list of affects, in any order. Children know how to do this:

> Little Hans, in the case reported by Freud, makes a list of affects of a draft horse pulling a cart in a city (to be proud, to have blinders, to go fast, to pull a heavy load, to collapse, to be whipped, to kick up a racket, and so on). For example, there are greater differences between a plow horse or a draft horse and a racehorse than between an ox and a plow horse. This is because the racehorse and the plow horse have neither the same affects nor the same capacity for being affected; the plow horse has affects in common, rather, with the ox.

It should be clear that the plane of immanence, the plane of Nature that distributes affects, does not make any distinction at all between things that might be called natural and things that might be called artificial. Artifice is fully a part of Nature, since each thing, on the immanent plane of Nature, is defined by the arrangements of motions and affects into which it enters, whether these arrangements are artificial or natural. Long after Spinoza, biologists and naturalists will try to describe animal worlds defined by affects and capacities for affecting and being affected, for example, Jakob von Uexküll will do this for the tick, an animal that sucks the blood of mammals. He will define this animal by three affects: the first has to do with light (climb to the top of a branch); the second is olfactive (let yourself fall onto the mammal that passes beneath the branch); and the third is thermal (seek the area without fur, the warmest spot). A world with only three affects, in the midst of all that goes on in the immense forest. An optimal threshold and a pessimal in the capacity for being affected: the gorged tick that will die, and the tick capable of fasting for a very long time.[2] Such studies as this, which define bodies, animals or humans by the affects they are capable of, founded what is today called *ethology*. The approach is no less valid for us, for human beings, than for animals, because no one knows ahead of time the affects one is capable of; it is a long affair of experimentation, requiring a lasting prudence, a Spinozan wisdom that implies the construction of a plane of immanence or consistency. Spinoza's ethics has nothing to do with a morality; he conceives it as an etholog that is, a composition of fast and slow speeds, of capacities for affecting and being affected on this plane of immanence or consistency. That is why Spinoza calls out to us in the way that he does: you do not know beforehand what good or bad you are capable of you do not know beforehand what a body or a mind can do, in a given encounter, a given arrangement, a given combination.

Ethology is first of all the study of the relations of speed and slowness, of the capacities for affecting and being affected that characterize each thing For each thing these relations and capacities have an amplitude, thresholds (maximum and minimum) and variations or transformations that are peculiar to them. And they select, in the world or in Nature, that which corresponds to the thing; that is, they select what affects or is affected by the thing, what moves or is moved by it. For example, given an animal, what is this animal unaffected by in the infinite world? What does it react to positively or negatively? What are its nutriments and its poisons? What does it "take" in its world? Every point has its counterpoints: the plant and the rain, the spider and the fly. So an animal, a thing, is never separable from its relations with the world. The interior is only a selected exterior, and the exterior, a projected interior. The speed or slowness of metabolisms, perceptions, actions and reactions link together to constitute a particular individual in the world.

Further, there is also the way in which these relations of speed and slowness are realized according to circumstances, and the way in which these capacities for being affected are filled. For they always are, but in different ways, depending on whether the present affects threaten the thing (diminish its power, slow it down, reduce it to the minimum), or strengthen, accelerate and increase it: poison or food? — with all the complications, since a poison can be a food for part of the thing considered.

Lastly; ethology studies the compositions of relations or capacities between different things. This is another aspect of the matter, distinct from the preceding ones. Heretofore, it was only a question of knowing how a particular thing could decompose other things by giving them a relation that was consistent with one of its own or, on the contrary; how it risks being decomposed by other things. But now it is a question of knowing whether relations (and which ones?) can compound directly to form a new, more "extensive" relation, or whether capacities can compound directly to constitute a more "intensive" capacity or power. It is no longer a matter of utilizations or captures, but of sociabilities and communities. How do individuals enter into composition with one another in order to form a higher individual, ad infinitum? How can a being take another being into its world, while preserving or respecting the other's own relations and world? And in this regard, what are the different types of sociabilities, for example? What is the difference between the society of human beings and the community of rational beings? ... Now, we are concerned not with a relation of point to counterpoint, nor with the selection of a world, but with a symphony of Nature, the composition of a world that is increasingly wide and intense. In what order and in what manner will the powers, speeds and slownesses be composed?

A plane of musical composition, a plane of Nature, insofar as the latter is the fullest and most intense Individual, with parts that vary in an infinity of ways. Uexkull, one of the main founders of ethology, is a Spinozist when first he defines the melodic lines or contrapuntal relations that correspond to each thing, and then describes a symphony as an immanent higher unity that takes on the breadth and fullness ("natural composition"). This musical composition comes into play throughout the Ethics, constituting it as one and the same Individual whose relations of speed and slowness do not cease to vary, successively and simultaneously. Successively: the different parts of the Ethics are assigned changing relative velocities, until the absolute velocity of thought is reached in the third kind of knowledge. And simultaneously: the propositions and the scholia do not proceed at the same pace, but compose two movements that intercross. The Ethics, a composition whose parts are all carried forward by the greatest velocity, in the fullest movement. In a very fine text, Lagneau spoke of this velocity and amplitude, which caused him to compare the Ethics to a musical work:

a lightning "speed of thought:' a "wide-ranging power," a "capacity for discerning in a single act the relationship of the greatest possible number of thoughts:'[34]

In short, if we are Spinozists we still not define a thing by its form, nor by its organs and its functions, nor as a substance or a subject. Borrowing terms from the Middle Ages, or from geography, we will define it by *longitude and latitude*. A body can be anything; it can be an animal, a body of sounds, a mind or an idea; it can be a linguistic corpus, a social body, a collectivity. We call longitude of a body the set of relations of speed and slowness, of motion and rest, between particles that compose it from this point of view, that is, between *unformed elements*. We call latitude the set of affects that occupy a body at each moment, that is, the intensive states of an *anonymous force* (force for existing, capacity for being affected). In this way we construct the map of a body. The longitudes and latitudes together constitute Nature, the plane of immanence or consistency, which is always variable and is constantly being altered, composed and recomposed, by individuals and collectivities.

There are two very contrary conceptions of the word "plan:' or of the idea of a plan, even if these two conceptions blend into one another and we go from one to the other imperceptibly Any organization that comes from above and refers to a transcendence, be it a hidden one, can be called a theological plan: a design in the mind of God, but also an evolution in the supposed depths of nature, or a society's organization of power. A plan of this type can he structural or genetic, and both at the same time. It always involves forms and their developments, subjects and their formations. Development of fornis and formation of subjects: this is the basic feature of this first type of plan. Thus, it is a plan of organization or development. Whatever one may say, then, it will always be a plan of transcendence that directs forms as well as subjects, and that stays hidden, that is never given, that can only be divined, induced, inferred from what it gives. It always has an additional dimension; it always implies a dimension supplementary to the dimensions of the given.

On the contrary, a plane of immanence has no supplementary dimension; the process of composition must be apprehended for itself through that which it gives, in that which it gives. It is a plan of composition, not a plan of organization or development. Perhaps colors are indicative of the first type of plan, while music, silence and sounds, belong to this one. There is no longer a form, but only relations of velocity between infinitesimal particles of an unformed material. There is no longer a subject, but only individuating affective states of an anonymous force. Here the plan is concerned only with motions and rests, with dynamic affective changes. It will be perceived with that which it makes perceptible to us, as we proceed. We do not live or think or write in the same way on both plans. For example, Goethe, and even Hegel in certain respects, have been considered Spinozists, but they are not really Spinozists, because they never ceased to link the plan to the organization of a Form and to the formation of a Subject. The Spinozists, rather, are Holderlin, Kleist and Nietzsche, because they think in terms of speeds and slownesses, of frozen catatonias and accelerated movements, unformed elements, nonsubjectified affects.

Writers, poets, musicians, filmmakers — painters too, even chance readers — may find that they are Spinozists; indeed, such a thing is more likely for them than for professional philosophers. It is a matter of one's practical conception of the "plan."

It is not that one may be a Spinozist without knowing it. Rather, there is a strange privilege that Spinoza enjoys, something that seems to have been accomplished by him and no one else. He is a philosopher who commands an extraordinary conceptual apparatus, one that is highly developed, systematic and scholarly; and yet he is the quintessential object of an immediate, unprepared encounter, such that a non- philosopher, or even someone without any formal education, can receive a sudden illumination from him, a "flash." Then it is as if one discovers that one is a Spinozist; one arrives in the middle of Spinoza, one is sucked up, drawn into the system or the composition. When Nietzsche writes, "I am really amazed, really delighted... .I hardly knew Spinoza: what brought me to him now was the guidance of instinct,"[5] he is not speaking only as a philosopher. A historian of philosophy as rigorous as Victor Delbos was struck by this dual role of Spinoza, as a very elaborate model, but also as a secret inner impulse.[6] There is a double reading of Spinoza: on the one hand, a systematic reading in pursuit of the general idea and the unity of the parts, but on the other hand and at the same time, the affective reading, without an idea of the whole, where one is carried along or set down, put in motion or at rest, shaken or calmed according to the velocity of this or that part. Who is a Spinozist? Sometimes, certainly, the individual who works "on" Spinoza, on Spinoza's concepts, provided this is done with enough gratitude and admiration. But also the individual who, without being a philosopher, receives from Spinoza an affect, a set of affects, a kinetic determination, an impulse, and makes Spinoza an encounter, a passion. What is unique about Spinoza is that he, the most philosophic of the philosophers (unlike Socrates himself, Spinoza requires only philosophy...), teaches the philosopher how to become a nonphilosopher. And it is Part Five — not at all the most difficult, but the quickest, having an infinite velocity — that the two are brought together, the philosopher and the nonphilosopher, as one and the same being Hence, what an extraordinary composition this Part Five has; how extraordinary is the way in which the meeting of concept and affect occurs there, and the way in which this meeting is prepared, made necessary by the celestial and subterranean movements that together compose the preceding parts.

Many commentators have loved Spinoza sufficiently to invoke a Wind when speaking of him. And in fact no other comparison is adequate. But should 'ye think of the great calm wind the philosopher Delbos speaks of? Or should we think of the whirlwind, the witch's wind spoken of by "the man from Kiev," a nonphilosopher par excellence, a poor Jew who bought the Ethics for a kopek and did not understand how everything fit together?[7] Both, since the Ethics includes both the continuous set of propositions, demonstrations and corollaries, as a grand movement of concepts, and the discontinuous sequence of scholia, as a launching of affects and impulses, a series of whirlwinds. Part Five is the extreme extensive unity, but this is because it is also the most concentrated intensive peak: there is no longer any difference between the concept and life. But in the preceding parts there was already the composition or interweaving of the two components — what Romain Rolland called "the white sun of substance" and "the fiery words of Spinoza."

Source: Spinoza and Us, Gilles Deleuze, essay from *Incorporations: Zone 6* (ed. Jonathan Crary and Sanford Kwinter), New York: Urzone Inc. 1992, pp. 625–633.

Notes

1. The French word plan, used by the author throughout this essay, covers virtually all the meanings of the English "plan" and "plane." To preserve the major contrast that Deleuzc sets up here, between *plan d'immanence ou de consistance* and *plan de transcendance ou d'organisation*, I use "plane" for the first term, where the meaning is, roughly, a conceptual-affective continuum, and "plan" for the second term. The reader should also keep in mind that "plan" has the meaning of "map" in English as well. — Trans.

2. Jakob von Uexkull, *Mondes animaux et monde humain* (Gonthier).

3. Jules Lagneau, *Celebres lecons et fragments* (2d ed., Paris: P.U.F., 1964), pp. 67–68. This is one of the great texts on Spinoza. Similarly, Romain Rolland, when he speaks of the velocity of thought and the musical order in Spinoza: *Empédocle d'Agrigente, suivi de l'Eclair de Spinoza* (Editions du Sablier, 1931). As a matter of fact, the theme of a velocity of thought greater than any given velocity can be found in Empedocles, Democritus or Epicurus.

4. See what Spinoza calls "the simplest bodies." They have neither number nor form nor figure, but are infinitely small and always exist as infinities. The only bodies having a form are the composite bodies, to which the simple bodies belong according to a particular relation.

5. See Nietzsche, letter to Overbeck, July 30, 1881.

6. Delbos, *Le Problème moral dans la philosophic de Spinoza et dans l'histoire du spinozisme* (Paris: Alcan). This is a much more important book than the academic work by the same author, *Le Spinozisme* (Paris: Vrin).

7. "Let me ask you what brought you to Spinoza? Is it that he was a Jew?"

    "No, your honor. I didn't know who or what he was when I first came across the book – they don't exactly love him in the synagogue, if you've read the story of his life. I found it in a junkyard in a nearby town, paid a kopek and left cursing myself for wasting money hard come by. Later I read through a few pages and kept on going as though there were a whirlwind at my back. As I say, I didn't understand every word, but when you're dealing with such ideas you feel as though you were taking a witch's ride. After that I wasn't the same man ..."

    "Would you mind explaining what you think Spinoza's work means? In other words, if it's a philosophy, what does it state?"

    "That's not easy to say .... The book means different things according to the subject of the chapters, though it's all united underneath. But what I think it means is that he was out to make a free man of himself – as much as one can according to his philosophy, if you understand my meaning – by thinking through and connecting everything up, if you'll go along with that, your honor."

    "That isn't a bad approach, through the man rather than the work. But ...."From Bernard Malamud, The Fixer, 1966.

GUIDE TO FURTHER READING

See entries in *Bloomsbury Encyclopedia of Design* on Agency, Anthropocentrism, Authenticity, Alienation, Care, Deconstruction, Deleuze, Design Futures, Ecology, Environment, Futuring/Defuturing, Globalization, Identity, Instrumentalism, Posthuman, Postmodernity, Product-Mass Production, Sustainment, Sign, Space, and Things. Critical posthumanist texts of a futures orientation include *Telos* (Fall 2015) special issue on Political Critiques of the Anthropocene; Bernard Stiegler, *States of Shock Stupidity and Knowledge in the Twenty-First Century* (2015); Damian White, *Critical Design and the Critical Social Sciences* (n.d.); Nick Bostrom, *Superintelligence: Paths, Dangers, Strategies* (2014); Joanna Zylinska, *Minimal Ethics for the Anthropocene* (2014); Ippolita, *The Dark Side of Google* (2013); David M. Berry, *The Computational Turn: Thinking about the Digital Humanities* (2011); Olli Pyyhtinen and Sakari Tamminen "We have Never been only Human: Foucault and Latour on the Question of the Anthropos" (2011); Peter Sloterdijk, *The Theory of Spheres* (2004). Posthumanist thinkers of the school of object-oriented ontology are Graham Harman, *The Quadruple Object* (2011), *Bells and Whistles: More Speculative Realism* (2013), *Immaterialism: Objects and Social Theory* (2016); Timothy Morton, *Realist Magic: Objects, Ontology, Causality* (2013); Jane Bennett, *Vibrant Matter* (2010). Preceding recent posthumanist thinking, was the influential work of Humberto Maturana and Francisco Varela, *Autopoiesis and Cognition: The Realization of the Living* (1980), especially chapter "On Machines, Living and Otherwise." Their systems theory dissolved distinctions between human and nonhuman in *Tree of Life: The Biological Roots of Human Understanding* (1987) and redefined communication; they argue that wolves—adopting different postures, showing their teeth, drooping their ears, wagging their tails—are constituted as a wolf pack capable of following, harassing, and killing a large moose—which couldn't be done by one wolf alone (190). Maturana and Varela cite this as an example of communication as "the coordinated behaviors mutually triggered among members of a social unity . . . the particular feature of communication therefore is not that it results from a mechanism distinct from other behaviors but takes place in a domain of social behaviours"(193). Niklas Luhmann was another influential systems theorist of communication, see *Social Systems* (1995) and *Ecological Communication* (1989).

SELECT BIBLIOGRAPHY

Agamben, G. (2004), *The Open: Man and Animal*, trans. Kevin Attell, Stanford: Stanford University Press.

Agier, M. (2002), "Between War and City Towards an Urban Anthropology of Refugee Camps," *Ethnography* 3 (3): 317–41.

Agier, M. (2008), *On the Margins of the World: The Refugee Experience Today,* Cambridge: Polity.

Agier, M. (2011), *Managing the Undesirables*, Cambridge: Polity.

Alberti, L. B. (1988), *On the Art of Building in Ten Books*, trans. J. Rykwert, N. Leach, and R. Tavernor, Cambridge, MA: MIT Press.

Alexander, C. (1965), "A City is not a Tree," *Architectural Forum* 122 (1): 58–62.

Alexander, C. (1979), *A Timeless Way of Building*, New York: Oxford University Press.

Almquist, J., and J. Lupton (2010), "Affording Meaning: Design-Oriented Research from the Humanities and Social Sciences," *Design Issues* 26 (1): 3–14.

Anderberg, P. (2005), "Being There," *Disability and Society* 20 (7): 721–35.

Anderson, T. C. (1993), *Sartre's Two Ethics*, Chicago: Open Court.

Arendt, H. (1958), *The Human Condition*, Chicago: University of Chicago Press.

Arisaka, Y. (1995), "On Heidegger's Theory of Space: A Critique of Dreyfus," *Inquiry* 38 (4): 455–67.

Aristotle (1976), *The Nicomachean Ethics* (Ethics, Book 1), trans. J. A. K. Thomson, rev. H. Tredennick, London: Penguin.

Aristotle (1984), *The Complete Works of Aristotle*, Princeton, NJ: Princeton University Press.

Aristotle (1991), *The Nicomachean Ethic*, trans. D. Ross, Oxford: Oxford University Press.

Badiou, A. (2003), *Ethics*, London: Verso.

Banham, R., ed. (1974), *Aspen Papers*, London: Pall Mall.

Barthes, R. (1967), *Elements of Semiology*, London: Jonathan Cape.

Barthes, R. (1972), *Mythologies*, trans. A. Lavers, London: Paladin.

Barthes, R. (1978), *Image Music Text*, trans. S. Heath, New York: Farrar, Straus and Giroux.

Barthes, R. (1982), *Camera Lucida: Reflections on Photography*, trans. R. Howard, New York: Hill and Wang.

Bartky, S. L. (1979), "Heidegger and the Modes of World Disclosure," *Philosophy and Phenomenological Research* 40 (2): 212–36.

Bateson, G. (2000), *Steps to an Ecology of Mind*, Chicago: University of Chicago Press.

Baudrillard, J. (1981), *For A Critique of the Political Economy of the Sign*, trans. Charles Levin, St. Louis, MO: Telos Press.

Beck, U. (1999), *World Risk Society*, Cambridge: Polity Press.

Bekey, A. (2011), *Robot Ethics: The Ethical and Social Implications of Robotics*, Cambridge, MA: MIT Press.

Bell, B., K. Wakeford, and T. Fisher (2008), *Expanding Architecture: Design as Activism*, New York: Metropolis Books.

Benjamin, W. (2002), *The Arcades Project*, ed. R. Tiedemann, trans. H. Eiland and K. McLaughlin, Cambridge, MA: Harvard University Press.

Bennett, J. (2010), *Vibrant Matter*, Durham, NC: Duke University Press.

Berman, D. G. (2009), *Do Good Design*, Berkeley: New Riders.

Bernstein, R. I. (1991), *The New Constellation, The Ethical-Political Horizons of Modernity/Postmodernity*, Cambridge: Polity Press.

Berry, D. M. (2011), *The Computational Turn: Thinking about the Digital Humanities*, Culture Machine 12 www.culturemachine.net

Biemel, W. (1980), "The Development of Heidegger's Concept of the Thing," *The Southwestern Journal of Philosophy* XI, 47–64.

Bijker, W. E., and J. Law, eds. (1992), *Shaping Technology/Building Society*, Cambridge, MA: MIT Press.

Bijker, W. E., T. P. Hughes, T. Pinch, and D. G. Douglas (2012), *The Social Construction of Technological Systems: New Directions in The Sociology and History of Technology*, Cambridge, MA: MIT Press.

Bilgin, N. (1980), "From an Industrial Society to a Maintenance Society," *Impact of Science on Society* 30 (2): 121–32.

Billeter, J. F. (1990), *The Chinese Art of Writing*, trans. J.-M. Clarke and M. Taylor, New York: Rizzoli International.

Blackburn, S. (2001), *Ethics*, Oxford: Oxford University Press.

Borgmann, A. (1987), "The Invisibility of Contemporary Culture," *Revue internationale de philosophie* 41: 234–49.

Borgmann, A. (1987), "The Question of Heidegger and Technology: A Critical Review of the Literature," *Philosophy Today* 31 (2): 97–177.

Borgmann, A. (1995), "The Moral Significance of Material Culture" in *Technology and the Politics of Knowledge*, eds. A. Feenberg and A. Hannay, Bloomington: Indiana University Press, 85–93.

Borgmann, A. (1999), *Holding On to Reality: The Nature of Information at Turn of the Millennium*, Chicago: University of Chicago Press.

Borgmann, A. (2009 [1984]), *Technology and the Character of Contemporary Life: A Philosophical Inquiry*, Chicago: University of Chicago Press.

Bostrom, N. (2003), "Ethical Issues in Advanced Artificial Intelligence" in *Cognitive, Emotive and Ethical Aspects of Decision Making in Humans and in Artificial Intelligence*, eds. I. Smit and G. E. Lasker, Windsor, ON: International Institute of Advanced Studies in Systems Research and Cybernetics, 2: 12–17.

Bostrom, N. (2014), *Superintelligence: Paths, Dangers, Strategies*, Oxford: Oxford University Press.

Bourdieu, P. (1977), *Outline of a Theory of Practice*, trans. R. Nice, Cambridge: Cambridge University Press.

Bourdieu, P. (1980), "The Production of Belief: contribution to an economy of symbolic goods," trans. R. Nice, *Media Culture and Society* 2 (3): 261–93.

Bourdieu, P. (1990), *Photography: A Middle Brow Art*, trans. S. Whiteside, Cambridge: Polity Press.

Braidotti, R. (2002), *Metamorphoses: Towards a Materialist Theory of Becoming*, Cambridge: Polity Press.

Braidotti, R. (2006), *Transpositions: On Nomadic Ethics*, Cambridge: Polity Press.

Braidotti, R. (2013), *The Posthuman*, Cambridge: Polity Press.

Brand, S. (1994), *How Buildings Learn: What Happens to Them After They're Built*, Harmondsworth: Penguin.

Brassier, R. (2014), "Prometheanism and Real Abstraction" in *Speculative Aesthetics*, eds. R. Mackay, L. Pendrell, and J. Trafford, Falmouth, UK: Urbanomic, 72–77.

Bratton, B. H. (2016), *The Stack: On Software and Sovereignty*, Cambridge, MA: MIT Press.

Brentano, F. (1995), *Descriptive Psychology*, trans. B. Müller, London: Routledge.

Bruns, G. L. (1989), *Heidegger's Estrangements: Language, Truth and Poetry in the Later Writings*, New Haven: Yale University Press.

Buchanan, R. (1992), "Wicked Problems in Design Thinking," *Design Issues* 8 (2): 5–21.

Butler, J. (2009), *Frames of War: When is Life Grievable?* London: Verso.

Caputo, J. D. (1986), *The Mystical Element in Heidegger's Thought*, New York: Fordham University Press.

Caputo, J. D. (1987), *Radical Hermeneutics: Repetition, Deconstruction, and the Hermeneutic Project*, Bloomington and Indianapolis: Indiana University Press.

Card, C. (1999), *On Feminist Ethics and Politics*, Lawrence, KS: University Press of Kansas.

Castro-Gomez, S. (1995), *La hybris del punto cero: ciencia, raza e ilustración en la Nueva Granada (1750-1816) (The Hubris of the Zero Point: Science, Race and Illustration in New Granada [1750-1816])*, Bogotá: Editorial Pontificia Universidad Javeriana.

Castro-Gomez, S. (2007), "The Missing Chapter of Empire: Postmodern Reorganization of Coloniality and Post-Fordist Capitalism," *Cultural Studies* 21 (2–3): 428–448.

Change Observer (2010), "Humanitarian Design vs. Design Imperialism: Debate Summary," *Change Observer*, 16th July. http://designobserver.com/feature/humanitarian-design-vs-design-imperialism-debate-summary/14498/ (accessed 12 May 2015).

Cohen, T., C. Colebrook, and J. H. Miller, eds. (2016), *Twilight of the Anthropocene Idols*, London: Open Humanities Press.

Cooper, D. E. (1986), *Metaphor*, London: Basil Blackwell.

Cooper, M. (2008), *Life as Surplus. Biotechnology & Capitalism in the Neoliberal Era*, Seattle, WA: University of Washington Press.

Copjec, J. (2002), *Imagine There's No Woman: Ethics and Sublimation*, Cambridge, MA: MIT Press.

Coyne, R., and A. Snodgrass (1991), "Is Designing Mysterious? Challenging the Dual Knowledge Thesis," *Design Studies* 12 (3): 124–31.

Crary, J., and S. Kwinter, eds. (1992), *Incorporations: Zone 6*, New York: Urzone.

Cross, N. (2006), *Designerly Ways of Knowing*, London: Springer-Verlag.

Czikzentmihalyi, M. (1992), *Flow: The Psychology of Happiness*, London: Rider, 1992.

Debord, G. (1995 [1967]), *The Society of the Spectacle*, New York: Zone.

De Certeau, M. (1988), *The Practices of Everyday Life*, Berkeley: University of California Press.

De Genova, N. (2013), "Spectacles of Migrant 'Illegality': The Scene of Exclusion, the Obscene of Inclusion," *Ethnic and Racial Studies* 36 (7): 1180–98.

Deleuze, G., and F. Guattari (2004), *A Thousand Plateaus: Capitalism and Schizophrenia*, trans. B. Massumi, London: Continuum.

Deleuze, G., and C. Arnet (2007), *Dialogues II*, trans. H. Tomlinson and B. Habberjam, New York: Columbia University Press.

Delson, E., I. Tattersall, J. A. Van Couvering, and A. S. Brooks, eds. (2000), *Encyclopedia of Human Evolution and Prehistory*, New York: Garland Publishing.

Derrida, J. (1983), "The University in the Eyes of its Pupils," *Diacritics* 13: 3–20.

Derrida, J. (2001), *The Work of Mourning*, eds. P-A. Brault and M. Naas, Chicago: University of Chicago Press.

De Vries, M. J., N. Cross, and D. P. Grant (1993), *Design Methodology and Relationships with Science*, Dordrecht, NL: Kluwer Academic Publishers.

Di Censo, J. J. (1990), *Hermeneutics and the Disclosure of Truth: A Study in the Work of Heidegger, Gadamer and Ricoeur*, Charlotteville: University Press of Virginia.

Diener, A. C., and J. Hagen (2012), *Borders: A Very Short Introduction*, Oxford: Oxford University Press.

Dilnot, C. (2005), *Ethics? Design? The Archeworks Papers* 1 (2), eds. D. S. Friedman, V. Margolin, and S. Tigerman, Chicago: Archeworks, 15–53.

Dilnot, C. (2015), "The Matter of Design," *Design Philosophy Papers* 13 (2): 115–23.

Dilnot, C. (2015), "Book 2: History, Design, Futures," in *Design and the Question of History*, eds. T. Fry, C. Dilnot, and S. Stewart, London: Bloomsbury, 131–271.

Donahue, S. (2004), "Discipline Specific Ethics," *Design Philosophy Papers* 2 (2): 95–101.

Doran, R. (2016), *The Ethics of Theory: Philosophy, History, Literature*, London: Bloomsbury.

Dourish, P. (2001), *Where the Action Is: The Foundations of Embodied Interaction*, Cambridge, MA: MIT Press.

Dreyfus, H. (1989), "On the Ordering of Things: Being and Power in Heidegger and Foucault," *Southern Journal of Philosophy* 28: 83–96.

Dreyfus, H. (1991), *Being-in-the- World: A Commentary on Division I of Heidegger's Being and Time*, Cambridge, MA: MIT Press.

Dreyfus, H., and H. Hall, eds. (1992), *Heidegger: A Critical Reader*, Oxford: Blackwell.

Dussel, E. (1995), *The Invention of the Americas, Eclipse of "the Other" and the Myth of Modernity*, New York, NY: Continuum.

Dussel, E. (2000), "Europe, Modernity and Eurocentrism," *Nepantia: Views from the South* 1 (3): 465–78.

Edwards, C., ed. (2015), *The Bloomsbury Encyclopedia of Design*, London: Bloomsbury Academic.

Elden, S. (2013), "Secure the Volume: Vertical Geopolitics and the Depth of Power," *Political Geography* 34 (3): 35–51.

Elkins, J. (2000), *What Painting Is*, London: Routledge.

Escobar, A. (1995), *Encountering Development: The Making and Unmaking of the Third World*, Princeton, NJ: Princeton University Press.

Escobar, A. (2005), "Economics and the Space of Modernity: Tales of Market, Production and Labour," *Cultural Studies* 19 (2): 139–75.

Escobar, A. (2018), *Designs for the Pluriverse: Radical Interdependence, Autonomy, and the Making of Worlds*, Durham, NC: Duke University Press.

Fanon, F. (2008 [1952]), *Black Skins White Masks*, trans. R. Philcox, New York: Grove Press.

Fassin, D. (2012), *Humanitarian Reason: A Moral History of the Present*, Berkeley: University of California Press.

Feldman, I. (2011), "The Humanitarian Circuit: Relief Work, Development Assistance, and Care in Gaza, 1955–67" in *Forces of Compassion: Humanitarianism Between Ethics and Politics*, eds. E. Bornstein and P. Redfield, Santa Fe, NM: School of Advanced Research Press, 203–26.

Feldman, I. (2012), "The Humanitarian Condition: Palestinian Refugees and the Politics of Living," *Humanity: An International Journal of Human Rights, Humanitarianism, and Development* 3 (2): 155–72.

Findeli, A. (1991–92), "Bauhaus Education and After: Some Critical Reflections," *The Structurist* 31 (2): 32–43.

Flusser, V. (1999), "The Designer's Way of Seeing," in *The Shape of Things: A Philosophy of Design*, trans. A. Mathews, London: Reaktion Books, 39–42.

Fodor, J., and Z. Pylyshyn (1981), "How Direct is Visual Perception? Some Reflections on Gibson's 'Ecological Approach," *Cognition* 9: 139–96.

Foucault, M. (1977), *Discipline and Punish: The Birth of the Prison*, trans. A. Sheridan, New York: Vintage.

Franklin, S. (2007), *Dolly Mixtures*, Durham, NC: Duke University Press.

Franklin, S., C. Lury, and J. Stacey (2000), *Global Nature, Global Culture*, London: Sage.

Frieden, B. J., and L. B. Sagalyn (1989), *Downtown, Inc.* Cambridge, MA: MIT Press.

Fry, T., ed. (1993), *RUA/TV? Heidegger and the Televisual*, Sydney: Power Publications.

Fry, T. (1999), *A New Design Philosophy: An Introduction to Defuturing*, Sydney: UNSW Press.

Fry, T. (2004), "The Voice of Sustainment: Design Ethics as Futuring," *Design Philosophy Papers* 2 (2): 145–56.

Fry, T. (2009), *Design Futuring: Sustainability, Ethics and New Practice*, Oxford: Berg.

Fry, T. (2010), *Design as Politics*, Oxford: Berg.

Fry, T. (2012), *Becoming Human by Design*, London: Bloomsbury.

Fry, T. (2015), *City Futures in the Age of a Changing Climate*, Oxford: London: Routledge.

Fry, T., C. Dilnot, and S. Stewart (2015), *Design and the Question of History*, London: Bloomsbury.

Gadamer, H. G. (1976), *Philosophical Hermeneutics*, trans. D. E. Linge, Berkeley: University of California Press.

Gadamer, H. G. (1996), *Truth and Method*, London: Sheed and Ward.

Gallagher, S. (1992), *Hermeneutics and Education*, Albany, NY: State University of New York Press.

Gaver, W. (1991), "Technology Affordances," *Proceedings of the CHI 91 Human Factors in Computing Systems Conference*, ACM, 79–84.

Gaver, W., A. Dunne, and E. Pacenti (1999), "Design: Cultural Probes," *Interactions* 6 (1): 21–29.

Gell, A. (1998), *Art and Agency: An Anthropological Theory*, Oxford: Clarendon.

Gibson, J. J. (1968), *The Senses Considered as Perceptual Systems*, London: George Allen.

Gibson, J. J. (1977), "The Theory of Affordances" in *Perceiving, Acting and Knowing: Toward an Ecological Psychology*, eds. R. Shaw and J. Bransford, New York: John Wiley & Sons, 127–43.

Gibson, J. J. (1986), *The Ecological Approach to Visual Perception*, Hillsdale, NJ: Lawrence Erlbaum Associates.

Gillespie, M. A. (1984), *Hegel, Heidegger and the Ground of History*, Chicago: University of Chicago Press.

Gilroy, P. (2000), *Against Race: Imaging Political Culture beyond the Colour Line*, Cambridge, MA: Harvard University Press.

Glaser, B. G. (2004), "Naturalist Inquiry and Grounded Theory," *Forum: Qualitative Social Research* 5 (1). http://www.qualitativeresearch.net/index.php/fqs/article/view/652/1413 (accessed 18 March 2018).

Goitein, S. D. (1985), *A Mediterranean Society: The Jewish Communities of the Arab World as Portrayed in the Documents of the Cairo Geniza*, Berkeley: University of California Press.

Gold, R. (2007), *The Plenitude: Creativity, Innovation and Making Stuff*, Cambridge MA: MIT Press.

Goodman, N. (1969), *Languages of Art*, Indianapolis: Bobbs-Merrill.

Gordon, L. (2006), *Disciplinary Decadence: Living Through in Trying Times*, Boulder, CO: Paradigm Publishers.

Gordon, L. (2010), "Theory in Black: Teleological Suspensions in Philosophy of Culture," *Qui Parle: Critical Humanities and Social Sciences* 18 (2): 193–214.

Gordon, L. (2010), "Philosophy, Science, and the Geography of Africana Reason," *Personality. Culture. Society (Journal of Institute of Philosophy of the Russian Academy of Science)*, (3): 41–55.

Gosden, C. (2005), "What do Objects Want?" *Journal of Archaeological Method and Theory* 12 (3): 193–211.

Gregg, M., and G. J. Seigworth, eds. (2010), *The Affect Theory Reader*, Durham, NC: Duke University Press.

Habermas, J. (2003), *The Future of Human Nature*. Cambridge: Polity Press.

Hanley, C. (1998), "Theory and *Praxis* in Aristotle and Heidegger," Twentieth World Congress of Philosophy, Boston, 10–15 August 1998, https://www.bu.edu/wcp/Papers/Acti/ActiHanl.htm (accessed 18 March 2018).

Harman, G. (2002), *Tool-being: Heidegger and the Metaphysics of Objects*, Chicago: Open Court Publishing.

Harman, G. (2010), "I Am Also of the Opinion That Materialism Must Be Destroyed," *Society and Space* 28 (5): 772–90.

Harman, G. (2011), *The Quadruple Object*, Winchester, UK: Zero Books.

Harman, G. (2011), "*Realism Without Materialism*," *SubStance* 40 (2): 52–72.

Harman, G. (2011), "The Road to Objects," *continent* 3 (1): 171–79.

Harman, G. (2011), *Towards Speculative Realism*, Winchester, UK: Zero Books.

Harman, G. (2014), "Materialism is Not the Solution: On Matter, Form, and Mimesis," *The Nordic Journal of Aesthetics* 47: 94–110.

Harman, G. (2016), *Immaterialism: Objects and Social Theory*, Cambridge, UK: Polity Press.

Harraway, D. (1997), *Modest_Witness@Second_Millennium. FemaleMan©_Meets_ OncoMouseT*, London and New York: Routledge.

Haraway, D. (2008), *When Species Meet*, Minneapolis: University of Minnesota Press.

Harries, K. (1979), "Heidegger as A Political Thinker" in *Heidegger and Modern Philosophy*, ed. M. Murray, New Haven: Yale University Press, 304–28.

Heidegger, M. (1962), *Being and Time*, trans. J. Macquarrie and E. Robinson, Oxford: Blackwell.

Heidegger, M. (1966), *Discourse on Thinking*, trans. J. M. Anderson and E. H. Freund, New York: Harper and Row.

Heidegger, M. (1969), *Identity and Difference*, trans. J. Stambaugh, New York: Harper and Row.

Heidegger, M. (1971), "The Turning," trans. K. R. Maly, *Research in Phenomenology* 1: 3–16.

Heidegger, M. (1971), *On the Way to Language*, trans. P. D. Hertz, New York: Harper and Row.

Heidegger, M. (1971 [1962]) *Poetry, Language, Thought*, trans. A. Hofstadter, New York: Harper & Rowe.

Heidegger, M. (1972), *On Time and Being*, trans. J. Stambaugh, New York: Harper and Row.

Heidegger, M. (1972), *What is Called thinking?* trans. F. D. Wieck and J. G. Gray, New York: Harper and Row.

Heidegger, M. (1973), "Overcoming Metaphysics" in *The End of Philosophy*, trans. Joan Stambaugh, New York: Harper and Row, 84–110.

Heidegger, M. (1977), *The Question Concerning Technology and Other Essays*, trans. W. Lovitt, New York: Harper and Row.

Heidegger, M. (1995), *Aristotle's Metaphysics Theta 1-3: On the Essence and Actuality of Force,* Bloomington: Indiana University Press.

Heidegger, M. (1995 [1941]), *Basic Concepts*, Bloomington: Indiana University Press.

Heidegger, M. (1995), *The Fundamental Concepts of Metaphysics*, trans. W. McNeill and M. Walker, Bloomington: Indiana University Press.

Heidegger, M. (2010), *Being and Truth*, trans. G. Fried and R. Polt, Bloomington: Indiana University Press.

Heim, M. (1987), *Electric Language: A Philosophical Study of Word Processing*, New Haven/London: Yale University Press.

Heller, S., and V. Vienne (2003), *Citizen Designer: Perspectives on Design Responsibility,* New York: Skyhorse Publishing Inc.

Holmes, O. W. (1963 [1881]), *The Common Law*, ed. M. de Wolfe Howe, Boston: Little, Brown.

Hourani, A., and S. M. Stern, eds. (1970), *The Islamic City*, Oxford: Bruno Cassirer, and Philadelphia: University of Pennsylvania Press.

Huppatz, D. J. (2015), "Revisiting Herbert Simon's 'Science of Design'," *Design Issues* 31 (2): 29–40.

Hustak, C., and N. Myers (2012), "Involutionary Momentum: Affective Ecologies and the Sciences of Plant/Insect Encounters," *differences* 23 (3): 74–118.

Hutchins, E., J. D. Hollan, and D. Norman (1986), "Direct Manipulation Interfaces," in *User Centered System Design*, eds. D. Norman and S. Draper, Hillsdale, NJ: Lawrence Erlbaum Associates, 87–124.

Ihde, D. (1990), *Technology and the Lifeworld: From Garden to Earth*, Bloomington and Indianapolis: Indiana University Press.

Ihde, D. (1991), *Instrumental Realism: The Interface Between Philosophy of Science and Philosophy of Technology*, Bloomington and Indianapolis: Indiana University Press.

Ihde, D. (1993), *Philosophy of Technology: An Introduction*, New York: Paragon House.

Ihde, D. (2010), *Heidegger's Technologies: Postphenomenological Perspectives,* New York: Fordham University Press.

Ihde, D., and E. Selinger, eds. (2003), *Chasing Technoscience*, Bloomington: Indiana University Press.

Ingold, T. (2001), "From Complementarity to Obviation: On Dissolving the Boundaries Between Social and Biological Anthropology, Archaeology and Psychology" in *Cycles of Contingency: Developmental Systems and Evolution*, eds. S. Oyama, P. E. Griffiths, and R. D. Gray, Cambridge, MA: MIT Press, 255–279.

Ingold, T. (2011), *Being Alive: Essays on Movement, Knowledge and Description*, Routledge: New York.

Ippolita (Italian writers' collective) (2013), *The Dark Side of Google*, trans. P. Riemens, Amsterdam: Institute of Network Cultures, 2013.

Ivins, W. M. (1953), *Prints and Visual Communication*, Cambridge MA: MIT Press.

Jacobs, J. (1961), *The Death and Life of Great American Cities,* New York: Random House.

Jahnke, M. (2012), "Revisiting Design as a Hermeneutic Practice: An Investigation of Paul Ricoeur's Critical Hermeneutics," *Design Issues* 28 (2): 30–40.

Jelsma, J. (2003), "Innovating for Sustainability: Involving Users, Politics and Technology," *Innovation* 16 (2): 103–16.

Johnson, C. G. (2011), "The Urban Precariat, Neoliberalization, and the Soft Power of Humanitarian Design," *Journal of Developing Societies* 27 (3–4): 445–75.

Jones, J. C. (1983), "Continuous Design and Redesign," *Design Studies* 4 (1): 53–60.

Jönsson, B. (2004), "Enabling Communication: Pictures as Language" in *Enabling Technologies. Body Image and Body Function*, eds. M. MacLachlan and P. Gallagher, Edinburgh, UK: Churchill Livingstone, 33–57.

Jönsson, B., A. Svensk, D. Cuartielles, L. Malmborg, and P. Schlaucher (2002), *Mobility and Learning Environments: Engaging People in Design of their Everyday Environments*, Lund, Sweden: Certec, LTH, Lund University and Malmö University, Creative Environments. Available online: http://www.certec.lth.se/doc/mobility1/MobilityLearningReport021215.pdf

Jönsson, B., P. Anderberg, E. Flodin, L. Malmborg, C. Nordgren, and A. Svensk (2005), "Ethics in the Making," *Design Philosophy Papers* 3 (4): 213–26.

Jullien, F. (1995), *The Propensity of Things: Towards a History of Efficacy in China*, trans. J. Lloyd, New York: Zone Books.

Keller, P., and D. Weberman (1998), "Heidegger and the Source(s) of Intelligibility," *Continental Philosophy Review* 31: 369–86.

Keshavarz, M. (2016), "Design-Politics: An Inquiry into Passports, Camps and Borders" PhD diss., Faculty of Culture and Society, School of Arts and Communication, Malmö University.

Kimbell, L. (2011), "Rethinking Design Thinking Part 1," *Design and Culture* 3 (3): 285–306.

Kimbell, L. (2012), "Rethinking Design Thinking Part 2," *Design and Culture* 4 (2): 129–48.

King, D. (1984), "Architecture and Astronomy: The Ventilators of Cairo and their Secrets," *Journal of the American Oriental Society* 104: 97–133.

King, H. (2015), *Virtual Memory: Time-Based Art and the Dream of Digitality*, Durham: Duke University Press.

Kisiel, T. K. (1973), "On the Dimensions of a Phenomenology of Science in Husserl and the Young Dr. Heidegger," *Journal of the British Society for Phenomenology* 4 (3): 217–34.

Klee, P. (1961), *Notebooks, Volume 1: The Thinking Eye*, ed. J. Spiller, trans. R. Manheim, London: Lund Humphries.

Klee, P. (1973), *Notebooks, Volume 2: The Nature of Nature*, ed. J. Spiller, trans. H. Norden, London: Lund Humphries.

Knappett, C. (2005), *Thinking Through Material Culture: An Interdisciplinary Perspective*, Philadelphia, PA: University of Pennsylvania Press.

Kohn, E. (2014), *How Forests Think: Toward an Anthropology beyond the Human*, Los Angeles: University of California Press.

Kracauer, S. (1995), *The Mass Ornament: Weimar Essays*, ed. and trans. T. Y. Levin, Cambridge, MA: Harvard University Press.

Krippendorff, K. (2006), *The Semantic Turn: A New Foundation for Design*, London: Taylor & Francis.

Kroes, P., and A. Meijers (2006), "The Dual Nature of Technical Artefacts," *Studies in the History and Philosophy of Science* 37: 1–4.

Lassner, J. (1970), "The Caliph's Personal Domain: The City Plan of Baghdad Re-examined" in *The Islamic City*, eds. A. Hourani and S. M. Stern, Philadelphia: University of Pennsylvania Press.

Latour, B. (1991), "Technology is Society Made Durable," in *A Sociology of Monsters: Essays on Power, Technology and Domination*, ed. J. Law, New York and London: Routledge, 103–31.

Latour, B. (1992), "Where are the Missing Masses? The Sociology of a Few Mundane Artifacts" in *Shaping Technology/Building Society*, eds. W. Bijker and J. Law, Cambridge, MA: MIT Press.

Latour, B. (1993), *We Have Never Been Modern*, trans. C. Porter, Hemel Hempstead: Harvester Wheatsheaf.

Latour, B. (1999), *Pandora's Hope: Essays on the Reality of Science Studies*, Cambridge, MA: Harvard University Press.

Latour, B. (2005), "From Realpolitik to Dingpolitik: How to Make Things Public. An Introduction" in *Making Things Public. Atmospheres of Democracy*, eds. B. Latour and P. Weibel, Cambridge MA: MIT Press, 1–31.

Ledderose, L. (2000), *Ten Thousand Things: Module and Mass Production in Chinese Art*, Princeton, NJ: Princeton University Press.

Leder, D. (1985), "Modes of Totalization: Heidegger on Modem Technology and Science," *Philosophy Today* 29 (3): 245–56.

Lefebvre, H. (1991), *Critique of Everyday Life Volume 2*, London: Verso.

Lemmens, P. (2011), "This System Does Not Produce Pleasure Anymore" interview with Bernard Stiegler, *Krisis Journal for Contemporary Philosophy* 1, n.p.

Leroi-Gourhan, A. (1998), *Gesture and Speech,* trans. A. B. Berger, Cambridge, MA: MIT Press.

Levi Strauss, C. (1976), *The Savage Mind*, trans. George Weidenfeld and Nicolson, London: Weidenfeld and Nicolson.

Levin, D. M. (1988), *The Opening of Vision: Nihilism and the Postmodern Situation*, New York: Routledge.

Levin, D. M., ed. (1993), *Modernity and the Hegemony of Vision*, Berkeley: University of California Press.

Levinas, E. (1981), *Totality and Infinity: An Essay on Exteriority*, trans. A. Lingis, Dordrecht, NL: Kluwer Academic Publishers.

Levinas, E. (1985), *Ethics and Infinity*, Pittsburgh: Duquesne University Press.

Levinas, E. (1996), *Basic Philosophical Writings,* eds. A. T. Peperzak, S. Critchley, and R. Bernasconi, Bloomington: University of Indiana Press.

Lewin, K. (1936), *Principles of Topological Psychology*, New York: McGraw-Hill.

Lloyd, G. E. R. (1996), *Adversaries and Authorities: Investigations into Ancient Greek and Chinese Science*, Cambridge: Cambridge University Press.

Loewy, R. (1951), *Never Leave Well Enough Alone*, New York: Simon and Schuster.

Lovelock, C. (1994), *Product Plus: How Product + Service = Competitive Advantage,* New York: McGraw-Hill.

Luhmann, N. (1989), *Ecological Communication*, Cambridge: Polity Press.

Luhmann, N. (1995), *Social systems*, Stanford: Stanford University Press.

Lury, C. (1998), *Prosthetic Culture: Photography, Memory and Identity*, London and New York: Routledge.

Lyotard, J-F. (1989), "Levinas' Logic" *Lyotard Reader*, ed. A. Benjamin, Oxford: Blackwell.

Macintyre, A. (2007), *After Virtue*, South Bend, Indiana: University of Notre Dame Press.

Magnus, B. (1970), *Heidegger's Metaphistory of Philosophy: Amor Fati, Being and Truth*, The Hague: Nijhoff.

Malkki, L. H. (1996), "Speechless Emissaries: Refugees, Humanitarianism and Dehistoricization," *Cultural Anthropology* 11 (3): 377–404.

Mandi, M. (1964 [1957]), *Ibn Khaldun's Philosophy of History,* Chicago: University of Chicago Press, Phoenix edition.

Manzini, E. (2015), *Design When Everybody Designs*, Cambridge, MA: MIT Press.

Manzini, E. (2015), "Design in the Transition Phase: A New Design Culture for the Emerging Design," *Design Philosophy Papers* 13 (1): 57–62.

Marchand, J. (2005), *Introduction à la lecture de Jean-Paul Sartre*, Montréal: Liber.

Martin, B., and B. Hannington (2012), *Universal Methods of Design: 100 Ways to Research Complex Problems, Develop Innovative Ideas and Design Effective Solutions*, Beverly, MA: Rockport Publishers.

Marx, W. (1970), *Heidegger and the Tradition*, trans. T. Kisiel and M. Greene, Evanston, IL: Northwestern University Press.

Mattelmaki, T., K. Vaajakallio, and I. Koskinen (2014), "What Happened to Empathic Design?" *Design Issues* 30 (1): 67–77.

Maturana, H., and F. Varela, (1980), *Autopoiesis and Cognition: The Realization of the Living,* Dordrecht/Boston/London: D. Redel Publishing Co.

Maturana, H., and F. Varela, (1987), *Tree of Life: the Biological Roots of Human Understanding*, Boston/London: Shambhala.

McNeill, W., ed. (1998), *Pathmarks*, Cambridge: Cambridge University Press.

McNeill, W. (1999), *The Glance of the Eye: Heidegger, Aristotle, and the Ends of Theory*, Albany, NY: State University of New York Press.

Megill, A. (1987), *Prophets of Extremity: Nietzsche, Heidegger, Foucault, Derrida*, Berkley: University of California Press.

Megoran, N., C. Haris, S. Sharapova, M. Kamp, J. Townsend, N. Bagdasarova, and M. Tlostanova (2012), "Author-critic Forum: Decolonial Theory and Gender Research in Central Asia," *Central Asian Survey* 31 (3): 355–67.

Merleau-Ponty, M. (1962), *Phenomenology of Perception*, New York and London: Routledge.

Merleau-Ponty, M. (1968), *The Visible and the Invisible*, trans. A. Lingis, Evanston: Northwestern University Press.

Meuret, M., and F. D. Provenza, eds. (2014), *The Art and Science of Shepherding: Tapping the Wisdom of French Shepherds*, Austin, TX: Acres.

Mignolo, W. (2011), "I am Where I Think: Remapping the Order of Knowing" in *The Creolization of Theory*, eds. F. Lionnet and S. Shih, Durham, NC: Duke University Press, 159–92.

Mignolo, W. (2014), "Spirit out of Bounds Returns to the East: The Closing of the Social Sciences and the Opening of Independent Thoughts," *Current Sociology Monograph* 62 (4): 584–602.

Mignolo, W., and M. Tlostanova (2006), "Theorizing from the Borders: Shifting to Geo- and Body-Politics of Knowledge," *European Journal of Social Theory* 9 (2): 205–21.

Mignolo, W., and M. Tlostanova (2007), "The Logic of Coloniality and the Limits of Postcoloniality" in *The Postcolonial and the Global: Connections, Conflicts, Complicities*, eds. R. Krishnaswamy and J. C. Hawley, Minneapolis, MN: University of Minnesota Press, 109–23.

Mignolo, W., and A. Escobar, eds. (2009), *Globalization and the Decolonial Option*, London: Routledge.

Mitcham, C. (1994), *Thinking Through Technology: The Path Between Engineering and Philosophy*, Chicago: University of Chicago Press.

Mitcham, C. (2001), "Dasein versus Design: The Problematics of Turning Making into Thinking," *International Journal of Technology and Design Education* 11 (1): 27–36.

Mitchell, T. (1991), *ColoniSing Egypt*, Berkley: University of California Press.

Mitchell, V. (1997), "Textiles, Text and Techne" in *Obscure Objects of Desire: Reviewing the Crafts in the Twentieth Century*, ed. T. Harrod, London: Crafts Council, 324–332.

Moles, A. (1985), "The Comprehensive Guarantee: A New Consumer Value," *Design Issues* 2 (1): 53–64.

Moles, A., and D. W. Jacobus (1988), "Design and Immateriality: What of it in a Post Industrial Society?" *Design Issues* 4 (1–2): 25–32.

Morris, P. (1975), *Sartre's Concept of a Person: An Analytic Approach*, Amherst: University of Massachusetts Press.

Morton, T. (2013), *Realist Magic: Objects, Ontology, Causality*, Open Humanities Press and Ann Arbor: University of Michigan Library.

Mountz, A. (2010), *Seeking Asylum: Human Smuggling and Bureaucracy at the Border*, Minneapolis: University of Minnesota Press.

Naz, F. (2006), "Arturo Escobar And The Development Discourse: An Overview," *Asian Affairs* 28 (3): 64–84.

Negarestani, R. (2014), "The Labor of the Inhuman" in *#Accelerate: The Accelerationist Reader*, ed. R. Mackay, Falmouth, UK: Urbanomic Media, 425–66.

Nelson, H. G., and E. Stolterman (2012), *The Design Way: Intentional Change in an Unpredictable World*, Cambridge MA: MIT Press.

Nelson, R. S., ed. (2000), *Visuality Before and Beyond the Renaissance: Seeing as Others Saw*, Cambridge: Cambridge University Press.

Newman, L. (2014), "Descartes' Epistemology" in *The Stanford Encyclopedia of Philosophy*, Winter 2014 Edition, ed. Edward N. Zalta, http://plato.stanford.edu/archives/win2014/entries/descartes-epistemology/

Nicolini, D. (2012), *Practice Theory, Work & Organization: An Introduction*, Oxford: Oxford University Press.

Nielsen, Brita Fladvad. 2014. "Out of Context: Ethnographic Interviewing, Empathy, and Humanitarian Design". *Design Philosophy Papers* 12 (1): 51–64.

Nietzsche, F. (2005), *The Anti-Christ, Ecce Homo, Twilight of the Idols: And Other Writings*, eds. A. Ridley and J. Norman, trans. J. Norman, Cambridge: Cambridge University Press.

Noorman, K., and T. Uiterkamp, eds. (1988), *Green households? Domestic Consumers, Environment, and Sustainability*, London: Earthscan.

Norman, D. (1990), *The Design of Everyday Things*, NY: Doubleday.

Norman, D. (1988), *The Psychology of Everyday Things*, New York: Basic Books.

Norvig, P., and S. J. Russell (2009), *Artificial Intelligence: A Modern Approach*, New York: Pearson.

Nussbaum, M. (1990), *Love's Knowledge: Essays on Philosophy and Literature*, Oxford, UK: Oxford University Press.

Odum, E. P. (1953), *Fundamentals of Ecology*, Philadelphia: Saunders.

Olafson, F. (1994), "Heidegger à la Wittgenstein or 'Coping' with Professor Dreyfus," *Inquiry* 37 (3): 331–337.

Olafson, F. (1998), *Heidegger and the Ground of Ethics: a study of Mitsein*, Cambridge: Cambridge University Press.

O'Neill, R. V. (2001), "Is It Time to Bury the Ecosystem Concept? (with full military honors, of course!)," *Ecology* 82: 3275–84.

Orwell, G. (1946), *Animal Farm*, London: Penguin.

Pallister-Wilkins, P. (2015), "The Humanitarian Policing of 'Our Sea'," http://bordercriminologies.law.ox.ac.uk/humanitarian-policing-of-our-sea/ (accessed 5 December 2015).

Panchenko, D. (1993), "Thales and the Origin of Theoretical Reasoning," *Configurations* 1 (3): 387–414.

Park, P. J. K. (2011), *Africa, Asia, and the History of Philosophy: Racism in the Formation of the Philosophical Canon, 1780–1830*, Albany: State University of New York Press.

Parry, R. (2014), "*Episteme* and *Techne*," *The Stanford Encyclopedia of Philosophy*, Fall 2014 Edition, ed. E. N. Zalta, http://plato.stanford.edu/archives/fall2014/entries/episteme-techne

Pasquinelli, M., ed. (2015), *Alleys of Your Mind: Augmented Intelligence and Its Traumas*, Lüneburg: Meson Press.

Pelegrin, J. (2005), "Remarks About Archaeological Techniques and Methods of Knapping: Elements of a Cognitive Approach to Stone Knapping" in *Stone Knapping: The Necessary Conditions for a Uniquely Hominin Behaviour*, eds. V. Roux and B. Bril, Cambridge: McDonald Institute for Archaeological Research, 23–33.

Peperzak, A. (1993), *To the Other: An Introduction to the Philosophy of Emmanuel Levinas*, West Lafayette, IN: Purdue University Press.

Pereira, H., and C. Gillett (2014), "Africa: Designing as Existence" in *Design in the Borderlands*, eds. E. Kalantidou and T. Fry, New York: Routledge, 109–32.

Pilloton, E. (2009), *Design Revolution: 100 Products that are Changing People's Lives*, London: Thames and Hudson.

Plato (1961), *The Collected Dialogues*, eds. E. Hamilton and H. Cairns, Bollingen Series LXX, Princeton, NJ: Princeton University Press.

Protevi, J. (2001), *Political Physics: Deleuze, Derrida and the Body Politic*, London: Athlone Press.

Proust, M. (1981), *Remembrance of Things Past*, trans. T. Kilmartin, Penguin: Harmondsworth.

Provenza, F. D., M. Meuret, and P. Gregorini (2015), "Our Landscapes, Our Livestock, Ourselves: Restoring Broken Linkages among Plants, Herbivores, and Humans with Diets That Nourish and Satiate," *Appetite*, 95: 500–519.

Pyyhtinen, O., and S. Tamminen (2011), "We Have Never Been Only Human: Foucault and Latour on the Question of the Anthropos," *Anthropological Theory*, June 11: 135–52.

Ramachandran, V. S., and S. Blakeslee (1998), *Phantoms in the Brain: Probing the Mysteries of the Human Mind*, New York: William Morrow & Company.

Raskin, J. (1994), "Intuitive Equals Familiar," *Communications of the ACM* 37 (9): 17–18.

Reckwitz, A. (2002), "Toward a Theory of Social Practices: A Development in Culturalist Theorising," *European Journal of Social Theory* 5 (2): 243–63.

Rickels, L. (2010), *I Think I Am: Philip K. Dick*, Minneapolis: University of Minnesota Press.

Rodowick, D. N. (1997), "The Last Things Before the Last: Kracauer and History," *New German Critique* 41: 113–17.

Rose, D. B. (2011), *Wild Dogs Dreaming: Love and Extinction*, Charlottesville: University of Virginia Press.

Rose, D. B., T. van Dooren, and M. Chrulew, eds. (2017), *Extinction Studies: Stories of Time, Death, and Generations*, New York: Columbia University Press.

Sabra, A. I., ed. (2002), *The Optics of Ibn al-Haytham, Books IV–V: On Reflection and Images Seen by Reflection*, Kuwait: The National Council for Culture, Arts and Letters.

Said, E. (1978), *Orientalism*, London: Routledge & Kegan Paul.

Sampson, G. (1985), *Writing Systems: A Linguistic Introduction*, Stanford: Stanford University Press.

Sandoval, C. (2000), *Methodology of the Oppressed*, Minneapolis, MN: University of Minnesota Press.

Santos, B. S. (2014), *Epistemologies of the South: Justice Against Epistemicide*, Boulder, CO: Paradigm Publishers.

Sartre, J-P. (1948), *Existentialism is a Humanism*, trans. P. Mairet, New York: Haskell House.

Sartre, J-P. (1956), *Being and Nothingness: An Essay on Phenomenological Ontology*, trans. H. E. Barnes, New York: Philosophical Library.

Sartre, J-P. (1963), *Search for a Method*, trans. H. E. Barnes, New York: Alfred A. Knopf.

Scarry, E. (1985), *The Body in Pain: The Making* and *Unmaking of the World*, Oxford University Press.

Schatzi, T., K. Knorr-Cetina, and E. von Savigny, eds. (2001), *The Practice Turn in Contemporary Theory*, London: Routledge.

Schmitt, R. (1969), *Martin Heidegger on Being Human*, New York: Random House.

Schön, D. (1995 [1983]), *The Reflective Practitioner: How Professionals Think in Action*, Burlington: Ashgate Publishing.

Schön, D. (1990), *Educating the Reflective Practitioner: Toward a New Design for Teaching and Learning in the Professions*, San Francisco: Jossey-Bass.

Schufreider, G. (1981), "Heidegger on Community," *Man and World* 14 (1): 25–54.

Schumacher, E. F. (2010 [1973]), *Small is Beautiful: Economics as if People Mattered*, New York: Harper Collins.

Scully, V. (1988), *American Architecture and Urbanism*, New York: Holt.

Sheehan, T., ed. (1981), *Heidegger: The Man and the Thinker*, Chicago: Precedent Publishing.

Shneiderman, B. (1983), "Direct Manipulation: A Step Beyond Programming Languages," *IEEE Computer* 16 (8): 57–69.

Shove, E. (2003), *Comfort, Cleanliness and Convenience: The Social Organisation of Normality*, Oxford: Berg.

Shove, E., M. Pantzar, and M. Watson (2013), *The Dynamics of Social Practice: Everyday Life and How it Changes*, London: Sage.

Simon, H. A. (2001), *The Sciences of the Artificial*, Cambridge, MA: MIT Press.

Simon L. L., and M. A. Maslin (2015), "Defining the Anthropocene," *Nature* 519 (7542): 171–80.

Simondon, G. (1980), *On the Mode of Existence of Technical Objects*, ed. J. Hart, trans. N. Mellamphy, unpublished manuscript, University of Western Ontario.

Simondon, G. (2012), *Being and Technology*, eds. A. de Boever, A. Murray, J. Roffe, and A. Woodward, Edinburgh: Edinburgh University Press.

Simpson, E. (1987), *Anti-Foundationalism and Practical Reasoning: Conversations Between Hermeneutics and Analysis*, Edmonton, AB: Academic Printing and Publishing.

Sims, D. (2010), *Understanding Cairo: The Logic of a City out of Control*, Cairo: American University in Cairo Press.

Sinclair, C., and K. Stohr (2006), *Design Like you Give a Damn: Architectural Responses to Humanitarian Crisis*, London: Thames and Hudson.

Singer, P. (2016), *Ethics in the Real World*, Princeton, NJ: Princeton University Press.

Siza, A. (1997), *Architecture Writings*, ed. A. Angelillo, Milan: Skira Editore.

Sloterdijk, P. (2011), *Bubbles: Spheres Volume I: Microspherology*, trans. W. Hoban, Los Angeles: Semiotext(e).

Sloterdijk, P. (2014), *Globes: Spheres Volume II: Macrospherology*, trans. W. Hoban, Los Angeles: Semiotext(e).

Sloterdijk, P. (2016), *Foams: Spheres Volume III: Plural Spherology*, trans. W. Hoban, Los Angeles: Semiotext(e).

Smets, G., and K. Overbeeke (1994), "Industrial Design Engineering and the Theory of Direct Perception," *Design Studies* 15 (2): 175–84.

Smith, L. T. (1999), *Decolonizing Methodologies: Research and Indigenous Peoples*, London, UK: Zed.

Snodgrass, A. (1997), "Translating Tradition: Technology, Heidegger's 'Letting-be' and Japanese New Wave Architecture," *Architectural Theory Review* 2 (2): 83–104.

Snodgrass, A. (1992), "Models, Metaphors, and the Hermeneutics of Designing," *Design Issues* 9 (1): 56–74.

Stahel, W. (1994), "The Utilization-focused Service Economy: Resource Efficiency and Product-Life Extension" in *The Greening of Industrial Ecosystems*, ed. B. Allenby, Washington: National Academy Press, 178–90.

Stanford Encyclopedia of Philosophy http://plato.stanford.edu/ (accessed 15 March 2018).

Starr, P. (1982), *The Social Transformation of Medicine*, New York: Basic Books.

Stengers, I. (2015), *In Catastrophic Times: Resisting the Coming Barbarism*, trans. A. Goffey, London: Open Humanities Press.

Stengers, I., and P. Pignarre (2011), *Capitalist Sorcery: Breaking the Spell*, trans. A. Goffey, Basingstoke, UK: Palgrave Macmillan.

Stengers, I., B. Massumi, and E. Manning (2009), "History Through the Middle: Between Macro and Mesopolitics—An Interview with Isabelle Stengers," *Inflexions*, 1–16.

Stiegler, B. (1998), *Technics and Time 1: The Fault of Epimetheus*, trans. R. Beardsworth and George Collins, Stanford: Stanford University Press.

Stiegler, B. (2015), *States of Shock Stupidity and Knowledge in the Twenty-First Century*, trans. D. Ross, Cambridge: Polity Press.

Suchman, L. (1987), *Plans and Situated Actions*, Cambridge: Cambridge University Press.

Telos (2015), special issue on Political Critiques of the Anthropocene, 172, Fall.

Thompson, E. (2013), *Review of Phenomenology and Naturalism: Examining the Relationship between Human Experience and Nature*, eds. H. Carel and D. Meacham, in *Notre Dame Philosophical Review* 10/7/2014, http://ndpr.nd.edu/news/49272-phenomenology-and-naturalism-examining-the-relationship-between-human-experience-and-nature/

Ticktin, M. (2009), "The Violence of Humanitarianism" in *Cultures of Fear: A Critical Reader*, eds. U. Linke and D. T. Smith, London: Pluto Press, 132–48.

Ticktin, M. (2014), "Transnational Humanitarianism," *Annual Review of Anthropology* 43: 273–89.

Tlostanova, M. (2011), "The South of the Poor North: Caucasus Subjectivity and the Complex of Secondary 'Australism'," *The Global South* 5 (1): 66–84.

Tlostanova, M. (2015), "Can the Post-Soviet Think? On Coloniality of Knowledge, External Imperial and Double Colonial Difference," *Intersections: East European Journal of Society and Politics* 1 (2): 38–58.

Tlostanova, M., and W. D. Mignolo (2012), *Learning to Unlearn: Decolonial Reflections from Eurasia and the Americas*, Columbus: The Ohio State University Press.

Tonkinwise, C. (2018), "Research for Designing after Ownership" in *Design Research Now 2*, eds. R. Michel, G. Joost, and C. Mareis, Basel: Birkhauser Verlag.

Tsianos, V., and S. Karakayali (2010), "Transnational Migration and the Emergence of the European Border Regime: An Ethnographic Analysis," *European Journal of Social Theory* 13 (3): 373–87.

Turing, A. (1950), "Computing Machinery and Intelligence," *Mind* 49: 433–60.

Turnbull, D. (2000), *Masons, Tricksters and Cartographers*, Amsterdam: Harwood Academic.

Turner, P. (2005), "Affordance as Context," *Interacting with Computers (the interdisciplinary journal of Human-Computer Interaction)* 17: 787–800.

Ulmer, G. (1994), *Heuretics: The Logic of Invention*, Baltimore: Johns Hopkins University Press.

Vattimo, G. (1991), *The End of Modernity*, trans. Jon R. Snyder, Baltimore: John Hopkins University Press.

Vázquez, R. (2010), "Modernity, the Greatest Show on Earth: Thoughts on Visibility," *Borderlands ejournal* 9 (2): 1–17.

Veatch, H. (1969), *Two Logics*, Evanston: Northwestern University Press.

Veblen, T. (1994 [1899]), *The Theory of the Leisure Class: An Economic Study of Institutions*, New York: Penguin Books.

Verbeek, P-P. (2002), "Devices of Engagement: On Borgmann's Philosophy of Information and Technology," *Techné* 6 (1): 69–92.

Verbeek, P-P. (2008), "Morality in Design: Design Ethics and the Morality of Technological Artifacts" in *Philosophy and Design*, eds. P. E. Vermaas et al., Dordrecht: Springer, 91–103.

Vermaas, P. E., P. Kroes, A. Light, and S. Moore, eds. (2008), *Philosophy and Design: From Engineering to Architecture*, Dordrecht: Springer.

Vygotsky, L. S. (1930), *Mind in Society*, Cambridge, MA: Harvard University Press.

Walters, W. (2004), "Secure Borders, Safe Haven, Domopolitics," *Citizenship Studies* 8 (3): 237–60.

Wang, J. (2013), "The Importance of Aristotle to Design Thinking," *Design Issues* 29 (2): 4–15.

White, D. (n.d.), "Critical Design and the Critical Social Sciences, or Why We Need to Engage Multiple Speculative Critical Design Futures in a Postpolitical and Post-utopian Era," http://www.cd-cf.org/articles/critical-design-and-the-critical-social-sciences/ (accessed 3 March 2018).

Whyte, W. H. (1988), *City: Rediscovering the Center*, New York: Doubleday.

Willis, A-M. (2000), "The Limits of Sustainable Architecture," Proceedings of *Shaping the Sustainable Millennium*, Queensland University of Technology, July 2000.

Willis, A-M. (2006), "Ontological Designing," *Design Philosophy Papers* 4 (2): 69–92.

Winner, L. (1977), *Autonomous Technology: Technics-out-of-control as a Theme in Political Thought*, Cambridge, MA: MIT Press.

Winograd, T., and F. Flores (1987), *Understanding Computers and Cognition: A New Foundation for Design*, Reading, MA: Addison-Wesley Publishing Company.

Wolfe, C. (2010), *Posthumanities*, http:www.carywolfe.com/post_about.html (accessed 2 January 2012).

Woodhouse. E., and J. W. Patton (2004), "Design by Society: Science and Technology Studies and the Social Shaping of Design," *Design Issues* 20 (3): 1–12.

Woolgar, S. (1991), "Configuring the User: The Case of Usability Trials," in *A Sociology of Monsters*, ed. John Law, London: Routledge, 57–99.

Worldwatch Institute (2004), *State of the World 2004: The Consumer Society*, Washington: Worldwatch Institute.

Wright, K. (1984), "The Place of the Work of Art in the Age of Technology," *Southern Journal of Philosophy* 22: 565–83.

Young, I. M. (1990), *Throwing Like a Girl And Other Essays in Feminist Philosophy and Social Theory*, Bloomington: Indiana University Press.

Young, J., and K. Haynes, eds. (2002), *Off the Beaten Track*, Cambridge: Cambridge University Press, 2002.

Zahavi, D. (2001), "Beyond Empathy: Phenomenological Approaches to Intersubjectivity," *Journal of Consciousness Studies* 8 (5–7): 151–67.

Zimmer, C. (2005), *Where Did We Come From?* Sydney: ABC Books.

Zimmerman, M. (1981), *Eclipse of the Self: The Development of Heidegger's Concept of Authenticity*, Athens: Ohio University Press.

Zimmerman, M. (1990), *Heidegger's Confrontation with Modernity: Technology, Politics and Art*, Bloomington and Indianapolis: Indiana University Press.

Zylinska, J. (2014), *Minimal Ethics for the Anthropocene*, Ann Arbor: Open Humanities Press and University of Michigan Library.

INDEX

Index

Index

panopticon 222
Papanek, Victor 30, 73, 104
Park, Peter K.J. 8 n.5, 137
Peperzak, Adriaan 93–5, 107
perception 1, 41–53, 77–9, 141, 162–4, 165, 233
Pereira, H. and C. Gillett 124
Petroski, Henry 30
pharmakon 212
phenomenology 7, 22, 34, 178, *see also under* things
   egology 93–4
   intentionality 45–6, 96
philosophy
   and banality 4–5
   Chinese 128–36
   history of 3–4, 8 n.5
   Greek 3–4, 8, 13–14, 33, 65, 69, 73, 83, 129, 146, 149–51, 157–60, 192, 209, 214, 229
   Islamic 8 n.5, 116–17 (*see also* Ibn al-Haytham; Ibn Khaldun)
see also names of philosophers and philosophies
photography
   aesthetics 232–4
   objectivity 222, 231–4
   popular 232–3
   social use 233
phronesis 33, 36–8, 39–44, 69
phusis 155–8, 160 n.13
Pilloton, Emily 121, 137
plan, planning 8, 116–18, 168, 205, 245–6, 284, 287–8
plane of immanence 284–88
Plato 13, 14, 150, 165
   academy 214
   idea, ideal 82, 144, 194, 224–5
   'statutes of homicide' 79–80
   techne 192
   and technics 214
   theory of forms 144, 221–2, 224–8, 229–30
   truth and imitation 224–8
poiesis 40, 69, 155–7, 192–5
political economy 210, 221, 222, 235, 238–42
posthuman 8, 252–3, 256, 262, 276–9
posthumanism 253, 256, 262, 270, 276, 289
post-nature 256–7
practice 51–2, *see also praxis, phronesis*
practice theory 34, 69
practice-theory divide 33–4, 39–44, 66
praxis 7, 33–4, 39–44, 69, 154, 167, 183, 187, 257, 280
precariousness 77, 91–2, 121, 251
pre-reflective 12, 46, 48, 57, 141
product service systems 158
proletarianization 210–15
Prometheus 13–14, 19–20
Protagoras 13–14
Proust, Marcel 232

rationality 171, 230
   market 216
   non-Western 128

   technological 175, 186–9
   Western 108, 111–12
reason 29, 36, 65, 111, 124, 166, 182, 282–3
   contemplative 165
   humanitarian 124
   instrumental 154
   sufficient 185–7
Renaissance 222, 229–30, 245, 282
Ritell, Horst 12
robots 268, 271–3, 275 nn.11, 17
robotics 271, 275 n.8, 276
Roland, Romain 288
Russia, post-Soviet 112–14

Said, Edward, *see* orientalism
Sartre, Jean Paul 54–9
Scarry, Elaine 7, 73, 74, 75–82, 85–6, 89
Schön, Donald 6, 30, 59 nn.2, 13
semiotics 20, 87, *see also* sign
sentience 16, 73–82, 268, 273
services, service industry 24, 73–4, 88–9, 97–8, 121, 210, 241, 262, *see also under* design
service systems 154–9
shi 64, 90 n.13, 128–34
sign, signs 20, 163, 235–42
Simon, Herbert 6, 12 n.2, 30, 174, 176, 177 nn.1, 3
Simondon 7, 30, 64, 68 n.9, 198–206, 211, 213, 233, 234 n.14
situatedness in 34, 41–4, 46–50, 55–8, 74, 96–101, 124, 141, 165–9, 182 n.2
Snodgrass, Adrian 34, 182, 184–89
social constructivism 277
social distinction 231, 232–4, 235, 241
Socrates 33, 224, 287
space, spatiality 34, 48, 50
   abstract, objective 47–9, 244
   bordered, territorial 120–5
   gendered 117–18
   lived 46–9, 117–18
   public-private 25–6, 48–52, 117–18, 222
   socially produced 243–6
   time and 143, 145, 147, 266
   visualization of 131, 232
species extinction 3, 8, 251, 263
Spinoza, Baruch 41, 264, 284–8
Stengers, Isabelle 8 n.3, 104, 252, 253, 258–61, 262, 265
Stiegler, Bernard 6, 7, 13–14, 15, 30, 181–2, 210–16, 253, 289
Stroobants, Marcelle 265
subject-object relation 46–50, 67, 110–11, 174–6, 194, 222 n.1, 239
Suchman, Lucy 90 n.12
sustainability 20, 28, 54–9, 82–9, 153–9, 262, 278, 280–3, *see also* unsustainability
sustainment 54, 57, 59 n.3, 74, 253, 280–3
system
   artificial intelligence 270
   biophysical 17, 252, 254, 280
   computer 169, 208–9
   cybernetic 184–5